MEDIEVAL AND RENAISSANCE
SCHOLARSHIP

MITTELLATEINISCHE STUDIEN UND TEXTE

HERAUSGEGEBEN

VON

PAUL GERHARD SCHMIDT

BAND XXI

TUTA SUB AEGIDE PALLAS · 1683 ·

MEDIEVAL AND RENAISSANCE SCHOLARSHIP

Proceedings of the Second European Science Foundation
Workshop on the Classical Tradition
in the Middle Ages and the Renaissance

(London, The Warburg Institute, 27-28 November 1992)

EDITED BY

NICHOLAS MANN AND BIRGER MUNK OLSEN

E.J. BRILL
LEIDEN · NEW YORK · KÖLN
1997

960887

The paper in this book meets the guidelines for permanence and durability of the Committee on Production Guidelines for Book Longevity of the Council on Library Resources.

Library of Congress Cataloging-in-Publication Data

European Science Foundation Workshop on the Classical Tradition in the
    Middle Ages and the Renaissance (2nd : 1992 : London, England)
    Medieval and Renaissance scholarship : proceedings of the second
European Science Foundation Workshop on the Classical Tradition in
the Middle Ages and the Renaissance (London, Warburg Institute,
27-28 November 1992) / edited by Nicholas Mann and Birger Munk
Olsen.
        p.   cm. — (Mittellateinische Studien und Texte, ISSN
0076-9754 ; Bd. 21)
    Includes bibliographical references (p.   ) and index.
    ISBN 9004105085 (alk. paper)
    1. Classical literature—History and criticism—Theory, etc.)–
–Congresses. 2. Learning and scholarship—History—Medieval,
500-1500—Congresses.   5. Renaissance—Congresses.
    I. Mann, Nicholas. II. Olsen, Birger Munk. III. Title.
    IV. Series.
    PA3015.E87.   1996
    870.9'001—dc20   96-9830
                                                                   CIP

Die Deutsche Bibliothek – CIP-Einheitsaufnahme

Medieval and renaissance scholarship : proceedings of the Second
European Science Foundation Workshop on the Classical Tradition
in the Middle Ages and the Renaissance, (London, Warburg
Institute, 27-28 November 1992). / ed. by Nicholas Mann and
Birger Munk Olsen. – Leiden ; New York ; Köln : Brill, 1996
    (Mittellateinische Studien und Texte ; Bd. 21)
    ISBN 90-04-10508-5
NE: Mann, Nicholas [Hrsg.] Workshop on the Classical Tradition in
    the Middle Ages and the Renaissance < 2. 1992,. London>; European
    Science Foundation; GT

ISSN 0076-9754
ISBN 90 04 10508 5

PRINTED IN THE NETHERLANDS

Published with financial support from the European Science Foundation, the Commission of the European Community and the Warburg Institute.

The European Science Foundation is an association of its 54 member research councils, academies, and institutions devoted to basic scientific research in 20 countries. The ESF brings European scientists together to work on topics of common concern, to co-ordinate the use of expensive facilities, and to discover and define new endeavours that will benefit from a cooperative approach.

The scientific work sponsored by ESF includes basic research in the natural sciences, the medical and biosciences, the humanities and the social sciences.

The ESF links scholarship and research supported by its members and adds value by co-operation across national frontiers. Through its function as a co-ordinator, and also by holding workshops and conferences and by enabling researchers to visit and study in laboratories throughout Europe, the ESF works for the advancement of European science.

CONTENTS

MEDIEVAL AND RENAISSANCE SCHOLARSHIP

Second European Science Foundation Workshop
on the Classical Tradition in the Middle Ages
and the Renaissance

(London, The Warburg Institute, 27-28 November 1992)

PARTICIPANTS

ALEXANDRO COROLEU, Barcelona
VIOLETTA DE ANGELIS, Milan
A. C. DIONISOTTI, London
KARSTEN FRIIS-JENSEN, Copenhagen
COLETTE JEUDY, Paris
GEORGE KARAMANOLIS, Thessaloniki
MICHAEL LAPIDGE, Cambridge
CLAUDIO LEONARDI, Florence
NICHOLAS MANN, London
ALASTAIR J. MINNIS, York
BIRGER MUNK OLSEN, Copenhagen
LODI NAUTA, Groningen
PIERRE PETITMENGIN, Paris
L. D. REYNOLDS, Oxford
SUZANNE REYNOLDS, Birmingham
YVES-FRANÇOIS RIOU, Plougasnou
PAUL GERHARD SCHMIDT, Freiburg im Breisgau
KLAUS SIEWERT, Münster
MAX SPARREBOOM, Strasburg
CLAUDIA VILLA, Bergamo
J. B. VOORBIJ, Utrecht
RUTH WEBB, London

INTRODUCTION

In 1991 the European Science Foundation launched a Network on *The Classical Tradition in the Middle Ages and the Renaissance*, which was intended to run for a period of three years and to comprise three workshops and a final symposium. The first workshop took place at the Certosa del Galluzzo in Florence in late June 1992. On that occasion, we discussed the concept of reception, and the forms which it took in the Middle Ages and the Renaissance, focusing in particular upon some of its fundamental features: the availability of texts, their physical appearance, the different forms in which they circulated—from integral versions to abridgements and translations—and the public for which they were destined or which actually owned them.[1]

At the second workshop, whose proceedings are reflected by the present volume,[2] the centre of interest moved from quantitative to qualitative aspects, i.e. to medieval and early Renaissance scholarship, and its essential components: textual criticism, commentary on the texts, and critical discussions of authorship.

As far as the first of these is concerned, the critical activity of Byzantine scholars such as Demetrios Triklinios, Manuel Moschopoulos and Thomas Magistros has been amply studied, even if certain problems of attribution to the last-mentioned have not yet been resolved. In the field of Latin texts we are well informed about the period beginning with Petrarch, but have almost nothing to go on for the previous centuries: it is characteristic that even a standard work like Rudolf Pfeiffer's *History of Classical Scholarship* (no. 3)[3] leaps blithely from antiquity to Petrarch. We know that many *mutili* were completed, that texts were diligently collated, often with several manuscripts, that choices were made amongst variant readings, and that this in turn gave rise to large numbers

---

[1] The proceedings were published in 1995: *The Classical Tradition in the Middle Ages and the Renaissance. Proceedings of the First European Science Foundation Workshop on the Reception of Classical Texts* (Florence, Certosa del Galluzzo, 26-27 June 1992), ed. by Claudio Leonardi and Birger Munk Olsen (Biblioteca di medioevo latino, 15), Spoleto, 1995.

[2] Unfortunately for a variety of reasons it was not possible to include all the papers read at the workshop in the present volume.

[3] The numbers refer to the bibliography at the end of this volume.

of contaminated texts, which in most cases make it impossible to establish satisfactory stemmata. But we cannot tell to what extent the scribes and correctors of this period were capable of making emendations, or rather good emendations: there is no doubt that in the minds of the scribes the *lectiones faciliores* (for example) were intended to improve the texts. E. J. Kenney, in an article on 'The Character of Humanist Philology' (no. 12), is quite sceptical on this point, considering that 'conjecture, so far as it played a part at all, was generated by the tradition itself, not by the mind of the corrector'. It is in fact very difficult, given the present state of our knowledge, to settle such questions, the more so since modern editors usually do not consider scribal activity of this kind relevant to the constitution of their texts, with the result that interesting variants are often ignored because they are cloaked in anonymity. Yet allowance should at the very least always be made for the fact that good readings may go back to a lost manuscript. The organisers of the Workshop hoped that it might provide the occasion for some new light to be shed on textual criticism, especially in the pre-Petrarchan period, but it turned out to be impossible to find anybody actively doing research in this field.

The study of commentaries on classical texts is in contrast flourishing. Most of the important Greek scholia have been published, sometimes in monumental editions such as the *Scholia in Aristophanem* (no. 363-365). During the Workshop, Ruth Webb dealt with Byzantine grammatical commentaries of the late thirteenth and fourteenth centuries, with special reference to the unpublished commentary on the *Eikones* of the Elder Philostratos, and provided valuable illustrations of the practical problems posed by the study and the editing of such texts.

Commentaries on Latin texts are particularly numerous, and their tradition is somewhat complicated. The *Catalogus Translationum et Commentariorum* (no. 505) has marked a great step forward: in the volumes so far published many hitherto unknown commentaries and manuscripts have been brought to light, and the preparation of future volumes has already given rise to a considerable number of studies on, and editions of, texts relating to important authors such as Horace, Ovid and Virgil. The *Catalogus*, however, is essentially a repertory, even though it does provide comprehensive bibliographies and even biographies of the authors identi-

fied; much still remains to be done to enable us to distinguish the
old tradition from the new contributions, and to determine the
common characteristics of the different periods in a more syn-
chronic manner. Be that as it may, there is now a growing interest in medieval and Renaissance commentaries, as is clear from
the paper of Claudia Villa, who also discusses the evolution of the
genre and its influence on vernacular literature. More particularly, Alistair Minnis examines the way in which certain traditional
accessus idioms passed from Latin into the European vernaculars,
concentrating on the *accessus* to Ovid, and Klaus Siewert deals with
the significance of the vernacular glosses in Old High German,
which have been identified in a growing number of classical text-
books thanks to the German research programme on *Germanistische Glossenforschung*. Finally, there are valuable surveys of the commentaries on Horace by Karsten Friis-Jensen, on Statius by Violetta de Angelis and on Terence by Yves-François Riou.

Another interesting aspect of scholarship is the criticism of false
attributions. There was in fact an enormous body of pseudo-clas-
sical literature in circulation in the Middle Ages and the Renaissance, ascribed to most of the well-known authors, and in particular to Cicero, Ovid and Seneca. Some of these false attributions
go back to antiquity, others arose later on, either accidentally or
intentionally. Readers (and indeed scholars) had difficulty in dis-
tinguishing homonymous authors such as the Elder and Younger
Seneca or the Elder and Younger Pliny. In general, the Middle
Ages seemed inclined to accept the ascriptions which had come
down to them, but gradually more and more cases were queried,
beginning with the *Disticha Catonis* in the ninth century (no. 983).
There are however still many texts whose authenticity remains
open to doubt. This subject has not been much studied except for
the humanistic period (no. 982), and we are grateful to Paul Gerhard Schmidt for having concluded the workshop with a useful
outline of this topic.

As the need for a bibliography on medieval and early Renaissance scholarship was strongly expressed by the participants, a list
of about a thousand relevant studies has been compiled and added
at the end of this volume. Ole L. Smith, who spoke about Byzantine commentaries on classical Greek authors at the final symposium of the Network in Leuven in 1994, was persuaded to col-

laborate on this bibliography. His main contribution was received only a few months before his unexpected death, so that the final version of the Greek sections was regrettably deprived of his finishing touches.

BIRGER MUNK OLSEN

GREEK GRAMMATICAL GLOSSES AND SCHOLIA: THE FORM AND FUNCTION OF A LATE BYZANTINE COMMENTARY

RUTH WEBB*

The range of medieval Greek commentaries which contribute to the classical tradition is broad.[1] Rather than attempting to give a survey, I will concentrate on one commentary which can be dated to the very end of the thirteenth or the beginning of the fourteenth century, that composed by Manuel Moschopoulos to a text from the third century AD, the *Eikones* of the Elder Philostratos.[2] An analysis of the various components of this commentary in terms of their relationship to the text which they are supposed to elucidate, and with reference to other texts used in the teaching of grammar in the broadest sense, will help to show what the function of such a commentary was within the aims and methods of the Byzantine educational system.

In the context of the study of the classical tradition up to the Renaissance, the philological practices of the grammarians of the

* The original research for this paper was undertaken with the support of a British Academy Major State Studentship and the F.A. Yates Research Fellowship at the Warburg Institute. Grants from the British Academy and the University of London Central Research Fund allowed me to see the various manuscripts on which the study is based. The paper was written with the support of a British Academy Post-Doctoral Fellowship. I would also like to thank Jill Kraye who supervised the work for the thesis on which this paper is based and to Michael Reeve for his comments on the version presented at the colloquium.
[1] On Greek scholia and commentaries in general see for example N.G. Wilson, 'Scholiasti e commentatori', *Studi classici e orientali*, 33, 1983, pp. 83-112 and 'The Relation of Text and Scholia in Greek Books', in *Il libro e il testo*, eds C. Questa and R. Raffaelli, Urbino, 1984, pp. 105-110. On scholia in general see M.D. Reeve, 'Scholia' forthcoming in the new edition of the *Oxford Classical Dictionary*.
[2] Some excerpts from the commentary have been published in R. Browning, 'The So-called Tzetzes Scholia on Philostratus and Andreas Darmarios', *Classical Quarterly*, n.s. 5, 1955, pp. 195-200 and S. Lindstam, 'Die Philostratoskommentare und die Moschopoulos-Sylloga', *Göteborgs Högskolas Årsskrift*, 31, 1925, pp. 173-84. For a full transcription of the commentary see R. Webb, 'The Transmission of the *Eikones* of Philostratos and the Development of *Ekphrasis* from Late Antiquity to the Renaissance', Ph.D. diss., Warburg Institute, University of London, 1992, pp. 216-48.

Palaeologan period, such as Moschopoulos, are of particular interest since they formed the basis for the Greek studies of the Italian Renaissance.[3] There is a further advantage to studying the
commentaries to a text like the *Eikones*, which does not have an
illustrious place in the modern canon of classical texts: it can serve
as a reminder that the texts which were read in medieval schools
and whose influence in some form might therefore be expected to
be discernible in medieval literature, were not always those which
our civilisation considers to be of the greatest aesthetic importance.
Homer, the tragedians, Aristophanes and others did of course form
an important part of the Byzantine curriculum,[4] and the existing
studies of the manuscript transmission of these texts contain valuable clues as to the working methods, or lack of them, of Byzantine scholars of various periods.[5] Often, however, Byzantine grammatical scholia have been summarily discarded in the search for
clues to a pristine state of the text in question, or for comments
which correspond more closely to modern, literary interests.[6] The
scholia to Philostratos were similarly dismissed by a nineteenth-
century editor of the text as products of a 'less learned age' for
which no modern reader would find a use.[7] Such scholia, however, distant as they are from modern interests in classical texts, had
a precise function in their Byzantine context and it is this function
that I will seek to explore in what follows.

---

[3] See R.H. Robins, *The Byzantine Grammarians: Their Place in History*, Berlin,
1993, pp. 235-262.

[4] See N.G. Wilson, *Scholars of Byzantium*, London, 1983, pp. 18-27.

[5] See for example, R. Aubreton, *Démétrius Triclinius et les recensions médiévales de
Sophocle*, Paris, 1949; J. Irigoin, *Histoire du texte de Pindare*, Paris, 1952 and, for a
thorough demolition of earlier assessments of Moschopoulos and Thomas Magister's contributions to the text of Sophocles, R.D. Dawe, *Studies on the Text of
Sophocles*, I, Leiden, 1973, pp. 3-57.

[6] See for example the remarks of C.J. Herington who feels obliged to reas-
sure his readers that he has 'no more use than most people for mere scribblings
in the margins of the poets' and undertook his task in the hope that it would
lead 'to that strange and increasingly relevant historical phenomenon, the sur-
vival, through an era of collapse, of the best and most innocent that humanity
has created'. See *The Older Scholia on the Prometheus Bound*, ed. C.J. Herington, Leiden, 1972, p. ix. For a fascinating survey of the literary theories contained within older scholia see R. Meijering, *Literary and Rhetorical Theories in Greek Scholia*,
Groningen, 1987.

[7] Philostratos, *Opera*, ed. C.L. Kayser, Zurich, 1844, p. vi: 'Scholis destinatus
liber glossographos et schedographos valde exercuit, ut Manuelem Moschopulum
et Planudem, quorum Commentarios aetati parum litteratae olim utiles nemo
hodie desideravit.' The later editors also noted that there was nothing in the
scholia which could help in the interpretation or emendation of the text. See
Philostratos, *Imagines*, eds O. Benndorf and K. Schenkel, Leipzig, 1893, p. xviii.

Classical Greek poetry was read in the early stages of the Greek curriculum, as part of the mastery of grammar. The nature of the scholia to Philostratos, and the fact that the text is frequently found in manuscripts alongside grammatical treatises, show that the *Eikones* too were read at this stage in Late Byzantine schools. Like their Latin counterparts, Greek scholars were fond of referring to grammar as the foundation of all learning and the basis on which the subsequent stages of the curriculum were founded. Indeed, this stage of the curriculum provided, in addition to the rules of morphology and syntax, a general introduction to the literary heritage of the Byzantine élite.[8] Although the subjects of the quadrivium, arithmetic, geometry, music and astronomy, were still taught and were the subject of learned commentaries and intellectual debate,[9] the main focus of the education system was on the literary subjects of grammar, rhetoric and philosophy. The reasons for this were eminently practical since the ability to compose elegant speeches on imperial or religious subjects, following ancient models and in Atticising prose, was an important qualification for a successful career in Church or State.[10] A disagreement about literary style even formed part of the bitter polemic between two fourteenth-century statesmen, Theodore Metochites and Nikephoros Choumnos.[11]

The practical importance of a mastery of the classical language which they exemplified seems to have been sufficient in itself to justify the continued study of pagan texts.[12] Byzantine grammarians intermingled examples from classical and Christian texts with no apparent sense of contradiction or unease.[13] Most importantly,

---

[8] See the comments of P. Magdalino, *The Empire of Manuel I Komnenos, 1143-80*, Cambridge, 1993, p. 330.

[9] Constantinides, *Higher Education in Byzantium in the Thirteenth and Early Fourteenth Centuries*, Nicosia, 1982, pp. 113-58 and I. Ševčenko, *Études sur la polémique entre Théodore Métochite et Nicéphore Choumnos*, Brussels, 1962, pp. 68-75 on a debate on astronomy.

[10] E. Patlagean, 'Discours écrit, discours parlé: niveaux de culture à Byzance aux VIIIᵉ-XIᵉ siècles', *Annales*, 34, 1979, pp. 264-78 (267). For further discussion of the Byzantine literary idiom see R. Browning, 'The Language of Byzantine Literature', in *The 'Past' in Medieval and Modern Greek Culture*, ed. S. Vryonis, Malibu, 1978, pp. 103-33.

[11] Ševčenko, *Études* (n. 9 above), pp. 51-67.

[12] See Wilson, *Scholars of Byzantium* (n. 4 above), pp. 8-12.

[13] Ibid., p. 27. See also Robins, *The Byzantine Grammarians* (n. 3 above), p. 126. It is interesting to note, however, that a fourteenth-century prose version of the *Odyssey* not intended for school use omitted some episodes involving pagan gods.

although Byzantine authors did compose in verse, sometimes imitating the literary dialects of classical literature, most of the high-style literary output was in Atticising prose. This meant that, on the whole, poetry was read not as a model for imitation as a genre, but for the rules of grammar and for the vocabulary which it could provide.[14] It is against this background that commentaries used in teaching should be considered.

The Eikones *and its commentary*

The *Eikones* purport to be descriptions of paintings of mainly mythological subjects and were probably composed as models of *ekphrasis*, the vivid evocation of scenes. They were certainly recommended as such by Ioannes Sardianos in the ninth century and some were included in a miscellany of rhetoric and epistolography dating to the early thirteenth century.[15] Yet the commentary I will be discussing here shows that they were used in the teaching of grammar in Late Byzantium. The evidence from fifteenth-century manuscripts suggests that it was as a grammar book, too, that Philostratos' work first reached the Renaissance West.[16]

The commentary covers only the *Proem* and the first twenty-six descriptions of the first book (the modern editions follow the majority of manuscripts in dividing the *Eikones* into two books, the first of 31 and the second of 34 short chapters, each describing one 'painting'). The earliest manuscripts of the *Eikones* date from the thirteenth century: MS Florence, Laurentianus Pluteus LXIX.30 (containing the whole text), MS Oxford, Bodleian Library, Barocci 131 (excerpts from Book II) and MS Paris, Bibliothèque Nationale, suppl. grec 65 (the beginning of Book I). Only the last has any form of commentary and this differs significantly from the standard commentary found in later manuscripts. However, from

---

See R. Browning, 'A Fourteenth-century Prose Version of the Odyssey', *Dumbarton Oaks Papers*, 46, 1992, pp. 27-36.

[14] See R. Webb, 'A Slavish Art? Language and Grammar in Late Byzantine Education and Society', *Dialogos*, 1, 1994, pp. 81-103.

[15] See Ioannes Sardianos, *Commentarium in Aphthonii Progymnasmata*, ed. H. Rabe, Leipzig, 1928, p. 215 and Wilson, 'A Byzantine Miscellany: MS Barocci 131 Described', *Jahrbuch der österreichischen Byzantinistik*, 27, 1978, pp. 157-79.

[16] See Webb, 'The Transmission of the *Eikones*' (n. 2 above), pp. 142-68 for further discussion.

the fourteenth century there exist at least twenty manuscripts of the text with standard commentary, and seventeen dating from the fifteenth and sixteenth centuries. In some manuscripts only the commented portions of the text, i.e. *Eikones*, I, *Proem* and 1-26, are copied, but in others the uncommented chapters 27-31 are added at the end.

This section of the *Eikones* with commentary forms part of a selection of texts used for teaching grammar in the late thirteenth and fourteenth centuries and associated with the school of Maximos Planudes and his pupil Manuel Moschopoulos. This selection, christened 'Scholastic Anthology' by Gallavotti, includes, in addition to the *Eikones*, a selection of epigrams from the *Planudean Anthology* and excerpts from Marcus Aurelius' *Meditations* and Aelian's *Natural History*, all with grammatical commentaries of a similar kind.[17] The selection is at first sight an unusual one, but the works included share in common the practical advantage for the teacher of being divided into manageable sections. Moreover, they present the student with a range of linguistic styles and dialects. In the particular case of the *Eikones*, the variety of subjects in the 'paintings' described by Philostratos demands a varied and often recherché vocabulary.[18] Moreover, although Philostratos' terse and asyndetic style is often difficult to understand, he does not make use of complex periodic sentences.

Apart from the epigrams, therefore, the components of the 'Scholastic Anthology' are in prose, a departure from the traditional practice of teaching grammar through poetry. That works in poetic metre were still considered to be the essential medium through which grammar was taught is suggested by the cross-references to other authors in the commentary to the *Eikones*. The most frequently cited are Homer, Hesiod, Sophocles, Aristophanes and the Psalms. One can only speculate about the significance of, and motivation for, this development in its Byzantine context. It

---

[17] C. Gallavotti, 'Planudea II', *Bollettino del Comitato per la preparazione della Edizione nazionale*, n.s. 8, 1960, p. 13. The scholia to the epigrams have been published in A. Luppino, 'Scholia Graeca inedita in Anthologiae epigrammata selecta', *Atti della Accademia Pontaniana*, n.s. 9, 1959-60, pp. 25-62 and those to Aelian in L. Marcheselli Loukas, 'Note schedografiche inedite del Marc. gr. Z487 = 883', *Rivista di Studi Bizantini e Neoellenici*, 8-9, 1971-2, pp. 241-60.

[18] This was noted in the sixteenth century by Blaise de Vigenère, who made the first translation of the *Eikones* into French. See Philostratos, *Les Images ou tableaux de platte-peinture mis en François par Blaise de Vigenère*, Paris, 1578, p. 17.

is possible that the ever widening gap between the spoken and
written language called for new approaches to teaching. At this
period, the number of texts from the traditional canon of poets
which students were expected to read seems to have been dwind-
ling, to judge from the selections presented in the surviving manuscripts.[19] But the very existence of the 'Scholastic Anthology' suggests that, at the same time, new works were being added to those
read at this stage of the curriculum, perhaps in an attempt to find
texts which, while still suitable for grammatical and lexical dissec-
tion, were likely to be directly useful as models for prose composition.

The commentary: layout and attribution

The commentary is set out in three distinct areas of the page:
between the lines of the text; around the text in the side, top and
bottom margins (cf. Fig. 1, bottom) and in blocks following the
individual chapters and written in the space normally reserved for
the text (Fig. 2). In the majority of the manuscripts in which text
and commentary were copied simultaneously, Philostratos' text is
written in widely spaced lines with wide margins, while the blocks
of commentary with which the text is interspersed are written in
more closely spaced lines with narrower margins. In manuscripts
which contain the uncommented chapters 27-31 of Book I, these
are laid out in the same way as this text-space commentary: in
closely spaced lines with narrower margins (Fig. 1, top). In the
most carefully written manuscripts a separate column for the marginal comments is ruled so as to leave a narrow vertical band of
blank space between the text and the corresponding marginal comments. Where this is the case, the text-space commentary may
extend over this vertical band to the very edge of the column ruled
for marginal comments (Fig. 2). In manuscripts where more than
one component of the 'Scholastic Anthology' was copied by the
same scribe the same layout is used throughout.

The fact that the commentary is found in two main areas of the
manuscripts—around the text and after individual chapters—has
led to the view that there are in fact two, distinct commentaries.

---

[19] See A. Dain, 'A propos de l'étude des poètes anciens à Byzance', in *Studi
in onore di Ugo Enrico Paoli*, Florence, 1956, pp. 195-201.

This can be traced back as far as Bandini who, in his catalogue of Laurentian manuscripts attributed one commentary to Moschopoulos and the other to his teacher, Maximos Planudes.[20] This argument is supported by the fact that the first marginal comment and the first comment found in the text space are both to the first line of the *Proem* and make different points. The marginal comment refers to the structure of Philostratos' opening phrase, ὅστις μὴ ἀσπάζεται τὴν ζωγραφίαν... ('whosoever is not fond of painting') and explains that such a clause is incomplete in itself since it begins with the indefinite relative pronoun. The first comment found in the text-space refers to the same line, but discusses the meaning of the verb ἀσπάζομαι (in this context 'to be fond of'), its synonyms and opposites, and is followed by comments in a similar vein on the meaning of words in the first lines of the *Proem*. However, after the *Proem* there is no further such duplication.[21] Rather, the material in the text space, consisting largely of lengthy word-lists discussed below, is complementary to that in the margins, as will be evident from the examples cited below, and had a distinct pedagogical function. Moreover, such a layout is not a usual way of indicating authorship.[22] In fact from the eleventh century onwards scribes had commonly broken up texts into short sections and written the commentary below each short section, as well as in the margins, in order to synchronise text and comments.[23]

The layout of the commentary is largely dictated by practical problems and, to a certain extent, reflects the functions of the different components. The following sections will examine each of these components in turn, beginning with the interlinear comments.

---

[20] A.M. Bandini, *Catalogus codicum manuscriptorum Bibliothecae Mediceae Laurentianae*, Florence, 1764, II, p. 246.

[21] The division of the material into two commentaries proposed by S. Lindstam, 'Die Philostratoskommentare und die Moschopoulos-Sylloga', *Göteborgs Högskolas Årsskrift*, 31, 1925, pp. 173-84, is based on the distribution of scholia between margins and text-space in one highly idiosyncratic manuscript, MS Vatican, Biblioteca Apostolica Vaticana, Vat. gr. 97, and is not representative of the majority of manuscripts.

[22] When the authorship of individual comments was important, scribes used abbreviated forms of names or symbols to indicate the author and drew attention to this in an explanatory note as in MSS Vatican, BAV, Vat. gr. 47 and Naples, Biblioteca Nazionale, II.F.9. See R. Aubreton, *Démétrius Triclinius* (n. 4 above), pp. 64 and 74.

[23] See G. Prato, 'La presentazione del testo nei manoscritti tardobizantini', in *Il libro e il testo* (n. 1 above), p. 99.

Interlinear glosses and comments

The comments which are most closely bound to the text, in terms of their function and their place on the page, are those written between the lines of the text. These take several forms. Most are single word glosses or short phrases which paraphrase or otherwise explain the meaning of a word. Often they are introduced by ἤγουν ('that is to say', 'or rather') followed by an alternative term in the same number or case, if a noun, or number and tense for verbs. Occasionally the gloss adds further brief explanations, such as, for example, that a neuter plural adjective is being used as an adverb and that this usage is characteristic of Attic Greek.[24] Other interlinear comments explain the grammatical function of a word or small element of the phrase or supply words which need to be understood, such as the verb 'to be', frequently elided by Philostratos and other Attic or Atticising authors. They may clarify the syntax, identifying the antecedent above pronouns to ensure that the reference and the grammatical structure are clear.

Some longer interlinear comments give more extended paraphrases of difficult terms or discuss their etymologies. Thus the term ἀναλογία, in *Eikones*, I, 4 ('proportion') is glossed as follows: ἤγουν ὁμοιότης κατὰ τὸ προσῆκον ἑκάστῳ μέρει ('or rather, similarity in accordance with/in relation to what is fitting for each part).'[25]

In the same passage, the word for the dragon's lair beside which the hero Menoikeus is fated to die, ἡ χειά, is provided with an etymology derived from the *Etymologicum Magnum*: χειὰ παρὰ τὸ χεῖσθαι ὅ ἐστι χωρεῖσθαι. τοῦτο γὰρ ἐπιτηδεύεται ὁ ὄφις ('*Cheia* ('hole') derives from the verb *cheisthai* ('to be thrown out into a mound') which means to be withdrawn, taken away. For this is what the snake does').[26]

One frequent feature of the interlinear scholia, indicating a particular difficulty in comprehension, is the paraphrase of datives using the genitive with a preposition. For example, describing a

---

[24] In MS Vatican, Vat. gr. 97, f.25ᵛ, ἴσα used in this sense is glossed as follows: ἤγουν κατίσον, ἐπίρρημα ἀττικῶς. (Interlinear scholia not included in my transcription are cited from the manuscript in which they are to be found.)

[25] MS Vatican, Vat. Pal. gr. 143, f. 10ᵛ.

[26] Ibid.. Compare *Etymologicum Magnum*, ed. F. Sylburg, Leipzig, 1816, col.734: χειά...ἀπὸ τοῦ χεῖσθαι, ὅ ἐστι χωρεῖσθαι εἰς αὐτὸ γὰρ μηχανᾶται ὁ ὄφις χωρῆσαι τὸ σῶμα ὥσπερ εἰς ἔλυτρον.

wreath of flowers worn by the god Komos, Philostratos uses the instrumental dative of the colours 'with which' the painter may imitate the appearance of flowers: ξανθοῖς γὰρ καὶ κυανοῖς... χρώμασιν ἀπομιμεῖσθαι τὰς τῶν ἀνθέων εἰκόνας (297K) ('to imitate the appearance of flowers [with] light and dark colours (dat.)'). Here the interlinear comment replaces the dative with the genitive and preposition διά: ἤγουν διὰ ξανθῶν χρωμάτων, διὰ κυανῶν ('or rather through light colours, through dark [colours] (gen.)'.[27]

The dative, however, which had begun to disappear from spoken Greek in the Alexandrian period, appears to be the only case which presented even the novice reader with any great problems of comprehension, although in their writings Byzantine authors often use prepositions with cases which contravene classical usage.[28] There is nothing comparable to the systems of symbols or numbers used in Latin manuscripts to indicate which words agree, nor is the case found written above nouns or adjectives as occurs in Latin manuscripts with grammatical commentaries.[29] Spoken Greek retained the distinction between nominative, accusative and genitive, although with different forms and uses from classical Greek, so that the basic comprehension of the case system probably caused few problems. Indeed it was the Italian visitors to Constantinople, such as Guarino and Filelfo, who argued, on the basis of their experience of contemporary Greek speech, that classical Latin could have been spoken—and that it was not impossible even for women to decline nouns.[30]

In general, these glosses serve to aid comprehension of the text, a purpose which is not as self-evident as it may seem, as will become clear. However, the function is not always simply explanatory. The same word may be both glossed and used as a gloss on another within the same passage, suggesting that the purpose of some of these interlinear glosses was to extend the pupils' vocab-

---

[27] MS Paris, Bibliothèque Nationale, suppl. gr. 65, f. 187[r].

[28] R. Browning, *Medieval and Modern Greek*, Cambridge, 1983, pp. 36-7 and 82-3.

[29] See S. Reynolds, 'Learning Latin in the Twelfth Century: A Study of the Grammatical and Rhetorical Glosses on Horace's Satires', Ph.D. diss, Warburg Institute, University of London, 1991; R.J. Hexter, *Ovid and Medieval Schooling*, Munich, 1986, p. 38.

[30] See Filelfo's letter to Sforza Secondo in M. Tavoni, *Latino, grammatica, volgare: storia di una questione umanistica*, Padua, 1984, pp. 278-9.

ulary by providing synonyms. As the examples above show, these comments also provide further information about the word in question: its etymology or the register of literary language to which it belongs. This manner of placing words against a larger linguistic background is characteristic of the marginal scholia which are the subject of the next section.

Marginal comments

It is difficult to draw a strict distinction between interlinear and marginal comments on a formal level. Although single word glosses and longer paraphrases tend to be interlinear, slightly longer comments may be written either between the lines or in the margins, or may begin above the word in question and extend out into the margin. To this extent, the arrangement of the scholia depended on the scribe, and different manuscripts show different tendencies. However, some general differences in function between the short interlinear comments and the more extended marginal comments can be discerned, and the relation of commentary to text on the page reflects these differences. On the whole, the interlinear comments are closely linked to the word above which they are written and aim to help the reader to understand words and elements of syntax in their immediate context. The marginal comments, however, rather than helping the reader to understand a word and its relation to other words in the phrase, depart from this context and place the word or grammatical point in question against a broader linguistic background.[31]

Some of these marginal scholia make straightforward points of morphology, explaining the contracted forms of adjectives or perfect participles which occur in Philostratos' text and providing further examples to illustrate these rules. Others discuss points of accentuation, vowel length, rough and smooth breathings. Often, however, the marginal comments take their starting point from an explanation of the meaning of a particular term but go on to develop this in ways which are no longer relevant to the understanding of the word in the immediate context of Philostratos' text.

---

[31] M.L. Rosenkranz, 'Gli "atticismi" negli scoli ad Aristofane', *Helikon*, 4, 1964, pp. 261-78 provides a useful typology of grammatical scholia.

For example, in his description of the hero Menoikeus on the battlements of Thebes, Philostratos, in a rare reference to pictorial composition, describes how the painter has placed figures of armed men around the walls. The phrase he uses, περιβάλλων τοῖς τείχεσιν ἄνδρας ὡπλισμένους (299K) can be interpreted in two ways, either as 'surrounding the walls (dat.) with armed men (acc.)' or 'surrounding armed men (acc.) with the walls (dat.)'. Since he goes on to describe how, in the painting, the battlements hide most of the figures so that only the helmets or the spears are visible, it would seem that the second interpretation is to be preferred. The interlinear gloss to περιβάλλων is περιτιθείς suggesting, without further comment, the interpretation 'surrounding the walls with armed men'. The marginal comment takes the text as a starting point from which to make a general point about usage:

> περιβάλλω τινά, ἤγουν περιπλέκομαι. καὶ περιβάλλω τί τινι, ἤγουν περιτίθημι. καὶ περιβάλλει ὁ Θεὸς τὸν οὐρανὸν ἐν νεφέλαις, ἤγουν ἐνδύει. (I surround or enfold someone (acc.). And I put something (acc.) around someone (dat.). And God envelops, or clothes, heaven (acc.) in clouds.)

The student is shown how to use the verb in different ways and how to interpret it when he meets it in a new context, but the comment does nothing to help the comprehension of this difficult passage in Philostratos' text.

But by far the most informative comments for our understanding of Byzantine approaches to the literary language are those which deal with the range of meaning of words or phrases. A comment explaining the word ἀφρός, referring to the foam which is said to cover the horses in *Eikones*, I, 17 ('Hippodameia'), reads as follows:

> ἀφροῦ: ἀφρὸς τὸ ἀπὸ συγκρούσεως καὶ κοπῆς καὶ λεπτύνσεως τῶν ὑγρῶν ἐν τῇ ἐπιφανείᾳ λευκόν. φρὶξ δὲ ἀφ᾽ οὗ τὸ φρίττειν ἐπὶ τῆς ἐπιφανείας τῆς θαλάττης, ὅταν ὑπὸ τῶν πνευμάτων τραχύνηται. διαφέρει δὲ τοῦ ἀφροῦ τῷ τὸν μὲν ἀφρὸν εἶναι λευκόν, τὴν φρίκα δὲ μέλαιναν, ὡς παρ᾽ Ὁμήρῳ μελαίνῃ φρικὶ καλυφθείς. (Foam (aphros) is the whiteness created by liquids hitting and striking against each other and becoming rarefied on the surface. A ripple (phrix), whence the verb to bristle or shiver (phrittein), [occurs] upon the surface of the sea whenever it is roughened by the winds. It differs from foam in that foam is white, while ripples are dark, as in Homer: 'hidden by the dark ripple'.)

The comment begins with an account of the nature of the substance and how it occurs. It is evident from what follows that the type of foam which is referred to in the comment is that which appears, like ripples, on water. The context and meaning of the word within Philostratos' description are therefore ignored in favour of a more general definition. Although the accounts of both phenomena appear to refer to the rules of the natural world, the quotation from Homer with which the comment ends shows that these are, above all, literary phenomena whose attributes derive from texts, not from observation of the material world.

The scholia take their cue from one word in the text to build such distinctions between terms, often introducing quotations from other sources to illustrate the use of one of the related terms. Rather than explaining the word in its context, they make the pupil aware of the shades of meaning. A comment on the word ἀτμός ('vapour'), referring to the smoke rising from the torch held by the god Komos in *Eikones*, I, 2, explores the various words for smoke—κνίσσα ('the vapours arising from meat'), καπνός ('wood smoke'), ἀναθυμίασις ('exhalation, evaporation')—which can be covered by this term and the precise context in which each should be used. The range of precision in terms which is typical of classical Greek, like other literary languages, and a feature of which Byzantine grammarians and rhetoricians were acutely aware.[32]

Word-lists

This tendency in the marginal scholia to work outwards from the text is continued and taken further in the element of the commentary which follows the individual chapters in the manuscripts. The field below the text of the individual *Eikones* serves as an overflow for comments which will not fit into the margins as well as for lengthy word-lists which are related to the exercise of schedography, a specifically Byzantine development in the teaching of grammar.[33] In a typical schedographic text a short passage, often

---

[32] See, for example, Joseph Rhakendytes, *Synopsis Rhetorikes*, in *Rhetores Graeci*, ed. C. Walz, III, Stuttgart, 1834, p. 529: πλουσία πάνυ ἐστὶν ἡ Ἑλληνικὴ γλῶσσα καὶ οὐκ ἄν τις ἀπορήσειε διαφόρων ὀνομάτων πεπαιδευμένος ὁπωσοῦν ἐν τοῖς λόγοις. The classical, literary form of Arabic is also characterised by a wider range of vocabulary than is found in the colloquial form. See S.J. Altoma, *The Problem of Diglossia in Arabic: a Comparative Study of Classical and Iraqi Arabic*, Cambridge, Mass., 1969, p. 4.

[33] See R.H. Robins, *The Byzantine Grammarians* (n. 3 above), pp. 125-48; H.

no more than a few lines, is exhaustively analysed. Each word in discussed in terms of its etymology, declension or conjugation and, as in the marginal scholia to Philostratos described above, further examples are frequently adduced to illustrate the point as thoroughly as possible. In the collection of schedographic texts attributed to Moschopoulos himself,[34] the proportion of commentary to text is significantly increased by the inclusion of lists of words beginning with the same syllable, or with syllables which were written differently but sounded the same in Byzantine, and modern, pronunciation and which were therefore liable to be mis-spelt by Byzantine schoolboys.

It is lists of just this kind which are found written in the text-space following most of the *Eikones*. They take their starting point from one word in the text and develop a complex network of inter-related terms through associations of sound, sense and literary connotation. The meaning of each word cited is discussed and sometimes illustrated by a quotation from a classical author. One common approach in these lists is naturally to identify groups of words with common roots, which therefore share the same opening syllable. The first list (Fig. 2)—words beginning υ and οι, both pronounced 'i'—contains various words related to ὑγίεια ('health') with some discussion of their meaning (noting that ὑγιεινός means both 'healthy' in the sense of a body which is in good health and 'health-giving' of a medicine) and examples of how to use them in phrases. Distinctions in register are also mentioned in the word lists. The list of words in υ begins with a distinction, derived from the second-century AD Atticising lexicon of Moeris, between the Attic spelling of the word for glass (ὕαλος) and the *koine* spelling (ὕελος). Also included in these word lists are forms from dialects other than Attic, such as ὕσδος, the Aeolic form of ὄζος ('branch'), accompanied by the line in Sappho in which it occurs and an explanation of the dialect form, explained as a transformation of the Attic form which is thought of as standard.[35]

Hunger, *Die hochsprachliche profane Literatur der Byzantiner*, II, Munich, 1978, pp. 24-9.

[34] Manuel Moschopoulos, *Peri schedon*, Paris, 1545.

[35] This passage reads as follows: ὕσδος ὁ ὄζος παρ'Αἰολεῦσιν. οὗτοι γὰρ τρέπουσι τὸ ο εἰς υ καὶ τὸ ζ διαλύουσιν εἰς τὸ σ καὶ δ, ὡς παρὰ Σαπφοῖ ἀμφὶ δὲ ὕδωρ ψυχρὸν κελαδεῖ δι' ὕσδων μαλίνων. For a similar approach to the Doric dialect from elsewhere in the commentary to the Scholastic Anthology see Luppino, 'Scholia graeca inedita in Anthologiae epigrammata selecta' (n. 17 above), p. 38.

Only extremely rarely is any word which could be described as vernacular used at any point in the commentary. Some exceptions are the terms of Latin origin such as καβαλλάριος, introduced as a *koine* equivalent to ἱππεύς ('horseman') in the list of words beginning ιππ, ηπ and ειπ, all pronounced 'ip', which follows *Eikones*, I, 5, or ὄρδινος ('row, line') similarly introduced as an equivalent to στίχος in the list following *Eikones*, I, 8. Both the above terms are referred to as *koine*, a register which can equally well include words used by Aristotle. In the list of words beginning πυ and ποι, pronounced 'pi', which follows *Eikones*, I, 6, the classical word πυελίς (strictly, the setting for a precious stone) is described as 'what we call *sphragidophulakion*' (τὸ ὑφ' ἡμῶν λεγόμενον σφραγιδοφυλάκιον) in a direct quotation from the ninth-century lexicon by Photios, which is the earliest instance of the word.[36] In one other case a specifically Byzantine use of a classical term is mentioned: that of φροντιστήρια (a term originally coined by Aristophanes for Socrates's 'Thinkery' in the *Clouds*) to mean 'monasteries', a usage which dates back to Evagrius in the sixth century.[37]

The lexical and grammatical network thus created works on more than one level. On the one hand, words are juxtaposed with near synonyms, the difference between them serving to sharpen the distinction between their respective semantic ranges. Words formed on comparable patterns are related. Moreover, a further level of complexity is added by the distinctions made between the various registers or dialects of Greek literary language. Attic usages are juxtaposed with poetic and Homeric terms as well as with the language of the Septuagint and 'common' *koine* forms. This last category covers a wide range—from vocabulary used by Aristotle to Byzantine terms of Latin origin. The diversity of literary Greek was noted by Lorenzo Valla in the fifteenth century. Comparing the unity of Latin to the multiplicity of forms of Greek he asked how, if the Greeks cannot agree amongst themselves, they could possibly expect anyone else to learn their language.[38]

---

[36] Photios, *Lexicon*, ed. R. Porson, II, Leipzig, 1823, p. 407.

[37] This occurs in a discussion of words ending -ηριον which is found following *Eikones*, I, 16, the starting point for which is the mention of Daedalus' workshop (ἐργαστήριον).

[38] L. Valla, Preface to the First Book of the *Elegantiae*, in *Prosatori Latini del '400*, ed. E. Garin, Naples, 1952, p. 598: 'Graeci interse consentire non possunt, nedum alios ad sermonem suum se perducturos sperent. Varie apud eos loquuntur auctores, attice, aeolice, ionice, dorice, κοινῶς: apud nos, id est apud multas nationes, nemo nisi romane, in qua lingua disciplinae cunctae libero homine

References to contemporary practices of any sort are absent from the commentary as a whole. What may at first sight appear to be such, for example the mention of ἀνακαλυπτήρια, defined as 'the gifts given to brides when they are unveiled for the first time so as to be visible to men', turn out to be quotations from ancient lexica.[39] This reluctance to refer to *realia* extends even to the contents of Philostratos' text. Despite the many references in the text to places, customs, articles of clothing and equipment, the commentary confines itself to grammatical and lexical points. The word lists do contain a large number of names of ancient Athenian institutions, all derived from Harpocration's lexicon to the Attic orators in which such terms are defined.[40] But within the context of the word lists such terms are important not for their referents but rather for the shape of the word itself and its place within the network of associated words.

The result is a commentary which, rather than serving to interpret the text, uses individual words and phrases taken out of context to illustrate general points.[41] The degree to which the usefulness of the commentary was independent from the text is shown by the fact that an entirely independent work, the *Sylloge of Attic Words*, was compiled from this and other Moschopoulean commentaries. Arranged in alphabetical order and slightly emended to include new information from other sources, the comments were as useful as they had been in their original context.[42]

---

dignae continentur, sicut in sua multiplici apud Graecos.' I am grateful to Jill Kraye for this reference.

[39] Ibid.: ἀνακαλυπτήρια δὲ τὰ διδόμενα δῶρα ταῖς νυμφαῖς, ὅταν τὸ πρῶτον ἀνακαλύπτωνται ὥστε ὁραθῆναι τοῖς ἀνδράσιν. Compare Pollux, *Onomasticon*, ed. J. Bekker, Berlin, 1846, III, p. 115.

[40] On Moschopoulos' use of Harpocration see J. Keaney, 'Moschopoulos and Harpocration', *Transactions of the American Philological Association*, 100, 1969, pp. 201-207.

[41] For suggestions as to how such a commentary might have been used in the classroom see Webb, 'A Slavish Art?' (n. 14 above).

[42] The version published in Venice in 1524 was entitled Τῶν ὀνομάτων Ἀττικῶν ξυλλογὴ ἐκλεγεῖσα ἀπὸ τῆς τεχνολογίας τῶν εἰκόνων τοῦ Φιλοστράτου ἣν ἐξέδοτο ὁ σοφώτατος κύριος Μανουὴλ ὁ Μοσχόπουλος, καὶ ἀπὸ τῶν βιβλίων τῶν ποιητῶν. (*Sylloge of Attic Words Selected from the Commentary to the Eikones of Philostratos which the Most Wise Manuel Moschopoulos Published, and from the Books of the Poets.*)

The aims of the commentary and the nature of grammar

The nature of the commentary described above is entirely compatible with an education system whose final aim was the active use of the classical language, rather than the interpretation of classical texts. The pupils were receiving a training in which words to use in which context and how. This can be seen to apply even to the discussions of the literary dialects which can be read as prescriptive instructions for the formation of pseudo-dialect forms where required by the genre, rather than as accounts of historical phenomena.[43] This means of course, that the only words and phrases which are commented are those which can be paralleled in the regular usage of other authors. Philostratos' language is highly elliptical and many of his usages, such as the nominative absolute, were considered to be grammatical faults by Byzantine standards. Indeed Philostratos was one of the main targets of Ioannes Glykys, a slightly later contemporary of Moschopoulos and Planudes, in his treatise 'on correct syntax'.[44] The commentary, however, nowhere draws attention to this feature of Philostratos' style. At most, the interlinear glosses tacitly substitute the regular genitive absolute for the nominative absolute which so enraged Glykys.

This lack of interest in the idiosyncracies which, to a modern reader are perhaps the most fascinating aspect of the language of the *Eikones*, can be explained by reference to the definition of grammar current in Byzantium. This was set out in the treatise on grammar attributed to Dionysius Thrax (fl. c. 100 BC),[45] and was repeated unchanged by Moschopoulos in one of his own grammatical works, the *Erotemata*. Grammar according to Dionysios was 'acquaintance with what is generally said by poets and prose writers'.[46] As the Byzantine commentators explain, the grammarian cannot be concerned with every single *hapax legomenon*.[47] Words are

[43] On the use of dialect forms in Byzantine poetry see Browning, 'The Language of Byzantine Literature' (n. 10 above), pp 112-13 and 124-5.

[44] I. Glykys, *Opus de vera syntaxeos ratione*, ed. A. Jahn, Bern, 1839, pp. 53-4. For further discussion see Robins, *The Byzantine Grammarians* (n. 3 above), pp. 173-200 (198-9).

[45] See Robins *The Byzantine Grammarians* (n. 3 above), p. 42, on the text and its attribution.

[46] Dionysios Thrax, *Techne Grammatike*, ed. G.B. Pecorella, Bologna, 1962, p. 31: γραμματική ἐστιν ἐμπειρία τῶν παρὰ ποιηταῖς τε καὶ συγγραφεῦσιν ὡς ἐπὶ τὸ πολὺ λεγομένων.

[47] See *Grammatici Graeci*, ed. A. Hilgard, III, Leipzig, 1901, pp. 11, ll. 13-14 and 301, ll. 11-12.

of interest to the grammarian in so far as they are representative and can be related to other words.

Such commentaries aimed to provide a range of vocabulary, to make pupils aware of the literary registers of individual words and the appropriateness of particular words in particular contexts. This demanded a fine grasp of shades of meaning as well as an awareness of the register to which a word belongs. It was this understanding of the proprieties of all aspects of literary language, including vocabulary, subject-matter and, in the context of poetry, metre which prepared the student for the highest part of grammar. According to Dionysios Thrax, again repeated by Moschopoulos in the *Erotemata*, this was the κρίσις ποιημάτων—the judgement of works of poetry. As the scholia to Dionysios once more make clear, this is not an aesthetic judgement—that would have been the job of a poet, and grammarians are not poets.[48] According to these scholia the 'judgement' in question was primarily linguistic, involving the ability to distinguish the genuine from the spurious text. What is clear is that such commentaries do not aim to give aesthetic insights into a text but use it as a treasury of examples from which to build up a network of cross-references to other texts. The words in question derive their significance not from their reference to reality, nor primarily from their immediate context, but from their relation to the other words with which they are constantly compared and contrasted.

The attitude towards the literary language as a system of signs which this commentary reveals and which, in the fourteenth century, it helped to generate in its users, underlies Byzantine rhetoric.[49] The study of such grammatical commentaries against the background of the larger aims of the curriculum can shed light both on the nature and function of the commentaries themselves and on the high-style literary productions of their period.

---

[48] Ibid., pp. 170, ll. 2-5 and 304, ll. 2-3.

[49] See P. Lemerle, *Le premier humanisme byzantin*, Paris, 1971, p. 307: 'La rhétorique byzantine représente *l'autre* aspect du langage... Elle appartient à ce monde des *signes* qui double et transcende celui des formes, et qui est l'autre face du réel.'

1. MS Paris, cliché Bibliothèque Nationale de France – Paris, suppl. gr. 1164, f. 3ᵛ
The end of *Eikones*, I, 31 and beginning of extracts from Marcus Aurelius, showing the difference in layout between commented and uncommented parts of the Scholastic Anthology.

2. MS Paris, cliché Bibliothèque Nationale de France – Paris, suppl. gr. 1698, f. 45ᵛ
The end of *Eikones*, I, 1, *Skamander*, with the word-list in the text-space.

I COMMENTI AI CLASSICI FRA XII E XV SECOLO

CLAUDIA VILLA

Se è opportuno iniziare con una osservazione di carattere generale, vorrei sottolineare che l'interesse per gli esercizi di commento si è fatto, per molte discipline, assai vivace in questi ultimi anni: e mi li mito a ricordare il convegno di Parigi nel 1988, un ciclo di lezioni— mai pubblicate—organizzate presso l'Università di Pavia nella primavera dell'89 e il seminario di Ascona nell'autunno dello stesso anno, il seminario di Bressanone sull'autocommento nel luglio del 1990.[1] Si è dunque precisato un interesse specifico per un settore letterario che è stato, nella maggior parte dei casi, totalmente ignorato dalle storie delle letterature nazionali; mentre ha ottenuto finalmente udienza in imprese come *Lo spazio letterario di Roma antica*, III—dove Margherita Spallone ha presentato 'I percorsi medievali del testo: *accessus*, commentari, florilegi'[2]—e *Lo spazio letterario del Medioevo*, III, con il previsto contributo di L. Holtz, *Le glosse e i commenti*. Così cominciamo anche a disporre di sintesi teoriche, come quella di Cesare Segre, presentata ad Ascona;[3] e di singoli, specifici contributi dedicati a uno dei generi che la cultura mediolatina ha sommamente diletto: come aveva lucidamente avvertito Paul O. Kristeller, avviando negli anni '60 il monumentale censimento dei commenti medioevali con il titolo di *Corpus translationum et commentariorum*.[4]

È infatti importante ricordare quanto, fra XII e XIII secolo, gli uomini di cultura abbiano considerato il commento come un esercizio altissimo; se Guillaume de Conches si spinge fino a dichiarare

---

[1] *Les commentaires et la naissance de la critique littéraire, France/Italie (XIVᵉ-XVIᵉ siècles). Actes du Colloque internationale sur le commentaire. Paris, mai 1988*, Textes réunis et présentés par G. Mathieu-Castellani et M. Plaisance, Paris, 1990; *Il Commento ai testi. Atti del Seminario di Ascona. 2-9 ottobre 1989*, a cura di O. Besomi e C. Caruso, Basel-Boston-Berlin, 1992.

[2] *Lo spazio letterario di Roma antica*, III: *La ricezione del testo*, Roma, 1990, pp. 387-471.

[3] C. Segre, 'Per una definizione del commento ai testi' in *Il Commento ai testi* (n. 1 sopra), pp. 3-14; utili osservazioni anche in J. Fohrmann, 'Il commento come unità discorsiva delle scienze', *Allegoria*, 1, 1989, pp. 57-72.

[4] P. O. Kristeller, *Catalogus translationum et commentariorum*, I-VI, Washington, 1960-1986.

perentoriamente, nelle sue *Glose in Priscianum*: 'Sumus relatores et expositores veterum, non inventores novorum';[5] dove il compito della sua generazione è riassunto e definito dal termine tecnico *expositores*, gli addetti alla *expositio*, cioè alla lettura con commento di un autore. Anche fra gli scrittori che scelgono di esprimersi in volgare si avverte l'importanza della glossa. Marie de France ricorda l'attività dei glossatori che producono nuovo senso:

> K'i peussent gloser la lettre
> E de lur sen le surplus mettre,

mentre Wace, nel Roman de Rou, sottolinea quanto, come custodi della memoria, si adoperino per sottrarre i fatti all'oblio:

> Si escripture ne fust feite
> E puis par clers litte et retraite,
> Mult fussent choses ubliees.[6]

Poco dopo il *Libro del Buen amor* ricorda che '... pequeño libro de texto; mas la glosa no creo que es pequeña';[7] e ancora ser Brunetto Latini, ben distinguendo la 'littera sottile', dimostra di considerare il commento autorevole quanto il testo, quando volgarizza contemporaneamente Cicerone e una anonima glossa al *De inventione*, redatta nel secolo XII.[8]

Se crescono gli interessi sul valore dei commenti anche in sede di critica letteraria[9] è invece ancora assai difficile tracciarne una storia generale fra XII e XV secolo; perché gli strati di postille, accumulate dai maestri sui materiali loro consegnati dalle generazioni precedenti, già seriamente impegnate, fin dal secolo IX, nei lavori di esegesi, sono per lo più inedite e, non catalogate, giacciono sui margini dei manoscritti di autori molto popolari. Lo stesso problema della loro edizione si presenta particolarmente grave; e lo stato fluido di queste tradizioni suggerirebbe, al mo-

---

[5] E. Jeauneau, 'La lecture des auteurs classiques à l'école de Chartres durant la première moitié du XIIe siècle', in *Classical Influences on European Culture*, ed. R. R. Bolgar, Cambridge, 1971, p. 96.

[6] Questi testi sono ricordati da P. Zumthor, 'La glose créatrice', in *Les commentaires* (n.1 sopra), p. 14.

[7] L. Spitzer, 'The Prologue to the *Lais* of Marie de France and Medieval Poetics', nelle sue *Romanische Literaturstudien 1936-56*, Tübingen, 1959, p. 3.

[8] G. C. Alessio, 'Brunetto Latini e Cicerone (e i dettatori)', *Italia medioevale e umanistica*, 22, 1979, pp. 123-69.

[9] In particolare può essere ricordata l'antologia *Medieval Literary Theory and Criticism c.1100-c.1375. The Commentary Tradition*, ed. A. J. Minnis and A. B. Scott, Oxford, 1988.

mento, di preparare edizioni fondate sul criterio del buon manoscritto, secondo il modello proposto da J. Bédier; o, meglio, di proporre un particolare codice, quando vi sia stato riconosciuto l'insegnamento di un maestro o, quanto meno, il luogo in cui questo
insegnamento fu impartito. E, in ogni caso, i processi di stratificazione impongono accertamenti preliminari ben rigorosi, prima
di dichiarare qualsiasi attribuzione.[10] Infatti solo il censimento dei
codici di un autore può permettere di ricostruire, in tutta la complessa dinamica dei suoi commenti, gli acquisti, gli scambi e le
sottrazioni che caratterizzano questo tipo di trasmissione, per la
quale è ancor oggi difficile stabilire esattamente precise coordinate
storiche e cronologiche.[11]

È tuttavia accertato che fra l'età di Carlo Magno e quella di
Dante, il rapporto con i classici ha subìto alcune modifiche: come
immediatamente dimostrano i ritocchi e le trasformazioni che si
raccolgono negli schemi degli *accessus*. In particolare, verso la fine
del secolo XI assistiamo all'avvio di un imponente lavoro di mo-
difica e di revisione degli apparati ermeneutici, anche segnato
dall'abbandono dei commenti di tradizione tardo-antica. Di questa
operazione ebbero lucida coscienza gli stessi maestri, se in un *accessus* alle *Metamorfosi* di Ovidio, attribuibile alla scuola di Manegoldo
di Lautenbach (sec. XI/XII)) raccogliamo la dichiarazione:

> Cum multa possint inquiri in capite uniuscuiusque libri, moderni,
> quadam gaudentes brevitate, tria principaliter inquirenda statuere: id
> est materiam, intentionem et cui parti philosophie supponatur.[12]

Contemporaneamente Bernardo di Utrecht (1076-1099) presenta uno schema analogo, aggiungendo la 'causa finalis'[13] mentre

---

[10] Importanti osservazioni sono state fatte dagli studiosi di glosse giuridiche,
che, ben distinguendo fra *lectura redacta* e *lectura reportata*, riflettono poi sugli strati
'alluvionali' che caratterizzano la formazione di questo tipo di *lecture*; mi limito
a citare M. Bellomo, 'Sulle tracce d'uso dei *Libri Legales*', in *Civiltà comunale: libro,
scrittura, documento. Atti del Convegno. Genova 8-11 novembre 1988*, Genova, 1989, pp.
40-49.

[11] J. E. G. Zetzel, 'On the History of Latin Scholia', *Harvard Studies in Classical Philology*, 79, 1975, p. 354 ha sottolineato 'a continous flow of ancient scholarship into and out of commentaries, margins, glossaries'.

[12] L'*accessus* è pubblicato da K. Young, 'Chaucer's Appeal to the Platonic
Deity', *Speculum*, 19, 1944, p. 4; per questo codice B. Munk Olsen, *L'étude des
auteurs classiques latins aux XIe et XIIe siècles*, II, *Apicius-Juvénal*, Paris, 1985, p.176;
ho discusso alcuni dei problemi qui ripresi in C. Villa, 'I classici', in *Lo spazio
letterario del Medioevo*, I: *La produzione del testo*, I, Roma, 1992, pp. 502-506.

[13] *Accessus ad auctores. Bernard d'Utrecht, Conrad d'Hirsau*, ed. R. B. C. Huygens,
Leiden, 1970, p. 11, n. 1.

l'idea che i moderni potessero usare partizioni diverse da quelle degli antichi è ribadita nel commento ai *Disticha Catonis*, conservato nel codice di Lucca, Bibl. Governativa 1433, f. 83ʳ (sec. XII):

> In exordio uniuscuiusque libri septem apud antecessores nostros prae-libenda erant ... Sedmodo apud modernos tantummodo tria requiren-tur: vita poetae, titulus operis et ad quam partem philosophie spectet.[14]

Si dichiara dunque l'abbandono delle sette *circumstanciae* imposte da Servio e dunque delle più complesse partizioni seguite nelle introduzioni carolingie—dove peraltro si può anche ritrovare un più breve schema composto da 'locus, tempus, persona'; mentre è ben chiara l'idea di una distinzione fra antichi e moderni, dove, quale che sia il significato da dare ad antiqui (i classici? o i maestri delle precedenti generazioni?),[15] si sommano coscienza di modi-fiche e volontà di diversificazione.

Il secolo XII rappresenta certamente un momento fondamen-tale nella storia della esegesi ai classici: quando, come ben ci illu-strano le statistiche di Munk Olsen,[16] si sostituiscono i nuovi appa-rati interpretativi ai commenti tardo antichi. Questa letteratura di servizio, prodotta nella scuola, spesso povera di articolate rifles-sioni teoriche, vive in simbiosi con un altro testo ma riesce a orien-tarne i processi di ricezione: e rappresenta un grande collettore di memorie, come lucidamente intuisce Wace: perché chi si impegna in un nuovo commento non può tralasciare l'ermeneutica di chi lo ha preceduto e contemporaneamente è costretto ad impegnare le proprie personali capacità di associazione, qualora sia necessario integrare ed approfondire i risultati già acquisiti. Successivamente il commento, caricato di spiegazioni, di parafrasi e di varianti sino-nimiche, favorisce e suggerisce i passaggi semantici, le digressioni e gli incroci mentali con i quali gli scrittori riescono a trasformare, occultandola, la loro prima fonte di ispirazione, spesso rappresen-tata da un altro testo letterario. Quindi il commento mediolatino a un classico si propone come il custode e il garante di una idea di letteratura, prodotta da generazioni di lettori, nel confronto con un modello—il testo poetico proposto all'imitazione—; e collabora anche a mantenerla e a diffonderla, con autorità maggiore di quella

---

[14] H. Silvestre, 'Le schéma "moderne" des *accessus*', *Latomus*, 16, 1957, p. 686.
[15] Villa, 'I classici' (n. 12 sopra), p. 491, n. 28.
[16] B. Munk Olsen, 'La popularité des textes classiques entre les IXe et les XIIe siècle', *Revue d'histoire des textes*, 14-15, 1984-85, pp. 169-81.

riconosciuta a qualsiasi altro testo teorico. Si presenta infine come il più vasto e accessibile deposito di quelle notizie erudite che, in forma di postille eclettiche, possono ricomparire nelle più diverse letture, prima di essere utilizzate nella produzione di nuove opere letterarie.

Riflettendo sulla osservazione di Marie de France, possiamo domandarci quale sia il nuovo senso prodotto dai commentatori del secolo XII, cioè quali siano gli elementi che i commenti tardo-antichi forniscono in maniera tanto insufficiente da costringere i lettori del secolo XII a sostanziali revisioni degli apparati interpretativi.

È forse possibile rispondere sottolineando che i commenti ai classici, a partire dal secolo XII, sembrano soprattutto destinati a costruire una teoria della letteratura, concedendo ampio spazio alla tipologia delle classi letterarie, quando definiscono origini e ragioni etimologiche di generi come satira, commedia, elegia, ode, tragedia; e aggiungono gli inevitabili esempi dei tre livelli di stile, entro cui rientrano tutte le esperienze letterarie. La quantità dei nuovi commenti e la qualità di interessi e cure riservate allo studio del sistema classico, analiticamente esplorato, suscitano l'impressione che in quel secolo fosse assolutamente necessario definire un quadro teorico, in risposta ad esperienze altrimenti incontrollabili.

Una deliberata ricerca di regole ineludibili sembra infatti caratterizzare le indagini letterarie dei maestri attivi fra la fine del secolo XI e il XII: che ai commenti tardo antichi, spesso fonte prima delle glosse disposte sui margini delle grandi edizioni di classici dell'età carolingia e ottoniana, sostituiscono i commenti in testo continuo—dove il lemma è seguito dalla glossa—raccolti in manoscritti modesti e di piccolo formato, con pagine fittamente coperte di minute grafie. Questo materiale, che comincia a diffondersi nel secolo XII, pone in genere complessi problemi di datazione e di localizzazione perché le glosse sono raccolte e compresse in pochi fascicoli e, sottratte al testo, rappresentano il personale sussidio di maestri che evidentemente conoscono a memoria l'autore commentato. Strumenti di lavoro per la costruzione di una teoria della letteratura di orientamento rigorosamente stilistico, sono in uso in un tempo in cui la lettura dei classici è raccomandata soprattutto per la conquista dello stile: come afferma il maestro del commento a Ovidio del manoscritto ora München Clm 4610, dove isoliamo la dichiarazione: 'Potest nobis et ad ostendendam pulchram dictionum compositionem. Quandam vero intentionem possimus dare poetis: scilicet ut sint latine lingue correptores et imitatores', variamente ripetuta da altri commenti ovidiani.[17]

Ma è fondamentale osservare che l'attività di commento non si esaurisce in uno sforzo di minuta descrizione dei generi letterari, le cui ragioni sono spesso ricavate dall'etimologia, come nei casi di commedia, tragedia e satira. La scuola si assume un più complesso impegno, fornendo consigli precettivi per la produzione letteraria, come dimostrano alcuni fatti connessi con la fortuna enorme della *Epistola ad Pisones* di Orazio.

Dal momento che i retori latini avevano preferito evitare le norme prescrittive i nuovi maestri—come gli stessi produttori di *Artes* mediolatini—bisognosi di regole più attuali, non si sottraggono allo sforzo di fissarle, attribuendo allo stesso Orazio l'intenzione di fornire una summa di proibizioni e di norme: 'ipse, sicut Victorinus praecepit, dupliciter tradit, dicendo primum quod vitandum, deinde quod tenendum sit'[18] e, con più precisa determinazione: 'docendo que sunt facienda et reprehendendo que sunt respuenda, partim communiter omnibus poetis, partim proprie ipsis comicis'.[19]

Così l'epistola oraziana, breviario di estetica privo di norme concrete, si trasforma, secondo una idea di Quintiliano che già lo aveva detto 'ars poetica', in un manuale di leggi, produttore di una severa normativa, secondo l'etimologia di 'Ars ab artando'; dunque in una poetria, dove si apprende a fingere, secondo la definizione 'poetria ars est poesis scientia' (Orazio, MS Vaticano Reg. lat. 1431, f. 36[r]). L'*Ars poetica* serve 'non de morum formatione sed de verborum compositione' (Orazio, MS Paris, Bibl. Nat., n. a. lat. 350, f. 40[r], sec. XII), e si occupa 'de disponendo, de variando, de properando, de sumendo materiam', secondo le rubriche dell'Orazio, MS Vaticano lat. 1590 (sec. X-XI). E lungo questa linea si muoveranno nella seconda metà del secolo XII, le *Artes*, cioè i manuali che dichiarano la volontà di fornire regole necessarie,

---

[17] Young, 'Chaucer's Appeal' (n. 12 sopra), p. 4.

[18] La glossa si trova nel commento *Materia* pubblicato da K. Friis Jensen, 'The *Ars Poetica* in Twelfth-Century France. The Horace of Matthew of Vendôme, Geoffrey of Vinsauf, and John of Garland', *Cahiers de l'Institut du moyen âge grec et latin*, 60, 1990, p. 338.

[19] Lo scolio, ben diffuso, è stato pubblicato in *Scholia in Horatium in codicibus Parisinis latinis 17897 et 8223*, ed. H. J. Botschuyver, Amsterdam, 1942, p. 457.

approfondendo settori appena sfiorati da Orazio, ma già esplorati dai commentatori.

È inevitabile chiedersi perché la scuola sia stimolata a produrre questo tipo di trattatistica, elaborata nei commenti e ridefinita nei manuali teorici; e una possibile risposta a questi interrogativi dovrebbe tener conto dello squilibrio provocato, in un secolo di corretto classicismo in latino, dall'irruzione del volgare: dunque dall'uso, in sede letteraria, di una lingua priva di leggi grammaticali e ancor più di norme retoriche. Con questo giudizio sul volgare ancora un secolo dopo un intellettuale come Giovanni del Virgilio esprimerà il suo dissenso a Dante, in una elaborata epistola metrica di tipo oraziano: dove lingua e stile della *Comedìa* sono deplorati nel confronto con un possibile poema epico in lingua latina.

È evidente che certi apparati interpretativi preparati nel secolo XII corrisposero pienamente alle esigenze della scuola e all'idea di letteratura che intendeva proporre: ed ebbero poi una lunga fortuna, fino all'età della stampa. Perciò, nei secoli successivi, è necessario distinguere fra i commenti, composti nel secolo XII e poi ancora copiati per la scuola, e le glosse totalmente nuove.

I commenti particolarmente vitali e perciò accompagnati da buon successo, sono numerosi e può perfino accadere che i manoscritti li attribuiscano a maestri più recenti. È significativo il caso della glossa oraziana *Materia*, già testimoniata in codici del secolo XII, assegnata dal Torraca a Paolo da Perugia, il vecchio amico napoletano del Boccaccio, sulla base del colofone del codice di Napoli, Bibl. Naz. V F 21: 'Glosa super Poetria Oratii edita per Paulum de Perusio';[20] l'attribuzione è entrata poi in tutta la letteratura successiva ed è stata mantenuta anche dal Kristeller. In realtà 'editus per' è formula molto ambigua, come dimostrano altri commenti in cui 'editus per' è seguito dal nome di un maestro che certamente si è servito di una tradizione più antica.

Andrà inoltre osservato che anche i commenti 'recentiores' a Terenzio continuano ad essere letti per diversi secoli, addirittura con attribuzioni illustri: se il 'recentior' inc. 'Auctor iste legitur', è detto 'erutum a vetustissimo codice' ed attribuito a Servio nel codice Vaticano Urbin. lat. 362 (sec. XV), preparato per la biblioteca di

---

[20] C. Villa, 'Due schede per *editus*', *Italia medioevale e umanistica*, 31, 1988, pp. 399-402.

Federico da Montefeltro; e poi ancora nell'edizione veneziana di Lazzaro Suardi del 1504;[21] così stampe di Prisciano esibiscono ancora commenti del secolo XII.[22]

Può quindi essere interessante sottolineare quanto la scuola umanistica si serva ampiamente dei commenti del secolo XII: e come le interpretazioni mediolatine sopravvivono nel secolo XV, contribuendo in maniera significativa a formare il gusto, e a fornire informazioni storiche e mitologiche, anche alle più avvertite e smaliziate generazioni del Quattrocento. Possiamo perciò raccogliere diversi esempi di questo uso di materiali medioevali: Pietro da Moglio ricupera, nella seconda metà del Trecento, il *Commento Monacense* a Terenzio di età carolingia, sovrappone glosse più recenti e fonde tutto nella sua lettura bolognese, che circola poi, in varia forma per tutto il Quattrocento, trasferita e divulgata dagli studenti anche in area tedesca.[23]

Analogo il comportamento di molti umanisti delle prime generazioni, come Coluccio Salutati, Sozomeno e Gasparino Barzizza, che continuano ad usare materiali del secolo XII: l'impiego dei vecchi commenti induce a riflettere sulla persistenza e vischiosità delle tradizioni scolastiche; e anche a valutare le effettive dimensioni dei rinnovamenti umanistici. La glossa *Materia* si ritrova correntemente in manoscritti oraziani del secolo XV: anche ridotta a scarni appunti, addirittura alla semplice numerazione da I a VI, accanto ai versi dell' *Ars poetica* da cui si ricava la dottrina dei sei vizi poetici. Questo commento riduce il testo oraziano ad un manuale dal quale è possibile ricavare le leggi della *congruentia*, cioè della simmetria, della proporzione e della regolarità; e l'interpretazione è ripresa e sostenuta, fra gli altri, dall'umanista siciliano Tommaso Schifaldo.[24]

È significativo osservare che un maestro come Guarino ricerca l'antico commento di Donato a Terenzio, che poi possiede anche il suo allievo Ludovico Carbone, nel manoscritto di Ferrara, Bibl. Comunale II 173. Tuttavia per l'insegnamento Carbone sembra

---

[21] C. Villa, *La 'lectura Terentii'*, Padova, 1984, p. 121, n. 67.

[22] M. Gibson, 'The Collected Works of Priscian: the Printed Editions 1470-1859', *Studi Medievali*, ser. 3, 18, 1977, pp. 249-60.

[23] Villa, *La 'lectura Terentii'* (n. 21 sopra), pp. 217-31.

[24] Per codici del *Materia*, Villa, 'I manoscritti di Orazio, III', *Aevum*, 68, 1994, pp. 134-46; Tommaso Schifaldo è stato studiato da G. Bottari, 'Tommaso Schifaldo e il suo commento all'*Arte poetica* di Orazio', in *Umanità e storia. Scritti in onore di Adelchi Attisani*, II, Napoli, 1972, pp. 221-59.

preferire il codice ora Napoli, Bibl. dei Gerolamini CF.1.10, già appartenuto a Matteo Gisso, grammatico dello studio bolognese e a un magister Palamede; ed è importante sottolineare che il codice di Napoli non esibisce il commento di Donato, forse troppo difficile e inadatto a un uso scolastico, ma la più facile e didattica lettura diffusa a Bologna da Pietro da Moglio.[25]

Francesco di Bartolo da Buti e il maestro di Sozomeno, Antonio da San Gimignano, usano antiche tradizioni diffuse in Toscana; fra le quali il Terenzio MS Laurenziano Conv. sopp. 510 (sec. XII), che ha un certo successo perchè fu copiato nella regione e circolò nell'ambiente del Salutati, per il tramite del suo allievo Antonio Corbinelli fratello di Angelo (MS Firenze, Bibl. Laurenziana, Conv. sopp. 79).[26]

Perfino il Boccaccio si appoggia a materiali più antichi quando trascrive le postille del commento Monacense (sec. IX) nel suo Terenzio ora Laurenziano 38, 18.[27] E il commento alla *Rhetorica ad Herennium*, che in Italia circola con il nome di 'Alanus' (di Lilla?), già usato a Bologna da Bartolino da Benincasa (sec. XIV in.), posseduto in età umanistica da Sozomeno da Pistoia, nel codice ora London, British Library, Harl. 6324, è conosciuto da Lorenzo Valla, da Guarino e dal Barzizza.[28] La glossa ripete e diffonde la riflessione normativa di rigorosa impostazione classicista esposta nell'oraziano *Materia* e poi nei *Documenta* di Goffredo di Vinosalvo: e certo è interessante sottolineare che i giudizi e le linee interpretative di maestri del remoto secolo XII contribuirono decisamente a formare il gusto dei primi umanisti.

Il commmento mantiene la sua autorità anche quando un autore classico è reso in volgare: al già ricordato esempio di Cicerone e Brunetto Latini possiamo accostare le *Allegorie ovidiane* di Giovanni del Virgilio, volgarizzate insieme al testo per il quale furono preparate, le *Metamorphoses* di Ovidio;[29] mentre sembra normale che il traduttore, volgendo il testo, lo amplii, trasportandovi le bre-

---

[25] Villa, *La 'lectura Terentii'* (n. 21 sopra), pp. 218-19.

[26] Villa, 'Terenzio (e Orazio) in Toscana fra IX e XIV secolo', *Studi italiani di filologia classica*, ser. 3, 10, 1992, pp. 1103-15.

[27] Villa, *La 'lectura Terentii'* (n. 21 sopra), pp. 234-35.

[28] P. O. Kristeller, 'Umanesimo e scolastica a Padova fino al Petrarca', *Medioevo*, 11, 1985, p. 3, n. 9; per questo commmento J. Ward, 'From Antiquity to the Renaissance' in J. J. Murphy, *Medieval Eloquence. Studies in the Theory and Practice of Medieval Rhetoric*, Berkeley-Los Angeles-London, 1978, p. 38.

[29] B. Guthmüller, *Ovidio Methamorphoseos Vulgare*, Boppard am Rhein, 1981.

vi glosse interlineari che trova nel suo manoscritto. Peraltro, nel secolo XIII e nel confronto con l'età precedente, i commmenti ai classici presentano qualche segno di novità, con l'adeguamento all'uso della terminologia aristotelica, che si impone negli *accessus* divisi in cause *(causa efficiens, materialis, formalis, finalis)*: ma le innovazioni non sono sostanziali e spesso si avverte che il nuovo commento, formato per stratificazione, incorpora e rifonde materiali già presenti nelle *lecture* dei secoli precedenti. Così Nicola Trevet commenta Boezio, utilizzando il più antico Guillaume de Conches[30] e il commento più diffuso nell'Italia del Trecento, la glossa a Orazio inc. 'Communiter a doctoribus traditur' rinnova la terminologia e presenta una riflessione sulla classificazione delle scienze sermocinali, già proposta da Alberto Magno, però utilizzando tutta la parte proibitiva del *Materia*. Un contemporaneo di Petrarca, Giacomino Robazzi costruisce una fortunata lettura di Terenzio usando una redazione della più vecchia *Expositio* o 'commento recentior'.[31]

Per il secolo XIII, periodo che in sede storiografica è già stato oggetto di un ampio dibattito sollevato da una presenza relativamente scarsa di autori classici, dovremo almeno ricordare l'esperienza e le imprese di lettori isolati, impegnati ad affrontare opere non ancora introdotte nei canoni scolastici: come Albertano da Brescia che, secondo quanto ci ha insegnato L. D. Reynolds, postillò, non per la scuola ma per uso personale, il testo delle *Ad Lucilium* di Seneca, che raggiunse nel codice di Brescia, Bibl. Queriniana B II 6.[32]

Non è facile trarre conclusioni sulla fortuna e continuità dei commenti scolastici, con un sondaggio ancor tanto limitato; ma è forse possibile affermare che gli umanisti a tutti i livelli tendono a rifiutare il commento di tradizione gotica, cioè, per semplificare, il commento che predilige la divisione aristotelica in cause. Il commento oraziano 'Communiter a doctoribus traditur' sparisce con la fine del secolo XIV; così non ha fortuna la glossa terenziana del codice di Napoli, Bibl. Nazionale IV D 34 (sec. XIV) che dichiara 'cause sunt quattuor: efficiens, materialis, formalis, finalis; efficiens est duplex, scilicet mediata et immediata...'.[33] Invece non c'è ripugnanza per il commento 'romanico', che adotta la divisione

---

[30] H. A. Kelly, *Ideas and Forms of Tragedy*, Cambridge, 1993, p. 127.
[31] Villa, *La 'lectura Terentii'* (n. 21 sopra), pp. 202.
[32] L. D. Reynolds, *The Medieval Tradition of Seneca's Letters*, Oxford, 1965, p. 100.
[33] Villa, *La 'lectura Terentii'* (n. 21 sopra), pp. 145-147.

'materia, intentio, utilitas': e se queste categorie infastidirono il
Petrarca quando ne scrive nella *Vita Terrentii*: 'De materia loqui
prolixum est, de expositione prolixius' non sembrano suscitare tanta avversione nella scuola umanistica, se proprio l'*Expositio* a Terenzio del contemporaneo Giacomino Robazzi che inizia 'Circa expositionem huius libri ' continua ad esserci ampiamente usata, come
testimoniano i numerosi manoscritti.[34]

Finalmente potremmo ricordare che, in una letteratura altamente
formalizzata e costantemente legata all'uso di un modello quale
quella mediolatina, le glosse restituiscono la trama di ogni processo intertestuale, risolvendo ambiguità di scrittura e molteplicità di
interpretazione. Posso fornire qualche esempio, ricordando gli
oscuri versi con cui Giovanni del Virgilio rivela a Dante il suo dissenso sull'uso del volgare, costruiti con una commistione di rife-
rimenti disparati, distribuiti in una struttura chiastica:

Ante quidem cythara pandum delphyna movebis,	(Orazio)
Davus et ambigue Spyngos problemata solvet	(Terenzio)
Tartareum preceps quam gens ydiota figuret	(Dante, *Comedia*)
Et secreta poli vix experata Platoni:	(Dante, *Convivio*)
Que tamen in triviis numquam digesta coaxat	(Terenzio)
Comicomus nebulo, qui Flaccum pelleret orbe	(Orazio)

Addirittura i primi due versi, che metonimicamente alludono a
due maestri di stile come Orazio, teorico dello stile comico e Terenzio, modello della commedia, sono due glosse rispettivamente
Pseudacron., in Hor. *Carm.* , IV 3, 18-19 e la postilla in *And.*, 194,
diffusa in manoscritti terenziani di tradizione bolognese.[35]

Il commento si fa testo nei *Documenta* di Goffredo di Vinosalvo,
che ripete fedelmente le glosse dell'oraziano *Materia*, come ci ha
appena indicato K. Friis Jensen. Molti autori sembrano dialogare
con questo commento, che fornisce una dottrina proibitiva, elen-
cando sei vizi, collegati al commento dei primi 32 versi dell'*Ars*:
'incongrua partium positio' (v. 1), 'incongrua rationis digressio' (v.
15), 'brevitas obscura' (v. 25), 'incongrua stili mutatio' (v. 27),
'incongrua materie variatio' (v. 29), 'incongrua operis imperfectio'
(v. 32).

La 'incongrua partium positio' stabilisce un principio che regola il gusto ancora nel Cinquecento, quando all'immagine del
mostro—ridefinito come Chimera nel *Don Chisciotte* di Cervantes—è

---

[34] Ibid., p. 201.
[35] Ibid., p. 186.

affidata la riprovazione del genere romanzesco, composto di membra tanto diverse da non riuscire a disegnare una figura proporzionata.

La 'incongrua rationis digressio' richiama ad una unità monocentrica, rivelando il ribrezzo e il fastidio per un testo senza punto di riferimento: e avvia una implicita polemica nei confronti della tendenza manifestata dal romanzo cortese, anche di ispirazione antica come il *Roman d'Eneas* che, nel confronto con il modello virgiliano, svela il suo gusto per le divagazioni e i procedimenti ad intreccio.

La regola che vieta la 'incongrua stili mutatio' è acutamente ridiscussa da Dante quando, nell'*Epistola a Cangrande* 29-30, avrà il coraggio di ribaltare l'interpretazione più corrente, chiamando proprio *AP* 93-96: 'sicut vult Oratius in sua Poetria, ubi licentiat aliquando comicos ut tragedos loqui' a garanzia delle proprie escursioni stilistiche e linguistiche.[36] Ma è interessante osservare che perfino un testo spirituale come il commento al *Cantico dei Cantici* di S. Bernardo non sfugge, nella polemica del suo avversario Berengario, all'esame impietoso di una lente tarata sui precetti dichiarati nei commenti oraziani:

> Tu vero terminos transgrediens quos posuerunt patres tui cantica in elegos, carmina in threnos sorte miserabili convertisti. Quod si tibi deessent ecclesiasticae scita censurae, recolere poteras etiam gentilis instituta prudentiae ... Concedit Ars quod velis incipias, sed non ut quemlibet finem inceptis tuis supponas.[37]

La 'incongrua materie variatio' è considerata un vizio e perciò la 'variacio materie' permessa ai soli poeti, in quanto 'fictores', suscita qualche perplessità:

> Hoc primum vitium est contra preceptum rhetorice de inventione, ut inventa a Virgilio materia de bello Troiano, si astrorum doctrinam vel aliarum rerum non convenientium conscripsisset (MS Lucca, Bibl. capitolare 532, f. 1ʳ, sec. XV).

Un esempio di 'congrua materie variacio' è invece rappresentato dallo stesso Virgilio perché: 'propter veritatem historie Eneam venire ad Didonem et ibi morari describit' (MS Milano, Bibl. Ambrosiana, M 9 sup, f. 129ᵛ, sec. XIII). Con questo tipo di esempi dovette confrontarsi Chrétien de Troyes che, per giustificare una

---

[36] Villa, 'Dante e Orazio', in *Dante e la 'bella scola' della poesia*, Ravenna, 1993, p. 102.
[37] Villa, 'I classici' (n. 12 sopra), pp. 514-515, con bibliografia.

sua digressione, quando precisa i particolari del manto di Erec:

> Lisant trovomes en l'istoire
> La description de la robe,
> Si an trai a garant Macrobe,
> ...
> Macrobes m'ansaigne a descrivre

ricorre proprio a Macrobio—un autore molto apprezzato e commentato dai contemporanei maestri di Chartres—perché ammette le descrizioni astronomiche 'de stellarum motus, de coeli conversione' in un'opera di altro argomento.[38]

La 'incongrua operis imperfectio' è un vizio perché un'opera deve essere finita: e se ciò contraddice quanto si sa di Virgilio e di Stazio, i commentatori provvedono a normalizzare l'eccezione, dichiarando che la morte non rende imperfetta l'opera:

> Est autem imperfectio congrua operis, id est non reprehendenda, quando aliquis, quod incepit vel morbo, vel exilio, vel morte interveniente ad finem non perducit, sicut imperfectio Eneidos et Achileidos.[39]

Così diventerà obbligatorio ricordare che il poeta è morto prima della fine; da Chrétien de Troyes:

> Ce nous dist Crestiens de Troie
> Qui de Percheval comencha,
> Mais la mors qui l'adevancha
> Ne li laissa pas traire affin,

allo Stazio di Dante, *Purgatorio*, XXI, 93:

> ma caddi in via con la seconda soma.

Finalmente possiamo terminare con un esempio che mi sembra significativo perché dimostra quanta importanza possano avere i commenti nella definizione dei generi letterari. In una autonoma riflessione Chrétien de Troyes sembra dialogare con Orazio, *AP*, 47-48:

> dixeris egregie notum si callida verbum
> reddiderit iunctura novum,

quando nel romanzo *Erec*, 13-14 dice di sè:

> E tret d'un conte d'avanture
> Une mout bele conjointure.

---

[38] Ibid., p. 511.
[39] Ibid., p. 514.

Meglio potremo intendere questo passo discusso, ricordando che i versi di Orazio furono ampiamente postillati e che in particolare un manoscritto conservato a San Pietro di Beauvais—biblioteca che Chrétien, nel *Cligès*, afferma di aver frequentato—interpreta la 'callida iunctura' affermando: 'Dicit vulgaria verba in metro, honesta compositione splendescere, et quasi noviter inventa resonare' (MS Leiden, Bibl. der Rijksuniver., BPL 28, f. 58^v, sec. X).

La glossa, fraintendendo Orazio, offre in realtà una definizione del romanzo cortese: un componimento narrativo in volgare, in versi, letterariamente strutturato come un esperimento del tutto nuovo.

Sembra dunque di poter concludere ora che, dal secolo XII, la 'enarratio poetarum' di Quintiliano si trasformò progressivamente in una pratica assai più complessa, la ricerca di norme e leggi immanenti alle poetrie dei singoli autori. Mentre generazioni di maestri, impegnati in una critica letteraria che si impose soprattutto come descrizione di generi e di stili, si sforzarono di ricavarne lo statuto di una disciplina nomotetica, l'arte apparve una somma organizzata di artifici che fu necessario riconoscere, descrivere e insegnare ai futuri letterati: le istituzioni del classicismo—cioè le regole desunte dagli *auctores* scelti come modelli nei canoni scolastici del secolo XII—ebbero una lunghissima tenuta fin dentro le scuole dove i maestri dell'Umanesimo educarono i loro allievi, secondo una tipologia e un modello di classicismo in cui ancor oggi ci riconosciamo.

LES COMMENTAIRES MÉDIÉVAUX DE TÉRENCE

Yves-François Riou

Avant d'aborder la présentation cursive des principaux commentaires médiévaux de Térence, je souhaite faire quelques observations.

J'entends par commentaire principal un texte qui possède une
tradition manuscrite. Le fait qu'il ait été copié et recopié témoigne
de l'intérêt qu'on lui a porté et mérite aujourd'hui le nôtre. J'éli-
mine donc de mon exposé le commentaire dont on ne connaît à
ce jour qu'un seul manuscrit; ce qui touche surtout quelques commentaires humanistiques du quinzième siècle.

Deuxième observation. Ce commentaire n'est pas une oeuvre de
substitution. Entendons par là que même s'il renouvelle les objec-
tifs du commentaire antérieur, tout en puisant à pleines mains dans
ce dernier pour certains, il ne remplace pas le commentaire antérieur qui continue à avoir une tradition manuscrite propre jusqu'à
la fin du quinzième siècle. Ainsi le *Commentum Brunsianum* n'a-t-il
jamais été détrôné par l'un des quelconques commentaires qui l'ont
suivi, lesquels ont inauguré pour eux-mêmes une tradition manuscrite parallèle à celle de leurs successeurs et ainsi de suite.

Il ne s'ensuit pas pour autant qu'ils s'ignorent. Mais en l'ab-
sence d'éditions, il serait aventureux d'avancer qu'à l'image du
commentaire perpétuel scolaire, qui grossit de génération en génération, ils reproduiraient mot à mot l'oeuvre de leurs prédécesseurs.
Au contraire, mon sentiment est que même dans son *explanatio*, où
il charrie les même scolies de tout genre (grammaticales, historiques,
mythologiques etc., selon les circonstances), chacun de ces commentaires a une individualité propre à un auteur, telle qu'elle nous
permet d'en retrouver la marque dans des versions diverses d'une
même oeuvre.

Enfin, dernière observation, ces versions, par exemple la double
version à l'aube du dixième siècle du *Commentum Brunsianum* et
Monacense, la quadruple version d'un commentaire de la deuxième
moitié du douzième siècle ('Auctor iste', 'Poeta iste', 'Terentius
Africanus', et 'Legitur'), nous livrent la problématique du commentaire médiéval à Térence: à mi-chemin du texte littéraire et de sa

reportatio, du texte dont la tradition manuscrite est assurée et de la *reportatio* sans tradition manuscrite véritable.

Muni de ces jalons, on peut avancer dans ce que j'ai appelé le maquis des commentaires médiévaux. Ceux et celles qui ont pratiqué la mine d'informations qu'est le beau livre de Claudia Villa sur la *Lectura Terentii*[1] se sont aperçu que le foisonnement des commentaires instaurait une sorte de dialogue continu entre Térence et les besoins successifs du présent.

I. Les Commentum Brunsianum *et* Monacense

Au début du dixième siècle, ce besoin s'exprime dans le *Commentum Brunsianum* et une autre version transmise dans un seul manuscrit: München, Bayerische Staatsbibliothek, Clm 14420. On sait que ce manuscrit mutilé du début, avait en tête ce qu'il est convenu d'appeler la *Praefatio Monacensis*, composée de la *Vita Terentii III* et d'un résumé ou argument à l'*A*.

La présence de cette *Praefatio*, dont il ne subsiste plus dans le manuscrit que les onze dernières lignes de l'édition Ballaira[2] s'explique sans doute par la nécessité d'une introduction au commentaire. Cet *accessus* est traditionnellement une *vita*. Comme cette *vita* fait corps dans les manuscrits avec l'argument de l'*A*, le copiste a recopié le tout. Mais, par la suite, on ne retrouve plus d'arguments aux autres comédies dans le *Commentum Monacense*. Le caractère littéral de cette version n'a que faire de ce type d'argument d'autant plus que ces derniers se retrouvent en tête de chaque comédie dans la version *Brunsianum*. Et la source étant commune, ni l'une ni l'autre n'ont de divisions en actes ni en scènes. Ceci éloigne l'éventualité d'une influence, même indirecte, de Donat sur l'auteur, car la division en actes de l'Antiquité à nos jours se fonde sur les propositions de Donat et non sur la tradition manuscrite des comédies.

---

[1] C. Villa, *La 'Lectura Terentii'. Volume primo. Da Ildemaro a Francesco Petrarca*, Padoue, 1984.

[2] G. Ballaira, 'Praefatio *Monacensis* ad Terentium quae integra in Cod. Vat. lat. 11455 asservatur', *Bollettino del comitato per la preparazione dell'edizione nazionale dei Classici Greci e Latini*, n.s., 16, 1968, pp. 13–24; édition reprise en regard de l'*Accessus ad Andriam* du *Commentum Brunsianum* par Y.-F. Riou, 'Essai sur la tradition manuscrite du *Commentum Brunsianum* des comédies de Térence', *Revue d'histoire des textes*, 3, 1973, pp. 79–113.

Le *Commentum Brunsianum* s'ouvre sur le rappel de la didascalie et son bref commentaire. Puis l'*expositio tituli* glose rapidement l'argument et le prologue afin d'arriver au résumé de la comédie proprement dite. Ceci est le schéma général de l'*accessus* à toutes les comédies. Mais le premier *accessus* a un traitement particulier puisqu'il sert d'introduction générale au commentaire. Il commence par la *Vita Terentii II* suivie de considérations sur le style de Térence et les opinions des *auctores* (Priscien et Rufin), un exposé sur la métrique avec le rappel de l'autorité d'Horace (*De Arte poetica*, 251-52, 259), quelques aspects de la représentation, réflexions qui s'appliquent à toutes les comédies. Puis il livre le nom de celles-ci dans l'ordre suivant: *A.E.H.Ad.He.Ph.*, c'est à dire celui qui rapproche les pièces empruntées à Ménandre (*A.E.H.Ad.*) et celles traduites d'Apollodore (*He.Ph.*). C'est l'ordre d'une classe de manuscrits représentée par les manuscrits Vatican, Vat lat. 3868 (neuvième siècle) et Paris, Bibl. nat. lat. 7899 (neuvième siècle) appartenant au rameau γ. Ordre qui diffère de celui adopté par Donat: *A.Ad.E.Ph.He* (et *H.*; ce dernier ne figure pas dans le commentaire de Donat, mais les numéros 1 à 5 étant pris par les autres pièces, il ne reste qu'à lui attribuer le numéro 6). Il diffère encore de l'ordre suivi par Eugraphius: *A.E.H.Ph.He.Ad.*

Après l'*accessus* vient le commentaire proprement dit. C'est un commentaire à lemmes, clairement cités et composés parfois d'une phrase de six à sept mots. Les gloses introduisent majoritairement aux scènes. Certes, chemin faisant, l'auteur ne s'interdit pas quelques explications de mots rares, de verbes défectifs, mais son but est clairement de dérouler le fil de la compréhension de l'action. Ceci n'intéresse que médiocrement le rédacteur de la version du *Monacense*. Son exposé de l'action est à l'image du lemme qu'il transcrit: court; une phrase, là où le *Brunsianum* développe plusieurs. Mais en revanche, il s'occupe du vocabulaire dont le *Brunsianum* ne se soucie pas. Il le glose mot à mot, presque mot pour mot, de l'argument à la fin de la pièce.

Si bien qu'en tenant de part et d'autre ces deux versions, on a le sentiment d'une complémentarité qui renvoie à un auteur unique, antérieur aux témoins manuscrits conservés. Dans un premier temps s'élabore une introduction générale d'ordre littéraire aux comédies, (*Commentum Brunsianum*) et celle-ci étant assimilée, apparaît une étude minutieuse du vocabulaire et de la synthèse (*Commentum Monacense*).

Certains manuscrits contemporains et postérieurs ne s'y sont d'ailleurs pas trompés quand ils ont accueilli, en marge, les gloses du *Brunsianum*, et, en interligne, les scolies du *Monacense*. Ce phénomène explique peut-être d'ailleurs la solitude du manuscrit Clm 14420. Car si la *Praefatio Monacensis* a fait, si j'ose dire, une belle carrière jusqu'à la fin du quinzième siècle—même si l'on rencontre dans bon nombre de manuscrits des gloses du *Monacense*—le *corpus* rassemblé dans le manuscrit Clm 14420 ne se retrouve intégralement, et même en partie, nulle part.

Ce n'est pas le cas du *Brunsianum*. Au manuscrit lacunaire du début du douzième siècle de Bruns[3] qui présente les arguments dans le texte mais le commentaire en marge, nous pouvons opposer six manuscrits antérieurs transmettant d'une manière continue le commentaire dans sa totalité ou partiellement à la suite de mutilations: quatre sont du dixième siècle, deux du début du onzième siècle et ceci sans préjudice des soixante-dix autres manuscrits qui, du dixième au quinzième siècle, transmettent les arguments ou les gloses de ce commentaire.

II.   *'Poeta iste africanus', 'Auctor iste africanus', 'Legitur auctor iste africanus', 'Terentius africanus ... '*

Abordant maintenant quatre commentaires de la deuxième moitié du douzième siècle, qui me semblent être autant de versions particulières d'une même oeuvre, je ne peux éviter la question du motif d'une telle situation. L'hypothèse la plus commune serait de tabler sur un enseignement oral ayant généré lui-même d'autres enseignements reportés sur manuscrits dans la deuxième moitié du douzième siècle. On touche ici à la particularité de la problématique de ce type de commentaire. Il n'est pas seulement objet c'est à dire le produit fini d'un enseignement qui l'a construit, il est aussi sujet de cet enseignement s'élaborant différemment dans un temps et un lieu donnés. C'est ce qu'a pressenti, me semble-t-il, C. Villa quand elle souligne que la *Lectura Terentii* de Brescia est en fin de compte le point de départ de quelques traditions de commentaires de classiques immédiatement communiquées de l'autre

---

[3] D. Paulus Iacobus Bruns..., *P. Terentii Afri comoediae sex. Textum ad fidem codicis Halensis antiquissimi criticis nondum cogniti edidit, variam editionum lectionem annotavit, scholia a vulgatis diversa ex eodem codice descripsit et Cel. Ruhnkenii dictata in Terentium necdum typis impressa adiecit*, Halle, 1811.

côté des Alpes. Nous verrons d'ailleurs que l'étude codicologique des manuscrits donne à réfléchir sur ce point.

Voici le plan général de cette oeuvre que je tire de la version 'Poeta iste..' mais qui vaut pour les autres versions. Après la *Vita*, on trouve des notes sur la comédie, son étymologie, son origine historique, son utilité morale quels que soient l'âge, le sexe et la condition des personnes. L'auteur s'étend alors sur la matière des comédies, qui met en scène des personnages familiers avec des comportements ordinaires qu'il décrit complaisamment. C'est le miroir de la vie commune dont chacun peut tirer profit dans sa vie quotidienne. Il aborde ensuite les notions d'arguments, d'actes, qui sont à ses yeux une question de mesure du temps, de scènes, qui ne peuvent contenir plus de trois personnages car s'ils sont quatre, ils ne proféreront que de rares paroles afin de ne pas rendre le discours confus. Puis il aborde le commentaire des comédies, dans la même succession que celle du *Commentum Brunsianum* (*A.E.H.Ad.He.Ph.*) selon l'ordre d'une *expositio* suivie d'une *explanatio*. Dans l'*expositio*, on trouve la présentation des personnages, l'annonce des cinq actes, chacun étant caractérisé en une ou deux phrases. Puis il en vient aux raisons de l'existence d'un argument et d'un prologue. Ce dernier a pour but la *captatio beneuolentiae*. Quant à l'argument, il donne à la fois les ressorts de la pièce et le résumé de l'histoire. C'est cette histoire qui est reprise ensuite, plus longuement dans l'exposition de l'argument non sans que l'auteur ait dit qu'il s'en expliquera mieux tout au long de la pièce. Revenant alors au prologue, il le commente mot à mot tant sur sa nature que sa finalité. Sa nature est bien de plaire au public mais sa finalité est, en fait, de répondre aux attaques des auteurs malintentionnés. Il traite aussi de l'authenticité des prologues en soulignant que Térence parle ici en son nom mais sous le couvert d'un récitant Calliopius (confusion sans doute avec le réviseur) dont le rôle, précise-t-il, consiste à lire en public un ouvrage en face d'autres personnes à l'image du *cantor* à l'église (f. 1ᵛ, colonne 1: *A*). L'*explanatio* est le commentaire de la comédie selon la succession des actes et des scènes. Si les premiers sont clairement décomptés, les secondes ne portent pas toujours l'indication *prima, secunda scena*. Mais leur répartition est cependant clairement perceptible à la fois par l'initiale et par la longueur de la glose. Alors que le commentaire est généralement littéral, glosant en phrases courtes, parfois en quelques mots tel terme de Térence, la glose de la première scène de chaque acte est littéraire, en ce sens qu'elle résume les données de l'intrigue et situe les personnages. Ce sont ces dernières gloses que l'on retrouve en marge des manuscrits, au début de chaque scène, les autres étant le plus souvent inscrites au-dessus de chaque mot dans l'interligne du texte.

Nous trouvons donc ici le point d'aboutissement des commentaires antérieurs et comme la synthèse de la double rédaction du *Commentum Brunsianum*: l'approche globale des arguments et des gloses littéraires associée à une démarche analytique de gloses littérales.

Le commentaire se clôt par les étymologies de noms des personnages de Térence. Ces étymologies se trouvent en partie dans le lexique de Papias (c.1050), *Elementarium doctrinae rudimentum*, ce qu'avait déjà vu R. Sabbadini en 1897 examinant le manuscrit du quinzième siècle de la Riccardienne 647 (f. 4). En partie seulement, car Papias ne donne que l'intitulé des noms de l'*A*, comme je l'ai vérifié dans l'édition de Venise de 1496, alors que le commentaire donne l'étymologie des noms de toutes les comédies. Et puisque j'en suis aux sources, je note qu'il cite nommément Donat, Virgile, Stace (*Thebais*), Horace (*De arte poetica*), Plaute, Priscien et ce qui est plus surprenant le *Waltherius*. La référence à ce poème anonyme du dixième siècle, produit de l'aire ottonienne, est une indication de poids pour la recherche en paternité de ce commentaire.[4]

L'allégation de l'autorité de Donat porte sur l'imitation de Ménandre dans les Adelphes. Ceci, le prologue de Térence omet de le rappeler. Il ne parle, en effet, que de l'emprunt secondaire à Plaute, dont la pièce *Commorientes* est une contamination des *Synapothescontes* de Diphile. L'auteur du commentaire renvoie donc à Donat ('Teste Donato') qui dans la préface de son commentaire aux Adelphes rappelle, en effet, la paternité de Ménandre mais sans citer Diphile et Plaute comme le fait le commentaire 'Poeta iste'. On pourrait croire que sa source est directe car les versions du commentaire antérieur, qui n'ignorent pas non plus la paternité de Ménandre rappelée dans la didascalie, glosent d'après les données du prologue sur Diphile et Plaute pour le *Brunsianum* et

[4] Mais l'attribution du poème à Eckehard Ier, doyen de Saint-Gall, est presque unanimement rejetée. On discute aussi de l'attribution à Gérald de Fleury, auteur du prologue, qui le dédia à l'évêque Erchambald d'Eichstätt (822–890). On note que B. Bischoff a remarqué une analogie de ton avec le prologue d'Odilon de Cluny à l'empereur Henri II; cf. T. de Moremberg, 'Eckehard Ier (doyen de S. Gall)', in *Dictionnaire d'histoire et de géographie ecclésiastiques*, 16, 1960, col. 1382–83.

sur Diphile, uniquement, pour le *Monacense*, sans aucune mention de l'autorité de Donat dans les deux cas.

Le fait que la tradition manuscrite actuelle du commentaire de Donat ne remonte pas au-delà du quinzième siècle, mis à part un seul manuscrit du onzième siècle et des fragments du treizième siècle, ne nous autorise pas à préjuger de son état antérieur. Si l'on en croit la lettre de Loup de Ferrières au pape Benoît, en 855/858, à qui il réclame avec insistance le commentaire sur Térence de Donat, cette tradition manuscrite ne devait pas être fournie. Il me semble donc qu'une telle mention isolée de l'autorité de Donat, renvoie plutôt aux grammairiens. Car l'étude des commentaires postérieurs nous apprend que leurs auteurs ne connaissent pas Donat commentateur de Térence avant le quinzième siècle.

Arrêtons-nous un instant sur la tradition manuscrite de nos deux versions 'Poeta iste' et 'Auctor iste'. La version 'Poeta iste' est transmise dans le manuscrit Vatican, Vat lat. 2912, de la deuxième moitié du douzième siècle. C'est un manuscrit de trente-six ff. sur deux colonnes, de 261 x 131 mm., ce qui nous donne un format oblong très fréquent dans les 'libri manuales'. C'est d'ailleurs un manuscrit de commentaires de classiques. L'écriture fine, serrée, est me semble-t-il d'une seule main. Elle est soignée car le manuscrit n'offre pratiquement pas de corrections ou d'annotations marginales. J'ai noté un bourdon, en début de ligne, corrigé à la ligne suivante, ce qui dénote une attention soutenue du copiste et une bonne connaissance du texte qu'il transcrit. Des fins de lignes vides de texte sont prolongées par un trait à l'intérieur de la colonne ce qui est une particularité paléographique assez rare pour cette époque. Les abréviations sont très nombreuses. Certaines sont rares, peut-être même personnelles, d'autres sont spécifiques à la Lombardie. Ce qui m'amène à avancer le nord de l'Italie ou peut-être le sud de la France comme origine probable du manuscrit.

Cette proposition d'origine est renforcée par la tradition manuscrite de l'autre version de ce commentaire: 'Auctor iste'. Aucun des dix-sept manuscrits n'est antérieur à la deuxième moitié du douzième siècle. Parmi ceux-ci l'un peut être attribué à l'Italie du nord ou, peut-être, au sud de la France et deux autres à l'Allemagne du sud. Les quatre manuscrits du début du treizième siècle, le manuscrit qui attribue ce commentaire à Servius, et les manuscrits du quinzième siècle, ont, soit une origine italienne du nord, perceptible dans la décoration ou les filigranes, soit une origine du sud de l'Allemagne, ou de la France. Il est plus délicat de tirer argument de l'origine géographique des manuscrits portant des gloses marginales tirées de ce commentaire, car dans les manuscrits tardifs une confusion est toujours possible avec les gloses tirées du commentaire de Giacomino Robazzi qui a intégré des pans entiers de ce commentaire dans le sien. Mais là aussi, la zone d'influence reste toujours l'Italie du nord, le Piémont d'après des filigranes, puis la France et peut-être l'Allemagne.

L'attribution à Servius d'un seul des dix-sept manuscrits de cette version ne manque pas d'intriguer. On la trouve dans le manuscrit Vatican, Urb. lat. 362. Daté du quatorzième siècle par C. Stornajolo, ce manuscrit me semble devoir être remonté à la charnière du quatorzième-quinzième siècle, d'après l'écriture humanistique cursive arrondie et la décoration rouge, azur, des petites initiales.[5] Il est entré dans la bibliothèque de Federico de Montefeltro après 1474, puisque ses armes tiercées avec l'anneau de rubis, insérées dans un encadrement d'or et d'azur au f. 1^r, sont accompagnées de ses initiales: 'F[edericus] D[ux]'. De la même époque date au f. 1^v la couronne de laurier cerclée d'or, contenant le sommaire du manuscrit en capitales, en lignes alternativement rouge et azur: 'IN | HOC CODICE | CONTINETVR COM | MENTVM IN TEREN | TIVM ERVTV[M] EX VETV | STISSIMO CODICE | ITEM ALIVD IN NO[N] | NVLLAS PLAVTI | COMOEDIAS'.

Cette mention d'un 'vetustissimus codex' et l'attribution rubriquée de ce commentaire à Servius, f. 85^r: 'SERVIUS | DEO GRATIAS. AMEN' ont donné à croire à l'existence d'un commentaire de Servius sur Térence. On se fonde pour cela sur une mention d'une liste de livres prêtés et de livres scolaires de la première moitié du onzième siècle provenant de la cathédrale Saint-Pierre de Cologne: '... Terentium cum Servio'.[6] Dans cet inventaire composite, transmis par le manuscrit Erfurt, Wissenschaftliche Allgemeinbibl., Amplon. 2° 64-II, f. 117vb (addition du onzième siècle *in.*), les articles sont distingués par des points et des majuscules. La mention '... cum Servio' peut donc sembler troublante.

---

[5] C. Stornajolo, *Codices urbinates latini*, I, Rome, 1902, pp. 332–34.
[6] Gottlieb, n° 36; cf. B. Munk-Olsen, *L'étude des auteurs classiques latins aux XIe et XIIe siècles*, III, 1ère partie, Paris, 1987, p. 82.

Mais contrairement à Donat: 'Terencius cum Donato..',[7] Servius n'est pas connu comme commentateur de Térence. Dans l'affirmative, il serait bien étonnant que nous n'en ayons gardé d'autre trace que celle d'un seul catalogue médiéval. D'autre part, le texte de ce commentaire appartient à la deuxième version d'une oeuvre dont toute la tradition manuscrite commence dans la deuxième moitié du douzième siècle. Il semble donc qu'il faille comprendre que l'article de l'inventaire porte sur le prêt d'un seul manuscrit contenant Térence et Servius. Je constate que ce type d'apparentement n'a pas, à ma connaissance, d'autre exemple mais des sondages dans les catalogues médiévaux apportent des formulations syntaxiquement comparables: 'Terentius cum Omero de excidio Troiae ...', 'Terentius cum Statio Thébaidos ...', 'Terentii liber et in eodem disputatio Karoli et Albani ... ', 'Terentius in quo et Statius ... ', 'Martialis totus et Terentius in uno vol. ...'.[8]

Peut-on tenter d'expliquer ce qui nous semble une bévue? Le manuscrit (α), cité dans l'inventaire de Cologne, contenait certainement les comédies de Térence, suivies ou non d'un commentaire, qui, compte tenu de la date, ne peut être celui transmis par le manuscrit Vatican, Urb. lat. 362. Il faut donc admettre que le 'vetustissimus codex' dont parle ce dernier n'est pas antérieur à la deuxième moitié du douzième siècle. Cet exemplaire 'vetustissimus' (β) a vraisemblablement copié les comédies d'après le manuscrit de Cologne (α), en y incluant le titre général du recueil repris de l'inventaire; puis, négligeant Servius, il continue le manuscrit en y ajoutant le commentaire: 'Auctor iste', abusant plus tard le copiste du manuscrit Vatican, Urb. lat 362. On notera que cet exemplaire supposé (β) n'existe plus car aucun manuscrit du douzième siècle au treizième siècle de la version: 'Auctor iste' ne transmet le commentaire avec le texte des comédies. Et la boucle est bouclée par le copiste du MS Vatican, Urb. lat. 362 quand il omet, à son tour, le texte des comédies de Térence du manuscrit 'vetustissimus' (β), car il constitue un recueil de commentaires de classiques, sur Térence et Plaute, à partir de sources différentes. En effet, le commentaire de Plaute est une oeuvre récente d'un

[7] Erfurt, Colleg. Universitatis; 'Standortsregister von etwa 1510', éd. P. Lehmann, *Mittelalterliche Bibliothekskataloge Deutschlands und der Schweiz*, II, Munich, 1928, p. 187.
[8] *Catalogi bibliothecarum antiqui*, éd. G. Becker, Bonn, 1885, pp. 232, 285, 191, 239.

italien, selon une note marginale au f. 86^r, de la main du Cardinal A. Mai: 'Est italici recentioris quaedam interpretatio. Vide infra 135^v. A Maius' (f. 135^v: 'More vulgarium io li impiro le schiauine de ciancie').[9]

L'édition de Venise de 1518, qui utilise le manuscrit Vatican, Urb. lat 362: *Terentius cum quinque commentis uidelicet Donati, Guidonis, Calphurnii, Ascensii et Servii*, a repris l'attribution. On doit la prendre pour un exemple de méprise d'un inventaire médiéval. Ce dernier n'est pas toujours à prendre à la lettre, ou alors nous aurions encore un nouveau commentateur de Térence: 'Euagrii commentum super Terentium'[10] ou, un peu plus étonnant, une nouvelle qualité d'un Térence, poète tragique! : 'Item 9. Item sex comediarum et tragediarum Terencii poete libri'.[11]

Mais qu'en est-il pour la version 'Legitur'? La tradition manuscrite de cette version est plus courte: sept manuscrits qui vont aussi de la deuxième moitié du douzième au quinzième siècle. Ils sont tous français sauf peut-être un manuscrit inachevé de la Riccardienne sur l'origine duquel je ne peux me prononcer. Une autre particularité de cette version est qu'elle ne se retrouve presque pas en gloses marginales. Car le manuscrit Madrid, B.N. 14753, d'origine italienne, ne cite que les premiers mots de la version 'Legitur' quand il indique, en marge, d'autres divisions en actes que celles qu'il donne d'après d'autres commentaires. Certaines de ces gloses ont le sigle L.V. ou Laur. V. (abréviation de Lorenzo Valla), qui a collationné d'autres manuscrits en vue de la division en actes.

On voit donc que la parenté textuelle que nous avons observée entre les versions 'Poeta iste' et 'Auctor iste' est confortée par une communauté d'origine. De même, le fait que la France soit à peu près la seule zone d'influence de la version 'Legitur' explique peut-être ses variantes textuelles.

La dernière version, sans titre comme les trois autres, 'Terentius africanus' est copiée dans le manuscrit Vatican, Vat. lat. 2912, ff. 23^v-25^v, sans séparation, sans initiale majeure, à la suite de la version 'Poeta iste', comme si elle en était le prolongement sous

---

[9] C. Questa, 'Plauto diviso in atti prima di G. B. Pio', *Rivista di cultura classica e medioevale*, 4, 1962, p. 229, n. 13. L'auteur rapproche ce commentaire de celui contenu dans le MS Vatican, Vat. lat 2711, dont l'ordre est identique.

[10] *Catalogi bibliothecarum antiqui* (n. 8 supra), p. 192.

[11] *Katalog des Amplonius Ratinck, 1410-1412*, éd. P. Lehmann (n. 7 supra), 2, p. 12.

forme de résumé. C'est en effet un texte beaucoup plus court, composé sur le même plan, avec le même ordre des comédies. On retrouve dans l'introduction les mêmes notes sur les différents genres de comédies, sur la nature du récit, qui est très souvent tirée de l'imagination de l'auteur ce qui, entre autres différences, l'oppose à la tragédie, dont le récit est tiré de l'histoire. Il aborde les conditions des représentations successives, leur mise en scène, l'intéraction entre les musiciens et les acteurs à la seule fin de la délectation du public, les stéréotypes de personnages, vieillards irascibles et dépités, serviteurs fourbes, fils désobéissants etc... Puis intervient l'argument avec la glose de la didascalie. On glose aussi sur le nom de la comédie, son numéro d'ordre dans l'oeuvre de Térence, et sur la *Vita*. Entre cet argument et le commentaire proprement dit, se placent des extraits, inspirés d'Evanthius ou tirés d'Isidore de Séville, sur la comédie de Térence et sa matière qui, répartie en cinq actes, se résume à cinq catégories de personnages: les vieillards, les jeunes, les matrones, les esclaves, la cinquième étant constituée des courtisanes et des entremetteurs. Le commentaire proprement dit répartit alors l'action en actes et selon une succession de scènes, variable, mais suivant toujours le même principe du plus grand développement de la glose de la première scène de l'acte. Elle institue en effet comme un résumé des faits passés et à venir et une introduction à l'action présente des personnages en scène.

Cette version se retrouve partiellement dans quatre manuscrits et en particulier dans un quaternion inachevé jusqu'à *E.*, I, 2, 84, inséré entre les ff. 9-16ᵛ, d'un manuscrit du onzième siècle, d'origine espagnole, qui transmet le *Commentum Brunsianum*, El Escorial, Bibl. del monasterio, s. III. 23. Le quaternion est d'une autre main du douzième siècle et l'on ne sait rien sur son origine. Les trois autres manuscrits nous renvoient à la Bavière, la France et l'Italie. La seule conclusion qu'on puisse en tirer est que, manifestement, on a plus utilisé les versions longues que leur résumé.

III. *Giacomino Robazzi (c.1359-60).*

Je serai très bref concernant le commentaire de Giacomino Robazzi (de Mantua), grammairien dont la carrière se déroula en grande partie à Vérone. Les études de R. Sabbadini en 1933, E. Franceschini en 1938, de G. Billanovich en 1974 (qui l'identifie à Gia-

comino Robazzi), nous l'ont fait connaître au point que c'est le
commentaire le plus facile désormais à identifier dans les marges
des manuscrits.[12] C'est aussi le plus répandu. Je renonce à aborder ici sa tradition manuscrite. Outre les nombreux témoins cons-
tituant le *corpus* de l'oeuvre, on trouve du Giacomino Robazzi
presque partout en gloses marginales. Et non seulement dans les
manuscrits humanistiques, mais aussi en additions dans des manuscrits antérieurs. Ce sont souvent des versions remaniées pro-
pres à des régions ou à des pays, comme l'Espagne par exemple.
On doit y voir le témoignage d'un enseignement toujours vivant
qui prend appui sur ce commentaire en l'adaptant; ce qui n'est
qu'un juste retour des choses. Car on sait que Giacomino Robazzi,
dont l'oeuvre suit le plan des commentaires antérieurs et l'ordre
des comédies du *Brunsianum*, a puisé à pleines mains dans la version 'Auctor iste'. Même amplifiée, augmentée d'intérêts nouveaux
sur la métrique ou la stylistique, cette version est la trame de son
travail, au point que dans les manuscrits humanistiques, à moins
de trouver en marge le sigle 'Ia', il est parfois délicat de décider
si la glose marginale est tirée de Giacomino Robazzi ou de sa
source 'Auctor iste'; elle aussi recopiée indépendamment jusqu'à
la fin du quinzième siècle.

IV. Commentum Laurentii

Je serai tout aussi bref touchant au *Commentum Laurentii* du nom
figurant dans deux manuscrits: Paris, Bibl. nat. lat. 7907 et Cambridge, Univ. Lib. Ff. VI.4. Il a été étudié par C. Villa en 1981
et C. Bozzolo en 1984, laquelle l'attribue à l'humaniste français
Laurent de Premierfait.[13]

Observant la tradition manuscrite assez restreinte de ce commentaire, elles ont été frappées par l'origine française des manuscrits et par la période assez courte de leur production. En janvier

---

[12] R. Sabbadini, *Classici e umanisti da codici ambrosiani* -IV: *Giacomino da Mantova commentatore di Terenzio*, Florence, 1933, pp. 69–85; E. Franceschini, *Studi e note
di filologia latina e medievale*, Milan, 1938, pp. 163–73; G. Billanovich, 'Terenzio,
Ildemaro, Petrarca', *Italia medioevale e umanistica*, 17, 1974, pp. 1–42, et 60.

[13] C. Villa, 'Laurencius', *Italia medioevale e umanistica*, 24, 1981, pp. 120–33, et
La 'Lectura Terentii'... (n. 1 supra), pp. 237–59; C. Bozzolo, 'Laurent de Premier-
fait et Térence', *Vestigia. Studi in onore di Giuseppe Billanovich*. A cura di R. Avesani,
M. Ferrari, T. Foffano, G. Frasso, A. Sottili, Rome, 1984, pp. 93–129.

1408, le duc de Berry reçoit en étrennes de Martin Gouge, évêque de Chartres, l'actuel manuscrit Paris, Bibl. nat. lat. 7907A, qui est le premier témoin de ce commentaire. Un autre exemplaire, le manuscrit Paris, Bibl. de l'Arsenal 664, datable des années 1411-12 lui sera prêté par Jean d'Arsenal, évêque de Châlon. Enfin, le troisième manuscrit, qui permet de reconstituer le corpus du commentaire, le Paris lat. 7907, peut être daté aux alentours de 1440. Ces trois manuscrits, luxueusement décorés, transmettent donc des états différents d'un commentaire qui suit l'ordre des comédies de Térence *A.E.H.Ad.Ph.He.*, qui par rapport à l'ordre adopté jusqu'ici par les commentaires antérieurs se caractérise par l'interversion des deux dernières comédies: le *Ph.* prenant la place de l'*He.* Le dernier manuscrit, lat. 7907, est une ample étude dont la copie s'arrête, malencontreusement, au début de l'*E.* On peut la concevoir comme le témoignage d'un enseignement destiné à une lecture publique alors que les deux premiers, qui donnent une courte présentation de l'auteur et un sommaire de ses comédies, renvoient à un public peu soucieux de la métrique et de la stylistique de Térence.

J'ai peu de choses à ajouter à la tradition manuscrite. Le manuscrit Gotha, Forschungsbibliothek, Membr. II 96 signalé en addendum d'après une indication de C. Villa, est un manuscrit du nord de la France ou de la Belgique. Il a appartenu à un certain Conrad de Castro qui l'a acheté à Louvain en 1550 (f. 1ᵛ). Les gloses marginales sont tirées du Paris lat. 7907 et surtout du Paris Arsenal 664. Un extrait du commentaire à l'*H.* de Laurent de Premierfait figure au f. 92 du manuscrit Montpellier, Bibl. Mun. et Univ. Méd. 114, du quinzième siècle et d'origine française. D'autres extraits, tirés du Paris, lat. 7907, sont copiés aux quatre premiers feuillets seulement d'un manuscrit dont la réglure de l'encre a prévu la présence du commentaire marginal: Stuttgart, Poetae et Philologici, F. 11 du quinzième siècle. La décoration des bordures et des initiales, inachevées, situent le manuscrit dans la France du nord ou dans la Flandre. On voit que ces additions confortent, l'origine française de ce commentaire et témoignent d'une certaine notoriété de son auteur.

V. Iniungitis. *Petrus Luder*

Je terminerai cette présentation cursive des commentaires à Térence par une oeuvre qui n'apparaît que dans la deuxième moitié du quinzième siècle et qui est connue par son incipit: 'Iniungitis'. Le nom de l'auteur nous est donné par une note contemporaine au revers du plat supérieur du manuscrit Colmar, Bibl. mun. Consistoire 26 (MS 1939): 'Petrus Luder, poeta paduanus is Terencii comedias Ulme exposuit 1460'. Il s'agit de l'humaniste Petrus Luder de Kislau, étudiant à Padoue en 1444 et qui enseignera à Ulm et Leipzig. Les quatorze manuscrits que nous avons repérés limitent la diffusion de cette oeuvre à l'Allemagne du sud et à l'Italie du nord-est. Le premier manuscrit daté remonte à 1452 et ses filigranes proviennent de la Vénétie et de la Carinthie. Les filigranes d'un autre manuscrit qui se situent entre 1441-1448, viennent soit de la Vénétie, soit de la Moyenne-Franconie soit enfin de l'Autriche. Quant aux douze autres manuscrits qui sont soit datés ou datables, de 1454 à 1499, ils se situent—sauf deux, un à Bâle en 1471-72 et l'autre à Florence c.1494—en Bavière, dans la Basse-Franconie, la Haute-Autriche, le Haut-Tyrol et le Haut-Adige.

Le commentaire est toujours introduit dans les manuscrits par la *Vita Terentii* de Pétrarque, puis par l'argument de la *Praefatio Monacensis*, suivi d'un *accessus* à l'*A.*, que clôt la *Vita Terentii* de Giacomino Robazzi. Puis vient le commentaire proprement dit, séparé dans les manuscrits, soit par un blanc, soit par la copie des comédies. La préface introductive reprend un peu les thèmes de l'ancienne *expositio* en insistant sur les personnages, leur nom, leur caractère et leur rôle dans l'action. Cet essai de notice biographique est d'autant plus nécessaire que parmi les cinquante-trois personnages actifs de Térence, certains portent le même nom d'une pièce à l'autre: Chremes figure dans l'*A.E.H.* et le *Ph.*; Bacchis dans l'*Ad.H.*et l'*He.*, Dromo dans l'*A.Ad.* et l'*H.*; Parmeno dans l'*Ad.E.* et l'*He*; Sostrata dans l'*A.H.* et l'*He.* etc. La notice veille à bien les caractériser dans chaque pièce: origine, filiation, caractère et rôle dans l'action. De celle-ci, l'auteur en fait un résumé; puis il expose la matière de la comédie et bien qu'il annonce que son exposé sera succinct, sa démarche est assez discursive. C'est qu'il adopte l'ancien argument des commentaires médiévaux, mais libéré des contraintes de l'explication textuelle. Privilégiant le déroulement

scénique, il met successivement en évidence les ressorts drama-
tiques des diverses situations provoquées par l'action des personnages qui, après avoir embrouillé les fils, concourent tous à
l'heureuse conclusion finale. Il agit de même pour chaque comédie
dans l'ordre du *Commentum Brunsianum*: *A.E.H.Ad.He.Ph.* Ce récit
global ne se retrouve jamais en gloses marginales. Quand ce commentaire est copié dans un manuscrit qui transmet aussi les
comédies, les gloses marginales sont tirées soit du commentaire de
Giacomino Robazzi dont on se rappelle la *Vita Terentii* figurant en
tête du commentaire 'Iniungitis', soit d'un autre commentaire que
j'appelle du nom du premier manuscrit où je l'ai découvert:
München, Bayerische Staatsbibl. Clm 369. C'est qu'en vérité il ne
s'agit pas d'un commentaire scolaire mais d'une leçon inaugurale
débouchant sur un enseignement universitaire sur Térence. Il est
permis de se demander si nous n'avons pas recueilli cet enseignement dans le manuscrit Clm 369. Car tout ce qui manque dans
la leçon 'Iniungitis' se retrouve dans le manuscrit Clm 369 et vice-
versa.

Il s'agit, en effet, dans le manuscrit Clm 369 d'un cours pro-
fessoral qui démontre une connaissance approfondie de Térence.
Cette analyse minutieuse nécessite aussi de la part de l'auditeur,
soit une mémoire des six comédies qui de nos jours paraîtrait
phénoménale, soit plus vraisemblablement la possession du manuscrit de ces comédies auxquelles le cours renvoie constamment. La
brève introduction comprend la *Vita Terentii I* (Ambrosiana) et des
extraits sur les thèmes déjà rencontrés, *De fabula, De comoedia*. Puis
le commentaire s'articule en deux parties inégales. La première, la
plus importante puisqu'elle occupe presque les deux tiers de
l'oeuvre, est un commentaire grammatical des comédies. Le lemme
souligné est cité longuement puis situé dans la scène, désignée par
ses premiers mots. Le mot expliqué est parfois porté en marge et
toutes ces explications sont regroupées sous le titre de chaque
comédie. Cependant, l'auteur renvoie aussi nommément aux autres
en donnant le lemme et la scène. Il passe ainsi en revue les fonc-
tions de tel mot du vocabulaire térentien selon l'ordre de son
apparition dans chaque comédie dont l'ordre est le même que celui
de la leçon inaugurale 'Iniungitis'.

La référence aux scènes, identifiée par son incipit, renvoie à la
deuxième partie du commentaire et montre bien l'unité de composition de l'ensemble. La première est grammaticale, la deuxième

littéraire. Elle ordonne la matière en actes puis en scènes qui suivent majoritairement les choix de Donat. La première glose de chaque acte est plus nourrie. Comme dans les commentaires médiévaux elle donne le sens général de l'acte puis elle situe chaque personnage, un peu comme la notice de la leçon inaugurale le faisait: père, fils, belle-mère, servante..., avant d'en expliquer le comportement par l'analyse de ses sentiments. Les gloses des autres scènes, plus courtes, seront de même nature car il s'agit de comprendre le déroulement de l'intrigue et de souligner sa progression. A l'encontre de Donat, qui accorde plus d'intérêt au commentaire grammatical qu'à l'explication littéraire qu'il ramasse en un bref résumé en tête de chaque comédie, cette oeuvre cherche un équilibre entre l'explication lexicale et l'explication textuelle. Ce faisant, elle me semble être le point d'aboutissement des commentaires médiévaux d'autant plus que j'ai identifié l'une de ses sources dans les gloses marginales du douzième siècle d'un manuscrit italien du onzième-douzième siècle: Florence, Bibl. Laurenziana, San Marco 244.[14]

Or, la zone d'influence de ce commentaire transmis dans le manuscrit Clm 369 recoupe entièrement celle de la leçon inaugurale de Petrus Luder tant sur le plan géographique que chronologique. Six manuscrits du quinzième siècle transmettent ce commentaire. Quatre sont respectivement datés de 1462, de 1464, 1469 et 1471. Le filigrane du cinquième a une marque spécifiquement italienne localisée à Trévise en 1467. Quant au sixième, conservé à Bucarest, il ne m'est connu que par microfilm mais le type d'écriture gothico-humanistique cursive rappelle les manuscrits du nord de l'Italie. Le manuscrit daté de 1462 est d'origine allemande car il a été écrit à Erfurt. Le manuscrit Clm 369 est un recueil écrit en partie à Nuremberg en 1464 et partie à Padoue en 1465, complété par une pièce en 1468, par Hartmann Schedel. Cet humaniste de Nuremberg, né en 1440, mort en 1514, était docteur en médecine et ès arts de l'Université de Padoue. Avec son frère Hermann, il constitua une des plus riches bibliothèques de l'Allemagne en textes de Pétrarque et d'auteurs classiques. Il termine à Nuremberg sa copie de la première partie du commentaire le 28 septembre 1464 et de la seconde le 2 octobre de la même année. Il l'effectue sur

---

[14] Y.-F. Riou, 'L'influence italienne dans le commentaire à Térence de l'humaniste allemand Petrus Luder de Kislau', in *Umanesimi medievali. II Congresso dell'Internationales Mittellateinerkomitee*, S.I.S.M.E.L., Florence, 1996, sous presse.

un manuscrit qu'il a acheté en Italie car les filigranes sont, pour l'un, localisé à Trévise en 1464 et, pour l'autre, une variante d'une croix de Malte répandue à Rome en 1463-64. L'autre manuscrit, daté de 1469, qui porte un ex-libris du quinzième siècle de la commanderie de Comburg, en Wurtemberg, n'a qu'un seul filigrane pour tout le manuscrit, variante d'un groupe que l'on trouve entre Bergame, Brescia et Wintherthur. Quant au manuscrit daté de 1471 dont j'ignore les filigranes car je ne le connais que par microfilm, on peut le situer par l'écriture en Allemagne du sud ou en Italie du nord.

Voilà donc cinq manuscrits, au moins, qui ont tous des liens étroits avec l'Italie, soit dans la Vénétie du nord (Padoue) ou du nord-est (Trévise), soit dans la Lombardie au pied des Alpes bergamasques ou bresciennes. Leur regroupement géographique rappelle celui de la tradition manuscrite de la leçon inaugurale de Petrus Luder, d'autant plus que le commentaire du manuscrit Clm 369 se retrouve en gloses marginales dans neuf autres manuscrits, tous d'origine allemande, selon une ligne qui part de Wurtemberg jusqu'au Tyrol autrichien en passant par la Haute et Basse-Franconie.

L'auteur du commentaire a donc enseigné en Allemagne du sud à partir de 1464, date des premières gloses d'un manuscrit écrit à Ulm, ce même manuscrit qui transmet aussi la leçon inaugurale et qui nous en donne le nom de l'auteur: Colmar, Bibl. mun., Consistoire 26 (MS 1939). Il n'est pas interdit de penser que la copie qu'en fait cette même année Hartmann Schedel, à Nuremberg, est le témoignage de cet enseignement dont nous retrouvons encore l'écho dans les gloses d'un manuscrit écrit à Sélestat, Bas-Rhin, en 1480. Un tel faisceau d'indications permet d'avancer pour le commentaire le même nom que celui de l'auteur de la leçon inaugurale: Petrus Luder, mais évidemment sous bénéfice d'une collation textuelle à faire.

Tous ces commentaires et ces gloses qui accompagnent les comédies de Térence sont bien le signe que ce texte classique est resté vivant. Au début de cet exposé, je rappelais que ce foisonnement des commentaires médiévaux instaurait une sorte de dialogue continu entre Térence et les besoins successifs du présent. En concluant avec Petrus Luder, je ne pouvais rêver plus belle illustration de ce propos.

MEDIEVAL COMMENTARIES ON HORACE

Karsten Friis-Jensen

The ancient commentaries on Terence, Virgil, and Horace are the oldest and most important remains of Roman literary criticism. Among them Servius's commentary on Virgil is by far the best, and Virgilian scholarship still owes him a great deal. In Horace's case the situation is different. We have two commentaries on Horace which contain ancient material, but the form in which they have been transmitted is heavily marked by later editing, and very little of the ancient material left adds to our understanding of Horace's poems as such. Their merits lie elsewhere: they inspired the Middle Ages to keep the study of Horace on a qualified level, and thus they helped to secure Horace's position and popularity until Renaissance scholarship took over. Moreover, the ancient commentaries themselves, and the medieval commentaries to which they gave inspiration, are highly interesting documents that illuminate the way in which Horace has been read through the centuries.

Porphyrio and Pseudo-Acro

Porphyrio's commentary is probably of third-century origin, but the text transmitted is a later abridgment.[1] Its main aim is to explain Horace's text in grammatical and rhetorical terms, and it is very little concerned with factual explanations. There are also no metrical scholia. The scope of Porphyrio's commentary is therefore limited, but what is there is sensible and useful. It survives in very few manuscripts: two of the ninth century, and some fifteenth-century manuscripts dependent on a third medieval manuscript now lost.[2] In all cases the text is transmitted separately, independent of the text of Horace. Porphyrio therefore had very little direct influence in the Middle Ages. However, the other ancient

---

[1] Cp. Nisbet-Hubbard 1970, pp. xlvii-xlix.
[2] See R.J. Tarrant on the transmission of ancient scholia on Horace in Reynolds 1983, p. 186.

commentary, the so-called Acro or Pseudo-Acro, uses Porphyrio extensively. As Pseudo-Acro became very popular and influential in the Middle Ages, it guaranteed wide circulation for a large part of Porphyrio's material.

Gottfried Noske has given a thorough analysis of the Pseudo-Acronian corpus in his Munich dissertation. Pseudo-Acro did not begin as one single commentary, but is a corpus which originates in the amalgamation of two different late antique commentaries. One of these, the so-called *Expositio A*, covered the lyrics only; the other, the so-called *Paragraph scholia*, originally covered the entire *oeuvre*, but when it was fused with the *Expositio A*, it had lost the part concerning Books I-III of the *Odes*, and the two first odes of Book IV.[3] According to Noske, Keller's otherwise useful edition of Pseudo-Acro does not take sufficient account of the origins of the single parts, but the whole question is extremely complicated. In any case Pseudo-Acro is much fuller than Porphyrio, including information on factual questions, and also on metre. These points probably explain why Pseudo-Acro became the more popular and directly influential of the two ancient commentaries in the Middle Ages. It has been transmitted in many manuscripts, and in the Middle Ages was always written in the margins of texts of Horace. About 1400 a detached version of Pseudo-Acro, independent of the text of Horace, was created by Italian humanists, and only then did the anonymous commentary receive its attribution to Acro.

Modern scholarship on the medieval commentaries

Only few medieval commentaries on Horace have so far been edited in their full form, and we do not know exactly how representative those which have been printed are. The Dutch scholar Botschuyver edited two medieval commentaries transmitted together with Horace's text and covering his entire *oeuvre*. The first volume of Botschuyver's series was published in 1935 and contains an edition of the so-called *Phi scholia*. According to Gottfried Noske they were probably composed in the early Carolingian period on the basis of older material related to Pseudo-Acro.[4] Botschuyver used four manuscripts of the late ninth and tenth centuries for his

---

[3] Noske 1969 *passim*; cf. his conclusions, pp. 280f.
[4] Noske 1969, pp. 189-91.

edition, but the *Phi scholia* are also found in later annotated manuscripts of Horace.[5]

Botschuyver's Volume IV, published in 1942, contains an edition of a series of scholia transmitted in a manuscript of about
1100, perhaps written at Mont-St-Michel in north-western France.
I call them the *Aleph scholia* after Botschuyver's signature for the
manuscript. These scholia are probably not much older than the
manuscript in which they have been transmitted, and the whole
series of scholia seems to have been composed by one master, most
likely from north-western France, as I shall argue later.

In the high and later Middle Ages it is probably the exception
to find commentaries on the whole of Horace composed by one
single master. At least in the case of commentaries transmitted
without the text of Horace, a commentary normally covers only
one of the four groups of works, that is the lyrics, including the
Epodes and *Carmen saeculare*, the *Art of Poetry*, the *Satires*, and the
Epistles.

Scholarship on the medieval Horatian commentary tradition
began in 1877 with an edition of a commentary on the *Art of Poetry*.[6] The interest in commentaries on the *Art of Poetry* has no doubt
been a side-effect of the general interest in medieval handbooks of
poetry-writing, the Arts of Poetry, since Horace's poem is one of
the most important models for these treatises. Even the title of one
of the most famous new arts of poetry, Geoffrey of Vinsauf's *Poetria noua*, indicates the rivalry with Horace's *Poetria uetus*, as it is
sometimes called. So far three medieval commentaries on Horace's
Art of Poetry have been printed. Zechmeister edited the so-called
Scholia Vindobonensia, transmitted in only one manuscript of the second half of the eleventh century. This commentary already shows
the fusion of rhetorical and grammatical doctrine so characteristic
of the later independent arts of poetry. There is no doubt that this
commentary was composed in the eleventh century, although the
editor believed it to be much older. Thus the *Scholia Vindobonensia*
are themselves one of the earliest known results of the renewed
interest in Horace's poems which followed the establishment of a
more classical canon of school authors in the early eleventh cen-

---

[5] A sample inquiry indicates that this may apply to, for instance, the heavi-
ly-annotated twelfth-century German MS Vatican, Chigi H. V. 165 (= Munk
Olsen Hor. C. 194, 1982 p. 498).

[6] Zechmeister 1877.

tury, a canon which also included all Horace's works.[7]

In contrast to the *Scholia Vindobonensia*, one of the other commentaries on Horace's *Art of Poetry* which has been edited is known in more than twenty manuscripts, and may even turn out to have been the standard commentary in the later Middle Ages (ed. Friis-Jensen 1990). This so-called *Materia commentary* is almost certainly French, and was composed before c. 1175, when Matthew of Vendôme used it in his own treatise on poetry-writing. The *Materia* commentator begins with an unusually long *accessus* in which the six vices of poetry-writing and their corresponding virtues are discussed at length, and then he goes on to give a detailed literal commentary, explaining points of poetological doctrine and of grammar, and antiquarian questions. The canon of six vices and virtues of poetry-writing probably originated in the *Materia commentary*, but it won wide recognition in the later commentary tradition and in the independent arts of poetry.[8]

Another twelfth-century commentary on Horace's *Art of Poetry* was published very recently, the so-called *Anonymus Turicensis*, which has been transmitted in two manuscripts (ed. Hajdú 1993). In terms of doctrine, the *Anonymus Turicensis* lies somewhere between the eleventh-century *Scholia Vindobonensia* and the *Materia commentary*, and it may even be the actual link between the two commentaries.

Apart from Botschuyver's two editions, no medieval commentaries on Horace's lyrics, *Satires* and *Epistles* have been published in their entirety. The nearest equivalent is a series of *accessus* and introductory glosses to every single poem written in the margins of a twelfth-century English manuscript now in Magdalen College, Oxford, which I edited in an article in 1988. This so-called *Oxford commentary* will be discussed later.

In the same article I also published an *accessus* and introductory glosses to the *Odes* from the margins of a Vatican manuscript. In the meantime I have found the entire commentary in two later manuscripts, this time detached from the text of Horace.[9] In this version it also covers the *Epodes* and the *Carmen saeculare*, and comprises a full literal explanation. I shall call this commentary the *Auctor-iste-Uenusinus commentary*, after its incipit.

---

[7] See Glauche 1970, pp. 62-100, and Munk Olsen 1991, pp. 32-37 & 120.

[8] For the question of the six rules of poetry see now Friis-Jensen 1994.

[9] Cp. the note on MSS to the *Auctor-iste-Uenusinus commentary* in the Appendix below.

Except for a small number of *accessus* to Horace,[10] and quotations from commentaries in various articles, I know of no other medieval exegetical texts on Horace that have so far been published. When we consider that hundreds of medieval annotated manuscripts of Horace and dozens of separately-transmitted commentaries have not yet been investigated, it it obvious that any statement about the way Horace was read in the Middle Ages must be of a very preliminary nature. Luckily scholars have taken up other aspects of scholarship concerning the medieval Horace, apart from editing commentaries, and I should like to mention some important recent publications in this field.

Birger Munk Olsen has laid a solid basis for all manuscript studies concerning the period before 1200 with his monumental catalogue of manuscripts of the Latin classics (Munk Olsen 1982-89). The section on Horace comprises about 250 manuscripts, many of which are annotated, and about thirty manuscripts containing independent commentaries, described by *incipit* and *explicit*.

Claudia Villa recently published a check-list of all Horatian manuscripts, a total of 815 containing a text of Horace; this list makes a very welcome extension beyond the year 1200 (Villa 1992-93). It is to be hoped that she will supplement it with a list of manuscripts of independent commentaries on Horace, even if such a list cannot be as definitive as the one already published.

Günter Glauche's and Birger Munk Olsen's monographs on the medieval canon of school authors give the necessary background for an understanding of Horace's position among the most-read Latin classics, together with for instance Virgil, Terence, Lucan, and Juvenal (Glauche 1970 and Munk Olsen 1991).

In 1989 Jürgen Leonhardt published a very interesting study of metrical theory which sheds new light on the medieval tradition of quantitative lyric metres. Horace with his proverbial *uarietas metrorum* is one of the chief models of this tradition.

Some recent publications have even taken medieval glosses and commentaries on Horace as their main subject. Klaus Siewert's edition of Old High German glosses to Horace not only presents the evidence for an intensive study of Horace in German schools from the tenth to the beginning of the twelfth century, but his

---

[10] See the texts printed in Huygens 1970, pp. 49-53 & 111-14, and in Jeudy 1971.

thorough linguistic discussion of the possible time of composition
and region of origin of the glosses also contributes significantly to
our knowledge of the commentary tradition (Siewert 1986).

Suzanne Reynolds's interesting article about syntactical glosses,
above all in medieval manuscripts of Horace, is the first fruits of
a larger survey concerning the grammatical aspects of medieval
scholia on Horace, as far as I have understood (Reynolds 1990).

Claudia Villa is also in the middle of a larger project about how
Horace was read in the Middle Ages and the Renaissance. Her
recent article about commentaries on Horace's *Art of Poetry* contains much new information (Villa 1992).

My own interest in medieval commentaries on Horace was
aroused by a wish to know how some specific Horatian odes and
satires were interpreted in the twelfth century. The shortest way
to that sort of knowledge is probably via the commentary tradition. It is therefore my aim to edit and publish some of the most
representative or interesting of the twelfth-century commentaries
on Horace which have come down to us. I believe that the *Materia commentary* is such a standard commentary. Similarly, a rough-
ly contemporary commentary on the *Satires* and another on the
Epistles are both transmitted in several manuscripts, and may turn
out to be what I am looking for.[11] In the case of the *Odes*, it is
more difficult to decide which of the several commentaries is the
most rewarding to edit.

A last item among research projects in progress is the article on
Horace for the *Catalogus Translationum et Commentariorum*. A team has
been formed, of which I am a member. But since the driving force
behind the Horatian team is also a member of the Virgil team
which is working hard to finish that very large and difficult article, work on Horace has been proceeding only at a moderate pace.

I have postponed mentioning Bernhard Bischoff's more than
twenty-year-old article 'Living with the Satirists' (Bischoff 1971).
In it Bischoff gives a penetrating and amusing characterization of
a group of un-published commentaries on Horace and Persius
transmitted in a St Gall manuscript. If we accept that the entire
series of commentaries on all of Horace's works, with certain lacu-
nae and overlaps, has a common origin in the same scholastic envi-
ronment, as Bischoff himself seems inclined to do, then they offer

---

[11] Selected passages from the twelfth-century standard commentaries on
Horace's *Satires* and *Epistles* are now published in Friis-Jensen 1993.

a kind of landmark in a sea of uncertainty. References to contemporary events show that the commentaries were written in the last quarter of the eleventh century, and vernacular glosses in Old High German and French indicate that they were composed in the borderland between Germany and France. Klaus Siewert also discusses the St Gall commentaries, as I shall call them, in his book. Siewert corroborates Bischoff's localization and dating from a linguistic point of view, and proposes the region around Liège as a possible place of origin. We shall return to the St Gall commentary on the *Odes*.

Six medieval commentaries on the Odes

In order to give an impression of the medieval Horatian commentary tradition, I have decided to take commentaries on the *Odes* as an example. There are various reasons for this. One point is that since Horace's poems in hexameters seem to have enjoyed a steady popularity throughout the Middle Ages, signs of a serious study of his *Odes* are a good index of a particular boom in medieval Horatian scholarship.

I am also for the time being concentrating on commentaries transmitted separately, detached from the text of Horace. There is to my knowledge no fundamental difference between commentaries transmitted in the margins of a text of Horace and those transmitted separately. We have several examples of commentaries which change from one form into the other in the course of their life. But for the modern scholar the texts transmitted separately offer one advantage. Marginal and interlinear glosses in a manuscript may have been added on many occasions by different readers or scribes, and need not have anything at all to do with each other. A sequence of scholia transmitted independently is not necessarily the product of one single author, or a commentary proper, but at least the person who first collected the scholia believed that they made sense in conjunction.

In the appendix below I have set out the discussion of Horace's Ode I, 20 from six different medieval commentaries, besides Porphyrio and Pseudo-Acro. Two of these are marginal commentaries, whereas the other four have been transmitted separately. They were probably all composed in the period between 1050 and 1200.

A few other independent commentaries have been registered by Birger Munk Olsen, but I have begun with the most promising or most easily accessible. Some of the commentaries are defective as we have them in the manuscripts, although there is no reason to believe that they were not once complete. As for the following centuries, there may be several commentaries on Horace's *Odes* of the thirteenth and fourteenth centuries concealed in separate manuscripts or in the margins of texts of Horace, but manuscripts of this period have not yet got their Munk Olsen. It should also be mentioned that there exist at least five manuscripts containing a detached version of Pseudo-Acro's commentary on the *Odes* only, all of them of the fifteenth century, and probably all Italian. The humanists clearly felt a need to return to the ancient commentary tradition. In contrast to the complete detached version of Pseudo-Acro of the fifteenth century which I mentioned earlier, this partial version, on the *Odes* only, does not carry Acro's name.

On the basis of the six commentaries I have chosen it should be possible to get a more general impression of the commentary tradition of Horace's *Odes* in the important 150 years which are so often labelled collectively 'the twelfth-century Renaissance'.

All the commentaries are headed by a prologue or *accessus*, although of greatly varying length. They all belong to the most common type in the twelfth century, Richard Hunt's 'type C', which Alastair Minnis discusses in detail in his book on *Medieval Theory of Authorship*.[12] However, they do not all of them include all the standard headings of this type. Since the books of *Odes* form the first work in the canon of Horace's works, *accessus* to the *Odes* often contain a life of Horace, which is one of the standard headings of the *accessus* scheme, the *uita auctoris*. Four of my six *accessus* actually do so. The other three best represented headings are *materia libri*, *intentio auctoris*, and *titulus libri*.[13]

In the six *accessus* the discussion of the 'subject-matter of the book', *materia libri*, almost always takes Horace's own definition of the lyric genre in his *Art of Poetry* (lines 83ff.) as a point of departure. Among types of lyric poetry Horace here mentions hymns and *encomia*, love-poems and drinking songs, all subgenres which he uses himself. The commentators almost always stress the variety of Horace's subject-matter, and the *St Gall commentary* is isolat-

---

[12] Hunt 1948 pp. 126ff. [=94ff.]; Minnis 1988, pp. 18-28.

[13] A more substantial discussion of some of the *accessus* to commentaries on Horace's *Odes* is to be found in Friis-Jensen 1993, esp. at pp. 275-89.

ed in its short moralizing statement that 'est igitur materia Horacii in hoc opere uitia et uirtutes hominum'.

Another recurring heading is the 'intention of the author'. Here the Horatian terms of benefit and delight, *prodesse* and *delectare* (*AP* 333), are normally pointed out as the double intention of the author, so that benefit always implies moral edification. We should not be surprised by the medieval interest in moral edification, but note that the other side of the pair, the delight aspect, is normally also represented, and, what is more, as a legitimate purpose of poetry.

Under the heading the 'title of the work', *titulus libri*, the commentators often discuss the etymologies of the words *oda* and *lyricus*, since the work is called either *liber carminum, liber odarum*, or *lyrica*. The word *lyricus* they interpret as 'varied', following a strange etymology transmitted by Isidore of Seville, and thus they make a connection between the name of the lyric genre and the variety of both its metre and its subject-matter.

The characteristic diversity of metrical forms in Horace's *Odes* is almost always mentioned in the *accessus*, but without any definitions of the single lyric metres. Of the two ancient commentaries, Pseudo-Acro is the only one which gives metrical definitions, not collectively but as glosses in connection with the single odes. In the case of Ode I, 20, Pseudo-Acro gives only the name of the metre, since the sapphic stanza was described in detail when it occurred for the first time, at Ode I, 2. The only one among the medieval commentaries transmitted separately which has adopted and integrated this system consistently is the *Auctor-iste-Uenusinus commentary* (cp. Appendix below, last entry). The other commentaries do not deal with metrical questions. However, since most manuscripts of Horace's *Odes* either contain a separate metrical treatise, such as Servius's 'On the metres of Horace', or simply carry metrical glosses to the single poems, we cannot take this lack of metrical information as a sign that students were not supposed to know Horace's metres.

It is a common feature of the commentaries on the *Odes* that every single poem is provided with its own small prologue or *accessus*, stating for instance to whom the poem is addressed and what its subject matter is. Porphyrio and Pseudo-Acro had already set an example. Some of the medieval commentators clearly thought in terms of standard headings when they composed these introductory glosses, in analogy with the *accessus* proper. There is nothing strange in that, since they often phrased the *accessus* to the *Odes* as if it were an introduction to Horace's very first ode, only provided with extra information relevant to all of the *Odes*. The *Auctor-iste-Uenusinus commentary* is again instructive, because it mentions such headings explicitly. Even in the comparatively condensed introductory gloss to Ode I, 20 we find the standard headings used in this commentary: *metrum*, subject matter (*negotium*), which on the whole corresponds with the *materia* of the main *accessus*, and finally the rhetorical heading of the ode, in this case the term *prosphonetice*. As in the case of metrical identification, this commentary is the only one I know which systematically takes account of these somewhat obscure rhetorical headings,[14] and tries to explain them, although they recur in many glossed manuscripts of Horace.

Other commentaries structure their introductory glosses almost as schematically as the *Auctor-iste-Uenusinus commentary*, without actually mentioning their headings explicitly. An example is the *Oxford commentary*, which always begins by mentioning the addressee and the general background of the poem, and Horace's intentions in it. And, invariably, it concludes by telling us what moral benefit we may obtain by reading the poem. This last category corresponds with the heading *utilitas* of the ordinary *accessus* scheme.

Medieval commentaries on carm. I, 20

I should also like to say something about the way the medieval commentators build up their exegetical text. But before I do that we should perhaps take a quick look at the Horatian ode which I have chosen. Ode I, 20 was convenient for my purpose, among other things because it is short, and because it is addressed to Maecenas. The relationship between Horace and Maecenas is one of the features of Horace's *Odes* which really interests the medieval commentators, as we shall see:

> Hor. carm. I, 20
> *Uile potabis modicis Sabinum*
> *cantharis, Graeca quod ego ipse testa*
> *conditum leui, datus in theatro*
> *   cum tibi plausus,*
> *care Maecenas eques, ut paterni*
> *fluminis ripae simul et iocosa*

---

[14] Cp. Faerber 1937.

redderet laudes tibi Uaticani
  montis imago.
Caecubum et prelo domitam Caleno
tu bibes uuam; mea nec Falernae
temperant uites neque Formiani
  pocula colles.

Nisbet and Hubbard give the following paraphrase of the ode in their commentary (Nisbet/Hubbard 1970): 'You shall have cheap wine which I laid down at the time of your ovation, Maecenas. It is all very well for you to drink vintage wines, but they are too grand for me'. Horace's modern commentators are not too enthusiastic about this particular poem. Among their judgments are phrases such as: 'Our poem has no exceptional literary merit ... the ode spends too much time on blatant flattery of Maecenas's ovation. The last sentence of the ode is in fact most elegantly balanced, and this gives the poem such charm as it possesses'. Nisbet and Hubbard's reservations do not however influence their thoroughness in annotating the poem, and their discussion fills about ten pages.

Our medieval commentators are more restrained (the full text of the commentaries are found in the Appendix below, with references to editions and manuscripts). The scope of their annotation corresponds more or less with that of the ancient commentators. I have already mentioned the introductory glosses, the small prologues. As for the explanation of the literal meaning of the poem, only the *St Gall commentary* is obviously different from the others with its bald list of very short unconnected glosses. The other five commentaries clearly intend to give a full discussion of the literal meaning of the text. There is a tendency in all of them to explain a whole sequence of words at a time, so that the syntax of Horace's text is kept intact. This manner is most pronounced in the *Auctor-iste-Uenusinus commentary* (the last text in the Appendix).

The discussion of Ode I, 20 gives a good picture of the method of the *Auctor-iste-Uenusinus commentary*, at its most comprehensive. Structurally speaking, the commentary is built up around the backbone of a syntactically coherent rearrangement of Horace's words, an *ordo* gloss. Such *ordo* glosses are common in cases of difficult word order. Glosses on single points are then inserted into this sequence in their appropriate places. This may be done in various ways. One is to introduce clarifying additions coherent with the syntax of the *ordo* gloss, as for instance the *o* before the vocative *MECENAS*, or the *est* before *DATUS*. Another common device is the insertion of *id est* or *scilicet* glosses. A third method is to insert whole sentences parenthetically, normally without causing the *ordo* gloss to abandon its syntactical progression. The *ordo* glosses used by the *Auctor* commentator sometimes coincide with the *ordo* glosses preserved in some manuscripts of the Pseudacronean tradition (V and the Γ group). This correspondence may be seen in the first long section of the *Auctor-iste-Uenusinus commentary* to Ode I, 20, which corresponds to the *ordo* gloss in Pseudo-Acro (second text of the Appendix).

The technique we see here of combining a rearrangement of the word order with glosses on single words is also a characteristic of the *Materia commentary* on Horace's *Art of Poetry*, and of several other twelfth-century commentaries on classical authors.

This is not the place to examine in detail the single glosses offered on Ode I, 20 in the medieval commentaries, but even a superficial glance will show that these commentaries either borrow a great deal from each other or use the same sources. On the whole the glosses are sensible, and the level of understanding reflected in the explanation of the literal meaning is quite impressive. All the medieval commentators have difficulties in understanding the relationship between the two halves of the third stanza, but so have modern commentators.

What I should like to look at in more detail here is the overall interpretation of the ode which we find in the introductory glosses of the medieval commentaries. Porphyrio and Pseudo-Acro both give a down-to-earth summary of the ode. However, five of the six medieval commentaries propose an interpretation of the ode which can only be reconciled with Horace's text with considerable contortions. They cannot understand the sophisticated relationship between the poet and his patron, and they therefore assume that the ego of the poem must be somebody other than the real Horace, that is, that the ego must be a fictitious person or a mask, a persona (cp. the *Aleph commentary*: *Oratius ... gerens personam rusticorum*). This interpretative strategy is obviously very useful for a medieval scholar faced with, for instance, some of Horace's most explicitly sexual odes and epodes,[15] but it seems hardly called for in this

---

[15] Cp. Friis-Jensen 1993, p. 288, for Horace, and Minnis 1991, pp. 14ff., for the concept of *persona* in thirteenth- and fourteenth-century exegesis, with suggestions of a late-classical origin for the concept.

poem. However, the man who with a smile promises his exalted guest a mediocre wine must be a hypocrite, a bailiff or tenant farmer who is unwilling to pay his due to his lord, or is even planning to extort gifts from him. The mention of Maecenas's ovation in the theatre must therefore also be fulsome flattery, according to the *St Gall commentary*[16]—an attitude which Nisbet and Hubbard were also inclined to take up, as we have seen. This complex interpretation of the ode can easily be explained as the product of a society in which the gap between poet and statesman patron was normally too wide to allow any friendship or friendly banter between them. Moreover, an interpreter who is looking for clear-cut moral truths will always be suspicious of light-hearted irony. It seems to me, however, that the similarities in interpretation, and sometimes also in the actual wording, between the five medieval commentaries point to a common medieval source, an influential commentary or schoolmaster. The *Auctor-iste-Uenusinus* commentator is independent of this interpretation, either by accident or by design. He does not hesitate to call Maecenas Horace's 'patron and friend', and acknowledge the bantering tone of the ode.

The similarities between five of the medieval commentaries entitle us to take a look at their background, to see whether they might have something more in common. The *St Gall commentary* has already been tentatively located by Bischoff and Siewert in the Liège region, on the northern borders between France and Germany, and may equally tentatively be dated to the late eleventh century.

The *Aleph commentary* edited by Botschuyver has been transmitted in a French manuscript of c. 1100, perhaps written at Mont-St-Michel. In any case the commentary is clearly French, since it contains several French glosses. We even have an example in Ode I, 20. Here the word *LEUI* is glossed with a vernacular synonym, the verb 'naier', although given in a Latinized form. I have collected the other French glosses in this commentary, and persuaded Birger Munk Olsen to take a look at them. He is inclined to see some linguistic features that point towards northwestern France

---

[16] St Gall comm. carm. I, 20,3 *DATUS IN THEATRO. ecce adulatio*, 'this is fulsome flattery'. The term *adulatio* is most likely a reference to the attitude of the ego of the poem towards Maecenas, and not to the spectators' giving Maecenas an ovation: the corresponding term *adulando* is used at line 5 in this way, '<YOUR> NATIVE <RIVER>, because Maecenas was from Tuscany, where the Tiber has its source, as if he said, with fulsome flattery: the others were foreigners, but you were a native of this country'.

or Anglo-French, an observation which of course concords well with the origin of the manuscript in which the commentary is transmitted. The *Oxford commentary*, which has several features in common with the *Aleph commentary*, is preserved in an English manuscript of the first half of the twelfth century. And finally, the Paris manuscript, Bibl. Nat. lat. 7641, which contains a commentary not known from any other source, was probably also written in northern France, in Normandy.

On the basis of this, admittedly very inconclusive, material, we have reason to believe that Horace's *Odes* were studied intensively in more than one centre of learning in northern France, possibly also in England and in the Liège region, in the second half of the eleventh and in the twelfth century. Considering what we know in general about literary culture in the high Middle Ages, this conclusion is not very surprising, but nevertheless welcome.

In the case of the dissident voice among the medieval commentaries, the *Auctor-iste-Uenusinus commentary*, I have one or two pieces of information that perhaps may help, in the future, to date and locate it, or one of its models. The oldest manuscript, which only contains the *accessus* and the introductory glosses, dates from the beginning of the thirteenth century. On the other hand the commentary uses Bernard of Utrecht's late eleventh-century commentary on Theodolus, so a twelfth-century date seems assured.[17] In the *accessus* the commentator applies the three verbs *uituperare*, *inuehi* and *reprehendere* to Horace's varying attitudes in the *Odes*, *Epodes* and *Satires* respectively, and says explicitly that this is what Magister Alfred has stated in his glosses.[18] It follows that a Mag-

---

[17] A long scholion on the nine Muses, at Hor. carm. I, 1,33 *Euterpe ... Polyhymnia*, has been lifted out of Bernard of Utrecht (ad Theodol. 286, lines 1054-85 in Huygens 1977). At carm. IV, 7,25, the *Auctor-iste-Uenusinus commentary* mentions that Theodolus's version of the Hippolytus story (vv. 125ff.) is different from Horace's; but in this case the wording cannot prove that Bernard's commentary was used. Bernard wrote his commentary some time between 1076 and 1099, cp. Huygens 1970, p. 7, n. 15.

[18] *Auctor-iste-Uenusinus* comm. acc. (MS Klosterneuburg fol. 1ra) *Intentio sua est partim laudare, partim uituperare. In odis siquidem uituperat, non reprehendit, quod magister Aluuredus in glosis suis scripsit, in epodon inuehitur, in sermonibus reprehendit. Inter que est hec differentia: uituperare namque est malefacta alicuius iocose narrare, quod facit in odis, inuehi est malefacta alicuius maligno animo representare, quod uidetur facere in epodon, sed non facit. ... Reprehendere est malefacta alicuius sub spe correctionis enarrare, quod facit in sermonibus*; the words *quod magister Aluuredus in glosis suis scripsit* are found in both MSS of the complete version, whereas the abridged version in Vat. Pal. lat. 1655 omits them.

ister Alfred probably wrote a commentary on one of Horace's works, possibly the *Odes*, but we also know, by inference, that it was not the *Auctor-iste-Uenusinus commentary*. Exactly the same definition of Horace's varying attitudes in his works is found in Hugutio of Pisa's *Derivationes*, probably written in the 1180s[19]—but whether Hugutio took it from Alfred, or vice versa, we cannot tell.[20] I can propose various candidates for this Master Alfred, who is the only scholar from the Middle Ages known by name who *may* have written a commentary on Horace's *Odes*—however, nothing can be said with certainty, except that he was most likely an Englishman, because of the name.

That the *Auctor-iste-Uenusinus* commentator uses an older commentary which may have been written by an Englishman does not say anything about his own background. It should be noted, though, that the library of Peterborough Abbey in the later Middle Ages possessed a copy of the *Auctor-iste-Uenusinus commentary*.[21] It is a curious fact that, besides Magister Alfred, the only other medieval author of a commentary on Horace known by name is the Englishman William of Doncaster, who lived in the twelfth century. William refers to his own glosses on Horace's *Art of Poetry* in a work of his on moral philosophy; although William's reference is unusually explicit, it has not yet been possible to identify any existing commentary as his.[22] My point in mentioning Magister Alfred and William of Doncaster is simply to stress the fact that Englishmen seem to have been just as active students of Horace as the French or the Germans.

None of the medieval commentators on Horace I have mentioned are particularly interested in allegory or natural philosophy, topics important for so many other twelfth-century commentaries on the classics. Their ambition seems to consist in explaining the literal meaning of Horace's text to the best of their abilities, and possibly in mitigating the effect of some of Horace's most outspoken poems by introducing the device we have already met, the fictitious ego or persona who can be explained away as a warning

---

[19] This passage is printed in Kindermann 1978, p. 57.

[20] Hugutio's source is clearly a commentary on Horace, but this commentary may of course also have been Alfred's source.

[21] The so-called Matricularium (s. xiv ex.) lists a codex (C..... = C.v.) containing various commentaries on the Roman poets, among others *Glosa que sic incipit 'Auctor iste Uenusinus'*, see James 1926, p. 43.

[22] See Weijers 1976, pp. 1ff. and 15f.

to others. It is often claimed in *accessus* to the *Odes* that Horace wrote this work for the young, for those who are particularly interested in love and entertainment.[23] The medieval commentaries on the *Odes* which I have seen indicate that Horace's *Odes* were actually read in the arts courses of eleventh- and twelfth-century schools, and that some of the texts we have are based on lectures in the classroom. The level of knowledge assumed on part of the reader is not too advanced, but relevant quotations from other school authors are often introduced. We also sometimes find remarks directed at the readers, or rather listeners, in the second person plural. A feature discussed by Bernhard Bischoff in his article on the *St Gall commentary* points in the same direction. Commentators now and then introduce analogies from the Christian religion and from contemporary society, or simply discuss ancient Romans as if they were Christians. I do not believe that such modernizations are unconscious anachronisms. It is far more likely that they are introduced quite consciously in order to make the texts more accessible to the students.

It is my hope that the rather uneven and scattered material which I have presented may nevertheless give an impression of the diversity and strength of the medieval interest in Horace's works. My material should at least suffice to refute one of the most inveterate misunderstandings about the study of Horace in the Middle Ages, namely that the *Odes* were very rarely read. The best way of making this fact clear to for instance our classicist colleagues, would be to publish one of the medieval commentaries on Horace's *Odes*. Since Botschuyver has already edited a representative of the more moralizing trend among commentaries on the *Odes*, I am at the moment most inclined to choose the *Auctor-iste-Uenusinus commentary*. This commentary represents the more classicizing trend of interpretation. However, its full exposition of the literal meaning of Horace's text is typical of the twelfth century, and it also gives the modern scholar an excellent opportunity to follow in detail the methods of a twelfth-century colleague.

---

[23] See Friis-Jensen 1993, pp. 266-69, 273, 285-88.

Textual examples

Porphyrio

carm. I, 20: UILE POTABIS MODICIS S.C. Maecenatem ad cenam inuitat, promittens se ei uinum Sabinum exhibiturum, quod in amphoram Graecam miserit, ut inde scilicet aliquid adduceret suauitatis. Quod UILE pro non uetusto uidetur dixisse. Alioquin Sabinum uinum si uetustum sit, non est uile.

1 MODICIS. Uidetur modicum pro paruo positum; quod quidam [quidem *codd.uet.*] negant, existimantes modicum a modo dici et significationem habere eius, quod Graece metr<i>on dicitur.

3 CONDITUM LEUI. Dicit se hoc uinum per semet ipsum in ueterarium condidisse. Leuisse se ergo gypso utique uult intellegi. Huic contrarium est Terentianum illud [*Ter. Haut.* 460] 'Releui dolia atque omnes serias', quod significat 'aperui, et quasi regypsaui'.

3 DATUS IN THEATRO CUM TIBI PLAUSUS. Diximus et supra claros et bonae existimationis uiros plausu populi solitos fuisse in theatro excipi, malos autem sibilari.

5 CARE MAECENAS EQUES. Constat Gaium Maecenatem in equestri dignitate sua uoluntate permansisse, cum utique facultas lati claui pateret.

5 UT PATERNI FLUMINIS RIPAE. Tiberis ex Etruria uenit, quem paternum Maecenati dicit, quia inde Maecenas oriundus. Uaticanum autem montem non longe a theatro Pompei esse scimus, quem resonuisse simul cum ripis Tiberis plausu populi dicit.

10 TU BIBIS UUAM. <Uua> pro uino μετωνυμίᾳ τρόπῳ [-μία -πος *trad.*] dicitur. Huic contrarium Plautus in Trinummo fecit, uinum pro uua dicens [*Plaut. Trin.* 526]: '[Is]tum uinum, priusquam coctum est, pendet putidum'.

11 MEA NEC FALERNAE TEMPERANT UITES NEQUE. Ordo est: Mea pocula nec Falernae uites temperant nec Formiani colles, per quod significat nec Falernum uinum se habere, quod ei in caena exhibeat, nec Formianum.

[*ed. Holder 1894*]

Pseudo-Acro

carm. I, 20: Ad Mecenatem. {Metrum Sapphicum endecasyllabum.}

1 UILE POTABIS MODICIS SABINUM. Maecenatem inuitat ad cenam, cui mediocritatem suam excusat, promittens ei uinum Sabinum nouitate uile, sed quod in amphoram Graecam miserit, ut inde aliquid traheret suauitatis, eo tempore, quo ille in theatro a populo laudabatur; aut uile uinum propterea quod ipsi uile sit, qui meliora potare consueuerat.

1 UILE aut nouum aut certe habundans, minoris pretii, ut Uirgilius [*Verg. Georg.* I 227] 'Uilemque phaselum', item [*Verg. Georg.* I 274] 'Uilibus aut onerat pomis'.

1 {Ordo est: care Maecenas eques, potabis uile Sabinum modicis can-

taris, quod ego ipse leui conditum Graeca testa, cum datus est tibi plausus in theatro, ut ripae paterni fluminis simul et iocosa imago Uaticani montis redderet tibi laudes.}

1 MODICIS aut paruis aut modum habentibus.

2 {CANTHARIS uasis uinariis ansas habentibus.}

3 LEUI aperui, protuli, ut [*Ter. Haut.* 460]: 'Releui dolia omnia'.

4 PLAUSUS fauor.

5 PATERNI FLUMINIS RIPAE. Paterni ideo, quia de Tuscia fuit Maecenas, unde oritur Tiberis, ut Uirgilius [*Verg. Georg.* I 499]: 'Qui Tuscum Tiberim et Romana Palatia seruas'; nam et Porsennae dicitur adfinis fuisse.

6 SIMUL ET IOCOSA R.L. Constat Maecenatem in equestri dignitate mansisse sua uoluntate, dum ei <lati claui> [*suppl. ex Porph.*] facultas pateret.

7 {LAUDES. Per echo scilicet Uaticani.}

7 UATICANI MONTIS I. Mons est uicinus theatro, in quo dicit per echo uoces auditas, ut [*Verg. Georg.* IV 50]: 'Uocisque offensa resultat imago'.

9 CECUBUM uinum Campanae regionis.

9 PRELO DOMITUM CALENO. Prelum dicitur, unde premi uuae consueuerunt.

9 CALENO. Ciuitas Campaniae.

10 FALERNAE UITES probati uini et optimi, de quo [*Verg. Georg.* II 96]: 'Nec cellis ideo contende Falernis'.

10 {TEMPERANT, id est non fruor uino illarum ciuitatum neque sunt mea pocula similia.}

11 {FORMIANI. Formia ciuitas est, unde est hoc diriuatiuum.}

[*ed. Keller 1902.* {...} = *not in* **A** *(Paris, BN lat. 7900 A)*]

St Gall commentary

carm. I, 20: UILE POTABIS. hic reprehendit illos uillicos qui, quando debent recipere dominos suos, inhoneste et sine omni apparatu recipiunt eos, tantummodo captando eos assentando. et dicit ille uillicus domino suo sic: o MECENAS.

¶ 2 CANTARIS cyphis.

¶ 2 EGO IPSE. non uetus.

¶ 3 LEUI, reposui.

¶ 3 DATUS IN THEATRO. ecce adulatio.

¶ 5 UT PATERNI. tantus plausus.

¶ 5 PATERNI, quia iste de Tuscia fuit, unde Tiberis uenit, quasi diceret: alii fuerunt aduene, sed tu fuisti de hac terra, adulando.

¶ 6 IOCOSA IMAGO, id est echo resonans de Uaticano monte.

¶ 10 MEA NEC FALERNE. et quare bibes ista mala uina, quia nec tantum habeo de bono uino ut commisceatur malum.

¶ 11 FORMIANI. bonum uinum ibi crescit.

[*Sankt Gallen, Stiftsbibliothek, 868, s. xii 1/2, p. 21, Munk Olsen 1982 p. 520: 'Suisse'; the commentary may have been composed earlier, probably at the end of the eleventh century, and possibly in the Liège region, cp. Siewert 1986 p. 216*].

Aleph commentary
carm. I, 20: Prosphonetice ad Mecenatem, inuitans eum ad uinum.

[*in marg.:*]   ¶ 1 UILE POTABIS. Hic tanguntur rustici, qui cum dominis suis debeant apparare conuiuium, nolunt eis rem debitam conuenienter persoluere. Oratius uero gerens personam rusticorum sic ad Mecenatem loquitur: o Mecenas, si ueneris ad domunculam meam uile prandium habebis.

1 quod dicit: tu POTABIS SABINUM uinum UILE, et non cum argenteo uase, et hoc est MODICIS CANTARIS. quod UILE uinum CONDITUM et repositum in Greco uase, quia de Grecia erat allatus [*sic*] uini. illud uinum, o CARE MECENAS EQUES, EGO IPSE LEUI, id est uulgaliter naiaui [*Old French: naier = étouper, boucher avec un chiffon*], tunc scilicet LEUI, CUM TIBI FUIT DATUS PLAUSUS IN THEATRO a populo. propter hoc populus tibi dedit plausum in theatro, UT RIPE FLUMINIS tui, scilicet Tusci fluminis, et MONTes UNDIQUE RESONARENT ad honorem tuum. Mecenas fuit infirmus, et quia conualuit, datus est ei plausus in theatro, propter congratulationem quia euasit. et tunc temporis id accidit quod ?naiauit [?nare(s) *cod.*, narrat *Botsch.*].

¶ 3 LEUI, id est signaui operculo apposito, releui, id est designaui remoto operculo.

¶ 9 Hec uina tibi dabo, et non Falernum. non habeo, nec causa tui emam.

¶ 11 NEQUE uinum quod crescit in Formianis collibus TEMPERANT MEA POCULA.

[*supra lin.:*] 3 <LEUI> pro releui. 3 <DATUS> scilicet est. 7 <UATICANI> pro(prium). 9 <CECUBUM> uile uinum. 9 <CALENO> illius loci ubi fit uile uinum. 10 Si tu ueneris, BIBES. 10 <UUAM> id est uinum.

[*Paris, Bibliothèque nationale, lat. 17897, f. 8ᵛ-9ʳ, Munk Olsen 1982 p. 489: 's. xi/xii. ... France: Mont-St-Michel (F. Avril)'; ed. Botschuyver 1942 (with several misreadings)*]

Comm. carm. Paris 7641
carm. I, 20: UILE POTABIS MODICIS SABINUM CANTARIS [A. *cod.*]. In hac oda quasi inuitat Oratius Mecenatem in domum suam uilia proponens ei, per hoc reprehendens eos qui nimium in promptu[m] dominis suis calliditate quadam circumueniunt, ut aliquid extorqueant ab eis. Et quasi aliquando inuitantes eos in domum suam proponunt uilia exibituros se. Ac si aperte dicat: non habemus meliora, nisi tu, domine, uelis addere. Tu POTABIS UILE SABINUM, uinum illud, et hoc MODICIS CANTARIS, id est si<m>pl<icib>us, quasi diceret: quod nec etiam nobis sufficit. et illud uinum non est uetus, sed QUOD IPSE EGO LEUI, id est signaui et obstruxi. Solent enim, priusquam uinum reconditum est in uase aliquo, superius obstruere foramen uel pice uel aliquo alio, ne uapor uini simul cum sapore exeat.

¶ 2 Uellem illud uinum reconditum in GRECA TESTA, id est in hoc uase. Uel LENI, id est plano [*?lege* planaui], in GRECA TESTA, id est in illa terra. Solebant enim accipere corticem et cum illa terra<m>, quia tenax est quasi pix, et apponere amphorę uel alicui uasi, ubi uinum recondebatur. ego LENI non diu ante, sed tunc tantum quando PLAUSUS DATUS est TIBI IN THEATRO. tantus scilicet fuit plausus ille, quod RIPÆ PATERNI FLUMINIS, scilicet Tibridis, ET IOCOSA IMAGO MONTIS UATICANI, id est echo, REDDERET TIBI LAUDES. Uaticanus est mons iuxta Romam qui resonuit dato plausu Mecenati.

¶ 9 TU BIBES CECUBUM uinum, a loco ubi non multum bonum uinum crescit. UUAM, accipit pro uino, DOMITAM PRELO CALONO. prelum est arbor qua calcantur uuę, Cales est opidum ubi non bonum uinum crescit. Istud uile uinum dabo tibi, quia non habeo illud tam bonum sicut crescit in FALERNo aut in FORiMIANo COLLe. Forimę quędam ciuitas fuit, ubi optimum uinum crescebat, et declinatur tantum in plurali numero. Per hoc quod superius dixit DATUS TIBI IN THEATRO PLAUSUS notat eos laudes et adulationes adhibere, ut eo magis attrahat eos.

[*Paris, Bibliothèque nationale, lat. 7641, s. xii med., f. 140ᵛ; Munk Olsen 1982 p. 518: 'France: ?Normandie'*]

Oxford commentary
carm. I, 20: Mecenas, in Calabriam iturus ubi predia sua erant et per Sabinos uillam Horatii transiturus, monuerat Horatium ut optimum uinum ei apud se pernoctare uolenti prepararet. Horatius uero excusat se apud eum quadam astutia, dicens se bonum uinum non habere, ut sic possit ab eo aliquas uineas extorquere, uel competenter eum ab hospitalitate illa reuocare. Possunt hic notari omnes qui summe ditati a dominis suis solent tamen aliquam indigentiam pretendere, ut sic a dominis suis possint maiora extorquere.

[*Oxford, Magdalen College, Lat. 15, f. 10ʳ, s. xii 1/2 uel med., England; ed. Friis-Jensen 1988*]

Comm. carm. Paris 8241
carm. I, 20: UILE. Mecenas in Apuliam [*p.c.*, Italiam *a.c.*] transiturus mandauit Horatio ut susciperet eum hospitio. Ad quem Horatius scribit hanc odam, quia non tam digne possit eum procurare ut deceret tantum uirum, ut diminuendo res suas callide commoneat eum adaugere presidium eius, ut dignius possit ei seruire, non quod Horatius excusaret se non posse, quia potius benigno ei animo exhibuit necessaria. sed transfert in se illos, qui callide querunt aliquid extorquere a dominis suis, paupertatem uel aliquod tale premittendo [*?lege* pretendendo].

¶ Et quia uinum uile diutina seruatione bonum fieri potest, remouet etiam eius uetustatem dicens tunc, scilicet CUM TIBI et cetera. Mecenas egrotauit, et quia conualuit, DATUS est ei PLAUSUS IN THEATRO propter congratulationem, quod euasit. et tantus scilicet datus est plausus, ut et unde Tyberis et Uaticanus mons, qui a theatri ?re..... remotior est, inde resonarent. Paternum flumen uocat Tyberim, quia ab Etruria uenit, quam pater et antecessores eius tenuerunt. IMAGO, id est echo.

DOMITAM CALENO PRELO. Cales est oppidum ubi item uilia uina nascuntur. prelum est superius lignum in torculari, quasi premens lignum. MEA. quasi ideo hec uilia tibi offero, quia bonum uinum non habeo, ut Falernum aut Formianum. quasi diceret: non dedisti mihi quicquam apud Falernum montem neque apud Formias ciuitatem. Tunc TEMPERANT POCULA quando modo hoc modo illud infunditur uinum.

[*Paris, Bibliothèque nationale, lat. 8241, f. 26vb, s. xii ex.; Munk Olsen 1982 p. 519: 'France ou Allemagne'*]

Auctor-iste-Uenusinus commentary

carm. I, 20: UILE POTABIS. Metrum quale illud: 'Iam satis terris' et cetera. Negotium: Mecenatem patronum et amicum suum ad potationem Horatius inuitauerat. Nunc quale uinum sit ei appositurus demonstrat. Et quoniam familiariter et quasi derisorie eum alloquitur, ideo pro<s>ph<on>etice, id est exclamatorie, hec oda inscribitur.

1 dicit itaque: o MECENAS CARE EQUES (bene dicit EQUES: cum enim Mecenas esset ab [*Hor. carm.* 1,1,1] 'atauis regibus', numquam ab equestri ordine ad celsiorem honorem uoluit sublimari), tu POTABIS UILE SABINUM (a Sabinis ubi erat rus Horacii), MODICIS CAN-TARIS, id est non magnis (cantarus est uas uimineum [*sic KA*] in quo reponitur uinum), QUOD EGO IPSE LEUI <CONDITUM> in TES-TA, id est in olla, GRECA, a Grecis facta (lino, linis, leui [*A*, lini *K*], linere est operculum dolio superponere; relino, -is, releui quando oper-culum tollitur. Unde illud [*Ter. Haut.* 460]: 'Releui omnia dolia mea'), CUM PLAUSUS est DATUS TIBI IN TEATRO, id est plano [*K*, pala-tio *A*] (Mecenas enim semel egrotabat; reddita autem sanitate maximum fecerunt gaudium et plausum Romani in [*A*, et(iam) *K*] theatro), tantus, inquam, PLAUSUS, UT RIPE PATERNI FLUMINIS, id est Tiberis, ET SIMUL IOCOSA IMAGO, id est echo, UATICANI MONTIS (mons est iuxta Romam qui ad plausum Romanorum resonabat per echo) RED-DERET LAUDES Mecenati.

9 CECUBUM. Adhuc ostendit quale uinum sit ei appositurus. Et hoc est: TU BIBES CECUBUM, illud mite uinum, ET UUAM DOMITAM CALENO PRELO, id est torculari (Cales opidum est ubi mite uinum crescit).

10 Tu, inquam, mala bibes uina, quia non sunt mihi bona. et hoc est: NEC FALERNE UITES TEMPERANT, id est meliorant [meliorem *K*, meliora faciunt *A*], MEA POCULA (Falernum adeo forte uinum, quod etiam fex illius cetera meliorat [*A*, melioriat *K*] uina), NEQUE FORMI-ANI COLLES TEMPERANT MEA POCULA (in illis enim collibus bon-um crescit uinum; Bachus enim semper amat colles).

[*K=Klosterneuburg, Stiftsbibliothek 1097, f. 7rb, s. xiii 1/2, corrected with the help of A=Assisi 303, f. 198rb, s. xv; accessus and introductory glosses edited from the fragmentary Vatican, Pal. lat. 1655, s. xiii in., in Friis-Jensen 1988*]

Bibliography

Bischoff, Bernhard, 1971: 'Living with the Satirists', *Mittelalterliche Studien*, III, 1981, pp. 260-70 [originally publ. 1971].
Botschuyver, H.J. (ed.), 1935 & 1942: *Scholia in Horatium*, I & IV, Amsterdam.
Faerber, H., 1937: 'Die Termini der Poetik in den Odenüberschriften der Horaz-Oden', *Philologus* 92, pp. 349-374.
Fredborg, Karin Margareta, 'Difficile est proprie communia dicere (Horats, A.P. 128). Horatsfortolkningens bidrag til middelalderens poetik', *Museum Tusculanum*, 40-43, 1980, pp. 583-97.
Friis-Jensen, Karsten, 1988: 'Horatius liricus et ethicus. Two Twelfth-Century School Texts on Horace's Poems', *Cahiers de l'Institut du Moyen-Âge Grec et Latin (Université de Copenhague)*, 57, pp. 81-147.
id., 1990: 'The *Ars Poetica* in Twelfth-Century France. The Horace of Matthew of Vendôme, Geoffrey of Vinsauf, and John of Garland', *Cahiers de l'Institut du Moyen-Age Grec et Latin (Université de Copenhague)*, 60, pp. 319-88 (with 'Addenda et Corrigenda', ibid., 61, 1991, p. 184).
id., 1993: 'The medieval Horace and his Lyrics', in *Horace. L'oeuvre et les imitations, un siècle d'interprétation* (Entretiens sur l'antiquité classique, 39), Vandoeuvres-Genève, pp. 257-98.
id., 1994: 'Horace and the Early Writers of Arts of Poetry', in Sten Ebbesen (ed.) *Sprachtheorien in Spätantike und Mittelalter* (Geschichte der Sprachtheorie, 3), Tübingen, pp. 360-401.
Glauche, Günter, 1970: *Schullektüre im Mittelalter. Entstehung und Wandlungen des Lektürekanons bis 1200 nach den Quellen dagestellt* (Münchener Beiträge zur Mediävistik und Renaissance-Forschung, 5), München.
Hajdú, István, 1993: 'Ein Zürcher Kommentar aus dem 12. Jahrhundert zur Ars poetica des Horaz', *Cahiers de l'Institut du Moyen-Age Grec et Latin (Université de Copenhague)*, 63, pp. 231-93.
Holder, Alfred (ed.), 1894: *Pomponi Porfyrionis commentum in Horatium Flaccum*, Innsbruck (repr. Hildesheim 1967).
Hunt, Richard William, 1948: 'The introductions to the "Artes" in the twelfth century', in id.: *The History of Grammar in the Middle Ages. Collected Papers* (Amsterdam Studies in the Theory and History of Linguistic Science. Series III. Studies in the History of Linguistics, 5), Amsterdam, 1980 [originally published in 1948], pp. 117-44
Huygens, R.B.C. (ed.), 1970: *Accessus ad auctores, Bernard d'Utrecht, Conrad d'Hirsau: Dialogus super auctores. Edition critique entièrement revue et augmentée*, Leiden.
id. (ed.), 1977: *Bernard d'Utrecht, Commentum in Theodolum (1076-1099)* (Biblioteca degli 'Studi Medievali', 8), Spoleto.
James, M.R., 1926: *Lists of Manuscripts Formerly in Peterborough Abbey Library* (Supplement to Transactions of the Bibliographical Society, 5), Oxford.
Jeudy, Colette, 1971: 'Accessus aux oeuvres d'Horace', *Revue d'histoire des textes*, 1, p. 211.

Keller, Otto (ed.), 1902-04: *Pseudacronis scholia in Horatium vetustiora*, I-II, Leipzig.

Kindermann, Udo, 1978: *Satyra. Die Theorie der Satire im Mittellateinischen. Vorstudie zu einer Gattungsgeschichte* (Erlanger Beiträge zur Sprach- und Kunstwissenschaft, 58), Nürnberg.

Leonhardt, Jürgen, 1989: *Dimensio syllabarum. Studien zur lateinischen Prosodie- und Verslehre von der Spätantike bis zur frühen Renaissance* (Hypomnemata, 92), Göttingen.

Minnis, A.J., 1988: *Medieval Theory of Authorship. Scholastic Literary Attitudes in the Later Middle Ages*, 2nd ed., Aldershot.

id., 1991: 'Theorizing the Rose. Commentary Tradition in the "Querelle de la rose"' in Piero Boitani & Anna Torti (eds.): *Poetics. Theory and Practice in Medieval English Literature*, Cambridge, pp. 13-36.

Munk Olsen, Birger, 1982-89: *L'étude des auteurs classiques latins aux XIe et XIIe siècles*, I-II-III:1-2, Paris 1982-1985-1987-1989.

id., 1991: *I classici nel canone scolastico altomedievale*, (Quaderni di cultura mediolatina, 1), Spoleto.

Nisbet, R.G.M. & Margaret Hubbard, 1970: *A Commentary on Horace, Odes. Book I*, Oxford.

Noske, Gottfried, 1969: *Quaestiones Pseudacroneae*, Diss. Munich.

Quint, Maria-Barbara, *Untersuchungen zur mittelalterlichen Horaz-Rezeption* (Studien zur klassischen Philologie, 39), Frankfurt am Main 1988.

Reynolds, Suzanne, 1990: 'Ad auctorum expositionem: Syntactic Theory and Interpretative Practice in the Twelfth Century', *Histoire épistémologie langage*, 12, pp. 31-51.

Siewert, Klaus, 1986: *Die althochdeutsche Horazglossierung* (Studien zum Althochdeutschen, 8), Göttingen.

Villa, Claudia, 1992: 'Per una tipologia del commento mediolatino: l'Ars Poetica di Orazio', in: Ottavio Besomi & Carlo Caruso [eds.], *Il commento ai testi. Atti del Seminario di Ascona 2-9 ottobre 1989*, Basel & Boston & Berlin, pp. 19-46.

ead., 1992-93: 'I manoscritti di Orazio. I-II', *Aevum*, 66, 1992, pp. 95-135; ibid., 67, 1993, pp. 55-103.

Weijers, Olga (ed.), 1976: *William of Doncaster, Explicatio aphorismatum philosophicorum* (Studien und Texte zur Geistesgeschichte des Mittelalters, 11), Leiden & Köln.

Zechmeister, Joseph (ed.), 1877: *Scholia Vindobonensia ad Horatii Artem poeticam*, Vienna.

I COMMENTI MEDIEVALI ALLA *TEBAIDE* DI STAZIO. ANSELMO DI LAON, GOFFREDO BABIONE, ILARIO D'ORLÉANS

VIOLETTA DE ANGELIS

I due recenti convegni sul tema del rapporto fra testo e commento, anche nella tipologia estrema dell'autocommento, attestano il crescente interesse per questa forma di metaletteratura, che Kristeller ha indicato come la principale produzione letteraria medievale.[1] Di conseguenza, può considerarsi acquisita, e appena da richiamarsi, la conoscenza delle modalità di tradizione, fra IX e XV secolo, di un commento ad un autore classico: tranne nei pochi casi, concentrati fra XII e XIII secolo, nei quali il commento è scritto in testo continuo, esso è in simbiosi costante, anche se al suo interno instabile, con il testo a cui si riferisce.[2] E dunque, per

---

[1] *Il commento ai testi* a cura di O. Besomi, C. Caruso, Basel-Boston-Berlin 1992; *L'autocommento*, Atti del XVII Convegno interuniversitario. (Bressanone 1990), a cura di G. Peron, Padova 1994. Anche potranno citarsi, senza pretese di esaustività, singoli articoli: che spaziano da speculazioni sul 'ventriloquismo' dell'autocommento boccacciano al *Teseida* (J. T. Schnapp, 'Un commento all'autocommento nel *Teseìda*', *Studi sul Boccaccio*, 20, 1991-92, pp.185-203), a indagini sul *nomen* attribuito nel XII e XIII secolo al commento (N. Häring, 'Commentary and Hermeneutics', in *Renaissance and Renewal in the Twelfth Century*, ed. R. B. Benson-G. Constable, Oxford 1982, pp. 173-200). Tanto mi esime da insistere su quest'ultimo punto, ricordando appena che nel XII secolo, nel campo dell'esegesi agli *auctores*, i commenti in testo continuo sono pressoché unicamente definiti con il termine *glosule*. L'opinione di Kristeller, non esente da critiche al suo apparire, può leggersi in 'Der Gelehrte und sein Publikum im späten Mittelalter und in der Renaissance', in *Medium aevum vivum. Festschrift für W. Bulst*, Heidelberg 1960, pp. 212-30 = 'The Scholar and his Public in the Late Middle Ages and the Renaissance', in *Mediaeval Aspects of Renaissance Learning*, Durham North Carolina 1974, pp. 1-25.
[2] Può essere istruttivo, a questo proposito, un rilevamento statistico sul numero dei commenti a Stazio tràditi in testo continuo, rapportato al numero dei manoscritti che contengono invece il testo staziano corredato di glosse: contro più di 460 MSS, per la maggior parte estesamente glossati, abbiamo poco meno di una trentina di commenti in testo continuo, la metà dei quali è costituita da manoscritti del commento di Lattanzio Placido, per lo più copiati nel XV secolo, nel periodo in cui esso viene riscoperto e riconosciuto come testo a sè, affine per autorità a quello di Servio. Tanto evidenzia la vita estremamente effimera del testo di un commento continuo, che sovente è consegnato ad un unico esemplare e poi subito ricongiunto col testo dell'autore cui si riferisce, e in quest'atto, e in tutti i successivi travasi nei margini di altri manoscritti dell'*auctor*, ricomposto, manipolato, arricchito con glosse di diversa provenienza. Questa tradizione atti-

discorrere di commento, si dovrà volgere l'attenzione al classico e
considerare la particolare 'facies' che esso esibisce: a disegnare la
quale contribuiscono e cooperano i singoli essenziali elementi che
configurano l'edizione medievale del classico: glosse, *argumenta*
metrici, *epitaphia*, carmi mnemonici, e soprattutto, *accessus*, la cui
rilevanza è ormai riconosciuta.[3]

La costante coesistenza, fra IX e XV secolo, entro il medesimo
volume, di due testi, il classico e il suo commento, di due sistemi
quindi reciprocamente interagenti,[4] pare dunque recepita a livello
di enunciato, anche se non ancora compiutamente acquisita in
tutte le sue implicazioni. Solo molto recentemente sono stati
mostrati, con una straordinaria messe di risultati, ottenuti studiando
il comico per antonomasia, Terenzio, gli esiti cui conduce la sovrap-
posizione del sistema, costituito dall'*auctor* e dal suo commento, alle
opere di autori che scrissero fra IX e XV secolo: e si è constata-
to che solo utilizzando questa griglia interpretativa si possono leg-

---

iva—che rende spesso inattuabile, e talora addirittura improponibile, un'edizione
'lachmanniana' del commento, mobile diasistema uguale e diverso al tempo stesso
ad ogni nuova fase della tradizione stessa—impone necessariamente un'estensione
della accezione del termine 'commento': sarebbe infatti fuorviante considerare
l'esegesi a un classico limitando l'esame ai pochi commenti in testo continuo. Essi
non renderebbero piena ragione del modo di leggere e intendere l'opera dell'autore, perché risulterebbe fortemente limitata la comprensione della fortuna dell'interpretazione del suo testo e perché infine, nel caso non esista più il testimone
in testo continuo di una *lectura*, verrebbe falsato ogni discorso complessivo sullo
sviluppo dell'interpretazione dell'auctor: è questo il caso, ad esempio, dei commenti all'*Achilleide* tràditi nei commenti marginali dei MSS London, B.L., Add.
10090, Stuttgart, Wurttemb. Landesbibl., 4°.34, Wolfenbüttel, Herzog August
Bibl., 13.10 Aug. 4°, chiaramente risalenti a una tradizione compatta e stabile di
esegesi.
[3] A. J. Minnis vi ha dedicato due ampi studi (*Medieval Theory of Authorship. Scholastic Literary Attitudes in the Later Middle Ages*, Aldershot 1984; Minnis-A. B. Scott,
Medieval Literary Theory and Criticism c. 1100-c. 1375, Oxford 1988); più recentemente M. Spallone, 'I percorsi medievali del testo: *accessus*, commentari, *florilegia*', in *Lo spazio letterario di Roma antica*, III. *La ricezione del testo*, Roma 1990, pp.
387-471, ha tracciato il profilo storico dell'evoluzione di questo strumento, all'interno del sistema didattico dalla grecità al tardo Medioevo, trenta anni dopo che
a Bruno Nardi ('Osservazioni sul medievale *Accessus ad auctores* in rapporto all'epistola a Cangrande', in *Studi e problemi di critica testuale*, Bologna 1961, pp. 268-305
= *Saggi e note di critica dantesca*, Milano 1966, pp. 268-305) riuscì di risuscitare l'attenzione sull'*accessus* evocandone la presenza nell'epistola a Cangrande. Per la
vasta bibliografia sull'*accessus* cf. P. Klopsch, *Einführung in die Dichtungslehre des
lateinischen Mittelalters*, Darmstadt 1980, pp. 48-55. Per gli *accessus* a inni e sequenze: J. B. Allen, 'Commentary as Criticism: Formal Cause, Discursive Form, and
the Late Medieval Accessus', in *Acta Conventus Neo-Latini Lovaniensis*, Leuven-
München 1973, pp. 29-48.
[4] Sulle relazioni tra i due sistemi si veda da ultimo C. Segre, 'Per una definizione del commento ai testi', in *Il commento ai testi* (n. 1 sopra), pp. 3-17.

gere a pieno i testi, perché ci si riesce a impossessare del codice di riferimento comune all'autore e al lettore, quello consegnato appunto alla *lectura* dell'*auctor*.[5]

Dell'applicazione ultima del metodo all'indagine sul Lucano noto a Dante può essere utile proporre qualche esempio a titolo illustrativo, assieme ad una breve incursione nell'esegesi ad un altro classico.

I versi di *Paradiso*, XVI, 10-12

> Dal voi che prim'a Roma s'offerie,
> in che la sua famiglia men persevra,
> ricominciaron le parole mie

erano stati sin qui commentati dai moderni come un probabile riferimento a Lucano (V, 385-86), ma corrotto e frainteso: ai commentatori trecenteschi appariva invece ovvio il debito dantesco col *Bellum civile*:

> namque omnes voces, per quas iam tempore tanto
> mentimur dominis, hac primum repperit aetas.

La *lectura* vulgata di questo luogo nel Duecento risolve immediatamente ogni ambiguità: appare infatti in piena evidenza che Dante altro non fa che tradurre nei suoi versi l'interpretazione del passo lucaneo corrente ai suoi tempi.

'Voces ... quibus mentimur dominis' non veniva inteso allora, qual è, come un'allusione a generici titoli adulatori attribuiti a Cesare, ma come un'esplicita e univoca indicazione del fatto che con Cesare si iniziò l'uso, che poi ampiamente si estese, di rivolgersi ai *maiores* con il plurale.

L'interpretazione non pare risalire oltre la fine dell'XI secolo, ma ha una straordinaria diffusione, sino all'Umanesimo, intrecciata com'è, nelle discussioni dell'epoca, con la restaurazione del *tu* classico nell'epistolografia propugnata da Petrarca. Egli stesso sembra sia stato irretito da questa interpretazione del passo lucaneo *(Varia* 32; *Sen.* XIV, 1; XVI, 1 e 5) e, se forse non convinto pienamente, non certo stimolato a demolirla, come è suo uso quando gli si porge il destro di mostrare l'ampio distacco fra sè e chi lo aveva preceduto.

> Sed venio ad rem ... quod quasi magni criminis te mihi purgas infamiam, ... in tuis me litteris singulariter compellasse. Itaque stilum

---

[5] C. Villa, *La 'lectura Terentii'. I. Da Ildemaro a Francesco Petrarca*, Padova 1984.

mutas, quasi vel ego blanditiarum egeam, *quas primum Iulii Caesaris fortuna* mundo intulit... hoc stilo... ad reges atque pontifices Caesaremque ipsum uti soleo, quos reverentius affari ius aequumque est. Verum ego reverentiam veram in mendaciis non repono: *mentiri autem dominis his vocibus,* quibus nunc vulgo utimur, *aetate ipsius Caesaris inventum* Lucanum asseruit. (*Var.* 32; mio il corsivo).

Mi pare che il contesto nel quale solo si discute dell'opposizione tra lo stile del *tu* e quello del *vos* e la doppia citazione quasi *ad verbum* del passo di Lucano non lascino dubbi sul modo di intendere il luogo da parte di Petrarca:[6] analoghe considerazioni suscitano i luoghi delle *Senili* XIV, 1; XVI, 1 e 5.[7]

Spetterà invece a Coluccio Salutati, in una delle sue replicate esortazioni all'adozione del *tu,* il merito di porre le premesse per sostituire alla tradizionale una diversa interpretazione. Infatti, se ancora non afferma esplicitamente che i versi lucanei devono altrimenti intendersi, mostra per lo meno il suo aperto scetticismo sulla plausibilità della collocazione cronologica dell'inizio della consuetudine al *vos* nei tempi di Cesare, pur dichiarando di non essere in grado di fornirne una giustificazione storica più attendibile.[8]

Anche in altri casi—tutti riferibili alla ricezione di Stazio—la conoscenza del sistema della *lectura* dell'*auctor* consente di vedere alcuni problemi interpretativi in diversa prospettiva, e di suggerirne una soluzione più economica rispetto alle concorrenti: come, ad esempio, quando si esaminano alcuni luoghi 'staziani' di Boccaccio *(Gen.* II, 70 [pp. 113-14] e *De casibus* I, 8), a proposito dei quali sono stati invocati, come necessario tramite di notizie assenti nel testo staziano e tuttavia recate dal Boccaccio, luoghi paralleli del *Roman de Thèbes.*

È stato rilevato[9] infatti che la narrazione della storia di Edipo

---

[6] Per Petrarca rinvio alla recentissima edizione di A. Pancheri (Francesco Petrarca, *Lettere disperse,* Parma 1994, p. 198). Il senso non è chiaramente inteso da Fracassetti nella sua traduzione (*Lettere di Francesco Petrarca,* V, Firenze 1867, pp. 322-38).

[7] Per un approfondimento del tema rinvio a 'Il testo di Lucano (e Dante)', in *Seminario Dantesco Internazionale/International Dante Seminar,* I, Firenze, Le Lettere, in corso di stampa.

[8] Ho discusso più ampiamente la questione in '...e l'ultimo Lucano', in *Dante e la 'bella scola' della poesia,* Ravenna 1993, pp. 145-203; e con maggiori approfondimenti in 'Il testo di Lucano' (n. 7 sopra). Fra i numerosi luoghi dell'epistolario nei quali Coluccio tratta del problema (e si veda G. Billanovich, 'La prima lettera del Salutati a Giovanni di Montreuil', *Italia medioevale e umanistica,* 7, 1964, pp. 341-42 e n. 1), quello cui si fa riferimento si legge in Coluccio Salutati, *Epistolario* a c. di F. Novati, II, Roma 1893, p. 418.

[9] L. Edmunds, 'A Note on Boccaccio's Sources for the History of Oedipus in

in entrambi i testi di Boccaccio presenta particolari che sono assenti nei classici di riferimento (la *Tebaide* di Stazio e l'*Edipo* di Seneca): e tanto ha indotto non solo a presupporre da parte di Boccaccio una contaminazione fra i due classici, ma anche a postulare come sua fonte l'ipotetico argomento perduto al primo libro della *Tebaide*, nel quale si sarebbero composte le opposizioni e si sarebbe trovato quanto mancava in Stazio e Seneca. Indizio dell'esistenza di questa tradizione sarebbe un tardo racconto della storia tebana (XIV ex.), posto a mo' di introduzione al ritmico *Planctus Edipi* 'Diri patris'.[10]

E invece, sin dall'XI secolo, come presto dimostrerò altrove, in un ampio numero di copie della *Tebaide*, sia negli *accessus*, sia in

---

De casibus illustrium virorum and the *Genealogie*', *Aevum*, 56, 1982, pp. 248-52. Su Boccaccio e il *Roman de Thèbes* come necessario presupposto delle incongruità pseudo classiche nel *Teseida* vedi ancora da ultimo W. Wetherbee, 'History and Romance in Boccaccio's *Teseida*', *Studi sul Boccaccio*, 20, 1992, pp. 173-84.

[10] Esistono due *Planctus Edipi*: il 'Diri patris', ampiamente testimoniato dal XII secolo, e più volte edito (ad es. da E. Du Méril, *Poésies inédites du Moyen Age*, Paris 1854, pp. 310-13 e più recentemente da C. P. Clogan, 'Planctus Oedipi', *Mediaevalia et Humanistica*, 1, 1970, pp. 233-39): ai manoscritti segnalati da H. Walther, *Initia carminum ac versuum Medii Aevi posterioris Latinorum*, I/1, Göttingen 1969, 4511 e p. 1231 posso aggiungere MSS Wrocław, Reh. 124, sec. XIV-XV, Bruxelles, B.R. IV 719, 1419, Paris, B.N., lat. 14140, XIII (f. 100ʳ), Madrid, B.N. 10039, XII (f. 45ʳ), Genève, Bibl. publ. et univ., lat. 96, XIII¹ (f. 99ʳ), Cambridge, St. John's College, D 12, XII sec., (f. 61ᵛ). Un altro codice, datato 1418 e posseduto da Gaselee, viene utilizzato per l'edizione del testo nella sua antologia (S. Gaselee, *An Anthology of Medieval Latin*, London 1925, pp. 29 e 79-82). Segnalo che due altri MSS, italiani del XIV ex. e XV sec. (Vat. lat. 11507 e Paris, B.N., n.a.l. 1102) attribuiscono il componimento a Giulio Cesare. La connessione del testo con manoscritti di Stazio è molto frequente, anche se non esclusiva: il *planctus* può accompagnare Seneca (MSS Cambridge, Trinity College, R 9.21 e Milano, Ambros., D 276 sup.) o Giovenale (MS Oxford, Bodl., Canon. class. lat. 37). Lo conosce, e cita come 'Stacius', Giovanni di Garlandia nella sua *Ars rithmica* (G. Mari, *I trattati medievali di ritmica latina*, Milano 1899, rpt. Bologna 1971, pp. 50 e 54): a segno dell'intrinseca connessione del complesso della glossa, intesa estensivamente, come abbiamo detto sopra, con il suo autore. Un altro *planctus*, molto meno diffuso, è il 'Trux Edipus' (Walther 19463): all'unico manoscritto noto, London, B. L., Burn. 258, XII sec., posso aggiungere MS Wolfenbüttel, Herzog August Bibliothek, 85.6 Aug. 2°, italiano settentrionale del XIV sec., che inserisce questo testo nei margini di Lucano (f. 84ʳ). Sottolinea l'importanza del *planctus* 'Diri patris' per la circolazione della storia dell'incestuoso Edipo, viva nella tradizione volgare e fors'anche nel *Mathematicus* di Bernardo Silvestre (sul quale vedi da ultimo P. Godman, 'Ambiguity in the *Mathematicus* of Bernardus Silvestris', *Studi medievali*, 31, 1990, pp. 583-648): P. Dronke, *Fabula. Explorations into the Uses of Myth in Medieval Platonism*, Leiden-Köln 1974, p. 79 n. 1; ma l'importanza di questo testo sarà da ridimensionarsi se, come si vedrà subito, ogni lettore della *Tebaide* sapeva perfettamente, attraverso le glosse al testo, tutti gli antefatti di quanto cantava Stazio: le vicende cioè di Laio, Giocasta, Edipo, l'indovinello della Sfinge etc.

brevi note che lo seguono e precedono il testo vero e proprio, sia infine nell'esposizione dei primi versi del poema si possono leggere tutti i particolari narrati da Boccaccio, ma irreperibili in Stazio e in Seneca, quali l'esposizione di Edipo nel bosco 'perforatis plantis', l'uccisione di Laio in Focide, l'occasione della rissa tra cittadini e stranieri durante la quale Edipo uccise il padre. E neppure è necessario sempre presupporre, a giustificazione delle incongruenze di Boccaccio rispetto ai suoi classici di riferimento, la mediazione del *Roman de Thèbes*: che se è testo indubbiamente molto rilevante per Boccaccio, dipende però per larga parte dei suoi ampliamenti dalle glosse delle *lecturae* alla *Tebaide* che correvano nell'XI e XII secolo.

Si considerano solitamente innovazioni del *Roman de Thèbes* rispetto alla materia tebana di Stazio l'accusa mossa a Edipo da parte dei coetanei di essere un bastardo (*Roman de Thèbes*, 152-64), oppure il testo dell'indovinello della sfinge *(Roman de Thèbes*, 317-60), e infine il riconoscimento del figlio da parte di Giocasta attraverso le cicatrici che egli aveva ai piedi. Tutti questi racconti trovano invece posto nella *lectura* della *Tebaide* sin dall'XI secolo: e per l'ultimo dei particolari proposti la *lectura* del classico offre l'opzione addirittura fra tre varianti: il marchio del figlio esposto si rivela o mentre Edipo si calzava, o mentre Giocasta gli faceva il bagno—e questo sceglie il *Roman de Thèbes*, 495-500—o mentre di notte la madre 'muliebri mansuetudine pedes depalparet'.[11]

Molto sembra dunque da rivedersi in quel che si dice sul metodo di lavoro di Boccaccio, che si dimostra per larga parte tributario alla tradizione di commento ai classici. Infatti non solo scopriamo che nelle glosse al suo Stazio, Laur. 38.6, egli accoglie glosse d'origine lattanziana mediate dal commento alla *Tebaide* oggetto del nostro studio, l'‘In principio uniuscuiusque auctoris’ (d'ora in poi ‘In principio’),[12] ma che frammenti dell' ‘In princi-

---

[11] Dei molti altri ampliamenti del *Roman de Thèbes* che si rivelano ricezioni nel testo di quella che era la consueta glossa al testo della *Tebaide*, in alcuni casi recepita anche dall'Ovidio moralizzato, mi occupo nel lavoro annunciato sopra. Segnala la possibilità del ricorso alle glosse Clogan, ‘New Directions in Twelfth-Century Courtly Narrative: le *Roman de Thèbes*’, *Mediaevistik*, 3, 1990, p. 60. Insiste ancora sul presupposto del *Roman de Thèbes*, per giustificare l'inserzione della storia di Laio nel *Teseida*, Wetherbee, ‘History and Romance...’ (n. 9 sopra), p. 187: da ricondursi invece certamente alla *lectura* della *Tebaide*.
[12] Nell'aprile di 1992 ho affidato ad un esperto di cose boccacciane, David Anderson, gli sviluppi di questo rapporto; cf. ora il suo ‘Boccaccio's Glosses on Statius’, *Studi sul Boccaccio*, 22, 1994, pp. 30-104, che sfrutta a pieno il suggerimento propostogli.

pio' sono messi a frutto anche nelle *Genealogie*. E solo annuncio qui, per riprendere altrove il tema, che anche nel caso del mitico, terribile padre di tutti gli dèi, il Demogorgon[13] (*Gen.* I, 1, pp. 13-15), le fonti di Boccaccio non dovranno andarsi a ricercare in complicati intrecci di tradizioni rare: già nel XII secolo il commento 'In principio' recepisce informazioni confluite più tardi nel racconto di Boccaccio, come s'è intravisto; e si tratta di materiale addirittura già diffuso nell'XI secolo, nei testi più disparati.

Gli esempi offerti inducono dunque a considerare con estrema attenzione il sistema costituito dal testo e dal complesso della sua glossa, *summa* di una cultura variamente stratificata attraverso processi di aggregazioni e disgregazioni, la quale tendeva a proporsi, come s'è visto, in quanto strumento che agevolava la comprensione del testo, quale insostituibile ed unico vettore del testo stesso.

Questa affermazione, constatabile *in factis* se si leggono i testi attraverso la griglia interpretativa dell'esegesi agli *auctores*, diviene pienamente comprensibile quando si esamina il dibattito che si sviluppa nella prima metà del XII secolo nella adiacente esegesi sacra e quando si pongono in serie alcune teorizzazioni relative alle modalità esegetiche esperibili nei due settori dei testi sacri e profani.[14]

Sarà opportuno iniziare dal più volte discusso prologo ai *Lais* di Marie de France, che bene sintetizza il rapporto fra testo e commento

---

[13] Di Demogorgon, dopo M. Pastore Stocchi, hanno recentemente trattato M. P. Mussini Sacchi, 'Per la fortuna del Demogorgone in età umanistica', *Italia medioevale e umanistica*, 34, 1991, pp. 299-310 e L. Cesarini Martinelli, 'Sozomeno maestro e filologo', *Interpres*, 11, 1991, pp. 80-92, la quale cita proprio la glossa del MS Riccardiano 842, del XIV ex., f. 46ᵛ-47ʳ, che ora potrà meglio valutarsi perché appartenente al commento 'In principio'. Concordo pienamente con quanto afferma la studiosa: potrei infatti completare il dossier delle testimonianze da lei addotte con un cospicuo numero di altre glosse tratte da commenti a Stazio, Lucano, Ovidio. Demogorgon ha una vivacissima vita soprattutto fuori della nostra letteratura (Milton, *Paradise Lost*, Shelley, *Prometheus Unbound*, ad esempio: ed è persino menzionato, con citazione proverbiale, da Ben Jonson ne *Il Dottor Sottile*), come segnalò M. Castelain, 'Démogorgon ou le barbarisme deifié', *Bulletin de l'Association G. Budé*, luglio 1932, pp. 29-40 e G. Cordié, 'Alla ricerca di Demogorgone', in *Studi in onore di A. Monteverdi*, I, Modena 1959, pp. 158-84. Per il rapporto del Demogorgon di Boiardo con Stazio, cf. C. Zampese, 'L'*Orlando innamorato* e Stazio', *Giornale storico della letteratura italiana*, 170, 1993, pp. 394-523 (400). Da ultimo potrà citarsi lo studio di H. Vierbrock, *Wer ist Demogorgon?*, Wiesbaden 1971.

[14] L. Valente, 'Arts du discours et *sacra pagina* dans le *De tropis loquendi* de Pierre le Chantre', *Histoire, épistèmologie, langage*, 12, 1990, pp. 69-102 (98).

> Custume fu as ancïens,
> ceo testimoine Precïens,
> es livres ke jadis feseient,
> assez oscurement diseient
> pur ceus ki a venir esteient
> e ki aprendre les deveient,
> k'i peüssent gloser la lettre
> et de lur sen le surplus mettre.
> Li philesophe le saveient,
> e par eus meïsmes entendeient,
> cum plus trespassereit li tens,
> plus serreient sutil de sens
> e plus se savreient garder
> de ceo k'i ert a trespasser.
>
> (prol. vv. 9-22)[15]

Esso postula la necessaria mediazione del commentatore per dar senso al suo testo, dichiarando non solo una stretta relazione fra testo e commento, ma la libertà del commentatore di sovrapporre alla *littera* del suo *auctor* quella interpretazione cui egli creda di poterlo piegare: è dichiarata dunque una sorta di sovratemporale connivenza fra autore ed esegeta, in cui l'autore offre, attraverso una sciente, consapevole *obscuritas*, materia al lavorio esegetico del glossatore.

Quanto mi pare risulti maggiormente significativo è l'affermazione che un testo non solo profano, ma anche in lingua volgare, presenta una delle caratteristiche tradizionalmente connaturate al testo sacro, l'*obscuritas*.

Come è stato osservato[16] l'oscurità per un testo di contenuto dottrinale rilevante è obbligatorio requisito: costringe il lettore ad un arresto, a concentrare l'attenzione sul passo e ad uno sforzo di comprensione nel quale la meditazione, la ricerca e infine l'acquisizione faticosa dei reconditi significati consentiranno il non secondario risultato di una duratura memorizzazione del luogo. L'oscurità del testo, a più riprese affermata necessaria da Agostino (*De*

---

[15] *Les Lais de Marie de France* par J. Rychner, Paris 1966, pp. 1-2. Sull'interpretazione di questo testo da ultimi T. Hunt, 'Glossing Marie de France', *Romanische Forschungen*, 86, 1974, pp. 396-418, con ampia rassegna delle precedenti discussioni; J. C. Huchet, 'Nom de femme et écriture féminine au moyen âge. Les *Lais* de Marie de France', *Poétique*, 48, 1981, pp. 409-10; J. C. Delclos, 'Encore le prologue des *Lais* de Marie de France', *Le Moyen Age*, 90, 1984, pp. 223-32; A. Leupin, 'The Impossible Task of Manifesting "Literature": on Marie de France's Obscurity', *Exemplaria*, 3, 1991, pp. 221-42. Sulle relazioni fra glossa e testo: P. Zumthor, 'La glose créatrice', in *Les commentaires et la naissance de la critique littéraire. France-Italie (XIV-XVI s.)*, cur. G. Mathieu-Castellani-M. Plaisance, Paris 1990, pp. 14-31.

[16] Hunt, 'Glossing Marie...' (n. 15 supra), pp. 396-418.

doctrina christiana IV, 61-62 p. 133; 27 p. 124; II, 10 p. 36), sostenuta con i medesimi argomenti dallo pseudo Dionigi e ampiamente
discussa e commentata da Giovanni Scoto[17] verrà ancora invoca-
ta da Abelardo—che ad Agostino rinvia—come necessario filtro
per non disperdere vanamente la *sapientia*.[18]

Quanto risulta ben chiaro è dunque che i paradigmi esegetici
collaudati sui testi sacri sono applicati tal quali in campi non solo
tradizionalmente antitetici, come quello dei classici, ma anche in
quello più recente e innovativo della poesia cortese in lingua volgare.

Se quindi un testo si presenta come un serbatoio di significati
dei quali spesso l'autore è inconsapevole,[19] o che addirittura sono
estranei e opposti al suo originario intendimento—e si arrivava ad
affermare, come fa Guglielmo di Conches, che le contraddizioni
implicite nelle diverse ed opposte interpretazioni di un medesimo
passo erano segno della ricchezza del testo stesso,[20] ecco che si
presentano le condizioni per delegare senz'altro al commentatore
il compito di leggere dietro il testo e di trovare i suoi tesori di verità. E infatti, già in un'opera dell'XI secolo destinata alla scuola,
la *Fecunda ratis*, troviamo, tradotta in una metafora molto cara all'
esegesi sacra, l'affermazione che Virgilio deve leggersi con un commento: 'Qui sine commento rimaris scripta Maronis/ immunis
nuclei solo de cortice rodis'.[21]

---

[17] *Iohannis Scoti Eriugenae Expositiones in Ierarchiam Coelestem*, II, 334-427, ed. J.
Barbet, Turnholti 1975, pp. 29-31. Ancora nel XVI secolo si insisterà sulla valenza positiva dell'oscurità, che conferisce fascino al testo generando nel lettore un
godimento estetico: cf. Barthelemy Aneau, *Trois premiers livres de la Metamorphose
d'Ovide*, Lyon 1556, f. 5r, citato da M. Jeanneret, 'Préfaces, commentaires et pro-
grammation de la lecture. L'exemple des *Métamorphoses*', in *Les commentaires*...(n. 15
sopra), pp. 31-39 (37).

[18] *Theologia 'Scholarium'* I, 158-65, in *Petri Abaelardi Opera Theologica* III, ed. E.
M. Buytaert-C. J. Mews, Turnholti 1987, pp. 383-86.

[19] Cf. ad esempio Abelardo, *Theologia 'Scholarium'* I, 180-83, ibid., pp. 394-96.

[20] E. Jeauneau, 'L'usage de la notion d'*integumentum* a travers les gloses de
Guillaume de Conches', *Archives d'histoire doctrinale et littéraire du moyen âge*, 34, 1957,
pp. 35-100 = *Lectio philosophorum*, Amsterdam 1973, pp. 125-92: 139: glosse a
Boezio, MS Troyes, B. M. 1331, f. 69r.

[21] *Egberts von Lüttich Fecunda ratis*, ed. E. Voigt, Halle 1889, p. 154 (I, 923-24).
La metafora verrà impiegata, seppur con minore frequenza, anche nell'esegesi ai
classici. La ripete ad esempio anche Alano di Lilla, *Anticlaudianus* II, 510-13 applicandola ad una categoria di gramatici paghi della *littera* e dimentichi della *sententia*: 'gramaticos humiles, qui sola cortice gaudent/ quos non dimittit intus
pinguedo medulle:/ si foris exposcunt framenta, pitamine solo/ contenti, nequeunt
nuclei libare saporem' (Alain de Lille, *Anticlaudianus* II, 510-13, ed. R. Bossuat,
Paris 1955, p. 87).

Gli espedienti dell'*integumentum* o *involucrum* e i meccanismi che essi mettono in atto, perfettamente coincidenti con quelli dell'allegoria collaudata nell'esegesi sacra, consentono la più ampia libertà al commentatore di piegare il testo a significare quanto egli ritenga opportuno, solo osservando, e non sempre, l'obbligo di mantenere distinti i due termini nei campi loro propri.[22] Questa operazione sviluppa e conclude le premesse già poste da Giovanni Scoto quando aveva affermato l'esistenza di una teologia poetica affine nei suoi procedimenti alla poesia, depositaria di significati etici.[23]

Esisteva, e se ne era coscienti, il pericolo dello stravolgimento del testo, già segnalato da Gerolamo nella *Epistola ad Paulinum* 53, 7,[24] dove è esemplificato proprio con l'interpretazione dei classici, e riproposto da Abelardo nel *Sic et non* XXV:[25] ma la polisemia, connaturata al testo, era accettata anche nei risultati estremi, come s'è visto, dell'interna contraddittorietà: una prova documentale, non aliena da *vis polemica*, di questa ricchezza verrà fornita in questi anni nel *Sic et non* di Abelardo, in una sorta di controcanto al metodo sentenziario.[26]

---

[22] Abelardo ad esempio userà 'integumentum' anche ove sarebbe stato necessario 'allegoria': cf. Jeauneau, 'L'usage de la notion d'*integumentum*...' (n. 20 sopra), p. 129, e Tomaso di Morigny sarà pronto a cogliere quest'errore (Häring, 'Thomas von Morigny *Disputatio catholicorum patrum adversus dogmata Petri Abailardi*', *Studi medievali*, 22, 1981, pp. 299-376: 368), individuandone l'ispirazione eriugeniana, come nota M.-T. D'Alverny, 'Le cosmos symbolique du XIIe siècle', *Archives d'histoire doctrinale et littéraire du moyen âge*, 28, 1953, pp. 31-81; cf. anche Wetherbee, *Platonism and Poetry in the Twelfth Century*, Princeton 1972.

[23] *Iohannis Scoti Eriugenae Expositiones in Ierarchiam...*, II, 142-51 p. 24: '...quemadmodum ars poetica, per fictas fabulas allegoricasque similitudines, moralem doctrinam seu physicam componunt ad humanorum animorum exercitationem—hoc enim proprium est heroicorum poetarum, qui virorum fortium facta et mores figurate laudant—ita theologia, veluti quedam poetria, sanctam scripturam fictis imaginationibus ad consultum nostri animi et reductionem a corporalibus sensibus exterioribus, veluti ex quadam imperfecta pueritia, in rerum intellegibilium perfectam cognitionem, tanquam in quandam interioris hominis grandaevitatem conformat'. Una rappresentazione iconica della dipendenza del concetto di *involucrum* da Giovanni Scoto trova M. D. Chenu in un disegno a commento della *Clavis Physicae* di Onorio d'Autun ('*Involucrum*. Le mythe selon les théologiens médiévaux', *Archives d'histoire doctrinale et littéraire du moyen âge*, 31, 1955, pp. 75-79): ma vedi le precisazioni di L. Moonan, 'Abelard's Use of the *Timaeus*', *Archives d'histoire littéraire et doctrinale du moyen âge*, 56, 1989, pp. 7-90: 58.

[24] *S. Eusebi Hieronymi epistulae*, I, rec. I. Ilberg, Vindobonae-Lipsiae 1910 [CSEL 54], 453.11-454.9.

[25] Peter Abailard, *Sic et non*, ed. B. B. Boyer-R. McKeon, Chicago-London 1976, pp. 168-69.

[26] M. L. Colish, 'Another Look at the School of Laon', *Archives d'histoire doctrinale et littéraire du moyen âge*, 53, 1986, pp. 7-22: 12; G. Bertola, 'Le critiche di Abelardo ad Anselmo di Laon ed a Guglielmo di Champeaux', *Rivista di filosofia*

La radicalizzazione di questi procedimenti esegetici condusse infatti presto a proposizioni inconciliabili con l'ortodossia: valga per tutte l'interpretazione dell'*anima mundi*, intesa come Spirito santo ed oggetto della solenne condanna del 1141 a Sens. E dopo la metà del secolo Giovanni di Salisbury è un acuto testimone della piena coscienza dei pericoli insiti in quella sorta di sincretismo di testi e nella unificazione dei procedimenti esegetici.

Egli dedicherà un intero capitolo del *Policraticus* (VII, 12) a spiegare che 'aliter legendi sunt libri divini, aliter gentiles'; e affermerà che chi non si ferma al significato 'historicus' del testo, cioè al primo livello di lettura, commette un errore, ancor più grave se cosciente è il suo intento di fuorviare il pubblico; e infine, negando categoricamente la ricchezza inesauribile del testo, dichiarerà che esso non deve essere forzato a significare altro da quanto intende esprimere.[27] Tutto questo testimonia una comprensibile reazione a posizioni che, soprattutto con Abelardo, avevano turbato profondamente, trovando voce nelle parole di chi aveva stigmatizzato l'errore di aver introdotto 'philosophos Platonem, Virgilium, Macrobium intonsos et illotos ad convivium summi regis'.[28] Ma ci dimostra anche che era molto cambiato il modo di approccio al testo.

Se infatti, sulla spinta della necessità di attingere ogni riflesso della polisemia del testo, si era giunti persino a costringere entro precise categorie le diverse modalità di commento, producendo la celebre e fortunata definizione di Guglielmo di Conches, che muove da una etimologia presunta di Prisciano:[29]

> comminisci est plura, studio vel doctrina in mente habita, in unum colligere, commentum vero vel commentarium est plurium, studio vel doctrina in mente habitorum, in unum collectio. Et secundum hoc, omne scriptum potest commentum dici, sicut in hoc loco dicitur. Sed aliquando restringitur nomen, et dicitur commentum liber alterius expositorius qui sentencie serviens non curat de littera. Qui differt a glosa. Glosa enim et sentenciam et litteram sic debet

---

neoscolastica, 5, 1960, pp. 495-522 (522); J. Châtillon, 'Abélard et les écoles', in *Abélard et son temps. Actes du colloque international...*, Paris 1981, pp. 133-60: 153-54.

[27] Cf. anche *Metalogicon* III,1 (Iohannis Saresberiensis episcopi Carnotensis *Metalogicon*, ed. J. B. Hall, Turnhout 1991, pp. 103-05).

[28] Häring, 'Thomas von Morigny *Disputatio*...' (n. 22 sopra), pp. 299-376: 368.

[29] La fonte indicata da Guglielmo non pare recare traccia del passo addotto, che viene invece ascritto a Boezio nel commento a Marziano Capella attribuito a Bernardo Silvestre (*The Commentary on Martianus Capella's 'De nuptiis Philologiae et Mercurii' Attributed to Bernardus Silvestris*, ed. H. J. Westra, Toronto 1986, p. 93).

exponere quod lingua magistri videatur presens hoc docere. Unde et glosa dicitur. Glosa enim lingua interpretatur[30]

ciò sottintende che all'interprete era ormai delegato il compito di esclusiva guida ai riposti significati del testo, filo d'Arianna in una selva di sensi possibili. E che il testo, al contempo, diveniva progressivamente sempre più remoto, anche in senso fisico, separato com'era ormai dalla glossa che lo spiegava e finiva per prevalere sul testo stesso, come ci dice Roberto di Melun:[31]

> ordinis ... magna confusio est et discipline intolerabilis perturbatio, secundarium principali adequare, nedum anteponere. Quod ab his fieri qua ratione negabitur, qui textu et serie legendorum librorum postpositis, totam lectionis operam in studio glosularum expendunt? Neque enim huius rei hanc causam pretendere possunt, quod textus sine glosulis intelligi non valeat, aut quod glosarum cognitionem textus intelligentia necessario sequatur ... Quid enim aliud in lectione queritur quam textus intelligentia, que sententia nominatur? Non enim ille bene legit a quo quid scriptura sentit diligenter non exponitur, nec sensus nec voluntas auctoris evidenter proponitur ... Nec ibi aliquis addiscitur ubi sententia omnino incognita preteritur. Hoc autem ibi fieri fatendum est, ubi lectioni glosarum, immo recitationi, tota incumbitur intentione. Nam ibi textus spernitur, glosa cum devota veneratione colitur, textus propter glosam legitur et non glosa causa textus exponitur et fit quod predictum est, secundarium principale et principale secundarium ... te itaque interrogo, utrum textum et glosam idem an diversa concedas? ... textus ergo et glosa idem non sunt ... quid enim aliud in lectione queritur quam textus intelligentia, que sententia nominatur? ... Non enim ille bene legit a quo quid scriptura sentit diligenter non exponitur, nec sensus nec voluntas auctoris evidenter proponitur ... nullum utilem esse in lectione, qui in sententiarum non valet discussione.

Insomma, il testo era divenuto pretesto all'esposizione di proprie dottrine: che è ciò di cui Pietro di Blois, nel 1160, lamenta gli effetti nella scuola moderna, perché non si inizia più lo studio dagli *auctores* e dalla grammatica, ma si studia piuttosto 'in quaternis et schedulis': probabilmente le *glosule* frutto delle *reportationes* delle lezioni, ormai avulse dal testo dal quale avevano tratto origine.

---

[30] Su questo testo, ripetuto, oltre che nelle *Glosae super Platonem* ed. Jeauneau, Paris 1965, p. 67, nel commento a Prisciano e in quello a Macrobio, cf. Jeauneau, 'Deux rédactions des gloses de Guillaume de Conches sur Priscien', *Recherches de théologie ancienne et médiévale*, 27, 1960, pp. 212-47—*Lectio philosophorum*, pp. 346-47. La definizione di Guglielmo ebbe notevole successo: fu spesso replicata *ad verbum* e venne in seguito inserita nei lessici, di Uguccione, di Giovanni Balbi e di Guglielmo Bretone, ad esempio.l

[31] R. Martin, *Oeuvres de Robert de Melun*, III, 1, Louvain 1947, pp. 8-12. Sul tema, proponendo anche altri giudizi negativi sulla glossa, cf. Jeauneau, 'Gloses

> ... Wilelmum predicas subtilioris venae et acutioris ingenii eo quod, grammaticae et auctorum studio pretermisso, evolavit ad versutias logicorum, ubi non in libris, sicut fieri solet, dialecticam didicit, sed in schedulis et quaternis ... que utilitas est schedulas evolvere, firmare verbotenus summas et sophismatum versutias inversare, damnare scripta veterum et reprobare omnia que non inveniuntur in suorum schedulis magistrorum? Scriptum est quia in antiquis est scientia.[32]

Si verifica dunque una tendenza centrifuga dei due sistemi, e una modificazione del rapporto gerarchico fra testo e commento, come esito del tentato sincretismo in direzione di un'unica tipologia di testo, dotato delle stesse caratteristiche e delle medesime regole. Ma nonostante i richiami degli spiriti più avvertiti queste tendenze avranno lunghe eco, di diverso segno.

La seduzione della polisemia sfrenata, e quindi la licenza consentita ad ogni commentatore di creare il proprio testo,[33] perdurò a lungo, se interpreto correttamente la decisione di qualche autore di comporre un autocommento come l'intenzione di tagliare al futuro esegeta la possibilità di 'le surplus mettre' alla propria opera.

Inutile elencare l'ampia e nobile casistica del genere che trova esempi antichi (Abbone di St. Germain, *Bella Parisiace urbis,* i *Gesta Berengarii regis*, Giovanni di Garlandia, *Dictionarius*, tra gli altri) e più recenti (il *Trattato delle volgari sentenze sopra le virtù morali* di Graziolo Bambaglioli, i *Detti d'Amore* di Francesco da Barberino, per tacere della *Vita Nuova* e del *Convivio* di Dante e del *Teseida* di Boccaccio);[34] e ancora puntuali teorizzazioni nel Trecento, quando si discute del nuovamente riscoperto genere bucolico: Petrarca, che si appellerà di nuovo all'*obscuritas* come requisito proprio del genere, dichiarerà necessario che l'autore fornisca la chiave interpretativa dei propri carmi: come egli farà, ma solo per alcuni.[35]

---

et commentaires de textes philosophiques (IXᵉ-XIIᵉ s.)', in *Les genres littéraires dans les sources théologiques et philosophiques médiévales*, Louvain-la-Neuve, 1982, pp. 117-31.

[32] *PL* 207, pp. 312-13, *ep.* 101: la polemica è diretta contro il nuovo metodo dei dialettici cui viene contrapposto quello più collaudato degli *auctoristae*. Intendo 'schedulis et quaternis' come 'appunti e scartafacci' tratti dalle lezioni. Cf. Villa, 'I classici', in *Lo spazio letterario del Medioevo*. 1, *Il medioevo latino*, I.1, Roma 1993, p. 488.

[33] Per il rapporto dinamico fra testo e glossa rinvio alle osservazioni di Zumthor, 'La glose créatrice' (n. 15 sopra).

[34] D. Goldin, 'Autotraduzione latina nei *Documenti d'Amore* di Francesco Barberino', *Atti dell'Istituto veneto di scienze lettere e arti*, 133.2, 1975, pp. 371-92; B. Sandhküler, *Die frühen Dantekommentare und ihr Verhältnis zur mittelalterlichen Kommentartradition*, München 1967, pp. 50-76 e ora *L'autocommento*, Padova 1994.

[35] *Fam.* X. 4 a Gerardo per la I *Egloga*; *Var.* 49, a Barbato, per la II e *Var.* 12, a Cola di Rienzo, per la V: consultabili ora nell'edizione a cura di Pancheri

Restano anche lunghe tracce degli effetti estremi della polisemia del testo nella sua disponibilità ad ammettere interpretazioni contraddittorie presentate simultaneamente dalla glossa. Ne potremmo produrre molti esempi, in parte giustificabili nella glossa in ragione della sua genesi, perché ivi depositati e recepiti attraverso un processo di giustapposizione di moduli esegetici di varia provenienza.[36] Questa spiegazione non mi pare però più sufficiente quando, a fine Quattrocento, troviamo affidati all'ampia circolazione della stampa fatti vistosamente inconciliabili.

Ne è esempio emblematico l'*Achilleide* con il commento, composto verso gli anni '80, di Francesco Matarazzi, il quale, dopo aver dichiarato nel proemio che l'opera è incompiuta e divisa in due libri di diversa estensione,[37] accosta poi il suo commento marginale a un testo segnato dai cinque incipit ai libri, sottolineati persino dall'*argumentum* metrico relativo, propri della tradizione medievale che così divideva l'epica minore di Stazio.[38]

(n. 6 sopra), pp. 94-102 e 34-38. Sull'autocommento petrarchesco: N. Mann, 'In margine alla quarta egloga: piccoli problemi di esegesi petrarchesca', *Studi petrarcheschi*, n. s., 4, 1987, pp. 17-32. Boccaccio fornisce un'interpretazione del proprio *Buccolicum carmen* nella *Epistola* XXIV a Martino da Signa (*Opere latine minori*, a cura di A. F. Massèra, Bari 1928, pp. 216-21, ora nell'edizione a cura di G. Auzzas, in *Tutte le opere di Giovanni Boccaccio*, a cura di V. Branca, Milano 1992, pp. 712-23). Di un autocommento completo sono fornite anche le *Egloghe* di Giovanni Quatrario da Sulmona: G. Pansa, *Giovanni Quatrario da Sulmona (1336-1402)*, Sulmona 1912.

[36] La genesi per giustapposizione produce anche, molto frequentemente, una incompatibilità fra il testo dell'*auctor* e le lezioni che la glossa commenta: ad esempio in MS Napoli, B.N., IV E 44.

[37] '... ex quo imperfectum opus colligimus et ne quidem completum esse. Nam que alii inepte, ne dicam stulte, librorum initia fecere, capita profecto sunt...'. Si consideri però che anche a fine XV secolo perdurava la discussione sulla compiutezza dell'*Achilleide*: ancora sostenuta con vigore polemico, contro gli oppositori, da Giovanni Britannico nel suo commento edito a Brescia nel 1485 (Proctor 6977): '... unde hinc facile eorum refelli potest opinio qui hoc opus imperfectum esse contendunt, hac una ratione addu<c>ti, quod ait poeta "nos ire per omnem".... Nam, si omnia eius facta descripturus esset, quomodo affirmaret se nihil de rebus gestis circa Troiam scripturum esse, cum ait "Nec in Hectore..."? Nam, si omnia Achillis facta canere statuisset, operis quidem fuisset et voluminis immensi, contraque propositionem suam fecisset poeta ... Opus autem suum in quinque divisit libellos ... Hec ideo subiunxi ut error eorum qui opus perfectum non censent, monitione nostra corrigatur et rem eo perductam cognoscant quo promisit poeta ... Sileant ergo qui, sensum poete non percipientes, opus ad calcem perductum esse negant'.

[38] La prima edizione del commento è datata Roma 1475 (Hain 14975) ed entro il Quattrocento se ne ebbero numerose ristampe: Venezia 1483 (Hain 14976), 1490 (Hain 14978), 1494 (Hain 14979), 1498 (Hain 14980). Sul Matarazzi: G. Zappacosta, *Francesco Maturanzio umanista perugino*, Bergamo 1970 e 'Il *Gymnasium* perugino e gli studi filologici nel Quattrocento' in *L'Umanesimo umbro*, Gubbio-

Infine segni del progressivo accostarsi e persino coincidere dei due campi, sacro e profano, possono cogliersi in alcune manifestazioni meramente formali: ad esempio quelle espresse dalla *mise en page* dei testi.

La *Glossa ordinaria*, il 'male necessario' al quale ci si piega per sistematizzare la mole di esegesi prodotta, a metà secolo assume la forma canonica di testo centrale con due margini laterali previsti per la glossa:[39] il procedimento è il medesimo che si era adottato dal IX secolo in poi dislocando i commenti tardoantichi nei margini dei classici.[40]

Parallelamente l'esegesi 'moderna' alla Bibbia in testo continuo che si continua a produrre viene consegnata a manoscritti di piccolo formato, ove una minutissima grafia occupa prevalentemente due colonne fittamente scritte: ed è questa medesima impostazione della pagina che verrà replicata per i nuovi commenti ai classici prodotti nel XII e XIII secolo, che sempre, e solo in questo periodo, corrono separati dal testo commentato.[41]

Altri segnali provengono dalla sfera del lessico tecnico: 'continuatio', termine proprio dell'esegesi agli *auctores*, passerà all'esegesi biblica;[42] la proposta di problemi, introdotta da 'queritur', 'ques-

Perugia 1977, 197-272. I suoi manoscritti della *Tebaide* e del commento di Lattanzio Placido si trovano ancora a Perugia, nella biblioteca Augusta: sono il C 53 (170), scritto nel 1399 e G 1 (412), del XV². Nella sua biblioteca confluì l'Apicio del IX secolo, New York Acad. Med. 1, prima appartenuto al cardinale Bessarione, poi a Nicolò Perotti (M. Ella Milham, 'Towards a Stemma and "Fortuna" of Apicius', *Italia medioevale e umanistica*, 10, 1967, pp. 259-320: 273) e utilizzato da Poliziano per la collazione del *De re coquinaria*: Angelo Poliziano, *Miscellaneorum Centuria secunda*, ed. V. Branca-M. Pastore Stocchi, I, Firenze 1972, p. 23b. Lettere del Maturanzio al cardinale Armellini sono contenute nel MS Vat. lat. 5890 (E. Billanovich, 'Angelo Colocci e Francesco Bellini da Sacile', *Italia medioevale e umanistica*, 13, 1970, p. 267 n. 4). Della questione della compiutezza dell'*Achilleide* mi sono occupata in '*Magna questio preposita coram Dante et domino Francisco Petrarca et Virgiliano*', *Studi petrarcheschi*, n. s. 1, 1984, pp. 103-209.

[39] R. H. Rouse-M. A. Rouse, '*Statim invenire*. Schools, Preachers and New Attitudes to the Page', in *Renaissance and Renewal*...(n.1 sopra), pp. 201-25: 207-08; 222; cf. C. F. R. de Hamel, *Glossed Books of the Bible and the Origins of the Paris Booktrade*, Woodbridge 1984, pp. 24-26; per il rapporto fra testo e commento nell'impostazione della pagina: G. Powitz, '*Textus cum commento*', *Codices manuscripti*, 5, 1979, pp. 80-89 e de Angelis 'Fedeltà all'antigrafo nell'impostazione della pagina. Il caso dei testi commentati', *Filologia mediolatina*, 2, 1995, pp. 57-67.

[40] J. E. G. Zetzel, 'On the History of Latin Scholia', *Harvard Studies of the Philological Association*, 79, 1975, pp. 337-54; N. G. Wilson, 'A Chapter in the History of the Scholia', *Classical Quarterly*, 17, 1967, pp. 244-56.

[41] Sulla *mise en page* dei manoscritti della Bibbia prodotti nel XII secolo cf. de Hamel, *Glossed Books*...(n. 39 sopra), pp. 1-36.

[42] R. W. Hunt, 'Studies on Priscian in the Eleventh and Twelfth Centuries,

tio oritur', propria dell'esegesi filosofico-teologica,[43] penetrerà anche nell'esegesi agli *auctores*; 'distinctio', dall'originale significato tecnico retorico si estenderà al lessico filosofico-teologico, caricandosi di significati più pregnanti;[44] infine, nel campo più specifico della prassi esegetica, notiamo che si insinuano in numero sempre maggiore 'auctoritates' classiche nell'interpretazione teologica[45] così come, parallelamente, in quella ai classici penetrano citazioni bibliche.[46]

I', *Mediaeval and Renaissance Studies*, 1, 1941-43, pp. 194-231 = *The History of Grammar in the Middle Ages*, ed. G. L. Bursill-Hall, Amsterdam 1980, pp. 1-38: 5 n. 1; D. van den Eynde, 'Autour des *Enarrationes in evangelium S. Matthaei* attribuées à Geoffroi Babion', *Recherches de théologie ancienne et médiévale*, 26, 1959, p. 69. Il termine, come spiega Hunt, indica il ritorno al filo logico dell'argomentazione, o della narrazione: non si riferisce invece all'analisi della struttura logica del testo, in contrapposizione a quella più aderente alla *littera*, come deduce Minnis da un passo delle *Glose in Platonem* di Guglielmo di Conches, 67 (Minnis, *Medieval Literary Theory* ...(n. 3 sopra), p. 222 n. 37). Alla luce di quanto afferma Hunt, e può confermarsi con numerosi esempi, forniti anche dal commento 'In principio', ove abbondano 'continuatio' e 'hoc est (quod dicit)', appare necessario non ripetere più che l'uso delle due locuzioni, a conclusione di una spiegazione (la 'formula regrediente' per A. De Libera, 'De la lecture à la paraphrase. Remarques sur la citation au moyen âge', *Langages*, 73, 1984, pp. 17-29: 23) sia caratteristica dello stile usato da Guglielmo di Conches nelle sue glosse, come ancora afferma P. E. Dutton, *The Glosae super Platonem of Bernard of Chartres*, Toronto 1991, p. 54; 'hoc est' è formula già utilizzata, ad esempio, da Giovanni Scoto nel commento al Vangelo di Giovanni, come rivela Jeauneau nella sua introduzione a Jean Scot, *Commentaire sur l'Evangile de Jean*, Paris 1972, pp. 40-41. Su 'continuatio' e 'hoc est' in Abelardo cf. R. Peppermüller, *Abaelards Auslegung des Römerbriefes*, Münster 1972, p. 9 e n. 49.

[43] Il ruolo di iniziatore era riconosciuto ad Abelardo, ma uno sporadico uso di queste formule si rintraccia già in Anselmo di Laon: E. Bertola, 'Le critiche di Abelardo ad Anselmo...' (n. 26 sopra), p. 506; F. P. Bliemetzrieder, *Anselm von Laon systematische Sentenzen*, Münster 1919, 12; Peppermüller, 'Zu Abelards Paulusexegese und ihrem Nachwirken', in *Petrus Abaelardus (1079-1142). Person, Werk und Wirkung*, cur. R. Thomas, Trier 1980, pp. 217-22; D. E. Luscombe, *The School of Peter Abelard. The Influence of Abelard's Thought in the Early Scholastic Period*, Cambridge 1969, p. 174. Cf. S. F. Brown, 'Key Terms in Medieval Theological Vocabulary', in *Méthodes et instruments du travail intellectuel au Moyen Age*, ed. O. Weijers, Turnhout 1990, pp. 82-96.

[44] L. M. De Rijk, 'Specific Tools Concerning Logical Education', in *Méthodes et instruments...* (n. 43 sopra), pp. 62-81; per le partizioni nel testo della Bibbia B. Smalley, *The Study of the Bible in the Middle Ages*, London 1952, trad. it. a cura di V. Benassi, Bologna 1972, pp. 310-14; cf. anche Rouse-Rouse, '*Statim invenire...*' (n. 39 sopra), p. 212 n. 29 e 223.

[45] Ad esempio Thierry di Chartres nel suo *Tractatus de sex dierum operibus*, (Häring, *Commentaries on Boethius by Thierry of Chartres and His School*, Toronto 1971): cf. Häring, 'Commentary and Hermeneutics', in *Renaissance and Renewal...* (n. 1 sopra), p. 182; ma anche Abelardo, *passim*: cf. ad esempio qui, p. 119.

[46] Ad esempio nei commenti attribuiti a Bernardo Silvestre, a Marziano Capella e all'*Eneide* (*The Commentary on Martianus Capella's De nuptiis...* (n.28 sopra); *The*

Nel periodo nel quale si elaborano queste riflessioni sul rapporto fra testo e commento e sulla sempre più esile linea di demarcazione tra esegesi sacra e profana viene scritto il commento alla *Tebaide* del quale ora ci occuperemo e che coinvolge due personaggi noti sinora solo per la loro attività nel campo della 'sacra pagina': Anselmo di Laon, promotore della *Glossa ordinaria* e Goffredo Babione, autore di fortunatissimi *Sermones*, se non anche, come credo, delle *Enarrationes*, un originale e molto significativo commento al Vangelo di Matteo.

Occorre subito presentare il commento alla *Tebaide* ed inserirlo preventivamente nel quadro generale di quanto è noto sui commenti medievali a Stazio.

L'età tardoantica aveva prodotto un commento alla *Tebaide* attribuito a Lattanzio Placido (d'ora in poi LP), conosciuto, sino a tutto il XII secolo, attraverso un numero di testimoni piuttosto esiguo, spesso sopravvissuti solo come brevissimi frammenti e prevalentemente tràdito nella forma di glosse inserite nei margini di manoscritti della *Tebaide*. Il più antico testimone appartiene a St. Amand (MS Valenciennes, B. M., 394), ma tutto il resto della tradizione pare saldamente radicato in Baviera, fatta eccezione per un manoscritto italiano del X secolo (MS Vat., Pal. lat. 1694), che rimarrà sterile nel luogo d'origine (Italia meridionale) sino alla fine del Trecento, per poi divenire il più antico testimone della vulgata italiana.

Corre, erroneamente edito sotto il nome di LP, anche un commento all'*Achilleide*, che non è certamente tardoantico ed è tràdito in forma continua soltanto da due manoscritti anteriori al XII secolo (MSS München, Clm 19482 e Vat., Pal. lat. 1694) e, come glossa marginale, da un terzo (MS Paris, B.N., lat. 8040). Esso scompare dal XII secolo e non sembra lasciare tracce nella successiva, ampia tradizione esegetica all'*Achilleide*.

Esiste infine, attribuito a Fulgenzio Planciade, un breve commento alla *Tebaide*, assolutamente ininfluente sulla sua esegesi, che è piuttosto un'interpretazione allegorica dei suoi personaggi, conservato in un unico ms. del XIII secolo (MS Paris, B. N., lat. 3012) e in una copia a mano di Pierre Daniel (MS Bern, Burgerbibl.,

---

Commentary on the First Six Books of the Aeneid of Vergil Commonly Attributed to Bernardus Silvestris, ed. J. W. Jones-E. Frances Jones, Lincoln-London 1977), ma non in quelli di Thierry di Chartres a Cicerone *De inventione* e alla *Rhetorica ad Herennium* (K. Fredborg, *The Latin Rhetorical Commentaries by Thierry of Chartres*, Toronto 1988). Su tali citazioni vedi oltre, pp. 116-17.

141, 323).[47] La diversità di tradizione esegetica tra le due opere epiche staziane riflette la loro distinta tradizione manoscritta: dopo una breve parentesi, conclusa nell'XI secolo, nella quale vengono copiate entro il medesimo codice, esse procedono separate sino all'Umanesimo.[48] Ciò è effetto della destinazione del 'Stacius minor' al livello elementare dell'istruzione scolastica, cui è assegnata l'opera dopo un'operazione editoriale che ne ripartì il testo in cinque, e talvolta quattro, tre o addirittura sei brevi libri di simile estensione e appose lo spurio verso di chiusa 'Aura silet...'.[49]

Il commento LP alla *Tebaide*, dopo la fine dell'XI secolo, sembra completamente sparire per poi essere 'riscoperto' nel tardo XIV secolo: quando se ne moltiplicheranno le copie, sempre in testo continuo; esso sarà inoltre l'unico commento[50] ad essere dato

---

[47] Per un elenco dei manoscritti che contengono il commento di LP alla *Tebaide* rinvio a R. D. Sweeney, *Prolegomena to an Edition of the Scholia to Statius*, Leiden 1969, pp. 10-18. Ai manoscritti noti posso aggiungere ora un testimone frammentario, (2 ff.= *Theb.* I, 595-660 e II, 63-128), della fine del X secolo, MS Gotha, Forschungsbibliothek, membr. I. 129, proveniente da una zona tedesca meridionale, forse S. Gallo, che, rispetto all'edizione e al MS Vat. Pal. lat. 1694, attesta una nuova glossa, a I, 622 'exanimis'. Per il quadro generale della tradizione anteriore al XII secolo si osservi che contengono il commento LP, collocato nei margini i manoscritti della *Tebaide*: Parigino BN, lat. 10317, del X secolo, proveniente da Echternach e—tutti dell'XI secolo—MSS Bamberg, Staatliche Bibl., class. 47, Wolfenbüttel, Herzog August Bibliothek, 54 Gud. lat. 2°, München, Bayerische Staatsbibliothek, Clm 17206, proveniente da Schäftlarn, Firenze, Biblioteca Laurenziana, 38.6, tedesco; sono invece solo minimi frammenti, databili fra X e XI secolo: MSS Montpellier, Faculté de Médecine, H 62 e Leipzig, Universitätsbibliothek, Rep. I 12a del X secolo; Bern, Burgerbibliothek, A 91, Düsseldorf, Universitätsbibliothek, F 49 e Pavia, bibl. priv., del X-XI secolo; Liège, Bibl. Univ., 660 dell'XI e Kassel, Gesamt-Hochschul-Bibliothek, 2° 8 poet., XI-XII secolo.

[48] Questa modalità di trasmissione dei classici pare confermata anche dalla tradizione di Orazio fra IX e XII secolo: Villa, 'Per una tipologia del commento mediolatino: *l'Ars poetica* di Orazio', in *Il commento ai testi...* (n. 1 sopra), pp. 19-42 e 'I manoscritti di Orazio', *Aevum*, 66, 1992, pp. 95-135; 67, 1993, pp. 55-103; 68, 1994, pp. 117-46.

[49] de Angelis, *'Magna questio...'* (n. 38 sopra), pp. 103-209.

[50] Nell'umanesimo si spegne l'interesse esegetico per la *Tebaide*, con qualche sporadica eccezione (ad esempio le lezioni di Filippo Beroaldo il vecchio nel bolognese Archivio di Stato, Studio Alidosi 44, segnalate da I. Mariotti, 'Lezioni di Beroaldo il vecchio sulla *Tebaide*', in *Tradizione classica e letteratura umanistica. Per Alessandro Perosa*, Roma 1985, pp. 577-94; o il commento di Pomponio Leto tràdito nel Vaticano lat. 3279), per concentrarsi sul nuovo testo delle *Silvae* (che riceveranno le cure di Domizio Calderini, del Perotti, di Poliziano, di Parrasio, di Biondo Flavio). Qualche commento umanistico all'*Achilleide* viene invece ancora prodotto e stampato: Giovanni Britannico lo pubblicherà nel 1485 a Brescia (Hain 14989) (ma lo aveva concluso prima, probabilmente nel 1481); un altro commento umanistico è contenuto nel MS Vat. Ottob. lat. 1261 e nella sua copia,

alle stampe nel XV secolo. Un antesignano della rivalutazione di LP sarà proprio Boccaccio, che ne possiederà un testimone ragguardevole d'origine tedesca, ora MS Laur. 38.6, senza molta influenza—pare—sulla tradizione umanistica italiana.

Si rintraccia, a dire il vero, un numero di manoscritti, molto più considerevole di quelli sopra rammentati (varie decine), che, secondo Sweeney—il quale li raggruppa sotto le rubriche 'B. MSS of doubtful value for the text of LP; C. MSS including condensed excerpts from LP'—potrebbero riuscire utili alla costituzione dello stemma della tradizione del commento LP: ma il fatto che essi contengano in realtà minimi frustoli, spesso rielaborati, di questo commento lo induce poi a considerarli inutilizzabili per ricostituire il testo di LP.[51]

La prolungata assenza del commento tardoantico lascia spazio ad un proliferare di esegesi medievali alla *Tebaide*: i cui manoscritti verranno sempre fittissimamente postillati, a segno di un interesse mai intermesso al suo testo.

Credo di poter spiegare il motivo della brusca interruzione nella tradizione di un testo, quale quello di Lattanzio, degno certo della considerazione che il Medioevo tributava ad un'opera tardoantica.[52] La spiegazione consentirà di chiarire inoltre le ragioni della disparità che si constata tra il numero di manoscritti di LP anteriori al XII secolo e la moltitudine di quelli che, nei due secoli successivi nei quali si assiste alla scomparsa di LP nella sua integrità (sia esso nella forma del testo continuo o in quella di glos-

---

2027. Resta inoltre, adespoto, un frammento di un commento umanistico in testo continuo allo 'Stacius minor', costituito da un solo fascicolo, che si trova entro il manoscritto Wolfenbüttel 65 Aug. 2º; esso contiene soprattutto una serie di glosse mitologiche (*Incunabula Guelferbitana*, Wiesbaden 1990, nº 2551; IGI 9154; Pellechet 10690; Bibliothèque Nationale, *Catalogue des incunables* II, Paris 1985, S-385 = GW 4422, circa 1470). Sarà da sottolineare a questo proposito la persistenza a fine Quattrocento, anche nei testimoni a stampa, della tradizione del commento continuo, e che tanto non pare fenomeno isolato: è in testo continuo, ad esempio, il commento di Domizio Calderini edito nel 1476 da Enrico di Colonia (IGI 2361; un esemplare a Padova, Bibl. univ. sec. XV, 774), il commento a Lucano di Ognibene da Lonigo stampato a Venezia 1475, 'existente Venetiarum duce Petro Mocenico' (HC 10029; IGI 6999; CR 3653; BMC V 219; IBP 3418; IG 1987): cf., per altri esempi, M. Flodr, *Incunabula classicorum*, Amsterdam 1973.

[51] Cf. Sweeney, *Prolegomena...* (n. 47 sopra), pp. 18-24.

[52] Basti pensare alla costante fortuna del commento di Servio alle opere di Virgilio: B. Munk Olsen, 'La popularité des texts classiques entre le IXe et le XIIe siècles', *Revue d'histoire des textes*, 14-15, 1984-85, p. 177, nonostante la flessione del numero di manoscritti prodotti nel XII secolo: Id., *I classici nel canone scolastico altomedievale*, Spoleto 1991, p. 40.

sa marginale), dimostrano invece di contenere frammenti del commento.

Il commento 'In principio'

Non oltre la metà del XII secolo venne copiato un manoscritto, il Berlinese, Staatsbibliothek, Preuss. Kulturbesitz, lat. 2°. 34[53] che è il più antico testimone di un nuovo commento alla *Tebaide*, molto ampio e dotto, che si sostituì interamente al commento LP con un immediato e vastissimo successo.

Restano infatti assai numerosi manoscritti, molto prossimi all'epoca nella quale presumibilmente esso fu composto: oltre che nel MS Berlin, lat 2°. 34, del XII med., il commento è tràdito nel londinese MS Add. 16380, del XIII sec., nel berlinese, MS lat 4°. 228, del XII-XIII sec., nel leidense MS Gronov. lat. 191 A, XIII sec., nel Riccardiano MS 842, XIV ex., tutti in testo continuo, e poi, ridotto a commento marginale, nei MSS Paris, B.N., lat. 16694, XII[2], Vat. lat. 1375, XII-XIII, Chig. H VI. 209, XII ex., Barb. lat. 106, XIII[1], Lincoln Cathedral, 130, XII med., Vat. Ottob. lat. 1977, XIII sec., Vat. lat. 1616, XII ex., Karlsruhe, Landesbibl., frg. Augiense 139, XIII in., London, B.L., Arundel 389, XIII in., Vat., Pal. lat. 1717, XII ex., Vat. lat. 3280, XII (con altro), Bern, Burgerbibl. 407, XIII in., Leiden, Voss. Lat. Q. 114, XII-XIII, Vat. Ross. 536, XIII-XIV, e ancora, più tardi, Wolfenbüttel, 146 Gud. lat. 2°, XV, Padova, Sem. 41, XIV, Milano, Ambr. M 60 sup., XV sec., Salamanca Univ., M 72, XV sec., Oxford, Bodl., Canon. class. lat. 74, XIV ex., e molti altri ancora.

Dimostra l'eccezionale successo di questa *lectura* anche il nascere immediato di una sua redazione abbreviata, oggi nel Par. lat. 5137, ascrivibile agli stessi anni nei quali fu copiato il berlinese lat. 2°. 34, (dei rapporti fra i due testi tratteremo altrove); e il fatto che ne viene estrapolato l'*accessus*, tramandato nella raccolta di cui è testimone il MS København, Kongelige Bibl. Fabric. 29. 2, f. 6rb,

---

[53] Per la descrizione rinvio à V. Rose, *Verzeichniss der lateinischen Handschriften der königlichen Bibliothek zu Berlin*, II. 3, Berlin 1905, pp. 1304-1308 e cf. Munk Olsen, *L'étude des auteurs classiques latins aux XIe et XIIe siècles*, II, Paris 1985, p. 563. É una collezione di commenti continui agli *auctores*—nell'ordine a Lucano, a Virgilio *Bucoliche, Georgiche, Eneide*, a Stazio *Tebaide*—scritti nella prima metà del XII secolo dalla stessa mano, con la medesima impostazione della pagina, su due fittissime colonne, tranne nella sezione iniziale di Lucano, scritta a piena pagina. Cf. anche n. 58.

del XIII secolo, e nel MS Leipzig, Universitätsbibl., 1617, f. 40, del XII secolo; l'*accessus*, pur rielaborato, è riconoscibile in un alto numero di manoscritti, come nel Vaticano, Arch. S. Pietro, A 15, del 1342, nell'Harleiano 2665, f. 53[rv], XIII sec., nel commento *Casualis eventus*.[54]

La fortuna del commento si prolunga, come vedremo, in tutto il XV secolo, ed è tanto vivace da produrre anche una *summa*, fatto che mi risulta piuttosto singolare nel quadro dell'esegesi 'moderna' ai classici. Qualcuno infatti, nel XIV secolo, e in area inglese, provvide a estrarre dal commento ai libri I-IV molte glosse, di argomento prevalentemente mitologico-astronomico e storico, raccogliendole sotto un titolo, 'Ex alio incognito expositore'[55] che dimostra come già allora non vi fosse memoria del loro autore, cui però ancora a distanza di due secoli era riconosciuta una indiscussa autorità. E poiché una simile operazione è inconsueta ritengo utile segnalare un manoscritto il cui testo appare risultato di un analogo procedimento: nel fiorentino Bibl. naz., Conv. soppr. I. 1. 28, del XIV sec., ff. 50[r]-64[v] abbiamo una serie di glosse mitologiche, tutte estrapolate da un commento ai primi due libri di Marziano Capella, *De nuptiis*.[56]

Prima di esaminare le ragioni di un successo tanto singolare ed anche, e soprattutto, del prevalere del commento medievale su quello tardoantico, diciamo che una prima lettura del suo testo, condotta sul testimone più antico, MS Berlin, lat. 2° 34, ci moltiplica la messe fra le mani. Riconosciamo infatti con assoluta certezza che il medesimo autore che ha scritto il commento alla *Tebaide* ha steso anche quelli alle altre opere di Virgilio.[57]

---

[54] Sui manoscritti che tramandano questo commento all'*Achilleide* cf. de Angelis, '*Magna questio...*'(n. 38 sopra), pp. 103-69.

[55] MS London, British Library, Harl. 2693, ff. 41[r]-45[v]: cf. C. E. Wright, *Fontes Harleiani*, London 1972, pp. 53 e 87. Suo possessore è Thomas Archer (1554-1630?), rettore di Houghton Conquest, poi Robert Burscough, prebendario di Exeter, dal quale gli agenti di Lord Harley lo acquistarono il 17 maggio 1715.

[56] Lo rilevò per primo Dronke, *Fabula...* (n. 10 sopra), pp. 100-18 e 'William of Conches's Commentary on Martianus Capella', in *Etudes de civilisation médiévale, IXe-XIIe siècles. Mélanges offerts à E.-R. Labande*, Poitiers [1974], pp. 223-235, il quale ritiene che il commento appartenga a Guglielmo di Conches. Recentemente ha proposto che nel commento siano serbate tracce dell'esegesi di Giovanni Scoto C. Leonardi, 'Der Kommentar von Johannes Scotus zu Martianus Capella im 12. Jahrhundert', in *Eriugena redivivus*, cur. W. Beierwaltes, Heidelberg 1987, pp. 77-88.

[57] Non posso affermare nulla ancora sul commento a Lucano: ma posso dire che esiste semmai una testimonianza in contrario. Infatti la glossa a un passo di Lucano, I, 321, che Arnolfo d'Orléans registra come commento del 'magister

Il risultato assume un certo rilievo perché il commento all'*Eneide* contiene memoria di un 'magister Ansellus', identificabile con Anselmo di Laon;[58] e l'essere l'autore dei quattro commenti la stessa persona consente di applicare all'intero *corpus* quanto può essere dedotto dalla presenza del nome illustre, non solo, ma anche di utilizzare liberamente quanto possa essere ricavato dai commenti virgiliani che appaia utile a dare soluzione a problemi che emergano da quello alla *Tebaide*.

L'affermazione della appartenenza dei quattro commenti al medesimo autore è autorizzata da perfette rispondenze di molti rinvii incrociati fra le diverse opere.[59]

Anselmus' (Arnulfi Aurelianensis *Glosule super Lucanum*, ed. B. Marti, Rome 1958, p. 46: 'insolita corona armatorum cum circa iudices sedentes soleat stare populus quasi in corona, unde alibi "et vulgi stante corona" [Ov. *Met.* 13.1], magister quoque Anselmus sic glosat "Domine, ut scuto bone voluntatis tue coronasti nos corona" [*Psalm.* 5.12]'), non si rinviene nel commento a Lucano contenuto nel manoscritto berlinese. Ma la tipologia della glossa, che rivela che l'associazione è stimolata da un'analogia stilistica, di figura, rinvenuta fra i due luoghi (Lucano: gladii... triste... iudicium... trepidum cinxere corona), induce a dar credito ad Arnolfo: le medesime caratteristiche infatti, inconsuete sino ad Abelardo, si presentano anche nelle citazioni bibliche esibite dai commenti a Virgilio e a Stazio contenute nel manoscritto berlinese. Peraltro gli interessi retorici e grammaticali di Anselmo sono testimoniati nelle *Glosule* e nelle *Note Dunelmenses*: R. W. Hunt, 'Studies on Priscian...' (n. 42 sopra), pp. 13, 16; M. Gibson, 'The Early Scholastic *Glosule* to Priscian's *Institutiones grammaticae*: the Text and its Influence', *Studi medievali*, 20, 1979, pp. 235-47; cf. qui p. 120.

[58] La segnalazione apodittica di Rose, *Verzeichniss...* (n. 53 sopra), pp. 1304-1308 viene replicata, con alcune imprecisioni, da M. Manitius, *Geschichte der lateinische Literatur*, III, München 1931, p. 238 e poi accettata con il beneficio di qualche dubbio: vedi da ultimo Munk Olsen, *I classici nel canone...* (n. 52 sopra), p. 37; sin qui non è stato dimostrato su quali basi si fonda l'attribuzione. Sul commento alle *Georgiche* contenuto nel manoscritto vedi da ultimo Alessio, 'Glossografia altomedievale alle *Georgiche*', in *Settimane di studio del Centro italiano di Studi sull'alto medioevo*, XXXVII. *L'ambiente vegetale nell'alto medioevo*, Spoleto 1990, pp. 55-102, alla bibliografia del quale faccio rinvio. Breve cenno, soprattutto sulle *Ecloghe*, in V. Brown, 'A Twelfth-Century Miscellany-Commentary of German Origin (Vatican MS Pal. Lat. 1695)', in *Scire Litteras, Forschungen zum mittelalterlichen Geistesleben*, hrsg. S. Krämer und M. Bernhard, München 1988, pp. 73-86 (82 n. 25); sull'*Eneide* in C. Baswell, *Virgil in Medieval England*, Cambridge 1994, pp. 63-68, 313-14. Auspicava uno studio delle glosse di questo manoscritto, 'forse di Anselmo di Laon', B. Bischoff, 'Living with the Satirists' in *Classical Influences on European Culture A. D. 500-1500*, ed. R. R. Bolgar, Cambridge 1971, pp. 83-94, ora in *Mittelalterliche Studien*, III, Stuttgart 1981, pp. 260-70: 261. Non menziona il manoscritto, insieme con i molti altri contenenti il medesimo commento, R. Cormier, 'Preliminary Checklist of Early Medieval Glossed *Aeneid* Manuscripts', *Studi medievali*, 32, 1991, pp. 971-79, che senz'altro lo ascrive a Anselmo; alla bibliografia ivi dichiarata sarà da aggiungere la voce 'Medioevo, manoscritti', in *Enciclopedia virgiliana*, Roma 1989, a cura di Alessio, che censisce tutti i manoscritti di Virgilio sino al XV secolo.

[59] Ad esempio f. 102va a *Theb.* VIII, 560 '*Sineret*: deest "si". Similis est igitur

Sarà sufficiente limitare l'esame a un esempio, tratto dal commento alla *Tebaide*, che darà anche la misura della qualità del commento.

L'esegeta che lo confeziona è un attento e sensibile lettore di Virgilio,[60] vigile a rilevarne ogni caratteristica stilistica.[61] Egli riesce a cogliere che Stazio imita il suo modello anche nelle più profonde strutture interne all'opera di Virgilio, quindi in luoghi che non

---

grammatica "Greculus esuriens in celum iusseris ibit". Nam teste Prisciano (*GL* III, 247.8) subiunctivus potest poni sine coniunctione', che si ripete identico ad *Aen.* 6. 31, f. 59rb; oppure a *Theb.* XII, 273, f. 112[ra] '*legens*, idest sequens; verbum est polisxenum'; f. 98[rb] a *Theb.* III, 306 '*legit* verbum est polissemum. Est enim lectorum—lego Virgilium—, est messorum—lego fruges—, est viatorum,—lego iter—, est navigantium—Virgilius: "sive horam Illirici legit equoris" (*E.* VIII, 7)'; f. 51[ra] ad *Aen.* III, 127 '*legimus* verbum est polissemum'.

[60] Ovviamente egli rileva gli episodi paralleli, in qualche modo indicati da Stazio stesso: ad esempio a *Theb.* X, 445 'sicut Nisus et Eurialus per Virgilium fuerunt sacrati, ita et vos Dyma et Opleum per me sacrati eritis ... propter consimilem fidelitatem videtur hic latenter innuere et, quasi per tapinosim, Thebaidos paritatem et equivalentiam cum Eneide'; a *Theb.* X, 453: '*ostendere*. Similiter fecerunt Rutuli de Niso et Eurialo; ad illius similitudinem tractaturus est iste locus (*sic*)'; anche all'inizio del X libro viene sottolineata la perfetta corrispondenza dei temi trattati da Stazio con quelli virgiliani (MS Add. 16380, f. 171[vb]: 'hic incipit liber decimus: maxima eius pars sumpta est ex illo Virgiliano, ubi introducit actor Nisum et Eurialum de nocte egressos...'); oppure, f. 112[ra], a *Theb.* XII, 348 '*parvo Polinice*, idest Tessandro. Virgilius (*Aen.* IV, 327): "saltem si qua mihi de te suscepta fuisset/ ante fugam soboles, si quis mihi parvus in aula/ luderet Eneas qui te tantum ore referret, non equidem omnino capta aut deserta viderer"'; MS Add. 16380, f. 166[vb] a *Theb.* VI, 540 '*generum*, Polinicem victum. Hoc simile dixit Virgilius de Sergesto: "illi serva datur operum haud ignara Minerve" (*Aen.* V, 284)'. Naturalmente tutte le associazioni riportate non sono nemmeno suggerite dal commento LP. L'attenzione stilistica si estende in qualche caso a Orazio: ad esempio a *Theb.* VII, 418 (MS Ricc. 842, f.77ra) '*Mi<cenae>*... sequens Horatium multis partibus subiunctivam particulam supponit, qui in sermonibus (I, 8, 2) ait "Cum faber incertus scamnum faceretne Priapum"'.

[61] Ad esempio sottolinea, come peculiarità virgiliana, tutti i casi nei quali il poeta utilizza il dimostrativo 'hic' in luogo del relativo 'illic': f. 89rb a *Theb.* I, 273 'hic, more virgiliano, usus est demonstrativo pro relativo'; f. 89vb a *Theb.* I, 327 '*hac*, pro illac, more virgiliano'; f. 95rb a *Theb.* II, 523 '*huc*, pro illuc, more virgiliano'; oppure l'abitudine ad usare 'continuativae particulae' nel passaggio dal *figmentum* alla *historia*: f. 92[rb] a *Theb.* II, 1 'actores qui figmentum historiis admiscent poeticum, ab historia ad figmentum, vel a figmento ad historiam transeuntes, continuativas apponunt particulas ...'; f. 93[rb] a *Theb.* II, 134 'a figmento transit ad historiam et ponit continuativam particulam, more suo'; f. 97[vb] a *Theb.* III, 218 'more suo transit actor ab historia ad figmentum, quod ita competenter iungit historie, ut videatur insitum, non assutum; ponit enim continuativam particulam, dicens "hec"'; o rileva la consuetudine virgiliana allo zeugma: f. 109[vb] a *Theb.* XI, 324 '*ligabant* hoc verbum, more Virgilii, refertur ad duos, cum recte non possit nisi ad unum applicari. Non enim tela ligantur, sed galea tantum'; f. 111vb a *Theb.* XII, 174 '*a<m>bire* hoc verbum refert ad duo, cum non possit nisi ad unum applicari'.

rientrano nella casistica dell'*imitatio* più spesso esemplificata, quella stilistico-lessicale; così commenta infatti *Theb.* III, 167 (f. 97rb):

> *Ite diu.* actor iste adeo diligenter voluit imitari Virgilium quod etiam in positione istorum duorum versuum et quorundam aliorum eum est imitatus, siquidem Virgilius in Bucolicis quendam versum benigne dixit, hunc scilicet: 'insere, Dampni, pyros, carpent tua poma nepotes' (*Egl.* IX, 51), in alium maligne, hunc scilicet: 'insere nunc, Melibee, pyros, pone ordine vites' (*Egl.* I, 74), similiter iste actor de istis fratribus hos versus benigne dixit: 'ite diu, fratres' et cetera; inferius autem de Ethiocle et Polinice maligne dicet (*Theb.* XI, 575): 'ite, truces anime, funestaque tartara leto/ polluite et totas Erebi consumite penas'.

Stazio cioè avrebbe appreso da Virgilio il sottile gioco di autocitazioni; e questa è osservazione assolutamente originale, forse solo debolmente stimolata da Servio.[62]

Se poi leggiamo il commento a *Egloghe* I, 73, troviamo puntuale rinvio ai due luoghi della *Tebaide* (III, 167 e XI, 575) nei quali Stazio ha riprodotto lo schema virgiliano.[63] Un segno fortemente significativo per stabilire uno stretto rapporto fra i due commenti.

Tralascio numerosi casi simili, ad eccezione di uno nel quale pare di riuscire a cogliere il metodo di lavoro del commentatore: che rimedita ed elabora gli spunti offerti da Servio, quando questi rileva simmetrie interne al poema virgiliano, e poi autonomamente applica lo stesso metodo nel suo commento alla *Tebaide*. Infatti, se la nota serviana ad *Aen.* III, 717[64] diventa nel commento a Virgilio (f. 52vb):

> *sic pater.* mire illa duo que in principio secundi libri in duobus posuit versibus, in huius tercii fine tribus repetivit versibus: 'conticuere' et cetera, modo 'conticuit', 'intenti' tunc silere, modo 'intentis omnibus',

---

[62] A *Egl.* IX, 50: '*carpent...* ac si diceret: nihil est quod possis timere. Nam illud respicit quod supra invidiose ait: "insere nunc Melibee piros" (*Egl.* I, 74)...'.

[63] F. 28ra a *Egl.* I, 73 'o *Melibee*, quasi dicat: miser fuisti, quando ad opus aliorum hoc fecisti; et maligne prolatus est versus iste, sicut in contrario bene profertur ille in sequentibus "Insere, Dampni, piros, carpent tua poma nepotes" (*Egl.* IX, 51). Et in hoc imitatur Statius Virgilium, duos versus benigne proferens, duos vero maligne: benigne de duobus fratribus Thespiadibus quos Tydeus occidit, "ite diu, fratres, indiscretique supremis ignibus" (*Theb.* III, 167) et cetera, maligne vero protulit illos duos de Etheocle et Polinice: "ite, truces anime" (*Theb.* XI, 575) et cetera'; f. 33va-b a *Egl.* IX, 50 '*insere...* et est positus versus iste benigne, sicut ille maligne "insere nunc, Melibee, piros" (*Egl.* I, 74)'.

[64] Ad *Aen.* III, 717 (*Servii grammatici qui feruntur in Vergilii carmina commentarii*, rec. G. Thilo-H. Hagen, I, Leipzig 1878-81, p. 458): 'sane in secundi principio duo poetae sunt versus, sicut hic tres, et similis est finis initio: "conticuit" et "intentis"'.

è assolutamente nuova nell'esegesi a Stazio l'osservazione, analoga a quella sopra rilevata, del parallelismo fra le chiuse dei primi due libri (f. 96ra):

> *Theb.* II, 715 *diva*. sicut primus liber hymnum Apollinis in fine continet, sic et iste secundus in hymnum Palladis terminatur.

Si tratta dunque di un commentatore in grado di stabilire un rapporto fra il modello e l'imitatore sul fondamento di una sicura padronanza dei classici (Ovidio, Orazio, Giovenale, Persio, Lucano, con un'assoluta preminenza accordata a Orazio, del quale vengono prevalentemente citate le *Odi*) che si traduce in associazioni brillanti (ad esempio quando rileva la dipendenza di Stazio da Orazio *Carm.* I, 15. 9 per Theb. III, 210-11).[65]

Entro le osservazioni più caratteristiche riservate all'*ornatus* del testo potranno annoverarsi quelle relative alle comparazioni (Stazio ne era maestro riconosciuto),[66] delle quali viene analizzata la formulazione secondo i precetti retorici (e taluna si rivela 'congrua' ma 'viciose inducta');[67] oppure quelle, molto sintetiche, che si limitano

---

[65] F. 97va a *Theb.* III, 210-11 '*quantus sudor* futurus est. hec sunt cum desolatione <pronuntianda>. Sumptus est hic locus ab Horatio, ubi Nereus Paridi cum Helena rapta fugienti mala futura predicit: "Eheu quantus equis, quantus adest viris sudor" (*C.* 1. 15. 9)'. Sottile è anche l'associazione con Giovenale: f. 168ra a *Theb.* VI, 759 '*voto erecto*: ad superos, ut servaretur Alcida(mas). Huic simile ait Iuvenalis (VI, 17-18): "cum furem nemo timeret/ caulibus ac pomis et aperto viveret orto". ibi non repetes negationem, sed ita leges: "et cum omnis viveret aperto orto", et hic similiter: "et omnis timeat spectacula" et cetera'.

[66] Come leggiamo, ad esempio, nel MS del XII secolo, Oxford, Lincoln College, lat. 27, f. 62^r '...iste poeta totum opus suum variis verborum ornamentis, et maxime comparationum venustate, compaginat'; lo sottolinea ancora Goffredo di Vinsauf, *Documentum* 2. 2. 21: 'infinita inveniuntur exempla comparationum in auctoribus et precipue in Statio' (E. Faral, *Les arts poétiques du XIIe et du XIIIe siècle*, Paris 1958, p. 275); lo ripete Gervasio di Melkley, *Ars poetica* (ed. H.-J. Gräbener, Münster 1965, p.152,17): 'Fama enim nobilissime Thebaidos ob comparationum frequentiam vix permansit illesa'; vi allude l'autore dell'*Apocalipsis Goliae*: 'Incomparabilis est status Stacio/ cuius detinuit res comparacio' (K. Strecker, *Die Apokalypse des Golias*, Rom 1928, p. 18, 13) e ancora all'inizio del XV secolo lo rammenta F. Villani, *Expositio seu comentum super 'Comedia' Dantis Alleghaerii*, ed. S. Bellomo, Firenze 1989, 116 p. 106: 'Comparatione aliqua crebro poete utuntur, in quibus inter poetas palma datur Statio'. Si osservi infine che in un certo numero di manoscritti, dopo l'*explicit*, viene registrato il numero di comparazioni contenute nell'opera: ad es. nel Vat. Pal. lat. 1690, toscano del XIV secolo.

[67] F. 93rb a *Theb.* II, 105 '*tu veluti*: hec comparatio non est viciosa, sed viciose inducta, quoniam a persona non introducta'; f. 93vb a *Theb.* II, 193 '*quam si*: comparatio hec vitiosa non est, sed viciose inducta. se et Tydeum comparat navi, que diu iactata tempestuoso mari, tandem potest in portu pervenire'; f. 168rb a *Theb.* VI, 857 '*reditura* ...: versus iste non potest adaptari, sed tantum ad proprietatem arboris respicit'; ibid., a *Theb.* VI, 858 '*non sic*...: alia comparatio gregis,

a segnalare la 'urbana positio', o 'transpositio', di molti luoghi[68] (l''urbanitas' è la cifra di Stazio sino al XV secolo).[69]

Frequenti, ma non sempre originali, le osservazioni metriche, spesso, anche se non esclusivamente, mutuate da Prisciano;[70] e ancora molto intriganti, a questa altezza, numerose chiose che paiono rivelare un vivo interesse per la storia della lingua latina e, marcatamente, per gli usi del suo tempo. La rilevanza di queste chiose, anche per le implicazioni con l'opinione premodista e dantesca sull'immutabilità della 'gramatica', impongono un cenno, anche se cursorio: basti dire che le osservazioni non si limitano a fatti meramente lessicali[71] ma si estendono a considerazioni non insignificanti sulla sintassi stessa.[72]

---

idest armenti coniunx, idest vacca. Hoc iterum non potest adaptari, nisi forte ad premium respexeris, quod fuit victor habiturus'.

[68] F. 91[rb] a *Theb.* I, 634-35 '*quis Sirius* ...: urbana positio est cum a propria significatione ad commune evocatur, ut Ovidius "Typhis et Antomedon dicar amoris ego" (*Her.* VI, 48) et ibi "Medee Medea forem" (*Her.* VI, 151)'; f. 109[ra] a *Theb.* XI, 47 '*terga Nemee* ...: est urbana positio'; f. 96[ra] a *Theb.* II, 713 '*superstans*: due dictiones, vel una; si sint due, urbana est transpositio'; f. 98[vb] a *Theb.* III, 395 '*Tydea circum*: ... vel sit urbana transpositio. Virgilius "transtra per et remos" (*Aen.* V, 663)'; f. 109[ra] a *Theb.* X, 833 '*Iovem contra*: urbana transpositio'; f. 109[rb] a *Theb.* XI, 175 '*me propter*: urbana transpositio'.

[69] Cf. de Angelis, 'Benvenuto e Stazio' in *Benvenuto da Imola lettore degli antichi e dei moderni*, a cura di C. Paolazzi e P. Palmieri, Ravenna 1991, pp. 139-63 e qui p. 109.

[70] F. 101[vb] a *Theb.* IV, 136 'antiquitus dicebatur *Nemeas*, sed moderni, extremam subtrahentes litteram, retinuerunt productionem vocalis et accentum (*Prisc. GL* II, 287.8)'; f. 106[va] a *Theb.* X, 342 '*trunca ar(ma) Ly(cie)* o Apollo, a Lycia regione ubi colitur; sed auctor, poetica licentia, produxit mediam, qua re et versus iste a Prisciano in exemplum adducitur (*GL* II, 41.18; 72.7)'; ibid. 347 '*hos inter*, scilicet Argivos, sed, metro cogente, fecit anastrophen'; f. 110[va] a *Theb.* XI, 631 '*num*, idest numquid, *abiit*. licentiam facit actor in tercio pede, quod nos facimus in secundo'; f. 165[va] a *Theb.* VI, 391 '*decori*: sistole est, ut propter metrum "co" sillaba brevis, que longa est, vel sit a decus decoris, quod modo non est in usu; alii vero sic emendant: decora ampla'; f. 166[vb] a *Theb.* VI, 486 '*illic* pro ilico, gratia metri'; e nel commento a Virgilio, f. 62[vb] ad *Aen.* VI, 514: '*egerimus*: deduxerimus. Testatur Servius quod "ri", longum naturaliter, breviatur necessitate metri cogente. Nam quod sit longa habemus ex O(vidio), qui ait (*Met.* VI, 350) "vitam dederitis in undis". Inde usus quorundam longam retinet, ut monachi qui dicunt: "si vocem eius audieritis"; communior tamen usus corripit'.

[71] Una glossa molto interessante sui mutamenti linguistici che potrebbe essere originata nell'ambiente della corte sveva segnala Claudia Villa in un manoscritto dell'*Ars poetica* oraziana: 'Dante lettore di Orazio', in *Dante e la 'bella scola'*... (n. 8 sopra), pp. 92-93.

[72] F. 99[vb] a *Theb.* III, 570 'antiquitus quicumque potens tirannus appellabatur, sed modernus usus sevos potentes tyrannos appellavit, et recte. tyrus enim dicitur angustia, inde tyrannus dicitur angustians, et tyrannis tyrannidos tyranni sevicia'; f. 104[rb] a *Theb.* IX, 493 '*amicior*: idest propinquior, gratia metri dixit, quod regula requirebat, cum usus noster dicat amicicior propter differentiam'; f. 104[vb] a *Theb.* IX, 585 '*felici robore*: idest fructiferi roboris, sed antique dixit per abla-

Nel novero delle minuzie, non utilizzabili per perizie di alloca-
zione, sono infine i volgarismi lessicali *(barbatus, palicium, palefridus)*[73]
e una sola osservazione geografica di scarso rilievo,[74]

La caratteristica che però più importa sottolineare in questo
commento è il rapporto filologico del commentatore con il testo,
o meglio con i testi, che usa: Stazio e Lattanzio Placido.

Nel commentare il poeta latino egli puntualmente segnala tutti
i casi nei quali gli risulta che la tradizione contenga versi spuri, o
quelli che egli tali ritiene;[75] inoltre, nel caso di presenza di varian-

---

tivum, cum usus modernus genitivum ponat...'; le stesse attenzioni anche nel commento all'*Eneide*. Ad es.: f. 45[va] ad *Aen.* III, 14 '*lato ferro*, quasi lati ferri, mulier
honesta forma'; f. 58[va] ad *Aen.* VI, 576 '*quinquaginta abu* (ma *hiatibus*): antiquum
est, sicut mulier honesta forma, quod nos dicimus honeste forme, et secundum
hanc lectionem nulla invenietur contrarietas'; f. 68[vb] ad *Aen.* VII, 483 '*prestanti
forma*: antiquum est, sicut mulier honesta forma, quod nos dicimus honeste forme'.

[73] F. 105[ra] a *Theb.* IX, 750 '*tergeminis*: idest triplici curvatura. huiusmodi sagit-
tas vulgo barbatas appellamus'; f. 106[rb] a *Theb.* X, 275 '*terga* boni, idest sessioni
utiles, scilicet palefridi'; f. 106[vb] a *Theb.* X, 457 '*vallum* Thebanorum, quod vulgo palicium dicimus'; a *Theb.* X, 351 (Berl. 4° 228, f. 27[r]) '*supinat*: idest facit sup-
pinari, quod vulgo rusare dicimus'. La prima annotazione rinvia prevalentemente
ad ambiente francese, ove intorno al XVI secolo era ancora attestato 'barbeleure',
ed era, come nel nostro testo, un ferro con uncini ad amo, voltati all'indietro,
che ne rendevano impossibile l'estrazione: cf. E. Huguet, *Dictionnaire de la langue
française du XVIe siècle*, I, Paris 1925, p. 481. I volgarismi sono più frequenti ovviamente nelle *Egloghe* e nelle *Georgiche*: cf. Alessio, 'Glossografia altomedioevale...'
(n. 58 sopra). Anche in questi casi essi rinviano univocamente ad area francese:
ad esempio f. 30rb a *Egl.* IV, 45 '*sandix*: herba est que vulgo dicitur garance';
f. 35va a *Georg.* I, 74 '*siliqua*: folliculus, ... a vulgo dicitur cossa'.

[74] F. 109ra a *Theb.* XI, 27 '*per arva Mas(sila)*: idest Affricana. Due sunt Mas-
silie: una est in Affrica, alia quam condiderunt Phocenses in via qua itur de
Alpibus ad montes Pyreneos'. La città francese era celebrata da un classico molto
letto quale Lucano, dal quale poteva assumersi anche la notizia dell'origine focese
(*Bellum civile* IV, 256-57; V, 53); e l'esatta collocazione, sulla via per S. Iacopo
di Compostela, poteva esser nota anche per via indiretta.

[75] F. 100vb a *Theb.* IV, 28 '*relicti amici* navigantium. Semper in hoc loco solet
haberi corrupta littera, sed hec est actoris: "Stant in rupe tamen, fugientia car-
basa visu/ dulce sequi patriosque dolent crebrescere ventos"'; f. 99[rb] a *Theb.* III,
508 '*pro altis rapinis*: idest agnis, non quas in aere faciant, sed quas in terris
fecerunt. Quidam libri habent "qui vultur", et tunc ita leges: non venit vultur,
qui est melior auguriis quam cetere aves'; f. 101[ra] a *Theb.* IV, 51 '*Stragilla* (v.l.
Bruxelles, B. R., 5337; Oxford, Magdalen College, lat. 18) vel *Langia*, ubi biberunt
sicientes Achivi, palus est quieta, unde dixit "pigra lambit vado tacenti"'; f. 101[vb]
a *Theb.* IV, 172 '... vel propter hoc quod dicit "torpens" notat esse paludem
pigram. quidam libri habent "torrens", sed referendum est ad ydram torrentem,
idest venenum evomentem'; f. 103[rb] a *Theb.* IX, 56 '*sunt dempta mihi*: quidam libri habent "empta" (Cambridge, St. John's Coll., D 12), et tunc ita leges: quo
diademate gaudia, idest cuius diadematis gaudia, sunt empta mihi tanti precii';
f. 103[rb] a *Theb.* IX, 107 '*excusso terrore*: idest crista, que terrorem importat. quidam
libri habent "excelso terrore", quia excelsam partem galee excussit, idest conum';

ti, il commentatore, in molti casi, non esita a dichiarare la sua adesione a quella che considera migliore (modo di operare, questo, piuttosto infrequente nei commenti), oppure saggia l'attendibilità delle lezioni della *Tebaide* che commenta alla luce dei lemmi staziani attestati da LP[76] o della tradizione indiretta di Prisciano.[77] Attraverso una lettura attenta del commento si può quindi intuire la fisionomia testuale della *Tebaide* che il commentatore ha sotto mano, le scelte che gli si propongono e che egli opera.

Tradizione non ignobile, da quanto fin d'ora[78] appare: infatti a *Theb.* IV, 29-30 dove l'autore sottolinea con forza la sua opinione su quale sia il testo corretto, la sua scelta, in opposizione all'errore di tutti gli altri 'libri', coincide con la lezione ritenuta cor-

---

f. 105[rb] a *Theb.* IX, 811 '*vultu* huius, idest Dircei. Quidam libri habent "vultum"'; f. 108[vb] a *Theb.* X, 858 '*spes una* (v.l. Bamberg class. 47 e Lipsia Rep. I 12): quidam libri habent "unde", sed tunc interrogative legetur'; f. 108[vb] a *Theb.* X, 930 '*acies* uterque exercitus. Quidam versus solent hic haberi (932-34), sed non sunt de libro, immo sic ordinanda est littera: "et terror utrimque/ quo ruat ardenti feriat quas corpore turmas (930-31). Stat tamen" (935), licet fulminatus'; f. 109[va] a *Theb.* XI, 270 '*potentem* funeribus patrie et lacrimis..; quidam libri habent "potitum"' (B N C r μ ν); f. 109[vb] a *Theb.* XI, 360-61 '*nefas* exclamative legendum est; quidam libri habent "incessantem", idest incessanter pulsantem'; f. 111[rb] a *Theb.* XII, 69 '*solatia forti*: idest Meneceo. Quidam libri habent "fortes" et refertur ad equos'; f. 111[va] a *Theb.* XII, 124-25 '*comes Dia(ne)... ducit postrema agmina*; sed opponitur de Euhadne, uxore Capanei, que eam subsequitur: ergo Athalanta non est extrema. sic ergo leges: "Athalanta et Euhadne", uxor Capanei, "gravis" (126), idest magna, "ducunt postrema agmina". Quidam libri habent: "it gravis Euhadne", sed hec littera legi non potest, sed hec est littera actoris: "et gravis Euhadne"; "hec" Atalanta, "illa" Euhadne, "astris irascitur" (128) propter maritum fulminatum, vel quia ipsa contemptrix erat numinum'; f. 113[rb] a *Theb.* XII, 646-47 '*agmina penarum exercita Thebis*: ypallage, idest Furie penis Thebarum fatigate; quod statim glosat dicens: "anguicome ducent" et cetera. Quidam sic legunt: "Thebis" adverbialiter, ex parte Thebarum, "stant agmina pe(narum) ex(ercita) The(bis)": sententia non mutatur'; f. 167[rb] a *Theb.* VI, 629 '*litus* improprie dixit pro clivo montis. quidam libri habent "latus hoc" (Bruxelles 5337), et tunc plana est littera'; f. 167vb a *Theb.* VI, 744 '*suadebat materiam* (D N μ ν) exercitium. Quidam libri habent "materie" et tunc sic iunges: "amor materie", idest ludi; etiam de Polluce legatur'. É inoltre evidente che nel testo della *Tebaide* sul quale veniva compilato il commento non comparivano i versi *Theb.* X, 100-105; 113-17; e *Theb.* VI, 227-33, sulla tradizione dei quali cf. A. Klotz, 'Probleme der Textgeschichte des Statius', *Hermes*, 40, 1905, pp. 341-72. Ho fatto ricorso agli apparati delle edizioni della *Tebaide* di A. Klotz-T. Klinnert, Leipzig 1973; H. W. Garrod, Oxford 1906 e D. E. Hill, Leiden 1983, controllando in alcuni casi le lezioni sui manoscritti.

[76] F. 88[va] a *Theb.* I, 200-01. Per il testo cf. pp. 104-105.

[77] Ad esempio f. 110ra a *Theb.* XI, 429 '*rogat externos*. Priscianus (*GL* II 85. 6-9) tamen, volens hoc probare, quod dicatur "exter, extera, exterum", hunc versum adducit in exemplum, dicens "si quid proficeret apud illos exter honos"' (la citazione è a memoria).

[78] Sto lavorando all'edizione del commento.

retta nelle edizioni critiche, lezione rarissima, perché attestata, a quanto consta, dall'unico manoscritto rappresentante la tradizione P (MS Paris, B.N., lat. 8051),[79] e, probabilmente per giunta posteriore, registrato a margine di MS Cambridge, St. John's Coll., D 12.

A *Theb.* X, 930-31 invece, quando con il medesimo rilievo il commentatore, optando con sicurezza, ancora una volta, per il testo corretto dei vv. X, 930-31, espunge i 'quidam versus' che 'solent hic haberi' (alludendo evidentemente ai versi 932-34), dà prova di conoscere l'esistenza dell'interpolazione che, a questa altezza, risulta attestata soltanto dal manoscritto proveniente dal priorato di S. Martino di Dover, l'attuale MS Cambridge, St. John's College, D 12, e da MS Oxford, Magdalen College lat. 18.[80]

E basti per ora accennare che l'interesse del commento coinvolge anche l'aspetto testuale di LP, al quale viene ascritta qualche glossa che non compare nel testo edito da Jahnke:[81] attribuzione di cui, beninteso, sarà da valutare l'attendibilità.

Non v'è dubbio, come si accennava, che al commentatore premesse il confronto con il suo autorevole predecessore tardoantico. Particolare rilevanza assume quindi l''In principio' in relazione a LP, sia come testimone indiretto e ancora piuttosto alto, della sua tradizione, sia—vedremo subito—per i rapporti di confronto, e di opposizione, che con questo egli instaura.

LP stava, assieme alla *Tebaide,* sullo scrittoio del nostro commentatore e veniva considerato un testo di assoluta autorità, le cui citazioni dovevano essere segnalate con l'indicazione del nome del-

---

[79] Klotz, 'Probleme der Textgeschichte...' (n. 75 sopra), pp. 358-59. Per il testo cf. n. 74.

[80] Su entrambi i manoscritti: Garrod, 'The St John's College (Cambridge) MS of the *Thebaid*', *Classical Review*, 18, 1904, pp. 38-42; inoltre H. Gneuss, 'A Preliminary List of Manuscripts Written or Owned in England up to 1110', in *Anglo Saxon England*, 9, 1980, p. 13 n° 152; M. R. James, *A Descriptive Catalogue of the Manuscripts in the Library of St. John's College*, Cambridge 1913, pp. 115-16; Id., *The Ancient Libraries of Canterbury and Dover*, Cambridge 1903, p. 431 n° 391; C. R. Haines, 'The Library of Dover Priory. Its Catalogue and Extant Volumes', *The Library*, 4, 8, 1928, pp. 109-110; H. H. E. Craster, 'Early Oxford College Manuscripts', *The Bodleian Quarterly Record*, 1, 6, 1916, Oxford 1917, p. 159. Sull'interpolazione cf. Klotz, 'Probleme...' (n. 75 sopra), p. 362.

[81] Potrebbe essere questo il caso della glossa, esplicitamente attribuita a Lattanzio, che leggiamo a *Theb.* II, 189: '*tales so(ceros)* idest talem socerum qualis Adrastus. plurale pro singulari; nam de uxore Adrasti nulla unquam fit mentio. hec figura a Lactentio appellatur enfaticos' (f. 93vb), se non è, come credo poco probabile, una trasposizione, entro questa glossa, dell'interpretazione applicata da LP a *Theb.* I, 10: '*Tyrios accedere montes.* emphaticos dixit montes pro saxis' (e cf. anche la glossa tràdita da Gotha, Forschungsbibl., membr. I 129, n. 47).

l'autore, come solo avveniva per Servio. Ma con acuto senso critico—assai raro nella esegesi medievale prima di Petrarca—il commentatore oppone alla interpretazione di LP nel commento alla
Tebaide (come anche alla interpretazione di Servio nel commento
alle opere di Virgilio) la propria, corroborata da altre *auctoritates*,
quando abbia motivo di ritenere l'opinione dei commentatori antichi insufficiente o ingenua.

In ogni caso, sia quando LP viene esplicitamente citato,[82] sia
quando esso viene utilizzato senza menzione dell'autore, le sue
informazioni sono sempre completate con quanto fornivano altre
fonti: insomma è sempre attentamente scandagliato, vagliato prima di essere immesso nel nuovo commento.

Nella glossa a *Theb.* I, 22, ad esempio, il commentatore oppone
polemicamente alla interpretazione di LP troppo favorevole a Domiziano quella che ritiene essere la verità storica:

> hoc dicit Vitellius familiam Sabinorum... ab hostili sevitia liberavit.
> Sed Suetonius (*Dom.* 1), hystorie veritatem attendens, ait: In Vitel-
> liano bello, cum prevaleret Vitellius et Sabini deficerent, Domitianus
> cum parte copiarum presentium in Capitolium aufugit ibique ea nocte
> apud edituum pernoctavit; mane vero facto, cum hostes irruerent et
> iam Capitolium arderent, Domitianus in Isiaco latens habitu pe-
> riculum evasit; quod auctor, ei blandiens, virtuti (veritati MS) eius
> deputat... (f. 86vb).

In due altri casi l'opposizione a LP poggia su una revisione critica del testo della *Tebaide*: a *Theb.* II, 431-32 viene evidentemente
restaurato e correttamente inteso 'Danaae (opes)', come aggettivo
da 'Danaus', rettificando LP che invece riferiva il passo a Danae:

> (95ra) *Danae opes cumu(lentur)* tibi, quia non invideo; sed hoc dicit sub
> interrogatione (431) *melioribus* (ma maioribus) *actis* idest tue prospe-
> ritati. Solent habere quidam libri *Dane* et tunc sic leges: regio illa in
> qua regnavit Dane filia Acrisii (è l'interpretazione di LP). Melior est
> tamen prima lectio[83]

e a *Theb.* I, 200-01 sottolinea che non è corretta la lezione del
testo di Stazio che anche LP accetta:

---

[82] Almeno una trentina sono le citazioni esplicite. Si noti che spesso negli
apparati esegetici meno stabilmente strutturati e posteriori all''In principio', il
nome di 'Lactantius' viene trascinato proprio in connessione con i luoghi nei
quali esso appariva menzionato nel commento 'In principio'.

[83] LP *ad loc.* p. 115: '*Te penes*. Ordo: te penes est regia Inachiae, dono con-
iugis, quam Danae Argiva possidebat. Hoc autem ideo dictum, ut doceat fratrem
habere, quod repetit'.

(f. 88va) hec littera (*scil.* effusa sub omni terra et unda) non est actoris, sed hec 'effusa sub omni terra atque ima die'; lege ergo sic... (ima corr. s.l. di Monaco, Clm 6396).

Altrove è l'interpretazione del testo offerta da LP a non convincere il commentatore: come nella protratta e ben motivata ipotesi esegetica per *Theb.* II, 45, ove preferisce l'ordo litterae' del testo a quello proposto da LP:

> 2. 45 *fessis* cursu rapido fatigatis. ordo sequentis littere secundum Lactentium (II, 43, p. 81): interiore sinu frangentia littora curvat Tenarus, expo(sitos) non audens (v.l. Par. 8063) scan(dere) fluctus; ast ubi prona dies lo(ngos) super equo(ra) fi(nes) exigit atque ingens me(dio) na(tat) un(bra) profundo, illic Egeo et cetera. lege littera: dicit actor curvari Tenarum ad invicem portus ubi Neptunus equos suos in nocte <s>tabulare consuevit... 'illic' et cetera. Aliter potes legere secundum ordinem libri: nam primus ordo secundum Lactentium est. lege ergo sic: 'ast ubi prona dies' (41), idest die advesperascente, 'interi(ore) si(nu)' (43), idest infra montem 'Tenaros' (44), idest umbra veniens de Tenaro, 'curvat' (43), idest curvata ostendit esse littora—umbra enim ad modum littoris curva esse videtur—'expo-(sitos) non au(det)': (44) probat quia littus illud Tenari curvum esse, quasi non audeat apparere vel fluctus ascendere; vel Neptunus 'non au(det) scandere fluctus ex(positos)', idest turbatos: confert se in tempestate ad portum quietum; vel 'expo(sitos)', quasi extra mare positos, idest terre vicinos, ubi aqua non est profunda; ibi in nocte quiescit. Cetera non mutantur (f. 93ra).

In altri casi il commentatore si schiera su opposte ipotesi interpretative, ad esempio:

> a *Theb.* I, 55 *ina(ne) solu(m)*: idest speluncam ubi erat inclusus, ubi nil erat, ubi inanis erat. Lactentius tamen dicit (p. 7) *inane so(lum)*: idest inferos (f. 87rb);
> a *Theb.* VI, 739 *nuda*: idest expedita, quia neque carnea mole, neque vestibus sunt oppressi Lacones. Lactentius tamen sic glosat (VI, 714 p. 331): *nuda* amore ceromatis, ad certamina preparata (Add. 16380, f. 167vb).

Oppure, dopo aver dato ampia rassegna della tradizione mitografica pertinente, opta per una soluzione diversa da quella di LP:

> f. 99ra a *Theb.* III, 479 *Brancus* secundum quandam fabulam pastor Thessalus erat, cuius amplexibus Phebus utebatur, qui cum mature moreretur, Phebus ei templum dicavit et divinandi scientiam prebuit. Secundum hoc leges 'patrio ho(nori)'(478): idest tali qualem pater filio conferret. Lactentius (p. 168) tamen dicit: Brancus fuit Tessalus puer, pudico amore dilectus Apollini, quem Apollo dolens acriter interfectum, sepulcro et templo honoravit. Alii autem dicunt eum fi-

lium Apollinis fuisse. Secundum hoc dices 'patrio ho(nori)': idest Apollineo....[84]

Alla luce di queste considerazioni può essere meglio compreso il successo di 'In principio', vasto e rapido al punto da quasi cancellare la presenza di LP, reso ormai inattuale dal commento nuovo, nel quale esso era in gran parte confluito. Lo provano le conclusioni che possiamo trarre dall'esame dei manoscritti posteriori al XII secolo che secondo Sweeney presentano tracce del commento LP: quasi tutti le presentano in quanto contengono il completo commento 'In principio' o sue glosse sparse (MSS Firenze, Ricc. 842, Leiden, B.P.L. 191A, London, B.L., Add. 16380, Berlin, lat. 4°. 228, lat. 2° 34, Karlsruhe, Landesbibl., frg. Augiense 139, Paris, lat. 5137, ma anche Venezia, Marc. lat. XII. 61 = 4097, etc.).[85]

*L'*accessus

Alla ricchezza e perizia esegetica del commento non poteva certo dimostrarsi inferiore l'*accessus*: sul quale occorrerà soffermarsi, anche al fine di illustrarne i rapporti con autori ed opere del XIV e XV secolo.

Anche l'*accessus*, molto ampio e articolato, è costruito con l'intento di fare il punto sulla tradizione esegetica sin allora elaborata ed eventualmente di superarla. Subito presenta, ad esempio, una duplice ipotesi per la 'causa finalis' della *Tebaide*: che sarebbe quella o di fornire un esempio negativo ai due fratelli, Domiziano e Tito, figli di Vespasiano che lottavano per il potere; oppure, collocando la composizione dell'opera nell'epoca in cui, morto Tito, Domiziano aveva ormai conquistato il potere, di procurare al suo autore fama e gloria.

La prima ipotesi è più motivata, fors'anche perché maggiormente diffusa all'epoca, e viene sostenuta dal commentatore allegando la

[84] Segnalo a questo punto l'opportunità di valutare con attenzione estrema il materiale mitologico che confluisce in questo commento. Come segno indiziario posso citare la notizia di una diversa genealogia relativa a Cadmo, cumulata a quella riportata da LP, che non compare in nessuno dei repertori consueti, nè nella scoliografia nota, ma che affiora, ad esempio, nelle *Genealogie* attribuite a Paolo da Perugia da T. Hankey ('Un nuovo codice delle *Genealogie Deorum* di Paolo da Perugia (e tre manualetti contemporanei)', *Studi sul Boccaccio*, 18, 1989, pp. 65-161, con le necessarie precisazioni di Cesarini Martinelli, 'Sozomeno maestro...' (n. 13 sopra), p. 82-83).
[85] Sweeney, *Prolegomena...* (n. 47 sopra), pp. 19-24.

fonte storica che attestava la profonda inimicizia fra Tito e Domiziano, Svetonio, *Tit.* 9. Proprio questa 'intentio' viene infatti
dichiarata nell'*accessus* dell'XI-XII secolo scritto a Schäftlarn (MS
München, Clm 17206), nel quale l'esistenza di una profonda inimicizia fra i due fratelli, provata da numerosi aneddoti, è avallata
adducendo, sia pur in modo impreciso, la testimonianza di alcuni
versi attribuiti a Svetonio.[86] La fonte svetoniana è utilizzata anche
nel nostro *accessus*, da cui, a differenza di quel che fa, come s'è
detto, MS Clm 17206, vengono però ricondotti ai corretti luoghi
di Svetonio i passi citati per documentare le inimicizie di Tito e
Domiziano.

La fonte storica che attestava la profonda inimicizia fra Tito e Do-

Altre informazioni fornite dall'*accessus* 'In principio' appaiono
invece del tutto senza precedenti ed avranno alterno, ma duraturo,
successo: le più significative appaiono essere il nome della madre
di Stazio, Agilina, e la notizia degli studi del poeta a Narbona e
a Bordeaux.

La fonte di queste affermazioni mi è ancora ignota e posso solo
ricordare, con Sabbadini,[87] che Agilina pare corruzione di Acilia,
madre di Lucano; la cui moglie, Polla Argentaria, giunse ad essere
identificata (e vi acconsente persino Poliziano)[88] con la vedova
Claudia, che era stata sposata da Stazio (*Silvae* III, 5 e V, 3).

Una certa confusione fra le donne di famiglia pare dunque
esistesse: ma se su Claudia affiora qualche dissenso in età uma-

---

[86] Ad esempio, commentando l'assedio di Vespasiano da parte di Vitellio e la
liberazione ad opera di Domiziano afferma: 'unde in historiis Romanorum quas
fecit Suetonius invenitur "Nec vita dignus nec morte Vitellius ut vir"' (Ausonio,
Monosticha de ordine imperatorum, Peiper 184, 10) e ancora sulla morte di Vespasiano:
'laudatum imperium mors lenis Vespasiani' (Auson., *De obitu singulorum monosticha*,
Peiper 186, 10); più oltre ancora sono citati 'ex versu Suetonii': 'At Titus orbis
amor rapitur florentibus annis' e 'Sera gravem perimunt sed iusta pericula fratrem'
(Auson. *De obitu*, ibid. 11-12). 'Nec vita dignus nec morte Vitellius' (ancora con
la variante 'vita', contro 'regno' dell'edizione Peiper) ricorre anche nel commento del Marc. XII. 61 (4097), del XV secolo, f. n.n., a *Theb.* I, 17. Questo manoscritto, che proviene da S. Giovanni da Verdara, al quale venne donato da Pietro
da Montagnana, contiene un commento parziale alla *Tebaide* che è frutto di un
parco rimaneggiamento umanistico dell'In principio'. Posso aggiungere che la
maggioranza dei luoghi nei quali viene qui segnalata a margine la fonte Lattanzio corrisponde a quelli contenuti nell'In principio', sia in essi esplicitamente
nominato o invece sottaciuto il nome del commentatore tardoantico.

[87] 'Giovanni Colonna biografo e bibliografo del sec. XIV', *Atti della reale Accademia di Torino*, 46, 1910-11, p. 846.

[88] Angelo Poliziano *Miscellaneorum centuria secunda* ed. Branca-Pastore Stocchi,
III, Firenze 1972, cap. 48, pp. 103-08; IV, pp. 86-89 'Uxor Statii', e Angelo Poliziano, *Commento inedito alle Selve di Stazio* a cura di Cesarini Martinelli, Firenze
1978, pp. 5-7.

nistica,[89] l'accordo sembra ben saldo sul nome di Agilina. Infatti, passando attraverso le vite di Stazio scritte da Giovanni Colonna e da Sicco Polenton, il nome della madre verrà recepito anche nelle biografie di Stazio compilate da Pomponio Leto e da Francesco Matarazzi, nelle quali se il poeta sarà restituito, sulla base di *Silvae* III, 5 e V, 3, a Napoli, cancellando definitivamente la nascita tolosana, non verrà sottratto alla madre Agilina.[90] Solo la più asciutta vita di Domizio Calderini[91] e poi quella di Giovanni Britannico non ne faranno menzione: Agilina scomparirà silenziosamente solo dopo la lezione di Poliziano,[92] che non reputerà la notizia degna di discussione o di rettifica, fors'anche perché il suo antagonista, Domizio Calderini, non gli aveva fatto il favore di mostrarsi invischiato in quest'errore.[93]

Ma se un personaggio della statura filologica e fortuna editoriale di Pomponio Leto recepì ancora questo elemento biografico, tanto

---

[89] Ad esempio in Pietro Crinito, *De poetis latinis* IV, 65: 'Uxorem habuit nomine Claudiam, que ingenio magno fuit, minimeque vulgari doctrina, ut Statius alicubi refert. quidam falso existimarunt eandem esse Pollam Argentariam que uxor Annei Lucani fuit' (*Petri Criniti viri eruditissimi de honesta disciplina lib. XXV de poetis latinis lib. V et poematum lib. II cum indicibus suis* in vico sancti Iacobi ab Iohanne Parvo et ipso Ascensio, 1508).

[90] Non tocca il problema V. Zabughin, *Giulio Pomponio Leto: Saggio critico*, Grottaferrata 1909-1910. La vita può leggersi nell'autografo commento alla *Tebaide*, Vat. lat. 3279, ff. 1ʳ-2ʳ: 'Ex Agilina uxore, quam unicam habuit et cuius superstes fuit, P. Papinium Statium suscepit, cuius pueritiam ac iuventutem litteris fovit, copia varietateque rerum refersit et omne eius studium, quoad vixit, iuvit operaque castigavit' (f. 1ᵛ). La vita di Pomponio comparirà in molte edizioni (ad es. per Petrum de Quarengis... Venetiis 1498 [Hain 14980]) e con minime variazioni verrà replicata nella vita che Francesco Matarazzi premette alle sue *Recollecta super Achilleida* (Venetiis per Octavianum Scotum Modoetiensem 1483 [Hain 14976]): 'Ex Agelina uxore quam unicam habuit cuique superstes fuit P. Papinium genuit cuius pueritiam et adolescentiam litteris fovit, copia varietateque rerum refersit et omne eius studium iuvit quoad vixit operaque castigavit'. La notizia, ancora replicando la vita di Pomponio Leto, verrà ripetuta da Lelio Gregorio Giraldi: 'Ex Agelina uxore, quam unicam habuit, et ei superstes fuit, P. Papinium Statium genuit cuius pueritiam ac iuventutem litteris fovit, copia varietateque rerum refersit et omne eius studium quoad vixit polivit operaque castigavit' (*Opera omnia*, Lugduni 1696, pp. 241-43). Accetta la notizia anche la vita premessa al commento all'*Achilleide* consegnato al MS Vat. Ottob. Lat. 1261, XV² (e alla sua copia, MS Vat. Ottob. lat. 2027, XV-XVI, come s'è detto).

[91] La vita di Domizio Calderini è quella premessa alla sua edizione delle *Selve*, dal 1475 (Hain 14976; 14983); quella di Giovanni Britannico (Hain 14989) appare indipendente dalle fonti succitate.

[92] Ad esempio nella vita di Stazio inserita da Pietro Crinito nel suo *De poetis latinis* IV, 65.

[93] Sulle polemiche 'post mortem' di Poliziano con Calderini cf. Cesarini Martinelli, 'In margine al commento di Angelo Poliziano alle *Selve* di Stazio', *Interpres*, 1, 1978, pp. 96-145.

è segno, credo, dell'alta considerazione di cui ancora a fine Quattrocento veniva circondato il commento, pur senza che ne venisse fatta—ovviamente—menzione esplicita.

Quanto alle città che secondo l'In principio' avrebbero dato formazione culturale a Stazio, nulla mi riesce di dire, se non che la rinomanza di entrambe per il livello degli studi era nota ed era stata celebrata, ad esempio, da Ausonio e da Sidonio Apollinare, l'ultimo testimone che dimostra di conoscere le *Silvae*:[94] ma una connessione diretta con Stazio non pare accertabile per questa via.

La notizia degli studi di Stazio a Narbona e a Bordeaux non viene accolta, a dire il vero, nelle vite premesse alle edizioni umanistiche a stampa, ma perdura sin nel Quattrocento, anche sospinta da un'altra significativa *auctoritas*.

L'informazione singolare, consegnata a questa isolata tradizione dell'In principio' e agli *accessus* che ne dipendono,[95] non lasciò insensibile il padre della filologia moderna, Petrarca che, nella *Laurea occidens*, 341-46, collocò Stazio (procedendo da Bordeaux, ove aveva incontrato Ausonio) nell'inclita Narbona, là dove sbocca il lento Aude.

> urbanior inde
> unus, aquis ubi fessus Atax languentibus exit
> occupat eloquio; notus procul ille Larisse,
> notus apud Thebas. Sedenim Tiberina Latine
> docti omnes per rura loqui; tuque, inclita Narbo
> carmina piscoso referens accepta Benaco.[96]

---

[94] *Carmina* 22, ep. 6; 9, 226-229 (Gaii Sollii Apollinaris *Epistulae et Carmina* rec. C. Luetjohann, MGH AA 8, Berolini 1887, pp. 250 e 223).

[95] La prolissità dell'*accessus* induce presto a compendiarlo, come ad esempio nella copia in testo continuo tràdita da Leida B.P.L. 191A.

[96] Come si può constatare Petrarca definisce Stazio attraverso le sue opere, la sua cifra stilistica, l'urbanitas' ('Urbanior inde / unus') e quella della 'imitatio' di Virgilio ('Carmina referens piscoso Benaco'). Sulla definizione di Stazio attraverso l'epiteto 'urbanus' sarà utile osservare anche che nel XII secolo almeno una testimonianza ci consente di affermare che Stazio era divenuto Statius Urbanus (e non più Ursulus o Sursulus): *Vita Meinverci episcopi Paderborniensis*, (MGH SS 11 140, 160). Per l'edizione e commento della X egloga: Francesco Petrarca, *Laurea occidens*. Testo, traduzione e commento a cura di G. Martellotti, Roma 1968 [Note e discussioni erudite 12]: per il passo pp. 35 e 82; cui dovranno aggiungersi Mann, '"O deus, qualis epistola!". A New Petrarch Letter', *Italia medioevale e umanistica*, 17, 1974, pp. 207-43; Martellotti, '*Censura severior*', ibid., pp. 244-47; M. Feo, '*Furius*', ibid., pp. 248-50. Per i commenti di Benvenuto da Imola e di Francesco Piendibeni si dipende ancora da Francesco Petrarca, *Il 'Bucolicum carmen' e i suoi commenti inediti*, a cura di A. Avena, Padova 1906. Segnalo ora D. De Venuto, *Il Bucolicum carmen di Francesco Petrarca. Ed. diplomatica dell'autografo Vat. Lat. 3358*, Pisa 1990.

Forse nel *De remediis* II, 125 Petrarca rimeditò il riferimento preciso a Narbona, sfumandone i contorni in un 'provincia Narbonensi', che Benvenuto da Imola sarà pronto a trasferire nella redazione definitiva del suo commento alla *Commedia*.[97] Certo è che la notizia fece scalpore e fu subito fatta propria da un buon numero di fedeli di Petrarca, da quelli noti, come Francesco da Fiano,[98] ad altri ancora anonimi, che sulla fine del XIV secolo e nel XV inserirono la notizia della nuova patria di Stazio nelle titolazioni o negli explicit dei loro manoscritti del poeta latino, seppur sempre solo accostandola all'altra di più consolidata tradizione.[99]

Se in quest'ultimo caso è la fede in Petrarca a garantire la sopravvivenza di una notizia che proviene dal nostro commento, almeno due altri autori del XIV e XV secolo dimostrano invece di accogliere la tradizione 'In principio' per via diretta: Sicco Polenton nei suoi *Scriptorum illustrium libri*[100] tramanda, nella vita di Stazio, la serie delle informazioni che caratterizzano il commento—nome della madre, studi a Narbona e a Bordeaux e inizio della *Tebaide* vivente Tito—e Giovanni Colonna, nel *De viris illustribus*,[101] ci consente addirittura di formulare qualche più puntuale ipotesi. Questi infatti non solo attesta il nome della madre e la notizia, peraltro al suo tempo vulgata, dell'intenzione dissuasoria di Stazio nei confronti degli imperiali fratelli, ma presenta almeno un errore congiuntivo con il testo del commento 'In principio'. Infatti la stranezza, segnalata da Sabbadini,[102] che si legge nel *De viris* del Colonna—'Titus Domicianum expellere et patri flagitabat succedere'— si spiega se leggiamo la non chiarissima formulazione dell'*accessus*, per lo meno nei testimoni MSS Add. 16380, f. 144[ra-b] (L), Ricc.

---

[97] de Angelis, 'Benvenuto e Stazio...' (n. 69 sopra), p. 163.

[98] I. Tau, 'Il *Contra oblocutores poetarum* di Francesco da Fiano', *Archivio italiano per la storia della Pietà*, 4, 1965, pp. 254-350: 317: 'Qui Statius natione Tolosanus, quem aliqui Narbonensem dicunt?...' (citato per la prima volta da Sabbadini, *Le scoperte dei codici latini e greci ne' secoli XIV e XV*, II, Firenze 1914, p. 268): l'opera fu stesa nel 1400.

[99] Ad esempio: MSS Vat. Pal. lat. 1693, XV sec.; London, B. L., Harl. 3754, XV sec.; Firenze, Laur. 18 sin. 4, scritto da Tedaldo della Casa; Vat. Reg. lat. 1375, XV sec.; Roma, Vallic., B 30, XIV²; Firenze, B. N., II. II. 55, XIV italiano; Vat., Archivio S. Pietro, H 15, datato 1342 (ma la notizia è nell'*accessus* mutilo premesso al testo, e quindi potrebbe essere di qualche anno posteriore).

[100] Ed. B. L. Ullman, Romae 1958, pp. 120-21.

[101] Sabbadini, *Giovanni Colonna* ..., p. 846. Nulla aggiunge a quanto noto G. Brugnoli, 'Statius christianus', *Italianistica*, 17 (1988), pp. 9-15: importa solo rettificare qualche lettura: Agilina, hostiliter, similiter e due errori non segnalati: qua MS, (qui), cavens MS, (canens).

[102] Sabbadini, 'Giovanni Colonna biografo...' (n. 87 sopra), p. 846.

842, f. 88ra-b (R), Paris 5137, f. 105ra, (P), tutti, parrebbe, acco-
munati da un 'saut de même au même'.

Questo doveva probabilmente essere il testo originario:

> Verum qui hoc dicunt ex Suetonio habere videntur, qui in libro de
> XII Cesaribus inter cetera de Tito et Domiciano agit, et dicit de
> Tito Domicianum fratrem suum vite sue insidiari nolentem desistere,
> exercitum adversum se excitantem, noluisse tamen cum posset occi-
> dere, nec seponere, nec in minori honore quam cepisset habere, sepe
> autem rogare, ut mutua apud se dilectione teneretur seque suum fore
> successorem in regno promittere
>
> --------
>
> qui vero P videntur habere LPR de Tito inter cetera P et Domi-
> ciano agit et *om.* PRL de Tito² *om.* PRL Domicianum *om.* P fratrem
> suum Domicianum RL insidiari vite sue RL desistere (desitere P)
> nolentem RLP sepe etiam *add.* P suscitantem R sollicitantem P tamen
> noluisse L voluisse P cum]co–L eum post se R neque...neque PRL
> apud se mutua R se *om.* L secum teneretur dilectione P mutua dilec-
> tione L dellectacione R fore *om.* L successorem suum L eumque fore
> successorem suum P

che, dopo l'omissione di testo registrata in apparato, presenta un
aspetto tale da giustificare il fraintendimento:

> ... qui in libro de XII Cesaribus, inter cetera, de Tito dicit fratrem
> suum (Domicianum) insidiari vite sue desistere nolentem ... voluisse
> tamen ... occidere ....

Inoltre potrebbe suffragare l'ipotesi di dipendenza diretta di Giovanni dall''In principio' anche la presenza della serie completa dei
titoli di lode attribuiti a Stazio, tràdita solo in questo commento[103]
e replicata, soltanto con qualche slittamento, da Giovanni Colonna:

> *In principio*
> Fuit igitur morum honestate preditus, acris intelligentie, tenacis me-
> morie, clarus ingenio, doctus eloquio, liberalium artium feliciter eru-
> ditus. Fuit etiam nimie facundie.
> *De viris.*
> morum honestate preditus, pollens ingenio, clarus eloquio, felicis intel-
> ligencie, tenacis memorie ac liberalibus eruditus artibus...

Infine, come già ho accennato, la conoscenza del nostro commento
'In principio' è documentabile anche per il Boccaccio.

---

[103] Diversa e molto più ridotta la serie-base originata dalla vita 'Queritur':
'Fuit enim nobili ortus prosapia, clarus ingenio et doctus eloquio'.

L'autore

Una così riconosciuta e vasta influenza di un commento invita a tentare di contornare, per quanto possibile, il suo autore. L'impresa si presenta difficile, per non dire disperata, perché nei materiali erratici che affiorano nel commento è spesso illusorio filo di Arianna una glossa, anche inconsueta, che lo colleghi a testi o ad autori coevi, e persino la dichiarazione di alcune posizioni filosofico-teologiche, che sono spesso ampiamente condivise e sovente riecheggiate in collezioni di anonime *sententie*, talvolta molto distanti dalla loro fonte originaria. Inoltre le acquisizioni dei molteplici studi sulle scuole filosofiche e teologiche del secolo difficilmente riescono utili nella valutazione di quei minimi lacerti ai quali sono ridotte, entro un commento a un'opera classica epica, proposizioni che parrebbero autorizzare all'individuazione di scuole: tali frammenti, nei casi più fortunati, riescono solo a serbare uno scialbo riverbero e un'ambigua traccia della formulazione originaria.[104]

Il pullulare di maestri, spesso fratelli, troppo spesso omonimi e gravitanti in aree prossime (Chartres, Laon e Parigi) e la citazione di loro *auctoritates* da parte dei più distanti epigoni delle loro scuole complica ancor più, se possibile, il problema dell'attribuzione di un commento.

Sarò dunque paga di illustrare quanto mi pare possa sinora estrarsi dal testo: e proporrò appena qualche cauta ipotesi, suggerita da singolari coincidenze.

Potremo iniziare dalla 'pars destruens', escludendo che il nostro testo debba ascriversi a qualcuno dei personaggi meglio noti: e ci serviremo di una glossa che presenta caratteristiche di qualche rilevanza.

Infatti, entro un commento platonizzante che potrebbe anche definirsi chartriano,[105] nel quale si fa ampio uso, dichiarato o

---

[104] Coglie bene i problemi connessi all'individuazione di rapporti di dipendenza fra testi mediolatini legati alla *lectura* scolastica A. de Libera, 'De la lecture...' (n. 42 sopra), pp. 17-29; cf. anche E. Filhol, 'Les limites de la liberté interprétative dans la *lectura* médiévale: le cas d'Abélard', *Neophilologus* 74, 1990, pp. 481-87; C. Mews, 'Orality, Literacy and Authority in the Twelfth-Century Schools', *Exemplaria*, 2, 1990, pp. 475-500, con ulteriore bibliografia.

[105] Si veda soprattutto per il dibattito intorno alle posizioni dell'ancor fondamentale A. Clerval, *Les écoles de Chartres au moyen âge*, Paris 1895: R. W. Southern, 'Humanism and the School of Chartres', in *Medieval Humanism and Other Studies*, Oxford 1970, pp. 61-85; Häring, 'Chartres and Paris revisited', in *Essays in Honour of Anton Charles Pegis*, ed. J. R. O' Donnell, Toronto 1974, pp. 268-329;

sottaciuto, di Macrobio, soprattutto nelle glosse di tema astrologico e astronomico, e si mostra interesse ai più consueti temi platonici (l'interpretazione dell''anima mundi', la spiegazione platonizzante della pluralità degli dèi come espressione delle diverse proprietà dell'unico dio),[106] ma pochissimo si ricorre all'allegoria e mai si invoca l'*integumentum* o *involucrum*, leggiamo una glossa evidentemente dipendente dal commento di Calcidio al *Timeo*,[107] alla quale si cumula però l'originale notizia che Demogorgon è identificabile con l'*anima mundi*.

> Demogorgontem significat, quem dicebant poete cuncta creasse, cuius nomen nullus audebat proferre et illum solum dicebant regnare super alios deos. Ideo dicit 'quem sciri nefandum est' quia sic tacebant nomen eius quasi nescirent. Philosophi vero ad philosophiam transtulerunt, et per hoc mundanam animam voluerunt intelligi, que vegetat omnia et preposita est omnibus naturis, de cuius semine firmamentum, solem, lunam et ceteras stellas natas esse dicebant: nam in his precipue potestas eius innuitur. Poete vero, causa sui, volentes deum venerari, de qualibet sui natura membratim sibi effigiaverunt quasdam personas de naturis rerum, ut Bachum de pulcris digitis

---

Châtillon, 'Les écoles de Chartres et de Saint-Victor' in *La scuola nell'Occidente latino dell'alto medioevo*, Spoleto 1972, pp. 795-839; Dronke, 'New Approaches to the School of Chartres', in *Intellectuals and Poets in Medieval Europe*, Roma 1992, pp. 15-38. Per Laon: V. I. J. Flint, 'The "School of Laon": a Reconsideration', *Recherches de théologie ancienne et médiévale*, 43, 1976, pp. 89-110 e M. L. Colish, 'Another Look at the School of Laon' (n. 26 sopra), pp. 7-22; Châtillon, 'Abélard et les écoles...' (n. 26 sopra), pp. 133-60; S. Martinet, *Montloon reflet fidèle de la montagne et des environs de Laon de 1100 à 1300*, Laon 1972, pp. 95-111; e 'L'école de Laon au XIIe siècle: Anselme de Laon et Abélard', *Memoires de la Fédération des sociétés d'histoire et d'archéologie de l'Aisne*, 26, 1981, pp. 57-63; B. Merlette, 'Ecoles et bibliothèques à Laon, du déclin de l'Antiquité au développement de l'Université' in *Enseignement et vie intellectuelle (IX-XVI siècle)*, I, Paris 1975, pp. 21-53.

[106] Su questi dibattiti cf. T. Gregory, *Anima mundi*, Firenze 1955; e ora *Mundana sapientia*, Roma 1992.

[107] *Timaeus a Calcidio translatus commentarioque instructus* ed. J. H. Waszink, Londinii-Leidae 1962, 128 p. 171: 'At vero in eo libro qui Philosophus inscribitur summa diligentia precipuaque cura omnes exequitur huius modi questiones: priscorum hominum genus omnia quae ad usum hominum vitaeque agendae facultatem divino consilio providentiaque demanant auxiliantibus atque operantibus tam potentiis quam rationibus, haec ipsa quae auxiliantur deos existimasse, propterea quod rudibus animis nondum insedisset veri dei sciscitatio. Erant enim pastores et silvicaedi ceterique huius modi sine studiis humanitatis, quos cladis publicae superstites fecerat opportuna habitatio ex tempestatum atque illuvionis incommodo. Quae poetae postea blandientes humanis passionibus propter cupiditatem lucri versibus suis formata membratimque effigiata amplis et reconditis nominibus exornaverunt usque adeo ut etiam vitiosas hominum illecebras turpissimosque actus deos cognominarent obnoxios passioni. Itaque factum ut pro gratia, quae ab hominibus debetur divinae providentiae, origo et ortus sacrilegio panderetur; cuius erroris opinio crevit inconsultorum hominum vanitate'.

laudabant propter palmites, virginea facie quia iuvenes ebriosi et etiam senes sibi videntur esse formosi; flavam dixerunt Cererem propter
aristas. Vel, ut melius dicamus, poete, licet diversos deos esse dixerunt,
sciebant tantum unum esse deum cuius potentia preerat ceteris, unde
Ovidius 'sic ubi dispositam, quisquis fuit ille deorum, congeriem secuit
sectamque in membra redegit' (*Met.* I, 32-33) et cetera. Divinitas
namque incomprehensibilis est iuxta illud: 'Accedit homo ad cor
altum et exaltabitur deus' (*Psalm.* LXIII, 8, 1).[108]

Mi si consenta di sottolineare cursoriamente qui, in attesa di quanto dirò altrove sui rapporti di Boccaccio con questo testo, la straordinaria coincidenza di questa affermazione con quanto egli scrive
nella sua difesa della poesia, *anima mundi*, come il Demogorgon:

> Multos autem deos scripsisse poetas, cum unum tantum sit deus,
> negari non potest ... eruditos viros (*philosophos*) ... absque ambiguitate
> novisse unum tantum deum esse, ad quam notitiam devenisse poe-
> tas eorum in operibus percipitur liquido ... Reliquam autem deorum
> multitudinem non deos, sed d e i m e m b r a aut divinitatis officia
> putavere ... (*Gen.* XIV, 13).

Ma limitiamoci per ora a confrontare questa glossa con quelle
analoghe di Guglielmo di Conches e di Bernardo di Chartres nei
rispettivi commenti al *Timeo*.
Ecco quanto dice in proposito Guglielmo di Conches:[109]

> ...quid sit credendum...de aliis deis. Ad cuius rei intelligentiam predi-
> camus quod primi philosophi, considerantes quod sine timore pote-
> statis homines a criminibus retineri non possent, nec iterum timore
> equalis, maiorem substantiam docuerunt quam divinam vocaverunt.
> Sed quia viderunt quod rudes homines veram divinitatem cognoscere
> non possent, nec intelligere quomodo unus deus omnia posset, plures
> finxerunt. Unde Statius 'Primus in orbe deos fecit timor'. Et voca-
> verunt planetas deos, quatuor elementa, proprietates eorum, ut natu-
> ralem potentiam terre producendi germina Cererem, producendi
> vinum Bachum. Sed ne viles essent, nominibus et figuris veritatem
> tegebant. Deinde poetae, ut placerent populo, res turpes vocaverunt
> deos ut Priapum, Venerem. Dicit ergo Plato sic esse credendum ut
> primi philosophi docuerunt, non ut poete: illud enim honestum est
> et utile, istud inhonestum et turpe.

Infine, Bernardo di Chartres:[110]

---

[108] A *Theb.* V, 513. Riporto il testo da London, B. L. Add. 16380, f. 164va,
perché il berlinese ha una lacuna fra *Theb.* IV, 191 e VIII, 358.
[109] Guillaume de Conches, *Glosae super Platonem* ed. Jeauneau, Paris 1965, pp.
201-02.
[110] Dutton, *The Glosae super Platonem...* (n. 42 sopra), pp. 192-93; 194. Segnalo che questa interpretazione è identica a quella proposta dal *Myth. Vat. Lat.* III.
5. 2.

... Philosophus docet unde orta sit haec superstitio, ut qui non essent dii pro diis haberentur. Ibi enim dicit quod priscorum genus hominum, silvicolae et pastores, rationes et potentias a deo hominibus ad usum vivendi datas, ut agriculturam et similia, pro diis colebant. Deinde poetae, pro lucro et favore, membratim effigiaverunt et propriis nominibus assignaverunt, scientiam colendi agros vocantes Cererem, scientiam colendi vineam Bacchum, turpes etiam actus hominum deos appellantes, ut luxuriam Venerem et ita loco religionis nata est superstitio; ... mundo pereunte diluvio, sapientes et eorum libri destructi sunt, solis pastoribus remanentibus in montanis, et sic unius dei noticia periit. Poetae vero, inducti blanditiis fabularum, figmenta locuti sunt.

Mi pare interessante rilevare, pur nel comune accostamento dei filosofi ai poeti, come traduttori dell'ineffabile e incomprensibile divinità unica in una pluralità di divinità adorabili, il ruolo diverso applicato agli uni e agli altri nei tre testi proposti.

Guglielmo attribuisce ai filosofi, a ciò mossi dalle necessità del vivere sociale, l'invenzione della divinità che si manifesta nell'universo, negli elementi e nelle potenze della natura fisica, mentre lascia ai poeti la responsabilità di avere assecondato gli istinti della più umana fisicità, alla quale furono dati nomi di divinità al mero fine di conquistare il favore del pubblico.

Bernardo, più aderente alla spiegazione di Calcidio, esclude invece senz'altro la necessità del divino per il vivere civile e ritiene che l'attività dei poeti si sia limitata a registrare e nobilitare letterariamente un dato di fatto, i culti animistici degli uomini primitivi. Collocando poi il diluvio in epoca successiva a questa operazione ed ascrivendo al cataclisma la totale perdita della cultura superiore, quella dei *sapientes* che conoscevano l'unicità del dio, Bernardo spiega il permanere della credenza nei molti dèi come una vittoria della cultura dei 'silvicolae' e 'montani'.

Profondamente diversa è invece la posizione del nostro commentatore che dà un'assoluta preminenza ai poeti. É il Demogorgon, che i poeti affermano creatore del cosmo e signore di tutti gli dèi, ad essere spiegato filosoficamente come *anima mundi*, e su questa astrazione filosofica intervengono ancora i poeti trasformandola in una pluralità di dèi: 'causa sui' certo, anche in questo caso, ma sulla spinta di un anelito religioso—'volentes deum venerari'—; e ancora al commentatore preme di spiegare meglio: i poeti, nonostante mostrino di credere a una pluralità di dèi, sanno bene che uno solo è Dio, come dimostrano, concludendo, i due luoghi allegati a pari titolo: Ovidio *Metamorfosi* I, 32-33 e *Salmi* LXIII, 8, 1, nell'ordine.

Parrebbe dunque, seguendo l'"In principio', che l'ineffabilità e incomprensibilità di Dio abbia forzato la poesia a trovare degli artifici o degli espedienti perché essa potesse cantare di Dio. La poesia quindi adotta procedimenti affini a quelli della teologia: proprio come aveva affermato Giovanni Scoto.[111]

Avremmo dunque nel nostro commento un precedente non trascurabile delle argomentazioni in difesa della poesia, della quale verrebbe sin da allora riconosciuto il valore teologico: ben prima dunque delle discussioni che tanta parte avranno nel Trecento, da Albertino Mussato e Petrarca sino all'articolato dibattito di Boccaccio nei libri XIV e XV delle *Genealogie*.

Troviamo dunque nell'"In principio', pur entro l'impostazione platonizzante e pure su temi comuni discussi dai maestri con l'appoggio delle medesime fonti, qualcosa che innova, che non riesce in tutto riconducibile a quanto conosciamo e che consente di escludere diretti rapporti con Guglielmo di Conches e con Bernardo di Chartres.

Come ulteriore argomento, sebbene in negativo, a conforto di quanto affermato potrà inoltre osservarsi che dall'"In principio' pare estraneo ogni interesse scientifico: interessi che, come noto, caratterizzano l'opera di Guglielmo di Conches e in genere la scuola di Chartres.

Ancora, sempre in negativo, posso affermare che non si rinvengono contatti significativi con i commenti attribuiti a Bernardo Silvestre (a Virgilio e a Marziano Capella): le sporadiche coincidenze di informazioni si riscontrano su notizie di ampia circolazione. Come presto vedremo, anche l'utilizzo, entro l'esegesi ad autori classici, di *auctoritates* bibliche nei commenti di Bernardo e nell' 'In

---

[111] *Iohannis Scoti Eriugenae Expositiones...*, II, 142-51: per il testo cf. n. 23 sopra. Per l'interpretazione di 'poetria' come personificazione della teologia, 'poetessa', cf. Dronke, '"Theologia veluti quaedam poetria". Quelques observations sur la fonction des images poétiques chez Jean Scot' in *Jean Scot Erigène et l'histoire de la philosophie*, cur. R. Roques, Paris 1977, pp. 243-52, ora in *The Medieval Poet and His World*, Roma 1984, pp. 39-53. Echi di posizioni di Giovanni Scoto serpeggiano in tutto il XII secolo, epoca nella quale si sviluppano, sino a maturo compimento, le premesse da lui formulate (Gregory, *Giovanni Scoto Eriugena. Tre studi*, Firenze 1963, p. 76). Non dovrà trascurarsi inoltre che l'"In principio' riflette l'insegnamento di un maestro, Anselmo di Laon, che aveva accesso alla stessa biblioteca nella quale aveva lavorato Giovanni: cf. Jean Scot, *Commentaire sur l'Evangile de Jean...* (n. 42 sopra), pp. 57-62; Smalley, 'Some Gospel Commentaries of the Early Twelfth Century', *Recherches de théologie ancienne et médiévale*, 45, 1978, p. 150.

principio' presenta caratteristiche che nettamente distinguono i loro autori.

Occorre allora verificare se le singolarità presentate dal commento possano indirizzare ad un'ipotesi di attribuzione o, almeno, di localizzazione.

Nella discussione, canonica entro l'*accessus*, 'cui parti philosophie' la *Tebaide* 'supponatur', la soluzione offerta dall''In principio' presuppone, secondo le consuetudini dell'epoca, una divisione della filosofia pratica in filosofia etica, economica e politica—ma con la variante dell'essere la filosofia etica a bipartirsi in filosofia economica e politica:

> Ethice supponitur per politicam, quia nobis morum informat doctrinam. Ethice autem sunt due partes: echonomica, qua proprie dispensamus familie—echonomus enim dispensator interpretatur—; politica vero est sciencia que ad regimen civitatis est necessaria: polis enim civitas dicitur.

Non risulta altrove attestata una partizione di questo tipo, ed è altrettanto inconsueto che la *Tebaide* venga inscritta entro la filosofia politica:[112] l'informazione infatti circolerà solo nei manoscritti che attingono alla tradizione di questo commento.[113] La bipartizione della filosofia etica non può tuttavia giudicarsi un mero errore perché riusciamo a trovare, almeno nella tradizione iconografica relativa alla divisione della filosofia e delle *artes*, una replica di questa informazione nel MS Admont, Stiftsbibliothek 73 (128), del XIII secolo.[114] Se siano postulabili precisi rapporti o se

---

[112] Voglio solo segnalare che un grosso rilievo alla filosofia politica, entro la consueta partizione triplice della filosofia pratica, verrà assegnato da Domenico Gundissalvi: cf. A. Levi, 'La partizione della filosofia pratica in un trattato medievale', *Atti dell'Istituto veneto di scienze lettere et arti*, 67, 1907-08, pp. 1225-50, e, per un'ampia rassegna delle partizioni nelle diverse scuole: G. Dahan, 'Une introduction a la philosophie au XII⁰ siècle. Le *Tractatus quidam de philosophia et partibus eius*', *Archives d'histoire doctrinale et littéraire du moyen âge*, 49, 1982, pp. 155-93. Cf. anche P. Delhaye, 'L'enseignement de la philosophie morale au XII⁰ siècle', *Medieval Studies*, 11, 1949, pp. 77-99; id., 'La place de l'éthique parmi les discipline scientifiques au XII⁰ siècle', in *Miscellanea moralia in honorem eximii domini A. Janssen*, Louvain 1947, pp. 29-44; *Enseignement et morale au XIIe siècle*, Fribourg-Paris 1988.

[113] Certo non riesce a non associarsi a questa affermazione la considerazione che proprio in questi anni verrà composto sulla materia tebana il *Roman de Thèbes*, opera che non pare inverosimile ritenere abbia trovato *humus* propizia in un contesto politico caratterizzato da conflitti familiari e da incesti: cf. Clogan, 'New Directions...' (n. 11 sopra), pp. 55-70.

[114] K. A. Wirth, 'Von mittelalterliche Bildern und Lehrfiguren im Dienste der Schule und des Unterrichts', in *Studien zum städtischen Bildungswesen des späten Mittel-*

la coincidenza sia poligenetica non sono in grado di dire.

Il poco sin qui emerso e descritto, che delinea un commento di ispirazione platonica (anche se con qualche autonomia), può completarsi evidenziando altre sue caratteristiche, che sarà sufficiente per ora solo segnalare.

Anselmo di Laon e Abelardo

Nell'*accessus* la proposizione di due problemi relativi alla *Tebaide* (se cioè con Stazio si fossero chiuse le *recitationes* pubbliche e le ragioni dei modi in cui si esprime il titolo) viene fatta in forma 'dialettica':

> Nemo enim Rome post eum declamavit. Sed opponitur: quia Iuvenalis et multi actores alii post eum fuerunt, ergo post eum multi declamaverunt. Non sequitur. Satyra enim non solebat declamari ...
>
> queritur quare tot nomina in titulis apponantur. responde: ut per ea, actore commendato, opus autenticum reddatur.[115]

L'introduzione di un problema attraverso una *quaestio*, e la formulazione degli argomenti in contrario con 'opponitur', 'non sequitur' divengono di uso corrente, come noto, solo con Abelardo, anche se qualche traccia di *quaestiones* si può reperire già in Anselmo.[116]

Infine si dovrà ancora una volta ricordare che non è infrequente l'impiego, a commento di un passo di Stazio, di luoghi biblici o patristici. La consuetudine che affiora qua e là anche nel commento a Marziano Capella attribuito a Bernardo Silvestre e, ancora più raramente, in quello ai primi sei libri dell'*Eneide*, nelle glosse al *Timeo* di Guglielmo di Conches e nei commenti a Boezio di Gilberto di Poitiers, ma non nelle glosse di Bernardo di Chartres a Platone o di Thierry di Chartres alla *Rhetorica ad Herennium* e a Cicerone *De inventione*, nè nelle glosse a Giovenale di Guglielmo di Conches, mi pare che nel commento 'In principio' assuma caratteristiche che consentono di distinguerlo nettamente dagli altri.

---

alters und der frühen Neuzeit, hrsg. B. Möller, H. Patze, K. Stackmann, Göttingen 1983, pp. 255-370: 330 n. 210.

[115] Un altro caso si presenta nel corpo del commento: a *Theb.* VIII, 334-427, 5 *et equos corpusque novum* leggiamo: 'idest insolitum quantum ad illos quia neque sepultus neque combustus erat. Sed opponitur de Hercule et Theseo et Perithoo qui et vivi et ante eum descenderunt. Responde: non venerunt armati sicut iste et ideo dixit novum' (Ricc. 842, f. 81ra).

[116] Cf. n. 43.

Mentre infatti in tutti i commenti appena ricordati la citazione biblica viene inserita nel testo con il valore preciso di un'*auctoritas* che conferma il testo classico o le asserzioni dell'esegeta, oppure come suggello di proverbiale sapienza, nel commento 'In principio' essa interviene prevalentemente come esempio di perfetta coincidenza, a livello retorico, grammaticale, sintattico, con l'uso linguistico e stilistico dell'autore classico nel passo commentato. Propongo un primo esempio (f. 49vb):

> Virg. *Aen.* II, 685 *trepidare metu* idest festinare. Nam quotiens due partes idem significantes ponuntur, alteram oportet evocari a sua propria significatione, sicut ibi 'preliare prelia domini dei tui', idest evince; sicut dominus dixit ad sanctum Dyonisium 'preliare prelia', similiter et hic 'trepidare metu', idest festinabant;

ed un secondo dove l'analogia è stabilita con un luogo patristico: a *Theb.* I, 227 (f. 88vb):

> *Imposta* improba, perversa, omni malo plena. Iheronimus: impono, -nis, -sui, -nere, inpostum, inpostu est decipio, -pis, et construitur cum dativo; unde illud (Iuv. IV, 103): 'facile est barbato imponere regi', idest regem barbatum decipere; inde inpostus et inpostor et inpostorius, idest deceptorius.

Giunge spontaneo osservare, a questo punto, che Abelardo presenta la medesima impostazione di lettura, in questo caso perfettamente simmetrica a quanto sopra abbiamo letto, nell'esegesi *in Epistolam Pauli ad Romanos* IV, 9 quando adduce un parallelo virgiliano della costruzione adottata nel passo del *Nuovo Testamento*:

> *Quos et vocavit.* Iuxta rei significationem, non premissi nominis proprietatem, relativum nomen subponit, dicens 'quos', masculino genere, non 'quae' neutro, cum tamen premissum nomen, quod est 'vasa', ad quod relatio fit, neutri sit generis. Talis est et apud Vergilium mutatio generis secundum significationem, cum dicitur 'Preneste sub ipsa'.[117]

E Abelardo, il primo ad inserire in commenti biblici citazioni dai classici, aveva frequentato, come si sa, la scuola di Anselmo di Laon, e forse con maggior frutto di quanto egli voglia lasciar credere. La sua solitaria voce dissonante nel coro di lodi tributate al maestro, vanto della scuola teologica del XII secolo, probabilmente trova giustificazione, come s'è visto, proprio nell'opposizione di metodo fra due grandi maestri, fors'anche in conflitto gene-

---

[117] *Commentaria in epistolam Pauli ad Romanos*, in *Petri Abaelardi Opera Theologica*, I, ed. Buytaert, Turnholti 1969, pp. 243-44.

razionale,[118] più che in una generica disistima del venerato maestro.

Per altra via da vari testimoni del XII secolo sono dichiarati gli interessi grammaticali di Anselmo di Laon : sue opinioni su questioni grammaticali sono citate nelle *Glosule super Priscianum* e nelle *Note Dunelmenses*;[119] e sulla base della testimonianza di Pietro Elia possiamo dedurre che le sue attenzioni si fossero appuntate proprio su problemi presentati dal testo scritturale.[120] Una qualche conferma a questo specifico interesse di Anselmo potrebbe venire anche dall'epitafio che gli dedica Marbodo di Rennes: 'artis gramatice penitus periere labores, rhetoricus color emarcet, causeque Catonis ...'. [121]

Ed allineo qui anche quanto già detto in apertura, che cioè chi

---

[118] Ben note sono le lodi quasi iperboliche tributate ad Anselmo, tra gli altri, da Ottone di Freising (Ottonis episcopi Frisingensis *Chronica* ed. A. Hofmeister, Hannoverae 1912, p. 227) e da Giovanni di Salisbury, *Metalogicon* I, 5, p. 21). Per una rassegna dei luoghi dedicati alla celebrazione di Anselmo dai suoi allievi: J. de Ghellinck, *Le mouvement théologique du XIIᵉ siècle*, Bruges 1948, pp. 133-34 e Châtillon, 'Abélard et les écoles...' (n. 25 sopra), pp. 146-48, oltre a Luscombe, *The School of Peter Abelard...* (n. 43 sopra), pp. 173-81. Dal coro di lodi si stacca, come noto, Abelardo nell'*Historia calamitatum* (ed. J. Monfrin, Paris 1950, p. 68), che concluderà il suo ritratto del celebre maestro con l'immagine della quercia lucanea alla quale Pompeo viene paragonato ('stat magni nominis umbra/ qualis frugifero quercus sublimis in agro': *Bellum civile* I, 135-36): metafora che subito Giovanni di Salisbury replicherà applicandola al suo maestro Roberto di Melun (cf. *Epist.* 175: *The Letters of John of Salisbury*, ed. W. J. Miller-C. N. L. Brooke, II, Oxford 1979, p. 156). Sui rapporti fra Abelardo e Anselmo e le ragioni dell'animosità dell'allievo cf. Bertola, 'Le critiche di Abelardo... n. 42 sopra), pp. 495-220; Colish, 'Another Look...' (n. 26 sopra), pp. 7-22; Châtillon, 'Abélard et les écoles...' (n. 26 sopra), pp. 149-50; cf. anche Martinet, 'L'école de Laon...' (n. 105 sopra), pp. 57-63. La considerazione nella quale era tenuto Anselmo appare anche dalla frequenza con la quale lo vediamo citato nei testi più diversi: in trattati grammaticali (cf. R. W. Hunt, 'Studies on Priscian...' (n. 42 sopra), 13, pp. 16-17 e *Summa super Priscianum* di Pietro Elia, 501, 65-74), nelle glosse al *De inventione* (C. Dickey, 'Some Commentaries on the *De Inventione* and *Ad Herennium* of the Eleventh and Early Twelfth Centuries', *Mediaeval Studies*, 6, 1968, pp. 1-40 e Fredborg, 'The Commentaries on Cicero's *De inventione* and *Rhetorica ad Herennium* by William of Champeaux', *Cahiers de l'Institut du moyen âge grec et latin*, 17, 1976, pp. 1-37), nel commento a Lucano di Arnolfo d'Orléans, come s'è visto (n. 58).

[119] R. W. Hunt, 'Studies on Priscian...' (n. 42 sopra), pp. 16 e 17.

[120] Petrus Helias, *Summa super Priscianum*, ed. L. Reilly, I, Toronto 1993, 501, 68-71: '...sin autem dicatur "in convertendo Dominum captivitatem Sion", ut magister Anselmus voluit, videbitur quod "Dominum" habeat significare rem ut pacientem, cum tamen Domini sit convertere, non converti'. Frequenti opinioni di Anselmo sono citate anche nei commenti retorici studiati da Dickey, 'Some Commentaries...' (n. 118 sopra), pp. 1-40.

[121] *PL* 171, 1722.

compone il commento 'In principio' conserva il ricordo diretto di una opinione di Anselmo a commento di *Aen.* II, 1[122]: 'Conticuere. Hic respirat auctor: hoc dicebat magister Ansellus'[123]. La glossa appare dunque la registrazione dell'insegnamento del maestro fatta da un discepolo che, prima del 1117, ne aveva frequentato le lezioni: dunque, l'attività di Anselmo di Laon si era esercitata anche nell'esegesi agli *auctores*. Ed abbiamo visto che nelle opere di esegesi biblica del suo illustre allievo Abelardo affiorano tracce di un tipo di interesse grammaticale che ritroviamo nel commentatore dell''In principio'—opera di un allievo di Anselmo—che, a sua volta, come dichiarano le testimonianze coeve, a tali interessi non era affatto estraneo.

Un altro fatto contribuisce tuttavia a far supporre un rapporto privilegiato fra il commentatore dell''In principio' e Abelardo.

Nel commento troviamo la prima e originaria formulazione di una glossa che è poi citata da ampia parte della tradizione esegetica alla *Tebaide*, e che da quest'opera migrerà anche, parzialmente, in quella di Lucano e in alcuni commenti alle *Metamorfosi*,[124] penetrando poi nei volgarizzamenti della *Tebaide* e nei commenti della *Commedia*:[125] glossa già edita e caricata del compito troppo oneroso di giustificare l'interpretazione cristiana di Stazio,[126] accolta da Dante nella *Commedia*.

---

[122] Rose, *Verzeichniss...* (n. 53 sopra), 1305; Bischoff, 'Living with the Satirists...' (n. 58 sopra); Manitius, *Geschichte...* (n. 58 sopra), III, p. 238 e nota 53.

[123] L'uso della forma verbale all'imperfetto non giustificherebbe per sè l'affermazione che si tratti di un ricordo diretto: dovrà però considerarsi che la frase non è inserita in un contesto nel quale venga riportato quanto altri ricordavano, come osserva Dutton ('The Uncovering of the *Glosae super Platonem* of Bernard of Chartres', *Mediaeval Studies*, 46, 1984, pp. 192-221: 194-95) a proposito delle espressioni 'Bernardus aiebat, dicebat Bernardus...' utilizzate da Giovanni di Salisbury, che pur non lo aveva udito direttamente. Sul valore tecnico di 'respiro' cf. *Mathei Vindocinensis Opera omnia*, ed. F. Munari, II, Roma 1982, p. 75 e A. Pannenborg, 'Über den Ligurinus', *Forschungen zur deutschen Geschichte*, 11, 1871, pp. 161-300 (204).

[124] Si veda ad esempio la glossa a *Met.* I, 32 riportata da F. T. Coulson, *The Vulgate Commentary on Ovid's Metamorphoses. The Creation Myth and the Story of Orpheus*, Toronto 1991, pp. 53-55.

[125] Filippo Villani, *Expositio seu comentum super 'Comedia'...* (n. 66 sopra), p. 89.

[126] C. Landi, 'Di un commento medievale inedito della *Tebaide* di Stazio', *Atti e memorie dell'Accademia di scienze e lettere in Padova*, 30, 1914, pp. 315-44: la glossa viene edita dal MS Padova, Seminario 41, XIV italiano, che posso ora affermare dipendente per ampia parte dal commento 'In principio'; G. Padoan, 'Teseo *figura redemptoris* e il cristianesimo di Stazio', *Lettere italiane*, 11, 1959, pp. 432-57, poi

Il commento del verso *Theb.* XII, 497 instaura una identità fra l'ara 'in qua mitis posuit Clementia sedem'—alla quale fa riferimento Stazio in *Theb.* XII, 481-511—e l'ara dell'Areopago presso la quale Paolo predicò, convertendo Dionigi l'Areopagita. Questo il testo della glossa:

> *fama est*: determinat qui fuerunt illius templi positores. Hylus, Deianire et Herculis filius, et reliqui ex eodem nati, postquam Hercules interiit pulsi ab Ericteo, Athenas confugerunt, a quibus facile impetrantes auxilium, hanc aram consecraverunt asserentes apud Athenas tantum misericordiam sedem posuisse. Ad eam igitur aram quicumque supplices accedebant misericordiam impetrabant. Cum beatus Paulus Athenas predicaturus advenisset, invenit Dionisium Ariopagitam, virum prudentissimum, quem cum non potuisset convincere, duxit eum per singulas aras deorum inquirendo cuius esset. Tandem ad hanc aram pervenit et inquisivit cuius esset. Cui Dionisius: 'ara est ignoti dei'. Tunc beatus Paulus: 'Quem ignotum appellas solus ille notus est' et sermonem suum sic incipit: 'Notus in Iudea deus' et cetera. (f. 112va)

Della predicazione di Paolo sull'Areopago e della successiva conversione di Dionigi l'Areopagita si espone in *Act.* XVII, 23-28. Si dovrebbe invece all'elaborazione di Pietro Comestore, (o del suo continuatore Pietro di Poitiers) *Historia scholastica, in Act.* LXXXIX (*PL* 198, 1702-03), la notizia che l'ara al dio ignoto fu eretta nell'Areopago a seguito dell'eclissi che, verificatasi alla morte di Cristo, indusse a credere alla sua divinità.[127]

La connessione dell'accadimento descritto negli *Atti* con il passo di Stazio, e cioè l'identificazione dell'ara Clementiae' descritta da Stazio con l'ara dell'Areopago, si ha però, a quanto risulta, per la prima volta nel commento 'In principio' e chi per primo mostra di essere a conoscenza di questa interpretazione è Abelardo nella *Theologia christiana*, e sin dalla prima fase della composizione del-

in *Il pio Enea e l'empio Ulisse. Tradizione classica e intendimento medievale in Dante*, Ravenna 1977, pp. 125-50.

[127] Sull'Areopagita inoltre, come noto, si cumulerà un'ulteriore leggenda che da Ilduino sino ad Abelardo, e oltre, lo identificherà con il primo vescovo di Parigi. La rettifica dell'indebita identificazione costerà ad Abelardo l'espulsione da St. Denis, come egli ci racconta nell'*Historia calamitatum* (n. 118 sopra), pp. 89-90, e una parziale ritrattazione nell'*epistola* XI all'abate Adamo (Peter Abelard, *Letters IX-XIV. An Edition with an Introduction* ed. E. R. Smits, Groningen 1983, pp. 249-55). Sul problema: Jeauneau, 'Pierre Abélard à Saint Denis', in *Abélard et son temps...* (n. 26 sopra), pp. 161-73 e da ultimo Luscombe, 'Denis the Pseudo-Areopagite in the Middle Ages from Hilduin to Lorenzo Valla', in *Fälschungen im Mittelalter*, V, Hannover 1988, pp. 133-52.

l'opera: quindi negli anni 1122-25.[128] Questo il testo che ci propone Abelardo, *Theologia christiana* III, 45:

> ...cuius quidem ignoti dei aram magnus philosophus Dionysius Are-
> opagita Paulo apostolo apud egregiam studiis civitatem Athenas legi-
> tur ostendisse. Haec quidem, ni fallor, illa est ara misericordiae, cui
> a supplicibus non immolabatur nisi illud Brachmanorum sacrificium,
> hoc est orationes et lacrymae; cuius videlicet arae et Statius in XII
> meminit, dicens: 'urbe fuit media nulli concessa potentum ara deum;
> mitis posuit Clementia sedem...'.[129]

Ma altro aggiunge singolare importanza alla coincidenza fra la
glossa di 'In principio' e il passo della *Theologia christiana*. Abelardo cita il passo di Stazio, nel quale l'ara è detta sede della *Clementia*, ma afferma che essa è l'ara 'misericordiae' riproducendo tal
quale l'opinione della glossa di 'In principio', che appunto alla
'misericordia' fa riferimento. L'accettazione dell'identità fra *Clementia* e *Misericordia* sembra però elemento fortemente congiuntivo
quando chi scrive è Abelardo, che a più riprese aveva discusso sulla differenza fra clemenza e misericordia, l'una virtù, l'altra colpe-
vole simpatia umana,[130] al punto da lasciar supporre che in qualche
modo Abelardo proprio dall''In principio' sia qui stato condizio-
nato.

Nel novero delle coincidenze che, seriate, rischiano di non essere
casuali, potrà anche annoverarsi che Abelardo propone in due sue
opere, secondo la consuetudine di scrittura che gli è propria, un
esempio relativo alla difficoltà che l'anima incontra nell'abban-
donare il corpo.[131] Del racconto, che non mi risulta topico, trovia-

---

[128] Mews, 'Peter Abelard's *Theologia christiana* and *Theologia scholarium* Re-exam-
ined', *Recherches de théologie ancienne et médiévale*, 52, 1985, pp. 109-58; id., 'The
Development of the *Theologia* of Peter Abelard', in *Petrus Abaelardus* (n. 43 sopra),
pp. 183-98; e sulla datazione delle opere, id., 'On Dating the Works of Peter
Abelard', *Archives d'histoire doctrinale et littéraire du moyen âge*, 60, 1988, pp. 73-134.

[129] Petri Abelardi *Theologia Christiana* III, 45, in *Opera Theologica*, II, ed. Buytaert, Turnholti 1969, pp. 212-13.

[130] Ne discute ampiamente nel *Dialogus inter philosophum, Iudaeum et Christianum*,
ed. R. Thomas, Stuttgart 1974, 2156-76 (pp. 122-23), ora migliorata nell'edizione
di C. Trovò, Milano 1992, che recepisce le correzioni proposte da G. Orlandi
alla precedente edizione ('Per una nuova edizione del *Dialogus*', *Rivista critica di
storia della filosofia*, 34, 1979, pp. 474-94), e nei *Problemata Heloisse*, PL 178. 700-
701; cf. anche J. Marenbon, 'Abelard's Ethical Theory: Two Definitions from
the *Collationes*', in *From Athens to Chartres. Neoplatonism and Medieval Thought*, cur. H.
J. Westra, Leiden 1992, pp. 301-14.

[131] *Dialogus...*, 3093-3097 p. 158: 'Scriptum et alibi repperimus quasdam sanc-
torum morientium animas timore pene dissolutionis sue tempore ad paratam sibi

mo una variante simile nel commento all'*Eneide*, composto anch'esso, come si è visto, dall'autore dell'*'In principio'*:

> *Aen.* III, 139 *dulces*: maxime indignatur anima quando disiungitur a corpore, unde illud: 'vitaque cum gemitu fugit indignata sub umbras' (*Aen.* XI, 831); Statius: 'Indignantem animam propriis non reddidit astris' (*Theb.* VI, 885). Anima quidem non vult a corpore exire et non audet, nisi debet cum deo ire; unde legitur de beato Hilario quod, cum infirmus esset et mori vellet, anima eius non audebat exire, cui dixit: 'anima mea, quinquaginta annos deo servisti; ne dubita, exi' et statim exiit. Ille in deo bene fidebat (f. 51ra).[132]

Babione

Suggeriti questi collegamenti con Abelardo dovremo ora appuntare la nostra attenzione su Goffredo Babione, un altro maestro del quale viene registrata memoria nel commento, col risultato di essere ancora un volta attratti nell'orbita di Abelardo.

L'*'In principio'* sottolinea con forte rilievo come 'inventio' di Goffredo Babione l'interpretazione di un passo della *Tebaide* che l'autore del commento condivide pienamente e propone come risolutiva:

---

beatitudinem egredi prorsus refugere, donec eas dominus iussisset ab angelis suscipi sine dolore'; *Theologia Scholarium*, I, 1640-59 in *Opera Theologica* III, p. 376: 'Unde et in vitis patrum scriptum esse meminimus quod, dum quidam frater videre vellet animam peccatoris et iusti quomodo abstrahatur a corpore et Deus non vellet contristare eum in desiderio eius, invenit hominem peregrinum iacentem in platea aegrotum, non habentem qui ei curam adhiberet. Et cum venisset hora dormitionis eius, conspicit frater ille Michaelem et Gabrielem descendentes propter animam eius. Et sedens unus a dextris et alius a sinistris eius, rogabant animam eius ut egrederetur et non exibat, quasi nolens relinquere corpus suum. Dixit autem Gabriel ad Michaelem: "assume iam animam istam ut exeamus". Cui Michael respondit: "Iussi sumus a Domino, ut sine dolore eiiciatur ideoque non possumus cum vi avellere eam". Exclamavit ergo Michael magna voce dicens: "Domine, quid vis de anima hac, quia non acquiescit nobis ut egrediatur?" Venit autem ei vox: "Ecce mitto David cum cithara et omnes psallentes Ierusalem, ut audiens psalmum ad vocem ipsorum egrediatur". Cumque descendissent omnes in circuitu animae illius cantantes hymnis, sic exiliens anima illa sedit in manibus Michaelis, et assumpta est cum gaudio'. Cf. Jeauneau, 'Note critique sur une récente édition de la *Theologia* "Summi boni" et de la *Theologia* "scholarium" d'Abélard', *Revue des études augustiniennes*, 37, 1991, pp. 151-58: 156.

[132] Tra i contatti di minore rilievo, ma non del tutto privi di significato nel complesso degli indizi, potremo annoverare l'*exemplum* relativo al martirio di Lorenzo inserito nel *Commentarius Cantabrigense in Epistolas ad Romanos*, IV, 698 e l'episodio ancora relativo al santo inserito nel commento 'In principio' ad *Aen.* VI, 334-427, 572: '*insultans*: alludens. insultare proprie est per cavillationem hosti illudere, unde illud: "subicientibus prunas insultat levita Christi", hoc est de beato Laurentio, qui dicebat: "versa et manduca"' (f. 63rb).

exclusit fidas voces (*Theb.* XI, 200): idest ad Adrasti consolationem expulit, quam prius recipiebat Polinices: hanc sententiam invenit Gaufridus Babio. Nam prius hec erat communis sententia: *exclusit*, idest emisit, *fidas voces* a Casside, sed prima est melior et vera (f. 109rb).[133]

I problemi relativi alla datazione di questa testimonianza impongono qualche maggiore indugio sulla elusiva e discussa identità di Babione.[134]

Sono ora a lui attribuiti senza contestazioni i *Sermones*, editi per la maggior parte nella *Patrologia Latina* sotto il nome di Ildeberto:[135] un'opera di grande successo, come attesta la vasta tradizione manoscritta.[136]

Sappiamo per certo che egli insegnò ad Angers dal 1097, quando subentrò a Marbodo, eletto vescovo di Rennes, al 1107 circa, quando gli succedette Ulgero;[137] sappiamo ancora che un ignoto partigiano dell'antipapa Anacleto, e quindi negli anni 1130-1145, ebbe motivo di scrivere contro Goffredo Babione un feroce mot-

---

[133] La ripropone, in forma diversa, anche il Parigino lat. 5137, XII[1], (f. 114[va]): 'oblacione cassidis Adrasti solacionem interrumpit. alii dicunt quod ipse habens cassidem in capite quasi fidas edidit voces'. Altri commenti anteriori a questo propongono in effetti solo l'interpretazione respinta da Babione.

[134] J. B. Schneyer, *Repertorium der lateinischen Sermones des Mittelalters*, II, Münster 1974, pp. 150-59 con relativa bibliografia, alla quale dovrà aggiungersi G.-M. Oury, 'Les sermons de Geoffroi Babion et la chrétienté bordelaise (1136-1158)', *Cahiers de civilisation médiévale*, 22, 1979, pp. 285-97; id., 'La vie contemplative menée en communauté d'après Geoffroi Babion († 1158?)', in *Etudes ligériennes d'histoire et d'archéologie médiévales*, Auxerre 1975, pp. 297-305; G. Pon, *Recueil des documents de l'abbaye de Fontaine-le-Comte (XII*[e]*-XIII*[e] *siècles)*, Poitiers 1982, pp. i-xviii. Sull'identificazione: J. P. Bonnes, 'Un des plus grands prédicateurs du XIIe siècle, Geoffroi du Loroux, dit Geoffroy Babion', *Revue bénédictine*, 60, 1945-46, pp. 174-215; J.-A. Brutails, 'Geoffroi du Louroux, archévêque de Bordeaux de 1136 à 1158 et ses constructions', *Bibliothèque de l'Ecole des chartes*, 83, 1922, pp. 54-64; Oury, 'Les sermons...' (sopra); ma soprattutto la voce compilata da J. Becquet nel *Dictionnaire de spiritualité ascétique et mystique*, VI, Paris 1967, pp. 229-31; per una sintetica ed utile biografia cf. la nota di F. Gastaldelli alla lettera di Bernardo (125) diretta 'ad Magistrum Gaufredum de Loratorio' (*Lettere di S. Bernardo* a cura di F. Gastaldelli, in *Bernardi Opera*, VI.1, Milano 1986, pp. 574-75).

[135] *PL* 171, 343-964.

[136] B. Haureau, *Notices et extraits des manuscrits de la Bibliothèque Nationale...*, 32.2, Paris 1888, pp. 107-66; W. Lampen, 'De sermonibus Gaufridi Babionis scholastici Andegavensis', *Antonianum*, 19, 1944, pp. 145-68; H. Wilmart, 'Les sermons d'Hildebert', *Revue bénédictine*, 47, 1935, pp. 12-51; per un completo elenco dei *Sermones* di Babione: Schneyer, *Repertorium...* (n. 134 sopra), II, pp. 150-59.

[137] E. Lesne, *Les écoles de la fin du VIIIe siècle à la fin du XIIe*, Lille 1940, pp. 128-29; J. Vezin, *Les scriptoria d'Angers au XIe siècle*, Paris 1974, pp. 11-13; C. Urseau, *Chartulaire noir de la cathedral d'Angers*, Paris-Angers 1908; cf. anche Oury, 'La vie contemplative....' (n. 134 sopra), 277-305 e Becquet in *Dictionnaire de spiritualité...* (n. 134 sopra), pp. 229-31.

teggio, nel quale coinvolse ingiuriosamente anche Angers;[138] e che
la fortuna di Babione era viva ancora a fine secolo, quando Pietro
Comestore e Pietro Cantore, indipendentemente l'uno dall'altro,
ne citavano con frequenza le *auctoritates* nelle proprie opere: traen-
dole però non dai *Sermones*, ma da un altro commento che essi dichiarano appartenere a Babione, le *Enarrationes in evangelium Matthaei*.[139]

I problemi nascono, per un verso, proprio dai testimoni del secondo XII secolo che, indipendentemente, ascrivono a Babione le
Enarrationes, opera un tempo attribuita, ed ora senza contestazioni
sottratta, ad Anselmo di Laon;[140] e, per altro verso, dalla interpretazione ormai accettata del pamphlet metrico su Babione: dal quale
risulterebbe che Goffredo Babione, il quale piuttosto dovrebbe dirsi
'bafio' (porco), essendo diventato vescovo 'stupri precium', plagian-
do badesse e regine, è una sola persona con il vescovo Goffredo
di Loreaux o di Loriol (de Laureolo), proveniente da un'esperienza eremitica nella quale, forte dell'appoggio del duca d'Aquitania,
Guglielmo il Tolosano, era riuscito ad ottenere per la sua comunità cospicui, anche se non sempre legittimi, doni, promosso poi
all'episcopato nel 1136, forse per i meriti acquistati nello scisma
schierandosi contro l'antipapa Anacleto, vivo sino al 1158, amico
di Pietro il Venerabile, di Bernardo di Chiaravalle, di Pier Lombardo, di Gilberto di Poitiers, di Sugero di St. Denis, riformatore
delle sue diocesi di Bordeaux e Poitiers e perciò osteggiato acer-
bamente dal clero.[141]

---

[138] W. Wattenbach, 'Mitteilungen aus Handschriften', *Neues Archiv*, 8, 1882-
83, pp. 141-43; Bonnes, 'Un des plus grand predicateurs...' (n. 134 sopra),
p. 182, n. 1.

[139] Sull'attribuzione delle *Enarrationes*: van den Eynde, 'Autour des *Enarrationes*...'
(n. 42 sopra), pp. 50-84; Smalley, 'La *Glossa ordinaria*: quelques prédécesseurs d'Anselme de Laon', *Recherches de théologie ancienne et médiévale*, 9, 1937, p. 368; id., 'Some
Gospel Commentaries...' (n. 111 sopra), pp. 147-80: 166-76; 'Peter Comestor on
the Gospel and his Sources', *Recherches de théologie ancienne et médiévale*, 46, 1979,
pp. 84-129 (95-105); H. Weisweiler, 'Paschasius Radbertus als Vermittler des Ge-
dankengutes der Karolingischen Renaissance in den Matthäuskommentaren des
Kreises um Anselm von Laon', *Scholastik*, 35, 1960, pp. 363-402; A. Ballantyne,
'A Reassessment of the Exposition on the Gospel according to St. Matthew in
Manuscript Alençon 26', *Recherches de théologie ancienne et médiévale*, 56, 1989, pp.
19-57.

[140] Edita sotto tale nome in *PL* 162, 1227-1500 e ancora ritenuta di Anselmo
da O. Lottin, *Psychologie et morale aux XIe et XIIe siècles*, V, Gembloux 1959, pp.
153-69.

[141] Bonnes, 'Un des plus grands...' (n. 134 sopra), pp. 190-98; Brutails, 'Geoffroi
du Louroux...' (n. 134 sopra), pp. 54-64; per le lettere di Pietro Venerabile: *The
Letters of Peter the Venerable*, ed. G. Constable, Cambridge Mass. 1967, ep. 106 e

Un personaggio dunque con una vita che appare nettamente divisa: quella di maestro ed eremita e poi di vescovo e politico (1136-1158) [142] E, ai due diversi momenti della sua vita corrispondono due nomi diversi: Babione al primo, Goffredo 'de Laureolo' al secondo.

La scomparsa del soprannome che gli era attribuito può trovare qualche ragione di opportunità, una volta asceso Goffredo alla dignità episcopale (anche se i copisti dei *Sermones*, che pur paiono essere frutto del magistero di questi anni, se ne ricorderanno ancora negli 'incipit' dei manoscritti). Il soprannome tuttavia altrove riaffiorerà negli stessi anni, nel titolo di una commedia che ha a protagonista un religioso evirato [143] e che un'interpretazione recente, allo stato attuale ben poco fondata, ma che potrebbe trovare qualche supporto in quanto verremo dicendo, considera ispirata da intenti satirici nei confronti di Abelardo. [144]

Le *Enarrationes* restano il problema più arduo connesso con Goffredo Babione: in esse si trovano espresse posizioni e discussioni teologico-filosofiche troppo affini a quelle di Abelardo e impiegati termini e formule da lui introdotti; nell'opera si individuano inoltre rapporti certi, ma incerti quanto a direzione della dipendenza, con *sententie* riportate da *florilegia* della scuola di Laon, e contatti sicuri, seppur non numerosi—come prevedibile in opere destinate a un pubblico diverso—con i *Sermones* quando vengano toccate tematiche affini. [145]

Tali considerazioni, che avevano indotto van den Eynde [146] a

---

note; l'amicizia pare incrinarsi verso il 1148-49 per divergenze sull'elezione del vescovo di Angoulême, Ugo (ep. 142 e note); per Bernardo di Chiaravalle: *Lettere...*, in *Bernardi Opera*, VI. 1, 125, pp. 574-77 (n. 134 sopra). Per le lettere di Goffredo a Sugero: *Recueil des historiens des Gaules et de la France*, XV, par M. J. J. Brial, Paris 1878, n[i] 82-84 pp. 514-15; 109-10 pp. 524-25. Per gli atti relativi alle donazioni di Fontaine-le-Comte cf. Pon, *Recueil des documents...* (n. 134 sopra), pp. 3-29.

[142] L'esperienza eremitica appare essere stata una tappa nella vita dei personaggi che la scelsero, e si conosce almeno un altro esempio di eremita divenuto vescovo, Ugo di Nevers (Becquet, 'L'eremitisme clerical et laïc dans l'ouest de la France', in *L'eremitismo in occidente nei secoli XI e XII. Problemi e ricerche*, Milano 1965, pp. 182-211), contro il quale si scaglierà Pagano Bolotino: cf. J. Leclerq, 'Le poème de Payen Bolotin contre les faux ermites', *Revue bénédictine*, 68, 1958, pp. 52-86.

[143] *Babio*, ed. A. Dessì Fulgheri, in *Commedie latine del XII e XIII secolo*, II, Genova 1980, pp. 131-301.

[144] *Three Latin Comedies*, ed. K. Bate, Toronto 1976, p. 8; D. Fraioli, 'The Importance of Satire in Jerome's *Adversus Iovinianum* as an Argument against the Authenticity of the *Historia Calamitatum*', in *Fälschungen...* (n. 127 sopra), III, pp. 167-200.

[145] van den Eynde, 'Autour des *Enarrationes...*' (n. 42 sopra), pp. 65-66; 69-79.

[146] Ibid., pp. 80-84.

concludere, pur con molti dubbi, per l'attribuzione dell'opera a
Babione, e ad una sua collocazione intorno agli anni 1140, vengono riproposte da Smalley, che ne trae però conclusioni del tutto opposte.[147] Alcune ragioni avanzate dalla studiosa per negare
l'attribuzione delle *Enarrationes* a Babione mi paiono però non
cogenti,[148] nè tali da costringere a rigettare come false le testimonianze indipendenti di due autori molto prossimi a Babione, Pietro
Comestore e Pietro Cantore.

E aggiungerò invece che collega strettamente l'opera di Babione
ad Abelardo anche l'originale tripartizione dell'esposizione del Vangelo di Matteo (secondo la *historia*, la *allegoria* e la *moralitas*) che
Pietro Comestore giudicherà eccessivamente pesante:[149] caratteristica replicata con il medesimo rigore e costanza anche nell'abelar-
diana *Expositio in Hexaemeron*,[150] ascrivibile agli anni 1132-37.[151]

[147] 'Some Gospel Commentaries...' (n. 111 sopra), pp. 166-76; 'Peter
Comestor...' (n. 139 sopra), pp. 95-105.
[148] L'appartenenza dell'autore delle *Enarrationes* a un ordine monastico (Smalley, 'Some Gospel Commentaries...' (n. 111 sopra), p. 174 e van den Eynde,
'Autour des *Enarrationes*...' (n. 42 sopra), p. 84, sarebbe difficilmente conciliabile
con l'episcopato di Babione/Goffredo 'de Laureolo', che è invece palese nei *Sermones*; inoltre sarebbero significative le differenze fra le due opere: e sarebbe inconsueto a questa altezza che nelle *Enarrationes* venga citato un classico, Lucano. Mi
pare però che l'appartenenza ad un ordine monastico non sia necessariamente
implicata dalla definizione di sè come 'religiosus' nè dall'allusione ad un 'abbas
meus' introdotta in un esempio delle *Enarrationes*: Babione, anche se non fosse
stato monaco nero, come crede Oury ('La vie contemplative...' (n. 134 sopra),
pp. 297-305; id., 'Les sermons de Geoffroi Babion...' (n. 134 sopra), pp. 285-97;
al periodo di vita monastica, anteriore al 1107, risalirebbero addirittura le *Enarrationes*), come eremita ben poteva essere definito 'religiosus' e indicare il capo
della sua comunità come 'abbas', etimologicamente giustificato, nonostante la non
appartenenza alla gerarchia ufficiale (Becquet, 'L'eremitisme clerical...' (n. 142
sopra), pp. 182-211; L. Milis, 'Ermites et chanoines reguliers au XIIe siècle',
Cahiers de civilisation médiévale, 22, 1979, pp. 39-80: 66). Se si considerano poi le
citazioni di autori classici entro un'opera esegetica quale le *Enarrationes*, dovrà
osservarsi da un lato che esse non sono certo inusuali nei *Sermones*, nè limitate a
luoghi proverbiali—si citano più volte Virgilio (*Aen.* VI, 733, 852; I, 630), Orazio
Epist. I, 10, 24 e altri—; e dall'altro che se le *Enarrationes* sono scritte dopo Abelardo, del quale recepiscono le più recenti innovazioni, le citazioni dei classici anche
in un testo esegetico non dovrebbero più apparire inconsuete, data la frequenza
con la quale il 'peripateticus Palatinus' le inserisce nei suoi testi di esegesi biblica.
[149] Smalley, *Lo studio della Bibbia...* (n.43 sopra), p. 323 e n. 106.
[150] Su quest'opera, poco studiata: Buytaert, 'Abaelard's *Expositio in Hexaemeron*',
Antonianum, 43, 1968, pp. 163-94; E. F. Kearney, 'Peter Abelard as Biblical Commentator: A Study of the *Expositio in Hexaemeron*', in *Petrus Abaelardus. Person...* (n.
43 sopra), pp. 199-210; M. T. D'Alverny, 'Abélard et l'astrologie', in *Pierre Abélard,
Pierre le Vénérable*, Paris 1975, pp. 611-30.
[151] Mews, 'On Dating the Works...' (n. 128 sopra); van den Eynde, 'Chronolo-
gie des écrits d'Abélard', *Antonianum*, 37, 1962, pp. 337-49.

Sembrano dunque confermabili, anche sulla base di quest'ultima osservazione, i rapporti molto stretti fra le *Enarrationes*, che ritengo opera di Babione, e l'opera di Abelardo.

Ma da un'opera che esce dalla scuola di quest'ultimo e che viene stesa intorno agli anni 1140, il *Commentarius Cantabrigensis* sulle *epistole* di Paolo, apprendiamo il motivo per il quale il maestro di Angers era chiamato Babione[152] e, al tempo stesso, il giudizio e l'apprezzamento di Abelardo:

> *imperitus sermone (2 ad Corinth.* XI): balbutiens enim sepe melius balbutientem docet quam perplexus philosophus, cui est sermo expeditissimus. Unde magister Babio, cum esset balbutiens, melius tamen docere sciebat quam multi qui hodie sunt expeditiores.

E che il maestro di Angers rientrasse nel corpo docente del quale la città andava fiera emerge, mi pare, da un'ellittica espressione— che ora potrebbe divenire di chiara interpretazione—che leggiamo nella lettera indirizzata da Herveus a Ilario d'Orléans per invitarlo a tornare a insegnare ad Angers.[153] Tra i maestri che egli elenca dopo Vasleto, Gurdo, Renulfo e Antelmo, ve ne sono alcuni che sono 'vel scientie minoris, vel lingue impeditioris':[154] quindi alcuni che non sono meno bravi di Vasleto e colleghi, ma che solo sono segnati da difetti fisici che impediscono un più ampio successo di pubblico; e tanto pare tratteggiare il ritratto di Goffredo Babione.

Nei rapporti dunque di Abelardo con i maestri di Angers[155] si

---

[152] *Commentarius Cantabrigensis in Epistolas Pauli e schola Petri Abelardi*, I, *In Epistolam ad Romanos*, ed. A. Landgraf, Notre Dame, Indiana 1937, pp. xv-xvii; II, *In Epistolam ad Corinthios*, 1939, p. 322; lo osservò per primo J. Rivière, 'Magister Babio Balbutiens', *Revue du moyen âge latin*, 1, 1945, p. 310 e cf. Bonnes, 'Un des plus grands prédicateurs...' (n. 134 sopra), p. 182, n. 1.

[153] Hilarii Aurelianensis *Versus et ludi, epistulae, Ludus Danielis Belouacensis*, ed. W. Bulst-M. L. Bulst-Thiele, Leiden 1989, nⁱ 7-8, pp. 89-90, e Häring, 'Hilary of Orléans and his Letter Collection', *Studi medievali*, 14, 1973, pp. 1069-1122: 1089-90. I dubbi sulla datazione dell'epistola, non risolti nella recente edizione, dipendono dalla incerta identificazione del mittente, Herveus.

[154] L'espressione è sicura definizione tecnica della balbuzie: non può intendersi come scarsa abilità nel campo dell'eloquenza. Lo stesso problema infatti affliggeva anche un maestro di geometria, il cui insegnamento non richiedeva ornato elocuto: è Guglielmo di Soisson, le cui lezioni seguì Guglielmo di Tiro ('habuimus... in geometricis et maxime in Euclide magistrum Wilhelmum Suessionensem, impeditioris lingue virum, sed acute mentis et ingenii subtilioris hominem': R. B. C. Huygens, 'Guillaume de Tyre étudiant', *Latomus*, 21, 1962, p. 823).

[155] 'Unus qui in Andegavensi pago magni nominis viget' (*Theol. Christ.* IV, 77, in *Opera Theologica*, II, 301) potrebbe essere Ulgero per de Rijk (Petrus Abaelardus, *Dialectica*, ed. L. M. De Rijk, Assen 1956, pp. xx-xxi), nonostante nell'anno

inserisce a pieno titolo Babione del quale apprendiamo, attraverso il nostro commento, era nota anche una *sententia* che aveva definitivamente risolto un difficile passo della *Tebaide*: un maestro quindi al cui *curriculum*, come già a quello di Anselmo, possiamo aggiungere almeno la *lectura* di Stazio.

Se è così potrebbe allora essere probabile che il rapporto di Abelardo con Babione fosse più noto di quanto non ci sia apparso sin qui: e che narrare nel *Babio*, o *Comedia Babionis*, vicende simili a quelle, notissime, del filosofo,[156] attribuendole ad un personaggio che era stato un suo stimato maestro, il cui nome anche si offriva al gioco paronomasico 'bafio', cioè porco, potesse suggerire al lettore del tempo allusioni precise e dirette, e ben oltre la semplice analogia di un infortunio, all'epoca peraltro piuttosto frequente.

A completare e concludere la rassegna di queste singolari coincidenze adduco ancora un ultimo fatto. All'altezza presumibile del nostro commento pochissimo esercitata era l'esegesi a Matteo ed è anzi su impulso della scuola teologica di Laon che si confezionano commenti ai libri del *Nuovo Testamento* che ne erano privi, fra i quali figura appunto il *Vangelo di Matteo*.[157] Si ascriverebbe ad

---

che egli propone, 1107, fosse 'scholasticus' Babione; M. T. Fumagalli ritiene più probabile invece Vasletus; e cf. *Theologia Scholarium* II, 63 in *Opera Theologica*, III, pp. 439-40. La ben nota celebrità delle scuole di Angers affiora anche nei commenti alla *Rhetorica ad Herennium* 'In primis' di Guglielmo di Champeaux (Dickey, 'Some Commentaries...' (n. 118 sopra), pp. 1-41 e Fredborg, 'The Commentaries...' (n. 118 sopra), pp. 1-39) ove il nome della città viene significativamente accostato a quelli di Manegoldo di Lautenbach e di Anselmo di Laon.

[156] Il 'love affair' di Abelardo ed Eloisa era di pubblico dominio e variamente cantato: si veda almeno Dronke, *Abelard and Heloise in Medieval Testimonies*, Glasgow 1976, ora in *Intellectuals and Poets...* (n. 105 sopra), pp. 248-94; 'Abaelardiana III. Orléans, Bibliothèque Municipale 284 (238): An Edition of the Poems and Fragment on pp. 183-84', *Archives d'histoire doctrinale et littéraire du moyen âge*, 49, 1982, pp. 277-81 e J. F. Benton, 'Poems from Orléans, Bibl. Mun. 284 p. 183-84', ibid., 50, 1983, pp. 273-76.

[157] Smalley, 'Some Gospel...' (n. 111 sopra), pp. 147-150. Glosse al Vangelo di Matteo parrebbero composte anche da Manegoldo di Lautenbach: Flint, 'The "School of Laon"...' (n. 105 sopra), pp. 92-93, che gli attribuisce anche il commento ai *Salmi* di Ps. Beda ('Some Notes on the Early Twelfth-Century Commentaries on the Psalms', *Revue de Théologie ancienne et médiévale*, 38, 1971, pp. 80-88, e G. Morin, 'Le Pseudo-Bède sur les psaumes et l'*Opus super Psalterium* de maître Manegold de Lautenbach', *Revue bénédictine*, 28, 1911, pp. 331-40). Andranno approfonditi i rapporti del commento 'In principio' col 'magister Manegaldus', spesso accostato ad Anselmo di Laon, autore di commenti al *De inventione*: (cf. Dickey, 'Some Commentaries...' (n. 118 sopra), pp. 1-41) e alle epistole di Paolo, che dovrebbe essere altra persona rispetto al primo: Fredborg, 'The Com-

Anselmo un commento ancora non precisamente individuato;[158] possediamo invece i commenti anonimi tràditi dai MSS Valenciennes, Bibl. Mun. 14 e Alençon, Bibl. Mun. 26, oggetto di discussioni non ancora risolte, e le *Enarrationes in Evangelium Matthaei* di Babione.[159]

É quindi degna di nota la singolare associazione operata dal nostro commentatore fra il titolo delle *Bucoliche* e il titolo del Vangelo di Matteo, *Liber generationis*;[160] che potrebbe essere osservazione suggerita da una recente attenzione esegetica a questo testo: sia essa di Anselmo di Laon o di Goffredo Babione.

La ricerca, come si comprende, è ancora aperta, e i frammenti proposti sin qui valgono solo a consentire qualche precisazione cronologica: che l'associazione fra la leggenda dell'Areopagita e l''ara Clementie' o 'Misericordie' di Stazio si produce prima del 1122-1126, in un commento che registra l'insegnamento orale di

---

mentaries...' (n. 118 sopra), p. 15). Oltre al noto commento alle *Metamorfosi* di Ovidio tràdito nel Monacense Clm 4610 (Meiser, 'Über einen Commentar zu den *Metamorphosen* des Ovids', *Sitzungsberichte der Bayer. Akad. der Wissenschaften*, Phil. Hist. Cl. 1885, pp. 47-89) e riconosciuto da Bischoff, 'Living with the Satirists' (n. 58 sopra), p. 261), C. Villa segnala ora nel Bernese 327 un commento ad Orazio nel quale viene citato Manegoldo (f. 1ra): 'Per una tipologia...' (n. 48 sopra), pp. 19-42: 34): ead., 'Dante lettore di Orazio' in *Dante e la 'bella scola'...* (n. 8 sopra), p. 99. Su 'Manegoldo' cf. Châtillon, 'Recherches critiques sur les différents personnages nommés Manegold', *Revue du moyen âge latin*, 9, 1953, pp. 153-70.

[158] Lo identifica con il commento tràdito dal ben noto manoscritto di Alençon, Bibl. Mun. 26: Ballentyne, 'A Reassessment...' (n.138 sopra), pp. 19-57.

[159] Le *Enarrationes* parrebbero utilizzare questi ultimi due: van den Eynde, 'Autour des *Enarrationes*...' (n. 42 sopra), pp. 54-61. Per il probabile commento di Manegoldo: Flint, 'The "School of Laon"...' (n. 105 sopra), p. 93 e bibliografia.

[160] f. 27ra 'Bucolica ...apo ton bucolon, idest a boum custodia, non quia de boum semper agat, sed a digniori parte rusticane possessionis, idest a bove, librum suum intitulavit, ut sepe invenitur: sicut "liber Genesis", non quod ubique Moyses de mundi genitura agat, et sicut Matheus "liber generationis Ihesu Christi", non quia semper de genitura Christi agat, sed a digniori parte sue materie intitulat: et sic totum hoc opus a digniori parte, idest a bove, intitulavit'. É quindi la 'dignior pars materie' che motiva il titolo, di *Bucoliche*, come del vangelo di Matteo. 'Liber generationis' e l'analogo 'Genesis' vengono invece prevalentemente spiegati dall'esegesi richiamando la tradizione ebraica di dar nome all'opera sulla base dell'argomento iniziale (Rabano Mauro a Matteo, *PL* 107, 751: 'Quare autem librum dixerit generationis, cum parvam libri particulam teneat generatio, hoc intelligitur quod consuetudinem gentis sue secutus est'; Thierry de Chartres [Häring, *Commentaries on Boethius...* (n. 45 sopra), p. 555]: '*Genesis* ... a primordiis suis sic nominatus, sicut evangelium Matthei a prima parte sua *Liber generationis*'...; Clarembaldo di Arras [Häring, *Life and Works of Clarembald of Arras*, Toronto 1965, p. 226]: '...Consuetudo enim fuit Hebreis secundum operum principia voluminibus imponere nomina. Unde et evangelium Mathei "liber generationis Iesu Christi" vocatum est...'; e cf. *Glossa ordinaria*, *PL* 162, 1227).

Anselmo e un'*auctoritas* di Babione. Ancora, si può accogliere che il punto di convergenza di alcune informazioni offerte dall''In principio' possa essere Abelardo, certo in ragione anche della maggiore accessibilità delle sue opere: e Abelardo aveva frequentato la scuola di Anselmo di Laon e aveva conosciuto e apprezzato Goffredo Babione. Non può quindi trascurarsi l'ipotesi che il commento sia opera di un contemporaneo di Abelardo, provvisto del medesimo curriculum scolastico del maestro.

'Aurelius': Ilario d'Orléans?

Ma l''In principio' consente di aggiungere ancora una tessera al mosaico, suggestiva ed ambigua come tutte quelle che abbiamo sin qui raccolto.

Ancora una volta lo stimolo è costituito da una ampia glossa che nel commento 'In principio' a *Theb.* IV, 442 esamina quattro diversi tipi di sacrifici:

> quattuor modis fiunt sacrificia. Libatio vocatur cum sete carpuntur (capiuntur B) de fronte et notato capite mola infunditur, unde probatur an accepta sit hostia, scilicet si pacienter sustinet est accepta; vel, sicut alii dicunt, mittebantur sete in ignem et si creparent (crepent L) accepta erat. Immolatio est cum sacerdos in iugulo victime ponit cultrum expectatque vocem auguris, qui observat ortum et occasum, idest tempus in quo bonum sit occidi (occidere L) victimam, et notato tempore (tempus L) exclamat: 'age, age' et tum (tunc RL) ferit sacerdos. Reddicio est cum carnes in holocaustum (hocaustrum R) ferimus super congeriem lignorum, unde holocaustum (-strum R) quasi totum incensum dicitur. Litacio est cum adhuc viventi vinum instillatur (inscilatur R), vel oleum, aut lac, aut aliquis alius liquor et tunc, si accepta fuerit, perpenditur. Est autem litacio de preterito, sed libacio de futuro.[161]

In un manoscritto con tutt'altro testo, il 5. 5. 13 della Biblioteca Capitular y Colombina di Siviglia, un codice italiano della prima metà del XV secolo, che contiene il commento di Benvenuto da Imola a Lucano,[162] a f. 49ʳ una mano diversa, ma coeva, riporta

---

[161] Utilizzo i manoscritti Berlin, lat. 4° 228, (f. 15ʳᵃ) (B), Add. 16380 (f. 164ʳᵇ) (L) e Riccardiano 842 (f. 45ᵛᵇ) (R) perché nel berlinese lat. 2° 34 manca questa sezione di testo.

[162] Lo segnala L. C. Rossi, *Benvenuto da Imola lettore di Lucano*, in *Benvenuto da Imola* (n. 69 sopra), pp. 165-203 (179).

nel margine inferiore la medesima glossa riferita sopra; la ripro-
duce con fedeltà assoluta al suo modello, sì da non sanare nemmeno errori manifesti (invece di 'instillatur' legge 'inscitatur': attin-
geva al Riccardiano?) e la introduce con queste parole: 'Aurelius
super Statium Thebaidos libro IIII ubi de Tiresia dicit:...'.

La glossa, assente nelle fonti accessibili—Isidoro, Servio, Macrobio, Marziano Capella, e nei testi patristici—pare verosimil-
mente frutto autonomo della dottrina del commentatore dell''In
principio' e rende pertanto difficilmente sostenibile l'ipotesi che il
postillatore del manoscritto di Siviglia l'abbia ricavata da una fonte
comune. In questo senso induce a giudicare anche il fatto che
l'anonimo compilatore inglese del florilegio dell''In principio', conservato nell'Harl. 2693, riporti tal quale questa glossa (f. 45^{r-v}).

Lo sconosciuto postillatore del commento di Benvenuto a Lucano
sembra dunque meritevole di credito: fors'anche quando ci offre,
per la prima volta, il nome dell'autore dell''In principio': Aurelius.

'Aurelius': chi era costui?

Da scartarsi subito la via 'facilior', che il postillatore voglia cioè
indicare Agostino, e perché la glossa non appartiene a nessun testo
agostiniano e perché il postillatore indica in Aurelio un commentatore della *Tebaide*, fornendo tutte le coordinate topografiche per
reperire il riferimento nell'opera classica: 'super Statium Thebai-
dorum, libro IIII, ubi de Tiresia dicit'. Ma Aurelio, maestro di
primo piano, autore di una *lectura* a Virgilio e a Stazio di amplis-
sima fama avrebbe un nome che assolutamente non appare fra
quelli dei numerosi maestri che furono spesso citati in un secolo,
quale il XII, molto loquace sulla cultura e sulle varie scuole,[163]
nome che peraltro non affiora, a quanto ci è dato conoscere, nel-
l'onomastica dell'epoca e della zona di produzione del commento.

---

[163] Una rapida ma nutrita rassegna può leggersi in Häring, 'Chartres and Paris
revisited...' (n. 105 sopra), pp. 268-329; Southern, 'The Schools of Paris and the
School of Chartres', in *Renaissance and Renewal*...(n. 1 sopra), pp. 113-137; R. W.
Hunt, *History of Grammar*...(n. 42 sopra), oltre alle informazioni offerte dalla *Meta-
morphosis Goliae*, 189-216 (Huygens, 'Mitteilungen aus Handschriften', *Studi medievali*,
3, 1962, pp. 764-72) o dalla *Captatio benevolencie* del *Karolinus* (M. L. Colker, 'The
Karolinus of Egidius Parisiensis', *Traditio*, 29, 1973, pp. 199-325: 317-25).

Non improbabile allora pensare ad una possibile corruzione del nome.

Tra i suggerimenti correttori che subito si propongono[164] v'è la sostituzione di 'Aurelius' con 'Aurelianus': di uso frequente per designare, per estensione antonomastica del toponimo, Arnolfo di Orléans, come appare almeno dall''explicit' dell'Harleiano 6502—commento a Lucano—('Aureliani expliciunt'), e forse anche dall'abbreviazione 'Aurel' ('Aurelianensis', o 'Aurelianus' per antonomasia) che contrassegna le glosse di Arnolfo riportate nel Vat. Ottob. lat. 1192.[165] Traccia chiara di questa corruzione del nome di Arnolfo serba il catalogo quattrocentesco della biblioteca del Sozomeno, che così descrive l'Harleiano 6502: 'Aurelii comentum super Lucanum...'.[166]

Non credo però che quanto siamo venuti dicendo sul commento autorizzi la sua attribuzione ad Arnolfo; che opera troppo tardi, nell'ultimo quarto del XII secolo, e che offre un tipo di esegesi del tutto diversa da quella dell''In principio' (ad esempio con interesse quasi nullo per fatti grammaticali, retorici e metrici).

Un altro maestro di Orléans meglio si attaglierebbe all'epoca del nostro commento, il celeberrimo maestro che Arnolfo stesso proclama iniziatore della gloriosa tradizione di lettura dei classici ad Orléans, Ilario:

> ... Homines illius terre magis quam alii in illa valent arte, sicut nos Aurelianenses in auctoribus a primo patre magistro nostro Hylario.[167]

Attraverso quanto ci resta (una decina di carmi, alcuni *ludi* ed un certo numero di lettere)[168] Ilario offre di sè solo un profilo di poeta. Sappiamo però che egli aveva insegnato ad Angers, con qualche interruzione, dal 1105 al 1123: quindi anche negli anni

---

[164] Non può trascurarsi nemmeno l'ipotesi, paleograficamente accettabile, anche se meno suggestiva, che Aurelius sia corruzione grafica per Ansellus: rinviando quindi ancora ad Anselmo di Laon.

[165] Lo segnala Marti, *Arnulfi Aurelianensis Glosule...* (n. 56 sopra), p. LV.

[166] G. Savino, 'La libreria di Sozomeno da Pistoia', *Rinascimento*, 16, 1976, pp. 159-72: 168 n° 42.

[167] *Arnulfi Aurelianensis Glosule...*, p. 72 a l. 584.

[168] Hilarii Aurelianensis *Versus et ludi...* (n. 152 sopra); per notizie biografiche pp. 15-18; cf. anche Häring, 'Hilary of Orléans...' (n. 152 sopra), pp. 1069-1122. Ormai vecchio, intorno al 1145, Ilario fu seguito anche da Guglielmo di Tiro: Huygens, 'Guillaume de Tyre...' (n. 153 sopra), pp. 811-27. É molto probabile, anche se non unanimemente accettato, che Ilario sia autore di un fortunato commento a *Inni* e *Sequenze*, che fu edito ancora nel 1500: Allen, 'Commentary as Criticism...' (n. 3 sopra), 31; H. Gneuss, *Hymnar und Hymnen im englischen Mittelalter*, Tübingen 1968, p. 31 e n. 9; cf. *Lexikon des Mittelalters*, s. v. (G. Bernt).

in cui la presenza di Babione è attestata nelle scuole della città.

Durante uno di questi allontanamenti, che provocarono insistenti richieste di un suo ritorno,[169] egli si recò a Parigi, verso il 1125, per seguire Abelardo. Lo prova un suo carme, 'ad Petrum Abelardum', nel quale troviamo qualcosa che potrebbe forse congiungere Ilario al commento 'In principio'.

La poesia, nella quale egli lamenta l'ingiusto distacco del maestro dai suoi discepoli, provocato da un'imprecisata calunnia diffusa da un 'rusticus', così si conclude:

> Per impostum, per deceptorium,
> si negare vis adiutorium
> huius loci non Oratorium
> nomen erit, sed Ploratorium
> Tort a vers nos li mestre

ove il primo verso, sottolineando la causa della reazione di Abelardo, pone sullo stesso piano 'impostus' e 'deceptorius', glossando quasi con il secondo termine il primo.

Tale valore di 'imponere', o meglio di 'impostus', non compare nei glossari anteriori al XII secolo, nemmeno in Papia e, quasi assente nei testi mediolatini, può essere stato veicolato da un passo di *Genesi*, XXIX, 25 nella traduzione di Gerolamo, sulla quale esiste qualche dissenso. Troveremo poi attestato questo valore nel *Catholicon*, in Uguccione, nella *Summa* di Guglielmo Bretone[170] sino al *Vocabularius Ex quo*.

Ma rileggiamo la glossa di 'In principio' a *Theb.* I, 227:

> *imposta*: improba, perversa, omni malo plena. Hieronimus: impono, -is, -sui, -ere, inpostum, inpostu est decipio, -pis et construitur cum dativo: unde illud (Iuv. IV, 103) 'facile est barbato imponere regi', idest regem barbatum decipere; inde 'inpostus' et 'inpostor' et 'inpostorius', idest deceptorius.

---

[169] Hilarii Aurelianensis *Versus et ludi...* (n. 152 sopra), pp. 89-90; cf. anche Häring, 'Hilary of Orléans...' (n. 152 sopra), pp. 1069-1122: 1089-90; 1106-08; 1112 e qui p. 129.

[170] Il testo della *Summa* (e quello di Uguccione donde deriva il suo testo) presenta un significativo contatto con il commento 'In principio', essendovi inserito l'esplicito riferimento al passo di Stazio *Theb.* I, 227: 'Impono, -is, -sui, -ere, impositum dicitur intus ponere, iniungere, inculpare, imputare. Item imponere idem est quod decipere et tunc construitur cum dativo. Unde Genesis xxix "quare imposuisti mihi?", ubi false biblie habent "quare Liam supposuisti mihi?". Et tunc facit supinum impostum, inpostu...Unde hic impostor, idest deceptor ... et hec impostura, idest deceptio... et impostus, -a, -um, idest malus, deceptorius et perversus. Unde Statius (*Theb.* I, 227) "Mens cunctis imposta manet". Et ita exponit Huguitio' (*Summa Britonis sive Guillelmi Britonis Expositiones vocabulorum Biblie*, ed. L. W. Daly-B. A. Daly, I, Padova 1975, pp. 331-32).

Come si vede, il difficile passo della *Tebaide*—'mens cunctis imposta manet'—stimola un'articolata glossa che descrive coniugazione e reggenza di 'imponere' nell'accezione di 'decipere', concludendo che 'impostus' equivale a 'deceptorius': che è appunto quanto dice il verso di Ilario.

Si potrebbe obiettare che nulla induce ad escludere che la glossa sull'uso intransitivo di 'impono' si sia originata nel luogo di Giovenale, e di qui sia poi trasmigrata nel commento a Stazio.

Ma l'unico commento a me noto che produce una glossa simile è il 'More omnium satiricorum': ed è commento i cui più antichi testimoni si rintracciano nei manoscritti Siviglia, Biblioteca Capitular y Colombina, 5. 5. 13 e London, B.L., Add. 16380, entrambi del XIII secolo,[171] il secondo dei quali contiene i commenti a Stazio e a Virgilio di cui ci siamo sin qui occupati (il codice di Siviglia contiene solo il commento a Giovenale). Non improbabile appare quindi l'ipotesi che tutti i commenti tràditi dall'Additional 16380 risalgano al medesimo ambiente di produzione.

Ecco il testo della glossa di Giovenale:

> facile igitur... regem decipere. Ut ait beatus Augustinus hoc verbum impono-nis, quando sine accusativo ponitur, decipere significat, cuius supina sunt impostum, impostu; inde impostor et impostorius, idest deceptor et deceptorius (Add. 16380, f. 90va).

V'è un'indubitabile aria di parentela con il precedente: ma ai nostri fini basterà notare che pur in un passo straordinariamente affine a quello che glossa la *Tebaide* non viene registrato il termine 'impostus' con il suo valore di 'deceptorius', che è proprio quello che viene scelto da Ilario nel suo verso.

Se dunque l'Aurelius supposto autore dell''In principio' è l'orleanese Ilario,[172] il fatto che la glossa del commento alla *Tebaide* venga ridotta alla misura di un verso[173] e inserita nel carme per Abelardo potrebbe quasi assumere il significato di un'autocitazione.

Ma basti, per ora, di aver così evocato questo nuovo fantasma: occorre finalmente, per questa volta, far punto.

---

[171] E. M. Sanford, 'Iuvenalis, Decimus Iunius', in *Catalogus translationum et commentariorum*, a cura di P. O. Kristeller, I, Washington 1960, pp. 175-238 (188-92) non registra questi manoscritti.

[172] Si richiami anche la minima suggestione offerta dalla glossa citata a p. 124: '...de beato Hilario...'.

[173] Secondo un procedimento che appare applicato da Ugo Primate nel carme 18, come ha rilevato C. McDonough, 'Hugh Primas: a Poetic Glosula on Amiens, Reims and Peter Abelard', *Speculum*, 61, 1986, pp. 806-35 (824).

VERNACULAR GLOSSES AND CLASSICAL AUTHORS*

Klaus Siewert

From the early Middle Ages onwards we find vernacular glosses existing side by side with a predominating number of Latin glosses, including those on manuscripts of the classical writers. Even though the great number of Latin explanations makes the vernacular glosses less significant, they gain in importance in the domain of the history of the individual languages, such as English, Irish, Breton, Spanish, or German, because they represent some of the oldest and most valuable sources.

Apart from their undoubted linguistic merits we should ask ourselves how vernacular glosses contribute to the knowledge we have of how classical literature was received in the Middle Ages. With regard to the other sources available, such for instance as the Latin glosses and commentaries, I am inclined to say: not much. Looking more closely, however: more than is obvious. This is what I would like to elaborate on using the example of the Old High German glosses.

I should first like to make a few preliminary remarks concerning the significance of the sources:

(1) The general knowledge that we can obtain about the reading of the classics in medieval monastic schools (that is, where and when people studied which writers) comes predominantly from the existence of manuscripts in monastic libraries, and especially from codicological and palaeographical data, medieval library catalogues, prescriptions for recommended reading, and other sources. The fact that we are dealing with vernacular glosses is of minor importance. They are seldom useful for resolving questions as to the location or date of origin of a manuscript, owing to the mostly unreliable quality of the scribal tradition.

(2) As regards questions of understanding and interpreting a given text, there are other more illuminating sources, such as the

* I am grateful to Birgitta Stratmann who read my proofs, and to Monika Mengede who helped me with problems of translation.

Latin glosses, which are greater in number, and the Latin scholia and commentaries, which give the reader more detailed information. Since the glosses consist of separate words, we cannot expect to get an interpretation or even a transformation of the texts.

(3) Like Latin glosses, vernacular glosses do not at first sight appear to have any distinctive qualities, if one leaves the question of their linguistic merits aside. This is why Alexander Schwarz rather prematurely repudiates any of their achievements.[1] During recent years we have developed new methodical approaches in the *Germanistische Glossenforschung*, opening up new fields of interest. By concentrating on the glossed authors and also taking into account the original manuscripts including their Latin annotations, Germanists can nowadays contribute, even if in a modest way, to questions relating to the tradition of studying the classics in the Middle Ages.[2]

After a few general observations on the knowledge of the sources and on Old High German glossing, I would like to deal with the following five questions:

(1) Which of the classical authors were glossed in Old High German?

(2) What is the main impression we get from the Old High German glosses written on Horace?

(3) Do vernacular glosses fulfil certain functions that Latin glosses do not in order to make the texts more intelligible?

(4) Do vernacular glosses stand out in other ways as well?

(5) And last of all: do vernacular glosses reflect a Christian criticism of the implications expressed by the Latin lemmata?

---

[1] A. Schwarz, 'Glossen als Texte', *Beiträge zur Geschichte der deutschen Sprache und Literatur*, 99, 1977, pp. 25-36 (31, see also 27): 'Unmöglichkeit ..., den althochdeutschen Glossen gesonderte Funktionen zuzuordnen'.

[2] First of all, and now used as a model: K. Siewert, *Die althochdeutsche Horazglossierung*, Göttingen, 1986 (Studien zum Althochdeutschen 8), with its technique of a 'selection process based on indicators'('Indizienbegründetes Selektionsverfahren', pp. 62-66), which involves a systematic search through manuscripts and texts which might contain glosses as yet undiscovered. Reviewed most recently by S. Sonderegger, in *Zeitschrift für deutsche Philologie*,111, 1992, pp. 471-72; K. Siewert, 'Die althochdeutsche Persiusglossierung im Lichte neuer Quellen', in *Althochdeutsch [Festschrift Rudolf Schützeichel]*, eds R. Bergmann, H. Tiefenbach and L. Voetz, with H. Kolb, K. Matzel, K. Stackmann, I. *Grammatik. Glossen und Texte*, Heidelberg, 1987, pp. 608-24; for other classical authors see nn. 28-41 (state of research and earlier literature).

I. *The Sources*

According to the present state of our knowledge there are about 1,300 manuscripts containing Old High German glosses.[3] This number tells us about the progress made in this field of study since the publication of Elias von Steinmeyer and Eduard Sievers' authoritative edition of Old High German glosses,[4] which includes only half this number of manuscripts. The additional newly-found glossed manuscripts and additional glosses, identified by the so-called 'Indizienbegründetes Selektionsverfahren',[5] are being carefully examined within the framework of a research project called 'Althochdeutsches Wörterbuch' (R. Schützeichel) under the tutelage of the Akademie der Wissenschaften in Göttingen.[6] Meanwhile the study of Old High German glosses has taken on an international character, as is shown by the Göttingen series 'Studien zum Althochdeutschen'[7] and by the publication of T. Starck and J. C. Wells' glossary.[8]

---

[3] R. Bergmann, *Verzeichnis der althochdeutschen und altsächsischen Glossenhandschriften. Mit Bibliographie der Glosseneditionen, der Handschriftenbeschreibungen und der Dialektbestimmungen*, Arbeiten zur Frühmittelalterforschung 6, Berlin-New York, 1973; Id., 'Liste der in dem Verzeichnis der althochdeutschen und altsächsischen Glossenhandschriften nachzutragenden Handschriften', in R. Schützeichel, *Addenda und Corrigenda zu Steinmeyers Glossensammlung*, Nachrichten der Akademie der Wissenschaften in Göttingen, I, Philologisch-Historische Klasse, Jahrgang 1982, 6, Göttingen, 1982, pp. [12]-[17] (236-41); R. Bergmann, 'Zweite Liste der in dem Verzeichnis der althochdeutschen und altsächsischen Glossenhandschriften nachzutragenden Handschriften', in Schützeichel, *Addenda und Corrigenda (II) zur althochdeutschen Glossensammlung*, Studien zum Althochdeutschen 5, Göttingen, 1985, pp. 49-56; R. Bergmann, 'Dritte Liste der in dem Verzeichnis der althochdeutschen und altsächsischen Glossenhandschriften nachzutragenden Handschriften (unter Einschluß der in der ersten und zweiten Liste nachgetragenen Handschriften)', in Schützeichel, *Addenda und Corrigenda (III) zum althochdeutschen Wortschatz*, contribs R. Bergmann, D. Ertmer, B. Meineke, K. Siewert, S. Stricker, B. Wulf, Studien zum Althochdeutschen 12, Göttingen, 1991, pp. 151-72; R. Bergmann, 'Vierte Liste der in dem Verzeichnis der althochdeutschen und altsächsischen Glossenhandschriften nachzutragenden Handschriften', in Schützeichel, *Addenda und Corrigenda (III)*, p. 173.

[4] E. Steinmeyer and E. Sievers, *Die althochdeutschen Glossen*, I-V, 1879-1922, reprint Dublin-Zürich, 1968-69.

[5] See n. 2 above.

[6] See n. 3 above.

[7] J.C. Muller, 'Bisher unbekannte Griffelglossen im Echternacher Evangeliar Willibrords und im Maihinger Evangeliar', in *Addenda und Corrigenda II* (n. 3 above), pp. 65-73; A. Quak, 'Addenda und Corrigenda zur Edition der Glossen aus Oxford BL. Jun. 83', in *Addenda und Corrigenda II* (n. 3 above), pp. 74-76; J.M. Jeep, *Stabreimende Wortpaare bei Notker Labeo*, Göttingen, 1987.—The whole series 'Studien zum Althochdeutschen' (ed. by the Kommission für das Althochdeutsche Wörterbuch der Akademie der Wissenschaften in Göttingen) so far includes the

Today the sources are more easily accessible than ever. Concerning the difficulties he experienced when trying to obtain access to the manuscripts in French libraries in October 1921, Steinmeyer noted: 'Man muss sich also gedulden, bis in den internationalen Beziehungen wieder Vernunft wird eingekehrt sein'.[9] Even up to 1989, it was still quite difficult to order microfilms or even get direct access to glossed manuscripts in the former German Democratic Republic, in Poland, and in the former Soviet Union.

Taking a broad view, we find some 250,000 Old High German glosses added to the manuscripts, that is to say a collection of c. 25,000 lexemes. For research devoted to the early German language, these glosses are a source of the most comprehensive and invaluable kind. The missionary work of Irish and Anglo-Saxon monks and Charlemagne's linguistic reforms were landmarks for the appearance of Old High German glosses, and led to an evaluation of the vernacular in written texts. We can ascertain that the first Old High German glosses appeared in manuscripts of the

---

following 18 vols: (1) B. Kölling, *Kiel UB. Cod. MS K.B. 145. Studien zu den althochdeutschen Glossen*, 1983; (2) E. Meineke, *Saint-Mihiel Bibliothèque municipale MS 25. Studien zu den althochdeutschen Glossen*, 1983; (3) H. Tiefenbach, *Xanten-Essen-Köln. Untersuchungen zur Nordgrenze des Althochdeutschen an niederrheinischen Personennamen des neunten bis elften Jahrunderts*, 1984; (4) R. Bergmann, *Prolegomena zu einem Rückläufigen morphologischen Wörterbuch des Althochdeutschen*, 1984; (5) R. Schützeichel, *Addenda und Corrigenda (II)* (n. 3 above); (6) E. Meineke, *Bernstein im Althochdeutschen. Mit Untersuchungen zum Glossar Rb.*, 1984; (7) L. Voetz, *Die St. Pauler Lukasglossen. Untersuchungen. Edition. Faksimile. Studien zu den Anfängen althochdeutscher Textglossierung*, 1985; (8) K. Siewert, *Die althochdeutsche Horazglossierung* (n. 2 above); (9) B. Meineke, *CHIND und BARN im Hildebrandslied vor dem Hintergrund ihrer althochdeutschen Überlieferung*, 1987; (10) J.M. Jeep, *Stabreimende Wortpaare* (see above); (11) Siewert, *Glossenfunde. Volkssprachiges zu lateinischen Autoren der Antike und des Mittelalters*, 1989; (12) R. Schützeichel, *Addenda und Corrigenda (III)* (n. 3 above); (13) S. Stricker, *Basel ÖBU. B IX 31. Studien zur Überlieferung des Summarium Heinrici, Langfassung Buch XI*, 1990; (14) U. Thies, *Graphematisch-phonematische Untersuchungen der Glossen einer Kölner Summarium-Heinrici-Handschrift. Mit Edition der Glossen*, 1990; (15) S. Stricker, *Die Summarium-Heinrici-Glossen der Handschrift Basel ÖBU. BX 18*, 1990; (16) B. Meineke, *Althochdeutsches aus dem 15. Jahrhundert. Glossae Salomonis im Codex Lilienfeld Stiftsbibliothek 228*, 1990; (17) Id., *Althochdeutsche -scaf(t)-Bildungen*, 1991; (18) U. Wessing, *Interpretatio Keronis in Regulam Sancti Benedicti. Überlieferungsgeschichtliche Untersuchungen zu Melchior Goldasts Editio princeps der lateinisch-althochdeutschen Benediktinerregel*, 1992.

[8] T. Starck and J.C. Wells, *Althochdeutsches Glossenwörterbuch (mit Stellennachweis zu sämtlichen gedruckten althochdeutschen und verwandten Glossen)*, Heidelberg, 1972-84.

[9] E. Steinmeyer and E. Sievers, *Die althochdeutschen Glossen* (n. 4 above), V, p. v.—Since this paper was given at the Warburg Institute, London, in 1992, investigation in the field of Old High German glossing has made further progress. This can be demonstrated by eleven new monographs (19-29) in the series 'Studien zum Althochdeutschen' and other publications, for example: J. Splett, *Althochdeutsches Wörterbuch. Analyse der Wortfamilienstrukturen des Althochdeutschen, zugleich Grundlegung einer zukünftigen Strukturgeschichte des deutschen Wortschatzes*, vol. I-II, Berlin-

8th century[10], and it is interesting to note that four of the manuscripts in question also contain Old English glosses.[11] The end of the Old High German language period in the middle of the 11th century does not at all imply the disappearance of the older German forms. Thanks to the tradition of copying texts, we still come across Old High German forms in manuscripts of the 15th century, and even later in printed texts.[12]

Vernacular glosses are for the most part by-products of monastic teaching. It is thus Echternach, Freising, Fulda, St. Gallen, Murbach and Regensburg that are the centres of glossing.

Like the Latin glosses, the forms appearing in vernacular glosses are not distinguished by any particularity. They are normally interlinear, or more rarely written in the margin or incorporated in the text itself. On a higher level they are also systematically arranged in glossaries, either in alphabetical order or according to the sequence of the Latin lemmata as they appear in a given text (textual glosses).

Basically every text that was available in the monastic libraries, or figured on a school list of recommended reading, could be glossed.[13] About half of the Old High German glosses refer to the Bible and its exegesis by the Church,[14] among whose representatives we should mention Gregory the Great in particular.[15] About one third of all the glosses have come down to us in form of dictionaries and glossaries,[16] such as the *Reichenauer Bibelglossen*, the

---

New York, 1993; bibliography: R. Schützeichel, *Althochdeutsches Wörterbuch*, 5th ed., Tübingen, 1995, pp. 42-62.

[10] R. Bergmann, *Die althochdeutsche Glossenüberlieferung des 8. Jahrhunderts*, Nachrichten der Akademie der Wissenschaften in Göttingen, I, Philologisch-Historische Klasse,Jahrgang 1983, 1, Göttingen, 1983.

[11] Ibid., pp. 12f. (no. 168); 16 (no. 275); 18 (nos 334, 335).

[12] E.g. B. Meineke, *Althochdeutsches* (n. 7 above, no 16).

[13] See G. Glauche, 'Die Rolle der Schulautoren im Unterricht von 800 bis 1100', in *La scuola nell'occidente latino dell'alto medioevo*, II, Settimane di studio del centro italiano di studi sull'alto medioevo, 19, Spoleto, 1972, pp. 617-36; G. Glauche, *Schullektüre im Mittelalter. Entstehung und Wandlungen des Lektürekanons bis 1200 nach den Quellen dargestellt*, Münchener Beiträge zur Mediävistik und Renaissance-Forschung, 5, München, 1970; B. Munk Olsen, 'Les poètes classiques dans les écoles au IXe siècle', in *De Tertullien aux Mozarabes*, II, *Antiquité tardive et christianisme ancien (VIe-IXe siècles). Mélanges offerts à J. Fontaine*, Collection des Etudes Augustiniennes, Série moyen âge et temps modernes, 26, Paris 1992, pp. 197-210; B. Munk Olsen, *I classici nel canone scolastico altomedievale*, Quaderni di cultura mediolatina, 1, Spoleto, 1991.

[14] Cf. Steinmeyer and Sievers, *Die althochdeutschen Glossen* (n. 4 above), I-II.

[15] Cf. ibid., II, pp. 162-322; W. Schulte, *Die althochdeutsche Glossierung der Dialoge Gregors des Großen*, Göttingen, 1993 (Studien zum Althochdeutschen 22).

[16] Cf. Steinmeyer and Sievers, *Die althochdeutschen Glossen* (n. 4 above), III.

Abrogans, and later dictionaries such as the *Glossae Salomonis*,[17] and the *Summarium Heinrici*[18] (based on Isidore's *Etymologiae*). Old High German glosses on grammar books[19] are of minor importance; Priscian's *Institutiones* is most intensively glossed of them. For the rest, there are only a few glosses added to Donatus, Eutyches, Phocas, and later on to the grammar books by the Anglo-Saxon Alcuin and the Irishman Clemence.

Among early Christian writers[20] Prudentius deserves special mention, since his *oeuvre* was very richly glossed, much more so indeed than any other Latin poet.[21] Other early Christian writers glossed in Old High German include Juvencus,[22] Sedulius,[23] Arator,[24] Alcimus Avitus,[25] and Prosper;[26] finally, we should note that Boethius's *De consolatione philosophiae* is unusually full of glosses.[27]

II. *Classical Authors glossed in Old High German*

Just a few years ago the impression one might have gained from the research being done in the field of vernacular Old High Ger-

[17] B. Meineke, 'Zu einem Münchner Fragment der sogenannten Glossae Salomonis', *Sprachwissenschaft*, 15, 1990, pp. 226-33; Id., 'Zu einer Edition der sogenannten Glossae Salomonis', in R. Bergmann (ed.), *Probleme der Edition althochdeutscher Texte*, pp. 18-37; Id., 'glose iussu salomonis ... sub breuitate collecte', in *Sprachwissenschaft*, 16, 1991, pp. 459-69.

[18] R. Hildebrandt, *Summarium Heinrici, I. Textkritische Ausgabe der ersten Fassung Buch I-X. II. Textkritische Ausgabe der zweiten Fassung Buch I-VI sowie des Buches XI in Kurz- und Langfassung*, Quellen und Forschungen zur Sprach- und Kulturgeschichte der Germanischen Völker, NS, 61, 78, Berlin-New York, 1974, 1982; S. Stricker, *Basel ÖBU. B IX 31* (n. 7 above, no. 13); Id., *Die Summarium-Heinrici-Glossen* (n. 7 above, no. 15); U. Thies, *Graphematisch-phonematische Untersuchungen* (n. 7 above, no. 14).

[19] Cf. Steinmeyer and Sievers, *Die althochdeutschen Glossen* (n. 4 above), II, *passim*.

[20] Ibid., *passim*.

[21] See for example: B. Kölling, *Kiel UB. Cod. MS K. B. 145* (see n. 7 above, no. 1), with the earlier literature.

[22] See R. Schützeichel, *Addenda und Corrigenda (III)* (n. 3 above), p. 137; D. Ertmer, *Studien zur althochdeutschen und altsächsischen Juvencusglossierung*, Göttingen, 1994 (Studien zum Althochdeutschen 26).

[23] See K. Siewert, *Glossenfunde* (n. 7 above, no. 11), pp. 56-60 (state of research, MSS); J.M. Jeep, [Review], *Language*, 66, 1990, pp. 652f.

[24] See for example: H. von Gadow, *Die althochdeutschen Aratorglossen der Handschrift Trier 1464*, Münstersche Mittelalterschriften 17, München, 1974; H. Tiefenbach, *Althochdeutsche Aratorglossen. Paris lat. 8318. Gotha Membr. II 115*, Abhandlungen der Akademie der Wissenschaften in Göttingen, Philologisch-Historische Klasse, Dritte Folge, 107, Göttingen 1977.

[25] Desideratum.

[26] See for example: P. Pauly, *Die althochdeutschen Glossen der Handschriften Pommersfelden 2671 und Antwerpen 17.4. Untersuchungen zu ihrem Lautstand*, Rheinisches Archiv 67, Bonn, 1968, *passim*.

[27] Steinmeyer and Sievers, *Die althochdeutschen Glossen* (n. 4 above), II, pp. 54-81.

man glosses on classical authors[28] was a somewhat misleading one. All that existed was a number of studies on Virgil, by far the most intensively glossed writer, to whose work approximately 6,000 glosses had been added in thirty-seven (medieval) manuscripts.[29] Such far-reaching ignorance of the Old High German glosses on other classical writers, together with the resulting erroneous evaluation of the significance of these writers to the school-teaching of medieval German monasteries, is clearly demonstrated by Herbert Thoma's concise statement in his twelve-page encyclopedia article, 'Old High German Glosses':

> German glosses on Horace are only numerous in Clm 375 [12th-century], in addition to which there are some shorter compilations. There are only a few German translations of Persius, Juvenal, Terence, Ovid, and Lucan. Avianus's book of fables, much read in the Middle Ages, was extensively glossed in a Treves manuscript. Classical Latin prose writing is mainly represented by glosses on Sallust.[30]

There is no mention whatsoever here of the Old High German glosses on Cicero,[31] Solinus,[32] Vitruvius,[33] or Statius.[34] Four recently identified glossed manuscripts of Statius make him a new centre of attention:[35] the discovery of the Old High German glosses in MS Vatican, Pal. lat. 1695 proves that even his *Achilleis* was glossed in the vernacular.[36] With regard to the other classical writers mentioned by Thoma, recent research has also given us new insights, even in relation to the extent of the sources. Virgil's special position, due substantially to the Christian reinterpretation of the fourth Eclogue,[37] has become more even prominent than before as a result of the identification of twelve new manuscripts with

---

[28] Ibid., *passim*; IV, *passim*; V, *passim*.

[29] See K. Siewert, *Glossenfunde* (n. 7 above, no. 11), p. 173, with nn. 56, 57. See also pp. 34f., 42, 104, 106, 138, 166-73, 175; R. Schützeichel, *Addenda und Corrigenda (III)* (n. 3 above), pp. 119-21.

[30] H. Thoma, 'Glossen, althochdeutsche', in *Reallexikon der deutschen Literaturgeschichte*, I, Berlin, 1958, pp. 579-89.

[31] Steinmeyer and Sievers, *Die althochdeutschen Glossen* (n. 4 above), II, p. 156.

[32] Ibid., II, p. 624.

[33] *Vitruvii de architectura libri decem*, eds V. Rose and H. Müller-Strübing, Leipzig, 1867, p. 88. The phenomenon of OHG glosses on the *Architectura* of Vitruvius demands a special explanation (Carlotta Dionisotti in the discussion following my lecture).

[34] See *Glossenfunde* (n. 7 above, no. 11), pp. 34f., 158, 160-65, 176.

[35] Ibid., p. 165.

[36] Ibid., pp. 160-62.

[37] See for example: B. Munk Olsen, 'Virgile et la Renaissance du XIIe siècle; lectures médiévales de Virgile', in *Actes du Colloque organisé par l'École française de Rome* (Rome, 25-28 octobre 1982), Collection de l'École française de Rome, 80, Rome, 1985, pp. 31-48.

glosses.[38] What has been particularly underestimated, however, is the significance of the satirists Horace,[39] Persius,[40] and Juvenal.[41] Among the writers of classical antiquity they are second only to Virgil in the number of glosses devoted to them.

Taking into account all the glossed manuscripts that are now known, we get the following list of classical writers with Old High German glosses:

(1) Virgil (36 MSS; c. 6,000 glosses)
(2) Horace (21; c. 300)
(3) Persius (18; c. 100)
(4) Juvenal (14; c. 50)
(5) Sallust (10; c. 300)
(6) Lucan (8; c. 80)
(7) Statius (6; c. 30)
(8) Terence (5; c. 10)
(9) Ovid (3; c. 10)
(10) Avianus (2; c. 100)
(11) Cicero (2; less than 10)
(12) Solinus (2; less than 10)
(13) Vitruvius (2; less than 10)
(14) Seneca (1; less than 10)

III. Horace

Two thousand years after Horace's death there is good reason to take a closer look at this great Roman poet and use him as a paradigm for further scrutiny of the field of vernacular glosses.

An analysis of the twenty-one glossed manuscripts of Horace[42] yields the following broad results: originating in the 10th century,

---

[38] See n. 29 above.

[39] K. Siewert, *Die althochdeutsche Horazglossierung* (n. 2 above); addenda in Id., *Glossenfunde* (n. 7 above, no. 11), pp. 96-114; 142-45; see also pp. 34f., 58, n. 42, 62 with n. 12, 80, 124, 174.

[40] Id., 'Die althochdeutsche Persiusglossierung' (n. 2 above); addenda in Id., *Glossenfunde* (n. 7 above, no. 11), pp. 115-129; state of research: pp. 34, 126 f., 129; Id., 'Unbekannte althochdeutsche Glossen in zwei Wolfenbütteler Handschriften der Sammlung Gude', in Schützeichel, *Addenda und Corrigenda (III)* (n. 3 above), pp. 262-68 (262-64).

[41] Id., *Glossenfunde* (n. 7 above, no. 11), pp. 35, 61-77, 126f., 138, 175f.; Id., 'Unbekannte althochdeutsche Glossen' (n. 40 above), pp. 264-68.

[42] See n. 39 above.

vernacular glosses on Horace are a phenomenon of the later phase of the Old High German language. The first Old High German gloss on an Horatian text is the cryptographic entry in a St. Gallen record:[43] *sicarius—mxchfrk*, which should be read as *mucheri* (see Fig. 1): the vowels are replaced by the consonants that follow them in the alphabet. This gloss represents the first step in a development which is continuous from then onwards, reaching its climax in the vernacular glosses added to Horace's work in the 11th century.

The handing down of Old High German glosses can be shown to have lasted for at least two centuries beyond the Old High German period, indeed well into the 13th century according to Mellicensis 1545.[44] Evidence for this can be found in the occurrence of a number of older forms which have survived unchanged in manuscripts which postdate Old High German times. One can prove that in the later phase of the Middle Ages and in the Renaissance the tradition of glosses on Horace underwent an active, even though proportionately insignificant, expansion.

At the same time the discovery of a belated development and flowering of Horace glosses within the lifespan of the Old High German language also needs further explanation. The fundamental prerequisite for the appearance of Old High German glosses on Horace is the existence of his texts in Germania, which can be shown already to have been satisfied by the beginning of the 9th century; the written tradition of his texts[45] seems therefore to provide a possible explanation; but the first medieval manuscripts of Horace in Germany are not contemporaneous with the first Old High German glosses in these manuscripts.

We need to pay some attention to the history of the poet's reception in Germania.[46] The Horatian text was still disdained in Carolingian times, so that its re-evaluation and treatment in school at the turn of the 10th century coincide with the writing of the first glosses on it. What contributed decisively to this development was the influence exercised by the missionary work of the two Irish-

---

[43] K. Siewert, *Die althochdeutsche Horazglossierung* (n. 2 above), pp. 386-90.

[44] Ibid., pp. 409-17 ('Zeiten').

[45] For the MSS: B. Munk Olsen, 'L'étude des auteurs classiques latins aux XIe et XIIe siècles', I, *Catalogue des manuscrits classiques latins copiés du IXe au XIIe siècle. Apicius-Juvenal*, Paris, 1982, pp. 421-522; C. Villa, 'I manoscritti di Orazio, I', *Aevum. Rassegna di scienze storiche linguistiche e filologiche*, 66, 1, 1992, pp. 95-135.

[46] See K. Siewert, *Die althochdeutsche Horazglossierung* (n. 2 above), pp. 416f. (with the earlier literature).

men Heiric and Remigius of Auxerre, as well as that of Martin de Laon.

As a consequence of their more favourable assessment of Horace, his work (which had only led a shadowy existence during the 9th century) had become an integral and actively studied part of the school curriculum by the end of the 10th century. In the 11th and even in the 12th centuries he was one of the authorities on questions of grammar; it was only in the 13th century that interest in him diminished considerably, as it did in classical writers in general.

The majority of Horace glosses were written down in Echternach, Regensburg, Tegernsee, and St. Gallen.[47] It was especially in relation to these monasteries, but using different sources, that Günther Glauche was able to give evidence for the treatment of Horace in the schools.[48] His findings also point to the obvious connection between the Old High German glosses and medieval scholarship. Furthermore Walahfrid Strabo, Thiofrid von Echternach and Otloh von St. Emmeram—all of them authors of vernacular glosses on Horace[49]—clearly show the significance of the glosses for teaching.

As far as the passages glossed in the vernacular are concerned,[50] quite a number of Horace's writings—with the exception of *Carmen Saeculare*—are accompanied by Old High German glosses. In this context the accumulation of vernacular glosses added to Horace's *Ars poetica*, and to his *Satires* and *Epistles*, is revealing as a consequence of the preferential treatment that they received in the schools. Indeed we notice a special interest in glossing those passages that had already undergone a certain re-evaluation in being selected for further explanation in Latin glossaries, commentaries, annotations, and in *florilegium* literature.

There is no doubt that there may be various reasons for the vernacular glossing of a particular passage. Such reasons may include, for example, the individual interests of the glossator concerned,[51] clearly demonstrated by the so-called 'dirty glosses' of a

---

[47] Ibid., pp. 417-21 ('Räume').

[48] G. Glauche, *Schullektüre* (n. 13 above), pp. 83-100.

[49] K. Siewert, *Die althochdeutsche Horazglossierung* (n. 2 above), pp. 421f. ('Personen'); see also Id., *Glossenfunde* (n. 7 above), p. 113.

[50] Id., *Die althochdeutsche Horazglossierung* (n. 2 above), pp. 428-32 ('Textgrundlage').

[51] Ibid., p. 432.

Leipzig manuscript of Terence (MS Leipzig, Universitätsbibliothek, Rep. I 12).

The Old High German glosses written on Horace are separate words. Syntagmatic compilations, in this case as in that of all the classical writers, are the exception.[52] We can find some examples in MS Vatican, Reg. lat. 1703. One instance: 'o utinam noua incude diffingas' (*Carm.* I, 35, 38-39), glossed with the vernacular sentence: 'taz tu uuidersmidōtīst'.[53] There is no visible tendency to give a complete translation. We can, however, recognize a need to systematize the German explanations,[54] as reflected by the Latin-Old High German glossary on Horace's satires in a Vatican manuscript (Chigi H.V. 165).

At this point I would like to turn to the question of the relationship between the vernacular glosses and the Latin language.

IV. *The Functional Achievements of Vernacular Glosses*

The idea behind Old High German and Latin glosses alike is to guarantee the reader's understanding of the text. Compared to the number of Latin glosses, however, that of Old High German glosses is fairly insignificant. Nonetheless in some cases they seem to offer a better alternative to the Latin explanations; this may be illustrated by a few examples.

Type 1: Latin expressions for certain animals and plants
We do not usually find Latin synonyms here, which is why an exact rendering of the word to be explained would be difficult, or rather no more than an attempt at paraphrasing. In such cases the glossator uses the corresponding vernacular word as a translation, as in MS Paris, Bibliothèque Nationale, lat. 9345, f. 27[r], l. 22 f. (see Fig. 2):
'Teque nec laevis uetet ire picus / nec uaga cornix' (*Carm.* III, 27, 15f.)—The two Latin lemmata for 'bird' are glossed with vernacular words: *spêt* for *picus* ('woodpecker'); *kre* for *cornix* ('crow').[55] The remainder was glossed in Latin.

---

[52] Ibid., p. 441 ('Glossierungsverfahren und Übersetzungstechnik').
[53] Ibid., pp. 281f.
[54] Ibid., pp. 434; 240-69.
[55] Ibid., pp. 306f.

Here and there the glossators first try to find a Latin solution, but realizing the inaccuracy of the explanation they then add a vernacular gloss, as for example in MS Vatican, Reg. lat. 1703, fol. 68ʳ, l. 3 marg. r. (see Fig. 3): With the term *hirudo* 'leech' *(Ars poetica* 476), Horace alludes to a rather untalented writer bothering his readers like a leech. By mistake the copyist of the text wrote *hirundo* which was consequently corrected, with the erasure still visible.This case is discussed in a scholium: 'Int arundinē & hirundinē & hirudi/nē multū int ē. harundo. canna. / hirudo /sanuuisu/ga. *hirun/do. auicu/la* .i *suale/uua*.[56]

As to the explanation of *hirundo* the Latin gloss *auicula* 'little bird' does not fulfil its function. Although not incorrect, the expression *auicula* is not an exact explanation for *hirundo*. Yet by inserting the vernacular gloss *sualeuua* the glossator is able to give a clearer explanation.

Type 2: Taken *per se,* the Latin lemma is polysemic. The vernacular interpretation singles out a special meaning of a polysemic word.

MS London, British Library, Harl. 2724, fol. 117ᵛ, l. 5 (see Fig. 4): the polysemic Latin term *forma* in *Sermonis* II, 3,106 is specified (in the context) by *sutor,* referring to the tool of a shoemaker. The vernacular gloss *leist* 'last'[57] guarantees the correct understanding of *forma.* It is also reasonable to suppose, as such cases indicate, that the glossators did not know the corresponding technical word in Latin—if indeed it ever existed.

Type 3: Synonymous Latin lemmata are juxtaposed in the text.

See for example *Sermones* I, 3, 119f.: *scutica, flagellum, ferula.* In order to avoid a semantic circle, that is to say a repetition of one of the words already mentioned, the glossator uses a vernacular gloss, as in the example given (see Fig. 5): MS Munich, Bayerische Staatsbibliothek, Clm 375, fol. 128ʳ, l. 25: *keisila.*[58] Furthermore, this passage is glossed in three other manuscripts: MS Vatican, Vat. lat. 3866, fol. 75ᵛ, l. 19: *riemo;*[59] MS Vatican, Chigi H.V. 165, fol. 170ᵛ, l. 3: *geisela;*[60] MS Paris, Bibliothèque Nationale, lat. 9345,

---

[56] Ibid., pp. 288f.
[57] Ibid., p. 324.
[58] Ibid., p.144.
[59] Ibid., pp. 231f.
[60] Ibid., p. 251.

fol. 68ᵛ, l. 3 marg. r.: *geisela*.[61] This may suffice to indicate the problem in question.

When one considers the functional significance of the Old High German glosses on Horace, one notices that the glossators occasionally prefer the vernacular interpretation of a word to a Latin gloss. This may lead one to question the resigned view of Alexander Schwarz as to the 'impossibility ... of attributing special functions to Old High German glosses'.[62]

V. Annotating Glosses

As we have already seen above, Latin and vernacular glosses alike are (primarily) words used to translate unknown expressions. For the more extended explanation, interpretation, and re-interpretation of a text, recourse was had to more substantial annotations and scholia added to the manuscripts—usually written in Latin. If one studies the Old High German glosses more closely, however, one can also discover evidence of the glossators' attempts to give a better elucidation of the text by the use of vernacular words. In such cases the glosses are not just simply used for purposes of translation; an example taken from the glosses on Horace will make this clear (see Fig. 6). We can see that the glossator has added the vernacular ornithological terms *taha*, *pirihhŏn* and *fasan*[63] to explain the proper name Itys. By so doing he establishes a connection between the name Itys and its mythological namesake in the Aedon legend, according to which Itys, Tereus, Progne and Philomena are turned into birds. In such cases the vernacular glosses fulfil another function. They serve as annotations which are meant to give a more profound understanding of the text rather than being mere translations.

VI. Ideological Glosses

Finally, I would like to call attention to another special instance of glossing, when a Latin word, in this case *statua*, is glossed in the Old High German vernacular.[64] These are glosses which neither

---

[61] Ibid., pp. 311f.

[62] See n. 1 above.

[63] K. Siewert, *Die althochdeutsche Horazglossierung* (n. 2 above), pp. 104-107.

[64] For the following section, see K. Siewert, 'Statua im Spiegel deutsch-

offer translations of a single Latin word nor give further explanations for a Latin lemma which will guarantee a better understanding
of the text. Instead they reflect the glossator's particularly Christian point of view as opposed to the pagan notions of antiquity.
Glosses of this character are somewhat rare; they in any case always
appear in connection with certain words I call *Reizwörter*, words
with an associative quality which made it difficult for the Christian glossators to maintain an objective stance.

The Latin word *statua* apparently constituted such a *Reizwort*. It
is associated with the iconomachical controversy between Christian and pagan beliefs, alluding to one of the central issues in this
tension between Christianity and the notions and demands of
Roman times: suffice it to mention the sacrifice in front of the
emperor's statue, the ability of statues to perform miracles etc. In
some of these cases the function of the Old High German gloss is
clear: since the translation of *statua* as *abcuti* 'idol' (MS Karlsruhe,
Badische Landesbibliothek, Aug. IC, fol. 58ra, l. 18) is not manda-
tory, it provides an obvious example of the glossator's Christian
point of view. For *Abgot*, a genuinely Christian word-formation, is,
in the mind of medieval glossators, the crucial linguistic antithesis
to any worship of false gods and idols. In a similar way the frequently used translation of *statua* as *manalich* 'man-made', which
can be found in at least twenty-five (medieval) manuscripts, is intended to counteract any attempt at reading a supernatural meaning into *statua*.

The controversy over the implications of *statua*, which began
with the Early Fathers and continued through the Middle Ages,
forms the background to its specifically Christian interpretation.
The fear of punitive measures, such as those laid down by Bish-
op Burchard von Worms (forty days bread and water for the man-
ufacturing of idols), kept the official condemnation of statues and
their worship alive in the mind of medieval man, and in particular in the minds of the glossators. The Old High German glossing of *statua* shows that in translating the word the glossators were
under the ideological sway of the iconomachy between Christians
and pagans: it would appear that this word tempted the commentators to propagate their Christian views. Consequently we are

---

sprachiger Kommentierung des Mittelalters', in *Migratio et Commvtatio. Studien zur
alten Geschichte und deren Nachleben [Thomas Pekáry zum 60. Geburtstag am 13. September
1989. Dargebracht von Freunden, Kollegen und Schülern]*, eds H.-J. Drexhage and J.
Sünskes, St. Katharinen, 1989, pp. 326-36.

confronted with a type of gloss which, by departing from the actual meaning of the term glossed, can also give us an insight into the glossators' state of mind.

VII. Conclusions

1. It is apparent from the number of glosses and glossed manuscripts[65] which have come to light in recent years that our knowledge of the tradition of writing vernacular glosses in Old High German has yet to be consolidated.

2. We have not yet finished investigating the philology of those glosses which are known; it is indispensable for future research that we should do so.

3. In order to answer questions about the study of the classics in medieval times, we must concentrate on all the glosses devoted to one single author. This will enable us accurately to judge his reputation and reception, while at the same time obtaining valid philological results. With regard to the Old High German vernacular glossing of the classical writers, we are still at the beginning of our investigations: the research on Horace's writings is complete, but much work still remains to be done with on the other classical authors, including Persius and Virgil.

4. A new attempt is under way to classify the achievements of the Old High German glosses according to their typology, but we still need to verify and expand the work completed so far. In this area, we can expect to find similarities between the Old High German glosses and the vernacular glosses in other languages such as Old English.

5. The various vernacular glossing traditions extant in Europe during the Middle Ages differ from each other solely in terms of language; initially therefore each individual language has to be evaluated on its own merits. Yet in relation to Latin, other languages have to be viewed as a whole. For this reason collaboration and the sharing of knowledge between those conducting research on

---

[65] Most recently: Siewert, 'Unbeachtete Williram-Glossen', in *Philologische Forschungen. Festschrift für Philippe Marcq*, ed. Y. Desportes, Heidelberg, 1994, pp. 235-52; Id., 'Althochdeutsche Glossen zur "Regula canonicorum" des Chrodegang von Metz. Mit einer Abbildung', *Sprachwissenschaft*, 18, 1993, pp. 417-24.

glosses would be highly productive, in terms both of the methods and of the results of research.

6. The widespread lack of interdisciplinary cooperation until the present time is regrettable. To turn once more to Horace: neither Ernst Doblhofer's recent monograph devoted to Horace research since 1957[66], nor Peter L. Schmidt's encyclopedic article[67] reflects any knowledge of the current work of the *Germanistische Glossenforschung*. And even a study of Horace's reputation and reception during the Middle Ages written by M.B. Quint fails to take into account the phenomenon of vernacular glossing.[68]

---

[66] E. Doblhofer, *Horaz in der Forschung nach 1957*, Erträge der Forschung 278, Darmstadt, 1992.

[67] 'Horaz', in *Reallexikon für Antike und Christentum*, ed. E. Dassmann, XVI, Stuttgart, 1992, pp. 491-524.

[68] *Untersuchungen zur mittelalterlichen Horaz-Rezeption*, Studien zur klassischen Philologie 39, Frankfurt a.M., 1988.

1. MS St. Gallen, Stadtbibliothek, cod. 312, fol. 90^v

Siquis erat dignus deserbi: quod malusae fur.
Quod mechus foret. aut sicarius. aut aliusqui
foret:
Famosus. multa cum libertate notabat.

mxchfrk (=mucheri)   Hor. sat. I,4,4

2. MS Paris, Bibliothèque Nationale, cod. lat. 9345, fol. 27^r

spét, kre   Hor. carm. III,27,15f.

4. MS London, The British Museum, Department of Manuscripts, cod. Harl. 2724, fol. 117^v

Siscalpra & formas ñ sutor: nautica uela

leist   Hor. sat. II,3,106

5. MS München, Bayerische Staatsbibliothek, Clm 375, fol. 128^r

e scutica dignum hofribili sectere flagello

keisila   Hor. sat. I,3,119

6. MS München, Bayerische Staatsbibliothek, Clm 375, fol. 62^v

idum ponit hythin flebiliter gemens

taha, pirihhŏn, fasan   Hor. carm. IV,12,5

3. MS Biblioteca Apostolica Vaticana, Reg. lat. 1703, fol. 68ʳ

hirundo auicula .i. sualeuua

Hor. ars poet. 476

LATIN TO VERNACULAR: ACADEMIC PROLOGUES AND THE MEDIEVAL FRENCH ART OF LOVE

ALASTAIR J. MINNIS

This paper will briefly review some of the ways in which idioms from academic prologues passed from Latin into Medieval French, with special reference to the *accessus Ovidiani*.[1] Ovid was the most ambivalent of all the grammatical *auctores*: the expert on both the art of love and its cure, a skilled seducer yet also a champion of legal, married love, an acclaimed mythographer (the *Metamorphoses* was called 'the Pagan Bible') but also the arch *praeceptor amoris*. These paradoxes afforded at once a challenge and an opportunity to medieval scholars, translators and imitators of the ancient poet, as they twisted the waxen nose of Publius Ovidius Naso in different directions, quoting him as an expert on physics or medicine here, using him as a source and model for fashionable love-poetry there. Moreover, he proved invaluable to vernacular poetics, since his text and gloss provided the means and the method for bestowing value on contemporary poetry in a way which would affirm its moral credentials while accommodating its interest in human desire.[2]

Then there is the all-important but exceptionally difficult matter of the intended and actual audiences of the several Medieval

---

[1] I am using *accessus* in the general sense which it has acquired in much modern scholarship, as a term of convenience to designate certain types of schematic introductions to 'set texts' in the medieval schools. The term had a far more limited circulation in the Middle Ages than this scholarship may imply. My term 'academic prologue' includes both the *accessus ad auctorem* and the broader type of introduction to an art or science in general, the type which in its various manifestations has been called, for example, the 'extrinsic' prologue (on which see pp. 162-63 below) and the 'type D' prologue (by R.W. Hunt, in his seminal article 'The Introductions to the *Artes* in the Twelfth Century', in *Studia medievalia in honorem R.M. Martin, O.P.*, Bruges, 1948, pp. 85-115; repr. in Hunt, *The History of Grammar in the Middle Ages: Collected Papers*, ed. G.L. Bursill-Hall, Amsterdam Studies in the Theory and History of Linguistic Science, ser.iii, 5, Amsterdam, 1980, pp. 117-44).

[2] On these developments see A.J. Minnis, 'Authors in Love: The Exegesis of Late-Medieval Love-Poets', in *The Uses of Manuscripts in Literary Studies: Essays in Memory of J.B. Allen*, ed. C.C. Morse, P. R. Doob and M.C. Woods, Kalamazoo, Michigan, 1992, pp. 161-91.

Ovids. While many of the French works which we will touch on could probably be assigned to the genre of the clerical *jeu d'esprit*—regarded as products of a world without women, texts written by *cognoscenti* for the recreation of their fellows—at least some of them seem to mark a point of transition. Ovid has left the medieval schoolroom and joined the secular society of medieval aristocrats (of both sexes, though the males certainly dominate). Consequently the scholarly apparatus of *accessus* and glosses which accompanied his work in manuscript, and above all else the scholastic literary attitudes which permeated those hermeneutic procedures, have been adapted to suit the needs of a larger, and more heterogeneous, interpretative community.

Thanks to recent research it is now known that 'the age of Ovid' started somewhat later than once supposed.[3] It was not until the time of Arnulf of Orléans (fl. 1175) that the *Metamorphoses* received full exegetical treatment, a set of largely philological glosses being complemented with an allegorical exposition.[4] Arnulf was a major influence on three thirteenth-century works of Ovid scholarship, William of Orléans' *Bursarii Ovidianorum*, John of Garland's *Integumenta Ovidii* (c. 1230), and the anonymous 'Vulgate' commentary on the *Metamorphoses* (composed c. 1250, possibly at Orléans).[5] According to Arnulf's *vita Ovidii*, which was adapted by the 'Vulgate' commentator,[6] both the *Remedia amoris* and the *Metamorphoses*

---

[3] See for example Birger Munk Olson, 'Ovide au moyen age (du IXe au XIIe siècle', in G. Cavallo (ed.), *Le Strade del testo*, Bari, 1987, pp. 67-96, together with the relevant material in his book *I classici nel canone scolastico altomedievale*, Spoleto, 1991, pp. 23-55, 120; also Frank T. Coulson's introduction to his edition, *The 'Vulgate' Commentary on Ovid's 'Metamorphoses': The Creation Myth and the Story of Orpheus*, Toronto, 1991, pp. 2-7. See further Coulson, 'Hitherto Unedited Medieval and Renaissance Lives of Ovid (1)', *Mediaeval Studies*, 49, 1987, pp. 152-207; also Coulson and U. Molyviati-Toptsis, 'Vaticanus latinus 2877: A Hitherto Unedited Allegorization of Ovid's *Metamorphoses*', *Journal of Medieval Latin*, 2, 1992, pp. 134-202.

[4] The main study of Arnulf as Ovid commentator remains F. Ghisalberti, 'Arnolfo d'Orléans, un cultore di Ovidio nel secolo XII', *Memorie del Reale Istituto lombardo di scienze e lettere*, 24.4, 1932, pp. 157-234. See further Frank T. Coulson, 'New Manuscript Evidence for Sources of the *Accessus* of Arnoul d'Orléans to the *Metamorphoses* of Ovid', *Manuscripta*, 30, 1986, pp. 103-7.

[5] On William of Orléans see Hugues-V. Shooner, 'Les *Bursarii Ovidianorum* de Guillaume d'Orléans', *Mediaeval Studies*, 43, 1981, pp. 405-424. For the John of Garland poem see the edition by F. Ghisalberti, *Integumenta Ovidii: Poemetto inedito del secolo XIII*, Messina and Milan, 1933. On the 'Vulgate' commentary see Coulson's partial edition (n. 3 above) and also his article 'The "Vulgate" Commentary on Ovid's *Metamorphoses*', *Mediaevalia*, 13, 1987, pp. 29-61.

[6] For Arnulf's *vita*, see Ghisalberti, 'Arnolfo d'Orléans' (n. 4 above), pp. 180-81, repr. by A.G. Elliott, '*Accessus ad auctores*: Twelfth-Century Introductions to

were written in an attempt to mollify the emperor Augustus, who was incensed by the *Ars amatoria* wherein the poet had taught young Roman men how to be adulterers and young Roman women how to be unchaste. Arnulf proceeds to emphasise Ovid's moral *intentio* in describing transformation: the poet was not concerned with teaching about external, physical changes which result in good or bad corporeal forms, but rather with making us understand the nature of internal, spiritual change, so that we may be led from error towards knowledge of the true Creator. The *utilitas* or ethical usefulness of the *Metamorphoses* is defined as the instruction in divine matters which is achieved through its account of the transformation of temporal things.

Elsewhere the apologetic, compensatory mission of the *Remedia amoris* is elaborated. According to the *accessus* to this work which has been edited by R. B. C. Huygens (MS Munich, Clm 19475 being taken as the base text), Ovid had written a manual of love, the *Ars amatoria*, 'in which he taught young men where to find mistresses', and how to be nice to them when they had found them, 'and he had given girls the same instructions. But some young men indulged their passion to excess' and were not in the least backward in having 'affairs with virgins, and even married women and female relatives, while the young women submitted themselves to married men just as much as to unmarried men. The result was that Ovid became very unpopular with his friends and with others. Afterwards he regretted what he had done, and, being anxious to be reconciled with those he had offended, he saw that the best way of achieving this was to discover the antidote for the love he had proffered to them'. So he set about writing the *Remedia amoris*, in which he advises young men and girls alike who have been 'trapped in the snares of love as to how they may arm themselves against unlawful love'.[7]

The poet's ultimate moral agenda was affirmed in *accessus* to the *Heroides*.[8] William of Orléans is utterly typical in describing its *mate-*

Ovid', *Allegorica*, 5.1, 1980, pp. 6-48 (12-17). For the 'Vulgate' commentator's, see Coulson, 'Lives of Ovid' (n. 3 above), pp. 78-82.

[7] R.B.C. Huygens (ed.), *Accessus ad auctores; Bernard d'Utrecht; Conrad d'Hirsau*, Leiden, 1970, p. 34; translated in A.J. Minnis and A.B. Scott, *Medieval Literary Theory and Criticism c.1100-c.1375: The Commentary Tradition*, rev.ed., Oxford, 1991, p. 25.

[8] For glosses on the *Heroides* see the relevant material in Ralph J. Hexter, *Ovid and Medieval Schooling. Studies in Medieval School Commentaries on Ovid's 'Ars Amatoria', 'Epistulae ex Ponto' and 'Epistulae Heroidum'*, Munich, 1986. See further the copious

ria as 'unlawful and foolish love', and its *intentio* as commendation and condemnation: commendation of certain women who, like Penelope, practise legal love, but condemnation of illicit lovers like Phedra and foolish lovers like Phyllida and Oenone.[9] Similarly, in the second of the *Heroides* prefaces edited by Huygens, the work's intention is stated to be commendation of lawful marriage and love. It pertains to ethics (*ethice supponitur*), because Ovid is 'teaching good morality and eradicating evil behaviour. The ultimate end (*finalis causa*) of the work is this, that, having seen the advantage (*utilitas*) gained from lawful love, and the misfortunes which arise from foolish and unlawful love, we may shun both of these and may adhere to chaste love'.[10]

Moralising scholarship of this type constitutes a rather vain attempt to police the meaning of Ovid's erotic poetry, by controlling it through moral structures and strictures. But of course the texts resist such imposition. Ovid's amatory verse was composed to entertain a sophisticated audience of young Roman aristocrats, who would find in the *Ars amatoria* at once sexual comedy, seduction techniques, and worldly cynicism—an unstable mixture of the serious and the scurrilous, the elevated and the obscene. This mixture became even more volatile, so to speak, within its medieval reception. Ovid's words could be appropriated in a wide variety of ways by his glossators and imitators. This elasticity will be illustrated by the following account of medieval French texts which, in different ways, teach the art of love, beginning with one of the earliest, *L'Art d'amours*, a translation into French of the *Ars amatoria* along with traditional gloss materials.[11]

The first two books of this translation have been assigned to the period between 1214/15 and the end of the first third of the century, while the third book (following the original in which Ovid

---

materials transcribed by M.C.E. Edwards (now Shaner), 'A Study of Six Characters in Chaucer's *Legend of Good Women* with reference to medieval scholia on Ovid's *Heroides*', B.Litt. diss., University of Oxford, 1970, esp. pp. 29-37.

[9] Cf. the text of this *accessus* from MS Vatican, Vat. lat. 2792 as transcribed by F. Ghisalberti, 'Mediaeval Biographies of Ovid', *Journal of the Warburg and Courtauld Institutes*, 9, 1946, pp. 10-59 (44).

[10] Huygens (ed.), *Accessus ad auctores* (n. 7 above), p. 30; trans. Minnis and Scott, *Medieval Literary Theory* (ibid.), p. 21.

[11] Fortunately, a team of scholars comprising R.J. Tarrant, Frank T. Coulson, Ralph J. Hexter and Ann Moss is currently engaged in the preparation of an annotated catalogue of the medieval and Renaissance commentaries on Ovid for the *Catalogus translationum et commentariorum*.

set himself up as an advisor to women) seems to be an addition which was produced during the age of Philippe le Bel; more precisely, sometime between 1268 and the end of the century. The specific set or sets of Latin glosses which the translators followed have not yet been identified—which is hardly surprising, given the present state of our knowledge of Ovid's medieval commentary tradition.[12] What is perfectly clear, however, is that both the anonymous writers sought to go beyond the staple fare of the schools. In *L'Art d'amours* an impressive array of Latin and French texts are brought together. As well as citations of a substantial number of Ovid's other poems, along with the Bible, Horace, and the *De consolatione philosophiae* of Boethius, contemporary French songs and proverbs are liberally cited. Moreover, in the third book the *Roman de la Rose* is referred to, while the first two books draw on French romances which were written towards the end of the twelfth century and the beginning of the thirteenth, namely Chrétien de Troyes' *Philomena, Athis et Prophilias, Li Fet des Romains*, and *Blancandin*.[13]

In the following discussion I shall focus on the earlier translator. It may be inferred that he was a cleric who enjoyed considerable professional contacts with members of the aristocracy, whose interests and life-styles were markedly different from that of a priestly caste which valued celibacy; certainly he himself was not in the business of implementing Ovid's 'commandments'. This comes across very clearly in his statement that 'When young men are at leisure, they want to practise the art of love. They want to amuse themselves, to ride horses, and to be prized and praised for having love and riches with which they are fat and puffed up'.[14] Here an element of clerical censoriousness has crept in. But in general he keeps such opinions in check, as when Ovid's recommendation that 'the contest of noble steeds'[15] should not escape the lover,

---

[12] This work has been edited by Bruno Roy, *L'Art d'amours. Traduction et commentaire de l' 'Ars amatoria' d'Ovide*, Leiden, 1974, and translated by Lawrence B. Blonquist, *L'Art d'amours (The Art of Love)*, Garland Library of Medieval Literature, Series A, 32, New York and London, 1987. This translation has been drawn upon in the following discussion, though I have made occasional alterations. Blonquist's introduction is marred by minor errors, which may be typographical, though it is disconcerting to find the plural of *accessus* being given as *accessi* on three occasions.

[13] Cf. *L'Art d'amours*, ed. Roy (n. 12 above), pp. 49-53, 56.

[14] Ibid., p. 64; trans. Blonquist, p. 2.

[15] *Ars amatoria*, I, 135-36; a passage much mangled in translation, though of course the French writer may have been misled by a gloss.

because there are many opportunities for courtship at events like
that, prompts the citation of material from the romance of Blan-
chandin, who won the love of his *amie* through a tournament[16].
Women, the French translator declares, take note of which of the
bachelliers is the most impressively armed and holds himself best on
his horse, and they are eager to see their menfolk bear certain
tokens of their love, though some knights dare not wear them openly for fear of blame. Moreover, the translator offers an example
of what women sing in their dance-songs (*karoles*), and goes on to
claim that they are eager to take part in such things, this being a
type of amusement ('maniere de deduit') which is pursued solely
for the opportunities it affords them for display of their jovial qualities and their hearts' delights.[17] Indeed, he adds, the more they
are censured for such activities, the more they indulge in them.
But no thoroughgoing moral condemnation follows.

The hypothesis that the anonymous translator is, so to speak,
endeavouring to pull his punches, finds further warrant in his strug-
gle with the meaning of Ovid's infamous *fallite fallentes*, 'deceive
the deceivers' (*Ars amatoria*, I, 645), often read as a statement that
since all women are untrustworthy men should have no scruples
about deceiving them. But in this case the anonymous Frenchman
seems to want to mute his original, at least initially;[18] his rendering singles out as targets for deception *only* those women who want
to deceive 'you' (the addressee being constructed as male, inevitably): 'Decevés ceulz que vous cuidiés qui vous vouldroient dece-
voir: c'est droiture'.[19] The concomitant is that 'we must be loyal
to all those whom we expect to be loyal to us'. But then he seems
to defect to the other side: Ovid is credited with the belief that
since no woman is loyal to men 'we' need not bear them any loyalty. However, he continues, we must not deceive anyone else ('nul
autre') if they do not deceive us first. Presumably he has in mind
here certain males who seem to be inappropriate targets of pre-
emptive 'traïson'? But his meaning is far from clear. Ecclesiastes
VII 28 is then brought in, 'Who will find a friend (*amie*) in a

---

[16] *L'Art d'amours*, ed. Roy (n. 12 above), pp. 84-85; trans. Blonquist, p. 16.

[17] Ibid., p. 86; trans., p. 17.

[18] This can be read, of course, as a response to Ovid's recommendation to
make women fall into the snare which they themselves have laid (*Ars amatoria*, I,
646), which implies reactive rather than gratuitous or universal deception.

[19] *L'Art d'amours*, ed. Roy (n. 12 above), p. 144-45; trans. Blonquist, pp. 61-
62.

woman?', which is interpreted 'as if he said openly: there is none'.

That would seem to settle the issue. Yet later, when amplifying Ovid's advice about not reproaching a woman with her faults, the translator goes beyond the motivation of sexual self-interest in advocating chivalrous gallantry of a more general sort. 'Above all else be careful not to say churlish things (de dire villenie) to women', and not only to the woman you love but to others, because if your beloved hears you speaking ill of another she will suppose that you really think the same of her.[20] The translator then refers to something which he has said elsewhere ('comme nous avons dit ailleurs'): the honour of the man who bears no honour to women must be dead.

> Qui aux dames honneur ne porte,
> La sienne honneur doit estre morte. (3384-85)

This seems to be a quotation from a poem (as yet unidentified, and perhaps lost) in which our anonymous writer spoke in the discourse of 'courtly love', a language which was often far more flattering to women than that found in the text of the Roman *praeceptor amoris*.

It may therefore be concluded that on the one hand the cleric responsible for the original *L'Art d'amours* is making his Latin text more accessible to relatively uneducated readers, and on the other, adapting it to tastes which often were different from those of the compiler of the Latin commentary on which, one may presume, he drew so substantially. The mark of the schools is very visible at the beginning of the text. The first twenty lines of our anonymous writer's preface follow the pattern of the *accessus ad auctorem*.[21] It begins by identifying 'Trois choses furent pour lesquelles Ovide fu esmeüs a faire ce livre', the three reasons or causes which moved Ovid to write. This reflects *accessus* terms like *causae suscepti operis* and *causae scribendi*; by the middle of the thirteenth century the variant *causae moventes ad scribendum* was in use,[22] due to the

---

[20] Ibid., p. 216; trans., p. 114.

[21] Ibid., pp. 63-64; trans., pp. 1-2. The first 12 lines or so (in Roy's edition) of this introduction are generally similar to the *accessus* to the *Ars amatoria* which may be the work of Fulco of Orléans [see the references in n. 95 below], but the French version represents a considerable adaptation and amplification of the Latin text as published by Hexter, *Ovid and Medieval Schooling* (n. 8 above), p. 219.

[22] On such terminology see A.J. Minnis, *Medieval Theory of Authorship: Scholastic Literary Attitudes in the Later Middle Ages*, 2nd ed., Aldershot, 1988, pp. 31, 41, 80, 244n, 249n. For the *causae scribendi* in Ovid commentary specifically see for

impact of the 'Aristotelian Prologue' which followed the structur-
al principle of the four causes (efficient, material, formal, and
final).[23] In this case the 'trois choses' consist of Ovid's wish to display his knowledge, to reveal the fickleness of his youth, and to
teach the art of love, how to win over women and young girls.

The last of these reasons, the French translator continues, is
'necessary, proper and profitable, for there are some young men
who love young women very much, but they do not know how to
court them, or how to find them, or how to do the things that
would win them'. So they may despair, and either kill themselves
or go mad. It was 'in order to remove this despair from the hearts
of the young' that Ovid wrote this book. Generally this is reminiscent of William of Orléans' remark that Ovid was moved to
write the *Ars* when he saw young men suffering because they were
doing the wrong things through ignorance of the art of love.[24] Or
the statement in an anonymous twelfth-century *accessus* to the *Ars
amatoria* (as edited by Huygens, and described by Ralph Hexter as
the 'canonical' introduction to that text)[25] that Ovid's *intentio* 'is to
instruct young men in the art of love, and how they should behave
towards girls when having a love-affair. ... The way he proceeds
in this work is to show how a girl may be picked up (*possit inveniri*),
how when picked up she may be won over, and, once won over,
how her love may be retained'.[26] Indeed, the French writer goes
on to remark that once an attractive woman is found, her lover
must know how to keep her, and so Ovid includes advice on this
matter in his teaching. Such remarks derive, of course, from Ovid's
own statement near the beginning of the *Ars amatoria*:

> Principio quod amare velis, reperire labore,
> Qui nova nunc primum miles in arma venis.

---

example Ghisalberti, 'Mediaeval Biographies' (n. 9 above), pp. 52, 59; Hexter,
Ovid and Medieval Schooling (n. 8 above), p. 219; Minnis and Scott, *Medieval Literary Theory* (n. 7 above), p. 26. For the term *causa intentionis* in Ovid commentary
see further Ghisalberti, 'Mediaeval Biographies', pp. 56, 58; Hexter, *Ovid and
Medieval Schooling*, p. 224; Minnis and Scott, *Medieval Literary Theory*, pp. 25, 26.

[23] For a basic description of this prologue form see Minnis, *Medieval Theory of
Authorship* (n. 22 above), pp. 28-29. On the four causes in Ovid commentary see
for example Ghisalberti, 'Mediaeval Biographies' (n. 9 above), pp. 45, 50-52; Minnis and Scott, *Medieval Literary Theory* (n. 7 above), pp. 361, 364.

[24] MS London, British Library, Add. 49368, f. 81ʳ.

[25] Hexter, *Ovid and Medieval Schooling* (n. 8 above), pp. 46-47.

[26] Huygens (ed.), *Accessus ad auctores* (n 7 above), p. 33; trans. Minnis and Scott,
Medieval Literary Theory (ibid.), p. 24.

Proximus huic labor est placitam exorare puellam:
Tertius, ut longo tempore duret amor. (I, 35-38)[27]

The text's *titre* (cf. the Latin *titulus*)[28] is given as 'Cy commence
l'Art d'amours', this being a version of the form commonly found
in the *accessus Ovidiani*.[29] Its *matiere* and *entent* (cf. *materia* and *intentio*) are given together as, 'His subject-matter is amorous men and
women who are occupied with the commandments of love, which
he intends to introduce', though the earlier account of the *causae
scribendi* had already offered a full explanation of the poet's intentions. Finally, the 'fin cause', 'c'est a dire l'accomplissement de ces-
te euvre', which is understood when one has read the book though
in its entirety, is stated to be that we should keep the commandments which Ovid provides. 'Fin cause' translates the Latin *causa
finalis*, a term which could be used within the earlier *accessus* as
largely synonymous with the terms *intentio* and *utilitas* or indeed as
an extension of either or both of them.[30] (It should be noticed that
this term appeared frequently as one of the 'type C' prologue headings, as R.W. Hunt called it,[31] before becoming one of the four
'introductory causes' that constituted the 'Aristotelian Prologue'.)

This *accessus* to his *auctor* having been completed, the anonymous
writer then comments on his own activity as translator. Rather
coyly, he claims that had he wanted to he could have given a
more careful exposé and extracted more meaning from the text.
But *science* which is open to everyone is supposed to be worth
nothing. By contrast, when words are obscure one is more eager
to pause over them in order to understand what is being said. The
clear implication is that there is much left to think about in *L'Art
d'amours*. This is not, of course, to be seen as some sort of invitation to delve deeply into our text to discover some profound meaning hidden underneath its literal sense. Rather the translator is

---

[27] Ovid, *'The Art of Love' and Other Poems*, ed. J.H. Mozley, London and Cambridge, Mass., 1939, p. 14.

[28] On this *accessus* term see Minnis, *Medieval Theory of Authorship* (n. 22 above),
pp. 19-20.

[29] See for example the *accessus* printed by Hexter, *Ovid and Medieval Schooling*
(n. 8 above), p. 219: 'Titulus talis est: O[uidii] Nasonis de amatoria arte liber
primus incipit'. Cf. the specifications of the poem's *titulus* in the *accessus* printed
by Ghisalberti, 'Mediaeval Biographies' (n. 9 above), pp. 45, 47.

[30] For examples of the use of the term *finalis causa* in *accessus Ovidiani* see Ghisalberti, 'Mediaeval Biographies' (n. 9 above), pp. 45, 47, 50, 51; Hexter, *Ovid and
Medieval Schooling* (n. 8 above), pp. 16, 103, 111-12, 147, 158, 161, 220, 226; Minnis and Scott, *Medieval Literary Theory* (n. 7 above), pp. 23, 24, 28, 361, 364.

[31] Cf. Hunt, 'Introductions to the *Artes*' (n. 1 above).

seeking to praise and recommend his work by giving it a faint aura of mystery, in claiming that it is replete with intriguing secrets; this was a device often used by the writers of the day, even in cases in which the meaning of what they had said was perfectly obvious.

The remainder of the French prologue and its greater part, lines 28-109 in Roy's edition, follows another form which was extensively used in the schools, this being what may be termed the *accessus ad artem*, by which I mean a general discussion of the art or science to which the text appertained rather than the actual text under study. The distinction was well expressed by Thierry of Chartres at the beginning of his *De inventione* commentary, in terms of what it is necessary to know concerning the art (*circa artem*) and concerning the textbook (*circa librum*).[32] Concerning the art of rhetoric, he explains, ten things must be considered: its genus and what the art is in itself along with its material, office, end, parts, species, instrument, master or practitioner, and the reason why it is called rhetoric. Thierry also used the *extrinsecus / intrinsecus* distinction to designate respectively what must be known in advance before practising an art and what must be known in practising the art itself. This technical vocabulary is followed, for example, in Alan of Lille's commentary on the *Rhetorica ad Herennium*, and it influenced William of Conches' commentary on Priscian.[33] But within the study of grammar the headings *extrinsecus* and *intrinsecus* took over the functions performed by the headings *circa artem* and *circa librum* in Thierry's paradigm: an 'extrinsic' discussion comprised a discussion of the place in the scheme of human knowledge occupied by grammar, together with a summary of the defining characteristics of this art, while the heading *intrinsecus* introduced a systematic discussion of the text itself, often in accordance with the vocabulary characteristic of the 'type C' prologue and which has in part been rendered into French in *L'Art d'amours*.

In short, the anonymous translator has reversed the *extrinsecus / intrinsecus* order: the latter comes first, then the former, with his own little piece of self-recommendation in between. While he does not actually use the term *extrinsecus* (or *intrinsecus* either, of course)

---

[32] See N.M. Häring, 'Thierry of Chartres and Dominicus Gundissalinus', *Mediaeval Studies*, 26, 1964, pp. 271-86 (281; cf. 286).

[33] See M.-T. d'Alverny, *Alain de Lille: Textes inédits*, Paris, 1965, pp. 52-55; also Minnis and Scott, *Medieval Literary Theory* (n. 7 above), pp. 122-24, 130-34.

his concerns are those which were traditionally introduced by that heading, particularly the specification of the place in the scheme of human knowledge which is occupied by the art of love. A fundamental distinction is made between the mechanical arts and the arts which combine art and knowledge ('science'), the latter category being divided into the liberal arts and the non-liberal arts ('ars non liberaux'). There are only seven liberal arts practised at the present time among Christians, the translator explains, these being branches of study which may be pursued without the prohibition of the law or of the clergy. By contrast there are certain non-liberal arts which are prohibited either by earthly justice and secular princes (including poisoning and killing by treason) or by earthly justice and by the church (such as sorcery and divination). Moreover, the clergy in particular are barred 'by the church', meaning by canon law, from taking part in such arts as gaming, wrestling matches, and tournaments, along with games of dice, chess and tables (elsewhere these are identified as aristocratic pursuits) and of course necromancy, 'qui est art d'enchantement'. Finally there are certain non-liberal arts which are not prohibited: these include astronomy (providing prediction [*sors*] and necromancy are not involved) and the art of love. Here then, at last, is where the *ars amandi* fits into the scheme of things, the place it occupies within the *ordo scientiarum*. It is not forbidden for two reasons: first, it encourages love in certain people who, had they never read about the art, would have lacked the desire or the will to pursue it, and secondly, it ensures that the lover, who without the art would not know how to woo and win his lady, will avoid death. This is reminiscent of the treatments of the end (*finis*) of the art in question which were characteristic of the extrinsic prologues of rhetoricians and grammarians.

Moreover, the manner in which the anonymous translator actually began his excursus *circa artem* (i.e. lines 28-41) is reminiscent of schoolteachers' discussions of the practitioner or *artifex* of the art under discussion. We are assured that love is rightly called an art, in accordance with the usual etymology and explanation of what an art is, since one who wishes to attain knowledge of love has 'to do, say, and think many things'. And because we are dealing with a true art, it can be known in several ways: *par nature, par coustume, par aprison* and *par orgueil et folie*. Women and young men of leisure ('les femmes et les joennes hommes oiseux') know it by nature. (A few lines later the category *par nature* is amplified to

include a specification of age: 'par nature et par jouvence'.) Love
is known by custom to poor people and ribalds, a statement which
presumably means that for such people it is merely a matter of
habit. Clerks know it by teaching inasmuch as they read the his-
tories, books and commandments (presumably he has Ovid's love-
commandments in mind) of the ancients. Peasants ('villains') know
it by folly and pride, which might mean that people of lower rank
engage in foolish, untutored amatory practices on the one hand,
and on the other fall into the sin of pride by attempting to pursue a form of love which is far above their station.

Here, then, are the different ways in which love may be said to
be practised, and the different kinds of practitioner. But clearly, it
is the natural occupation of a small section of society: young men
and women of the aristocratic, leisured class. And in this supposed
fact we can find a clue to what might be termed the secularising
impulse of *L'Art d'amours*. For our French writer seems to be draw-
ing on a discourse which counterbalances (or perhaps undermines)
the moralising discourse which he has inherited from the Latin
commentary-tradition on Ovid's love-poetry. He speaks a language
and conveys attitudes which often occur in, for example, commentaries on the chapter on 'heroic love' which is included in the
Viaticum of Constantine the African (who died c.1087 at the abbey
of Montecassino), a major textbook in university faculties of medicine.[34]

According to *L'Art d'amours*, love is known naturally by aristocrats, who moreover have the leisure to indulge their pleasures;
they enjoy being praised on account of their loves and their riches (cf. p. 157 above). But the illness can be fatal. Male sexual frus-
tration may lead to despair, which may result in suicide. Some
men hang themselves, explains the French translator, while others
die by the sword, fire or water. Still others lose their sense and
memory on account of love.[35] Similarly, in the first *Viaticum* commentary to survive, the work of Gerard of Berry (late twelfth century), 'wealth and leisure—that is, pleasure in daily life—are the
pregrogatives of the nobility, and it is they who suffer the disease

---

[34] In contrast with the beginning of *L'art d'amours*, this medical discourse is
not present in the remarks about the kinds of death love can cause which are
found in the *accessus* published by Ghisalberti, 'Mediaeval Biographies' (n. 9 above),
pp. 45, 47 (re the *Remedia amoris*) and Hexter, *Ovid and Medieval Schooling* (n. 8
above), p. 219 (re the *Ars amatoria*).

[35] *L'Art d'amours*, ed. Roy (n. 12 above), p. 63; trans. Blonquist, p. 1.

of love', to follow Mary Wack's cogent summary.[36] The Arabic medical texts that were the sources of such Western teaching do not mention a particular social class as more or less susceptible to the lovers' malady, but the medieval medical profession labelled 'love as an occupational hazard of the nobility. It became another mark of precedence, like wealth and leisure themselves'.[37] Thus 'heroic' love —there was considerable confusion between the terms *eros* and *heros*—was specified to be the love that belonged to a lord or nobleman,[38] as in Gerard of Berry's statement that 'Heroes are said to be noble men who, on account of riches and the softness of their lives, are more likely to suffer this disease'.[39] Indeed, Constantine himself had said elsewhere (in his *De coitu*) that 'a leisured heart (*cor ociosum*) and daily joy increase libido'.[40] In his *Viaticum* he explains that 'if erotic lovers are not helped so that their thought is lifted and their spirits lightened, they inevitably fall into a melancholic disease'.[41] If untreated or unchecked, this could prove terminal.

Cures recommended by Constantine included actual consummation of one's love (or, failing that, therapeutic sex with another woman—an idea which Christian *medici* found difficult to support!), recreational activities with friends, and the enjoyment of music, poetry, and beautiful gardens. Gerard of Berry does manage to include in his list of treatments 'consorting with and embracing girls, sleeping with them repeatedly, and switching various ones' (i.e. changing partners regularly).[42] But this apparent invitation to promiscuity is tempered by the thought that the lover's ardour may be lessened by instruction in the unlovely aspects of sex and the female body, which I presume is how this statement should be interpreted: 'the counsel of old women is very useful, who may

---

[36] Mary Frances Wack, *Lovesickness in the Middle Ages: The 'Viaticum' and its Commentaries*, Philadelphia, 1990, p. 39.

[37] Wack, *Lovesickness* (n. 36 above), p. 61. Love was linked with melancholy, also generated by the noble life-style; large amounts of leisure and pleasure allowed digestive products to collect which could in due course turn into black bile, and cause melancholy.

[38] Ibid., pp. 46, 60. For the history of the term *amor heroicus* see further Danielle Jacquart and Claude Thomasset, 'L'amour "héroïque" à travers le traité d'Arnaud de Villeneuve', in *La folie et le corps*, ed. Jean Céard, Paris, 1985, pp. 143-58.

[39] Ed. and trans. Wack, *Lovesickness* (n. 36 above), pp. 202-3; cf. p. 60.

[40] Cited ibid., p. 61.

[41] Ed. and trans. ibid., pp. 188-89.

[42] Ed. and trans. ibid., pp. 202-3.

relate many disparagements and the stinking dispositions of the desired thing'. At this point Gerard nears the territory occupied by Ovid's *Remedia amoris*.[43] The translator responsible for *L'Art d'amours* limits himself to the statement that his author Ovid wrote this treatise in order to remove despair from the hearts of the young; here then is a courtship manual which may help its readers to achieve their amatory ends and preserve their health.

This brings us to consider the importance of youth in the French translator's account of love. He notes that it was the hearts of the young that Ovid sought to ease; that the poet was addressing those young men who love young women very much but do not know how to court them; that when young men are at leisure they want to practise the art of love. But there is more to consider here than the supposed needs of Ovid's audience: for the author was a young man himself when he wrote the *Ars amatoria*.[44] The second of the three causes which lie behind Ovid's work is identified (rather damningly!) as his wish 'to reveal the fickleness of his youth'.[45] Later, after his discussion *circa artem*, the translator develops this idea, in stating that the poet, 'when he was an adolescent and when he was a young man ("comme il fut adolescent en sa joennesse"), wrote this book in the first flower of his age and of his life'.[46]

Thus the *Ars amatoria* is put firmly in its place, both physiologically and morally. When this translation was produced the notion that youth was the age in which men were particularly susceptible to love, given that this was the time when their bodily heat was at its greatest, was an utter commonplace, along with the concomitant that in one's maturity wiser counsels would, or at least should,

---

[43] In the *accessus* to the *Remedia amoris* which has been edited by Huygens Ovid is described as prescribing 'just like a doctor. For a good doctor gives medicine to the sick to heal them, and to the healthy so that they may escape illness' (trans. Minnis and Scott, *Medieval Literary Theory* (n. 7 above), p. 25). Conversely, Ovid was quoted as an authority in certain medical commentaries. See for example the citation of his comments on the effects of wine by Egidius and Peter of Spain in their *Viaticum* commentaries, ed. and trans. Wack, *Lovesickness* (n. 36 above), pp. 208-9, 248-49.

[44] For Ovid as a poet who wrote love-poetry in his youth and/or who addressed a youthful audience see the relevant remarks in the *accessus* printed by Edwards, 'A Study of Six Characters' (n. 8 above), p. 32, 34-35; Ghisalberti, 'Mediaeval Biographies' (n. 9 above), pp. 44, 45, 47, 51, 57, 59; Hexter, *Ovid and Medieval Schooling* (n. 8 above), p. 219; Minnis and Scott, *Medieval Literary Theory* (n. 7 above), pp. 24, 25, 27, 362.

[45] *L'Art d'amours*, ed. Roy (n. 12 above), p. 63; trans. Blonquist, p. 1.

[46] Ibid., p. 69; trans., p. 4.

prevail. There was some dispute over when precisely *adolescentia* began and ended within a person's life-cycle (depending on which scheme of the ages of man was being followed), but general agreement that this was the *aetas amoris*. Sexuality, as John Burrow puts it, 'was held to be a function' of that same natural body-heat 'whose gradual cooling, as the fuelling moisture ran out, caused the processes of ageing. Hence it was easy to see why the fires of love should die down in the later ages of life', when the colder humours dominated.[47]

Our French writer opts for the scheme of the seven ages of man, in providing an account of the sequence of the ages of man's life.[48] This scheme, which is Ptolemaic in origin, does not seem to have attained the level of popularity enjoyed in the Middle Ages by the 'four ages' model, which was reinforced by theories relating to the four humours and the four seasons. However, an elaborate version of the seven ages (related to the corresponding planets) is included in Jean Froissart's *Le Joli Buisson de Jonece* (1373), and we know that King Charles V of France possessed a tapestry representing 'Sept Ars et Estats des Ages des gens'.[49] The translator of *L'Art d'amours* may have been prompted to use the seven ages scheme by his earlier account of the seven liberal arts, but no such connection is made explicit in the text. And his interest is in the physiological and psychological changes which are characteristic of the various ages rather than their planetary associations. Thus he explains that the first age is infancy, when one is unable to talk; the second, boyhood, an age of innocence, wherein one can speak well; the third, adolescence, 'when one has his first beard'; the fourth, manhood, the time of full strength; the fifth, maturity, when a man has acquired all the virtues and enjoys 'all the beauty and natural intelligence that nature can give him'; the sixth, old age,

---

[47] J.A. Burrow, *The Ages of Man. A Study in Medieval Writing and Thought*, Oxford, 1986, p. 157. 'Adolescence is of a hot and moist complexion', declares the ninth-century Arabic scholar who was known in the West as 'Johannitius' (cited ibid., p. 22). Moreover, as Wack explains, a hot complexion was believed to be the most important underlying cause of the lovers' malady *(Lovesickness* (n. 36 above), p. 98-100). 'We see that it befalls the young most', asserts Peter of Spain in the B version of his *Viaticum* commentary (ed. and trans. ibid., p. 243). See further the A version of this commentary (ed. and trans. ibid., pp. 221-25) in which the time at which young men most desire intercourse is investigated. Unfortunately, Wack's summary of this argument (ibid., p. 86) is misleading.

[48] *L'Art d'amours*, ed. Roy (n. 12 above), p. 69; trans. Blonquist, p. 5.

[49] As is pointed out by Burrow, *Ages of Man* (n. 47 above), pp. 40-41.

when one is aged and white-haired; the seventh, decrepitude, when
one 'drivels' and 'returns to the actions and speech of children'.
The first age is one year and a half; the second, seven years; the
third, eighteen; the fourth, twenty-five; the fifth, fifty; the sixth,
sixty to eighty years; the seventh, one hundred years, this being
the time in which 'age chills man and woman, and they lose reason, strength, and memory'.

From our point of view, however, what is most important is that
this account of the seven ages follows on from the translator's statement that Ovid wrote the *Ars amatoria* 'comme il fu adolescent en
sa joenesse'. 'En la premiere fleur de son temps et de sa vie' he
may have been, but this age had its limitations also, as a time of
immaturity and passion. Hence the translator's remark near the
beginning of his work that one of the reasons why Ovid wrote was
to reveal the fickleness ('legiereté') of his youth. (While the translator's account of the seven ages does not specifically link love with
adolescentia, the implicit connection is too obvious to miss.) It may
be inferred that this was the age in which Ovid himself had acquired
his amatory experience, for the translator proceeds to gloss Ovid's
claim that he is 'maistre' of 'l'art d'amer' with the statement that
no one can know sickness as well as the person who has experienced it: 'Nulx ne puet si bien savoir la maladie comme cellui qui
l'essaiee'.[50] Because Ovid had tried love, he can 'speak better than
anyone else about what one must do to conquer it' ('a la con-
querre' probably has the sense here of 'to master it', though there
is of course the possibility of mild irony, a nod towards the tenets
of the *Remedia amoris*). In short, Ovid experienced and wrote about
lovesickness, what medieval writers could call *amor heros* or *heroicus*,
in his adolescence, and it is up to the reader to contemplate the
significance of that fact. Ovid may have the authority of vast experience, and sex may be a quite natural activity for the young,[51]
but the age of love is also a time of *legiereté*, removed from the
perfect age of man's life when one is in possession of all the virtues
and all the understanding that nature can bestow.

Moving away from *L'Art d'amours* to consider other French translations of Ovid, all of the following three texts (which seem to be

---

[50] *L'Art d'amours*, ed. Roy (n. 12 above), p. 70; trans. Blonquist, p. 5.

[51] Hence his French translator declares that Ovid wished 'to prove that it is
not a sin for a man and a woman to go to bed with each other, for it is a natural thing, and nature bestows it, nor is it an artificial thing' (trans. Blonquist,
p. 106; cf. the edition by Roy (n. 12 above), pp. 204-5).

later) do not exploit the *accessus* tradition as such, yet offer telling contrasts with *L'Art d'amours*, as well as affording further evidence of what I have termed the elasticity of Ovid in the hands of his medieval readers. The first two of these are the work of a poet who identifies himself as 'Jakes d'Amiens'.[52] This Jacques produced French versions of both the *Ars amatoria* and (as a separate unit and perhaps slightly later) the *Remedia amoris*; the former consists of 2384 verses and the latter, of 625. He takes great liberties with the *Ars amatoria*, employing the device of the amatory dialogue which had been used so elaborately by Andreas Capellanus. Here Ovid has become a poet of *fine amor*, and his medieval disciple is no distant *praeceptor* but someone who himself loves in this fashionable way; indeed, love for the 'debonnaire' one who holds his heart in her prison was what motivated his writing, and he hopes that it will further his suit (ll. 11-24). May Love grant that his poem is agreeable to the 'tres douce dame' who often makes his face pale (i.e. with love-suffering); indeed, without her love he cannot do anything that might ever please. In the epilogue to his *Art d'amors*, as a 'fine lover' Jacques sends everything in this book to his beloved, begging mercy with his hands clasped in prayer, pleading that she should take mercy and pity on him, lest he should die (ll. 2367-80).[53]

Jacques' *Art d'amors* includes advice to women (ll. 1720ff.), though it should be noted that this draws on only a small part of Book III itself; for the most part he adapts material from Book II to

---

[52] I have used the edition by Gustav Körting, *'L'Art d'amors' und 'Li Remedes d'amors'*, Leipzig, 1868; repr. Geneva, 1976. There is also an edition by D. Talsma, *L'Art d'amours van Jakes d'Amiens*, Leiden, 1925, which is reprinted by A.M. Finoli, *Artes amandi, da Maître Elie ad Andrea Capellano*, Milan, 1969, pp. 31-121. On Jacques see further G. Paris, 'Chrétien Legouais et autres traducteurs et imitateurs d'Ovide au moyen âge', *Histoire littéraire de la France*, 29, 1885, pp. 489-97 (468-72), and G. Kühlhorn, *Das Verhältnis der 'Art d'amours' von Jacques d'Amiens zu Ovids 'Ars amatoria'*, Lepizig, 1908.

[53] The atmosphere of courtly compliment created by this work is very similar to that found in the anonymous *Clef d'amors* (dated 1280 by Gaston Paris), a poem of some 3,200 octosyllabic lines which follows the *Roman de la Rose* in employing the figure of the God of Love, who appears to the poet and orders him to write on the art of loving. The poet hides his own name and that of his beloved in his text, which represents a highly individual adaptation rather than a translation of the *Ars amatoria*. This work has been edited by A. Doutrepont, *'La Clef d'amors'. Texte critique avec introduction, appendice et glossaire*, Bibliotheca Normannica, V, Halle, 1890; repr. in Finoli, *Artes amandi* (n. 52 above), pp. 123-228.

that end.[54] Even more remarkably, he manages to recommend his *Remedes d'amors* to his lady (ll. 1-96).[55] The matter of this work, he asserts, relates to honesty and courtesy, and does not contain anything which is badly spoken or villainous. To blame those who should be praised is a waste of intelligence, and such behaviour wins neither praise nor glory; rather those who act in this way make themselves hated by people who should love them. That is what happens when someone writes ill of women, being unable to write either praise or good of them. Jacques does not say that women are without blemish, for there is no mortal who does not sin—even the heavens themselves are flawed. Returning to his purpose, Jacques explains that he has sought matter from which he could make a poem that would profit and please, this being the objective to which all writers direct themselves. Whether the poem is good or bad the matter itself is subtle and noble enough and pleasing, he claims; it is not made of fable—

> ne de Renart ne d'Ysengrin
> ne de Biernart ne de Belin (45-46)

—but rather it is drawn from pity and rhymed and made by love.

Fine amor, then, is what motivates his writing, and gives him joy and happiness in his work. If his 'tres douce, cortoise et sage' lady, for whose love he has undertaken this enterprise, were pleased by it, he wouldn't take any notice of what anyone else thought. Indeed, it should be agreeable to her, if she hears and knows it by heart— and not just to her, for all those who suffer the penance of love could obtain comfort and relief if they knew this teaching well. Jacques proceeds to emphasize how his text may help his lady's love-suffering. Seeing the very sweet one looking pale and lost because of the wounds of love's dart, and not knowing what to do about it, he set about providing a cure, so that she might be diverted and at least better able to bear her suffering even if she cannot put an end to it. So he started to write out of pity for her. Henceforth, in the text which follows, you will be able to hear how 'one can have joy of love'—altogether a novel way to introduce remedies against love![56]

---

[54] As is noted by Roy, in the introduction to his *L'Art d'amours* edition (n. 12 above), p. 15.

[55] *'L'Art d'amors' und 'Li Remedes d'amors'*, ed. Körting (n. 52 above), pp. 69-71.

[56] There is a certain awkwardness here, of course. Who has his lady been suffering on account of? himself? someone else? One possible rationalisation is that

Our third Ovid translation is quite unlike the ones which have just been discussed, since it takes the Roman poet in a very different direction, in consolidating his position (as claimed in the *accessus Ovidiani*) as a moral writer whose texts ultimately 'pertained to ethics'. The translator, who refers to himself simply as 'Guiart, qui l'art d'amours vost en romanz traiter' (l. 5), says he will first teach how one may find and conquer the beloved one, secondly, how one should behave during the affair, and thirdly, how one rids oneself of a lover who is no longer pleasing![57] This takes *Ars amatoria* I, 35-38 (cf. pp. 160-61 above) one step further, in anticipating the objective of the *Remedia amoris*.[58] Guiart then declares that the accusation that might be levelled against him, namely that he is treating of the good and the evil at the same time, is not well-founded. For he proceeds just like the labourer who pulls out thistles and nettles in order to protect the seed, for earth which is poorly prepared yields little. Aristotle 'en son livre' says that a clerk may deceive his mistress, yet elsewhere in the same book he condemns such falsity. In the first instance, then, the writer wishes to demonstrate worldly vice; subsequently he will reveal the truth that consists in the service of God.

> Or vos voil je premier mostrer la fauseté
> La vanité du monde et la desloiauté;
> Puis determinerai apres la verité,
> Coment on doit servir le roi de majesté. (25-28)

In sum, the work has basically a bipartite structure. Ovid functions within the first part, material from the *Ars amatoria* giving way to material from the *Remedia amoris*, which paves the way for the homiletic ending. One should not lose God and His Mother just for a little pleasure which does not last long, as the Bible teaches. The world is old and full of falsity, lacking in either faith or loyalty. Whoever wishes to possess everlasting life must reject the

---

his nominal mistress is so far above this humble clerkly poet that all he can expect from her at best is polite attention and perhaps patronage, her love-life being conducted within the highest ranks of society. Perhaps this is the wrong way to approach a poet who may have had no mistress but his muse; what we are dealing with here is conventional courtly language and rhetorical posturing. However, such discourses have their own logic and hence the question may be asked.

[57] Here I use the edition by Louis Karl, 'L'Art d'amour de Guiart', *Zeitschrift für romanische philologie* 44, 1924, pp. 66-79, 181-87.

[58] Cf. the anonymous *Confort d'amours*, which imitates both the *Ars* and *Remedia* by advising lovers how to acquire love, how to keep love, and how to destroy feelings of love.

works of the devil and worldly pleasures. And so forth. Guiart, taking over 16 strophes from the poem *Des cinq vegiles*, advocates confession, repentance and penance, and recommends the virtues of humility, charity, patience and respect for the church. He proceeds to treat briefly of the seven sacraments and the ten commandments, then offers a kind of love which is very different from the one described earlier: all men should be loved and given good counsel, with hatred and war being despised.

> Porte pes et amor a toute gent en terre,
> Done loial counseil, s'on le te vient requerre,
> Envers touz les pechiez aies haine et guerre ... (217-19)

The poem ends with a prayer to the Virgin as *mediatrix*. Apart from the brief statement in the prologue in defence of treating 'ensemble bien et mal' (l. 14) no attempt is made in ideological terms to reconcile this explicit Christian doctrine with the teaching of the *Ars amatoria* as retailed earlier in the poem; Guiart seems to assume that the text's structure will support the burden of its meaning. And that structure very much reflects the schematisation of Ovid's works which is found in the *accessus Ovidiani*.

Much work remains to be done on these French *artes amandi*, which have been surprisingly neglected, especially by historians of the phenomenon of 'courtly love'. Given the limitations of space here we must move straight on to one of the most significant and challenging Ovidian poets of the thirteenth century, namely Richard de Fournival (1201-60). Richard, one of the greatest bibliophiles of the time, was successively canon, deacon and chancellor of the Chapter of Notre Dame, Amiens, and in addition held the ecclesiastic appointments of a canonry in Rouen and a chaplaincy to Cardinal Robert de Sommercote. Particularly intriguing in view of our previous discussion of the importance of medical discourse in *L'Art d'amours* is the fact that Richard was a licensed surgeon (as well as being the son of a medical man, namely Roger de Fournival, who was personal physician to King Philip Augustus).[59]

---

[59] It may be added that two other major figures in the history of medieval commentary-tradition were physicians: Evrart de Conty (c. 1330-1405), the author of the first substantial commentary on a text written originally in French, namely the *Echecs amoureux*, and the fourteenth-century scholar Dino del Garbo, who commented on Guido Cavalcanti's *Canzone d'amore*. On Evrart see A.J. Minnis, 'Late-Medieval Vernacular Literature and Latin Exegetical Traditions', in J. Assmann and B. Gladigow (eds.), *Text und Kommentar. Archäologie der literarischen Kom-*

Richard de Fournival may have been responsible for the Pseudo-Ovidian *De Vetula* (in Latin, but there is a French version), which
was often taken as an original work of Ovid's [60] Here is a *remedium amoris* with a vengeance, for the text (allegedly found in Ovid's
tomb!) narrates how its poet, sickened by his experience with a
deceitful old woman, becomes a Christian. Several amatory works
in French have been attributed to Richard; the *Commens d'amours*
and *Poissance d'amours* may not be from his pen, but his authorship
of the *Consaus d'amours* has been maintained.[61] There seems to be
no doubt, however, that Richard was responsible for a love-trea-
tise of a rather different kind, this being the *Bestiaires d'amours*, in
which, so to speak, Ovid finds himself thrust into the medieval
beast-fable tradition.[62]

Li Bestiaires d'amours begins with the first sentence of Aristotle's
Metaphysics: 'all men naturally desire to know'. That passage opens
the prologues to many scholastic commentaries and treatises produced during the thirteenth century and beyond, and Dante was
to use it at the beginning of his *Convivio*, a quite extraordinary
instance of 'autoexegesis' in which the poet places the full weight
of academic commentary-technique on three of his own *canzoni*.[63]
Here we may identify the influence on vernacular literature of a
development in the history of Latin scholastic prolegomena, this
being the appearance of the 'sermon-type' prologue, which could
function as one of the several possible variants of the later and
looser 'extrinsic' introduction to a text (cf. pp. 162-63 above, for

---

munikation IV, Munich, 1994, pp. 309-29; F. Guichard Tesson, '*La Glose des Echecs amoureux*: Un savoir à tendance laïque: comment l'interpréter?', *Fifteenth-Century Studies*, 10, 1984, pp. 229-60. Evrart's commentary, which draws on both the *Ars amatoria* and *Remedia amoris*, falls very much within the category of improving yet entertaining books which were produced for princes and high-ranking aristocrats, which also includes works like Giles of Rome's *De regimine principum* (on which Evrart draws) and Boethius's *De consolatione philosophiae*, both of which were avail-able in French translation. On Dino del Garbo see the brief discussion and ref-erences in Minnis and Scott, *Medieval Literary Theory* (n. 7 above) , pp. 378-79.

[60] See for example the *accessus* to *De Vetula* which is printed by Ghisalberti, 'Mediaeval Biographies' (n. 9 above), pp. 50-51.

[61] By G.B. Speroni, 'Il *Consaus d'amours* di Richard de Fournival', *Medioevo romanzo* 1.2, 1974, pp. 217-78.

[62] I have used the edition by Cesare Segre, *Li Bestiaires d'amours di Maistre Richart de Fornival e Li Response du bestiaire*, Milan and Naples, 1957. The earlier edition by C. Hippeau was reprinted in 1978 at Geneva.

[63] Cf. Minnis and Scott, *Medieval Literary Theory* (n. 7 above), pp. 377-78.

the more rigid twelfth-century paradigm).[64] In prologues to twelfth-century Biblical commentaries there was a formal development whereby a technique that for generations had been used in sermons was applied in textual exposition. At the outset an authoritative passage would be quoted, and divided up and discussed in the course of the ensuing prologue, at some stage being applied to the text in question. Originally the *auctoritas* was a Biblical one— hardly surprising, given the origins of this technique in the sermon and the fact that the prologues were introducing commentaries on biblical books. But in the thirteenth century secular *auctoritates* could be cited and used in the same way, Aristotle being a great source of pithy sayings. By the end of the thirteenth century any kind of *auctoritas*, whether secular or sacred, could appear at the beginning of a commentary, or indeed of a discrete treatise, on any subject whatever.

Richard's opening citation of the *Metaphysics* may be placed in this overall perspective. More specifically, his practice may be compared with that found in the Ovidian scholarship and imitation of the next century, including Giovanni del Virgilio's *Metamorphoses* commentary, which begins with Ecclesiasticus XLVII, 16, ingeniously read as intimating the text's 'four causes', and Pierre Bersuire's *Ovidius moralizatus*, wherein the initial *auctoritas* is II Timothy IV, 4, a biblical attack on *fabulae* which Bersuire manages to twist to mean quite the opposite.[65] Even more intriguing is the case of the Spanish prose preface to Juan Ruiz's *Libro de Buen Amor* (written in the early fourteenth century; the prose preface appears in the Salamanca manuscript of the *Libro*, which is dated 1343).[66] It may be identified as a sermon-type prologue which contains both 'extrinsic' and 'intrinsic' elements. The mysterious 'Archpriest of Hita', surely one of the most accomplished of all Medieval Ovidians, cites Psalm XXXI, 10 and interprets it in terms of what 'some schooled in philosophy' have identified as pertaining to the human

---

[64] On the 'sermon-type' prologue see Beryl Smalley, 'Peter Comestor on the Gospels and his Sources', *Recherches de théologie ancienne et médiévale*, 46, 1979, pp. 84-129 (109-10); Minnis, *Medieval Theory of Authorship* (n. 22 above), p. 64.

[65] See Minnis and Scott, *Medieval Literary Theory* (n. 7 above), pp. 360-64, 366-67.

[66] *'The Book of True Love' by Juan Ruiz, the Archpriest of Hita*, ed. and trans. S.R. Daly and A.N. Zahareas, University Park, Pennsylvania, and London, 1978, pp. 22-29. For discussion see Minnis, 'Authors in Love' (n.2 above), pp. 166-71, and John Dagenais, 'A Further Source for the Literary Ideas in Juan Ruiz's Prologue', *Journal of Hispanic Studies*, 11, 1960, pp. 23-52.

soul, namely understanding, will, and memory; the key idea being
that by true understanding man knows what is good and consequently knows what is bad. (The broad similarity between this
argument and Guiart's underdeveloped defence of combining both
the good and the bad in a single work should be obvious.) Ruiz
professes that his intention is a good one. He has written 'in mind-
fulness of the good'; a man or woman with true understanding
will choose and act upon it—which presumably means that such
a person will understand what is good and what is evil, and behave
accordingly. This leads into a recommendation of the *Libro* as both
a *remedium amoris* and an *ars amatoria*, which owes much of its discourse to the *accessus Ovidiani*. The case of Ruiz is one among many
which indicate that Ovid was a godsend to certain vernacular writers who wished to conceptualize and commend their own literary
efforts, and the Ovidian *accessus* supplied the terms of reference for
the self-construction of many a love-poet, as well as pointing
towards (though not actually providing)[67] a higher-order discourse
in which human love was transcended and its words and works
viewed *sub specie aeternitatis*.

But let us return to Richard de Fournival. Having enlisted the
auctoritas of 'the Philosopher' at the very beginning of *Li Bestiaires
d'amours*, he proceeds to discuss that faculty of mind which is called
Memory, with its two doors, of Sight and Hearing.[68] Science gives
way to sexuality when Richard declares that his beloved cannot
depart from his memory, his love for her being incurable. And
may he live forever in her memory! Throughout the work which
follows he constructs himself as the typical 'fine lover' who 'dies
the sort of death that is appropriate to Love, namely despair without expectation of mercy',[69] but as usual his 'sweetest' one can
resuscitate him:[70] 'The sovereign remedy to help me is to have
your heart'.[71] But this is sex in the head, for the adaptations of

---

[67] This refers to *accessus* of the type cited on pp. 155-56 above. Obviously,
such later developments of the *accessus* tradition, like those carried out by Giovanni del Virgilio and Pierre Bersuire (cf. the references given in n. 64 above),
are of a different order and would require comment of a different kind from
what is offered here.

[68] *Li Bestiaires*, ed. Segre (n. 62 above), pp. 3-8.

[69] Ibid., 44; trans. by Jeanette Beer, *Master Richard's Bestiary of Love and Response*,
Berkeley and London, 1986, p. 15.

[70] *Li Bestiaires*, ed. Segre (n. 62 above), pp. 54-55; trans. Beer (n. 69 above),
p. 19.

[71] Ibid., p. 57; trans., p. 20.

beast lore which follow subvert and ridicule the conventional antics
of lovers, presumably for the amusement of an audience which is
educated and wise enough to know better. As a whole the text
makes abundantly clear that love is eminently curable, particular
since the animal imagery through which woman's nature is
described is often highly derogatory.

An 'underlying acrimony' has been detected in the *Bestiaires
d'amours* by Jeanette Beer, who cites as an example the passage in
which Richard's prayers to his lady are equated with dog's vom-
it that has flown out through his teeth.[72] But the writer's use of
the beast-fable tradition may be said to have given him the licence
to indulge in such far-fetched analogies. In this area a taste-bar-
rier divides our time from that of Richard, a point which may be
supported by consultation of, for example, the 'hunt of love' tradition in French literature, wherein imagery may be found of a
kind which is far more grotesque and (to the present writer at
least) disgusting than anything which Richard managed to invent.[73]
Richard was probably far more interested in the construction of
clever conceits for the entertainment of his sophisticated audience,
than in the conscious elaboration of misogynistic clichés. As Jeanette
Beer brings out very well, his underlying style is highly refined and
often 'understated'; it exploits the literary traditions of *courtoisie*,
and 'is not devoid of courtly preciousness either'.[74] All those elements, together with a certain graciousness, are very much evident
in the style of, for example, the *Consaus d'Amours* (here I assume
that this was indeed written by Richard), which is altogether a
more gentle affair. A 'tres douce suer' has asked him to advise her
about loving 'par amours',[75] and he obliges by giving her far more
than that, seeking definitions of both spiritual and temporal love
with the aid of quotations from not only Ovid but also Cicero,
Horace, Virgil, the Bible, and the modern masters John of Garland and Peter of Blois.

---

[72] Beer, *Master Richard's Bestiary* (n. 69 above), p. XX.
[73] For example, in *L'amoureuse prise*, which Jean Acart de Hesdin wrote in 1332,
the lover is imaged as the quarry in terms such as these: 'just as it was proper
to feed the dogs after a hunt, so Love gave them the intestines and other matter woven about the entrails to devour. And he gave them my blood to drink ...
each of the hounds was led forth for the strewed feast that I was'. Quoted by
Marcelle Thiébaux, *The Stag of Love: The Chase in Medieval Literature*, Ithaca and
London, 1974, p. 140.
[74] Beer, *Master Richard's Bestiary* (n. 69 above), p. XXI.
[75] Speroni, 'Il *Consaus d'amours*' (n. 61 above), p. 242.

Quite extraordinarily, *Li Bestiaires d'amours* seems to have pro-voked a written response from a woman—at least, a few manu-scripts of the *Bestiaires* contain a short treatise by a writer who, having described herself (?) as 'a woman in conformity with Our Lord's good pleasure',[76] proceeds to offer a systematic critique of Richard's text. His initial citation of Aristotle prompts the argu-ment that 'a man who has intelligence and discretion must not employ his time or his attention to say or do anything by which any man or any woman may be damaged [*empiriés*]'.[77] The 'dam-age' described in the ensuing text is largely that caused to women by smooth-talking, mendacious men who say they are dying from unrequited love, in order to seduce the credulous objects of their lusts. The clear implication is that Richard (or rather his amato-ry persona) may be one of them, though at the end of the *Response* she politely grants that in fact he may have been trying to warn her against such men.

Adopting the persona of the woman to whom Richard had addressed the *Bestiaires*, the writer takes over his beast-analogies and turns them against him. Of particular interest, in view of Richard's own status, is the attack on certain 'diabolical birds of prey', meaning 'clerics who are so decked out with courtesy and fine words that there is no woman or maiden who can withstand them, whom they do not wish to take'.[78] The attraction of these clerics is considerable: they 'have every courtesy, as I have heard'; moreover, they are the handsomest of men. But they are 'the most devious in malice. They take the ignorant by surprise. Wherefore I call them birds of prey, and it would be good to have protec-tion against them'. The argument takes a highly practical turn when the writer notes that in any case clerics are not the best men for women to associate with, the clear implication being that mar-rying them is not a prudent course of action.[79] It ruins their careers, which is hardly to the woman's advantage, particularly when she could have married a knight who would have enabled her to enjoy a far better life-style.

In *Li Response du bestiaire*, then, the love-object becomes the inde-pendent and highly vocal subject, declaring that she has no inten-

---

[76] *Li Bestiaires*, ed. Segre (n. 62 above), p. 106; trans. Beer (n. 69 above), p. 42.

[77] Ibid., p. 105; trans., p. 41.

[78] Ibid., p. 133; trans., p. 56.

[79] Ibid., pp. 134-35; trans., pp. 56-57.

tion of clothing the suitor with her love, and warning against male deviousness of the type which was taught by Ovid and medieval-ized within the *fine amor* tradition. I myself see little evidence for the view that this putative woman writer was intimating a more philosophical defence of womankind in general, though certainly there are hints of that, as when at the beginning of the text it is pointed out that Eve was made of a better substance than was Adam, although she was not created equal.[80] In short, our mys-terious 'feme ... selonc che qu'il plaist a nostre Seigneur' was no Christine de Pizan.

Which brings us to consider Christine de Pizan herself, or rather a major debate in which she was one of the main protagonists, the early fifteenth-century *querelle* over the meaning and morality of Jean de Meun's part of the *Roman de la Rose* (written between c. 1269 and 1278), a text which owes much to Ovid. Here she set herself up in opposition to such formidable men of culture and high social position as the Col brothers and Jean de Montreuil. Pierre Col was Canon of Paris and Tournay; Gontier Col, First Secretary and notary to King Charles VI. Jean de Montreuil was Provost of Lille and sometime secretary to the Dukes of Berry, Burgundy and Orléans, and to the king. Christine did not stand alone, however; she found a powerful ally in Jean Gerson, chan-cellor of the University of Paris, though it should be emphasised that Gerson's agenda is often markedly different from hers. Chris-tine presented herself as a woman writing in defence of her sex, which had been defamed by Jean de Meun's art of love, a work which in her view had nothing to do with real love. Gerson wrote as a pastor who was incensed by writing, whether ancient or modern, which he held to be morally dangerous; as far as women were concerned, he worried lest the *Roman de la Rose* would put men off marrying them. They certainly agreed, however, in criti-cising Ovid alongside Jean de Meun. Indeed, both the defenders and the attackers of the Rose regarded Jean as a sort of 'modern Ovid', for better or worse as it were. Moreover, the critical vocab-ulary used in the *querelle de la Rose* sometimes reflects technical

---

[80] Ibid., pp. 107-9; trans., pp. 42-43. Here the anonymous writer even puts forward the heterodox view that the original partner of Adam was created equal. However, Adam killed her, because she was nothing to him and so he could not love her. Thus God made a second wife for him, out of one of Adam's ribs, whereupon he loved her far too much—as is evidenced by the Fall.

terms and ideas which are characteristic of the *accessus Ovidiani*.[81]

Christine de Pizan and Jean Gerson saw Jean de Meun as a modern Ovid not least because he was duplicating Ovid's great fault, i.e. he had written an 'art of love' which offended against public morality. Reading books which stimulate lust is particularly dangerous, declares Gerson in a sermon (preached on 17 December 1402); men who own them should be required by their confessors to tear them up—books like Ovid's, or Matheolus, or parts of the *Rose*.[82] In similar vein, writing to Jean de Montreuil in the summer of 1401, Christine declares that she did 'not know how ... to consider this book [i.e. the *Rose*] useful in any way',[83] the term *utilité* here being used in the technical sense which the Latin form *utilitas* bears in the *accessus ad auctores*, as designating the didactic effect and moral worth which one expects in an authoritative work of literature.

The *utilitas* or final cause of Ovid's *Heroides*, as has already been noted, was generally said to consist in its provision of positive and negative *exempla* of amatory behaviour, so that one 'may reject and shun foolish love and adhere to lawful love'.[84] Christine anticipates Jean de Montreuil as offering a similar defence of the *Rose*: 'I know well that you will excuse it by replying to me that therein he enjoins man to do the good but to eschew the evil'.[85] But this justification is unacceptable, she declares: 'There is no point in reminding human nature, which is naturally inclined to evil, that it limps on one foot, in the hope that it will then walk straighter'. Why, Christine continues, should the good in this book be praised (for she is prepared to admit that it contains some good things), when one can find far more virtuous things, which are more profitable to the decorous and moral life, in the works of certain philosophers and teachers of the Christian faith? The fact that she offers

---

[81] For a fuller version of the arguments presented below see A.J. Minnis, 'Theorizing the Rose: Commentary Tradition in the *Querelle de la Rose*', in P. Boitani and A. Torti (eds), *Poetics: Theory and Practice in Medieval English Literature*, Cambridge, 1991, pp. 13-36.

[82] *Le Débat sur le Roman de la Rose*, ed. Eric Hicks, Paris, 1977, p. 179; cf. the translation by Joseph L. Baird and John R. Kane, *La Querelle de la Rose: Letters and Documents*, North Carolina Studies in the Romance Languages and Literatures, 199, Chapel Hill, 1978, p. 158.

[83] *Le Débat*, ed. Hicks (n. 82 above), p. 20; trans. Baird and Kane (ibid.), p. 54.

[84] Trans. Minnis and Scott, *Medieval Literary Theory* (n. 7 above), p. 21.

[85] *Le Débat*, ed. Hicks (n. 82 above), p. 22; trans. Baird and Kane, p. 55.

this argument immediately after her protestation that the *Rose* lacks
utilité strengthens the suggestion that throughout this entire excursus she had stock medieval literary criticism of Ovid in mind, even
though Ovid himself is not named here.

The connection between Ovid and Master Jean de Meun is,
however, made quite explicit in Jean Gerson's reaction to these
same critical ideas. In his 1402 treatise against the *Rose* Gerson
imagines a supporter of de Meun saying that, while there is some
evil in the book, it contains much more that is good, and so
'praingne chascun le bien et laisse le mal!' ('Let every man receive
the good and reject the evil').[86] Gerson retorts, are the evil things
in the book thereby deleted? Indeed not—a hook does not injure
the fish less if it is covered in bait; a sword dipped in honey does
not cut less deeply. Indeed, the good things contained in the book
actually make it more dangerous. One should recall how
Mohammed, in order to attract Christians more readily to his own
law and to cover his own outrages, mixed in some Christian truths
with his impure errors. The message is hammered home in Gerson's sermon of 24th December 1402: 'Good people', he pleads,
'take these books [i.e. Jean, Ovid, Matheolus] away from your
daughters and children! For they will take the evil and leave the
good'.[87]

In the 1402 treatise this line of reasoning predictably leads Gerson to consider the salutary example of Ovid's exile.[88] The *Tristia* is cited as proof that he was exiled on account of his wretched
Ars amatoria; even his refutation of its false teaching, the *Remedia
amoris*, could not save the poet from his fate. This is standard *accessus* doctrine. In the introduction to the *Tristia* which has been edited by Huygens, several opinions are given concerning the reason
for Ovid's exile, one of which is that 'he had written a book, *On
the Art of Love*, in which he had taught young men how to deceive
and attract married women. This gave offence to the Romans, and
it was for this reason that he is alleged to have been sent into
exile'.[89] Similarly, in the extensive *vita Ovidii* included in the prologue to Giovanni del Virgilio's commentary on the *Metamorphoses*,
the composition of the *Ars amatoria* is described as having incurred

---

[86] Ibid., p. 65; trans., p. 75.
[87] Ibid., p. 182; trans., p. 163.
[88] Ibid., p. 76; trans., p. 83.
[89] Trans. Minnis and Scott, *Medieval Literary Theory* (n. 7 above), p. 27.

the wrath of the emperor Augustus: 'and according to some, this is why he was exiled from Rome, because he had taught unchaste [love] ...'.[90] And the *Remedia amoris* was commonly regarded as an attempt by Ovid to make up for this great mistake, as for example in the *accessus* to this work which was quoted above (p. 155) and in Giovanni del Virgilio's *vita*. Gerson was of the opinion that Augustus was absolutely right—and that his example could teach present-day rulers a thing or two. How amazing it is, he declares, that a pagan and infidel judge (i.e. Augustus) should condemn a book which incites people to engage in foolish love, while among Christians a work of the same kind is supported, praised and defended![91]

If Jean de Meun's resemblance to Ovid could cut both ways, so also could the notion that he had surpassed Ovid. For the *Rose*'s opponents, the supposition that it was more thoroughgoing and effective than the *Ars amatoria* made it all the more dangerous. But for the poem's supporters, this made it all the more praiseworthy, as may be seen from Pierre Col's ingenious amplification of a common defence of Ovid and its application to the *Rose*, which he produced in the summer of 1402.[92] By describing the way in which the Rose's castle was captured, Col claimed, Jean de Meun was giving actually aiding its defenders. Because they then knew how their fortress could fall, in the future they would block the gap or place better guards there and thus lessen the chances of the assailants. This may be compared with one of the reasons given by the translator of the third book of *L'Art d'amours*, in explaining why Ovid wanted to give women the same instruction as men: 'it would be an ugly thing for men to conquer those who do not know how and would not be able to defend themselves.'[93] Moreover, Col continues, Jean made this information widely available by writing in 'the common language of men and women, young

---

[90] Trans. ibid., p. 362.

[91] *Le Débat*, ed. Hicks (n. 82 above), p. 76; trans. Baird and Kane, p. 83.

[92] Ibid., pp. 104-5; trans., p. 108.

[93] *L'Art d'amours*, ed. Roy (n. 12 above), p. 228; trans. Blonquist, p. 123. Similarly, at the end of the translation of Book III it is claimed that from this text both men and women may learn how to guard and protect themselves. However, there follows a rather different (from the one quoted above) view of the usefulness to women of the text: 'by this they can conquer men and put them under their laws'. Moreover, first comes the statement that it is 'beneficial for men, for by this they can know the ruses and deceptions of women, and thus they can be more careful'. Ed. Roy, p. 281; trans. Blonquist, p. 184.

and old, that is, in French ('en franssois')'. By contrast, the *fin* of the *Ars amatoria* was exclusively to teach men how to assault the castle—being in Latin this work was not available to women. (This is an utter anachronism, of course.) Therefore Ovid, according to Col, served only the assailants, whereas Jean de Meun has taken the side of the defenders in preparing them for the stratagems which they will face.

Here *fin* is used in the technical sense carried by *finis* or *finalis causa* in the *accessus*.[94] Moreover, in the introduction to the *Ars amatoria* printed by Huygens (cf. p. 160 above) Ovid's aim for the first two books is expressed, as if the entire work were addressed to men only, and its final cause is analysed exclusively in terms of Ovid's male addressees.[95] Could Pierre Col have been influenced by an account such as this, wherein the contents of the *Ars amatoria* are imperfectly represented? By contrast, the *accessus* to the *Ars* which may be the work of the scholar Fulco who was criticized so roundly by Arnulf of Orléans,[96] declares with far greater accuracy that Ovid sought to instruct *both* young men and women in the art of love ('intendit iuuenes et puellas in amorem instruere'), a view reiterated in his account of the work's *materia* ('materia eius sunt iuuenes et puelle, quos uult docere et instruere in arte amandi').[97] Similarly, in the *accessus* to the *Remedia amoris* which we had cause to cite earlier (p. 155),[98] it is noted that Ovid not only taught young men how to acquire and keep mistresses but also gave girls the corresponding instruction. Clearly, Col does not reflect this tradition of glossing.

His realisation of the *Ars amatoria* is, however, broadly in line with what is commonly found in French translations of that Ovidian text. The original *L'Art d'amours* ended with the second book, the translation of book three being a later addition, as explained above. Even Jacques d'Amiens, who was so concerned to direct his Ovid translations to a 'douce dame', preferred to draw on the

---

[94] For uses of *finis* in academic prologues from the twelfth century onwards see Minnis, *Medieval Theory of Authorship* (n. 22 above), pp. 20, 29, 31, 32, 41, 52, 92, 93, 120, 126-27, 129-30, 132, 147-48, 179, 217, 240n.

[95] Huygens (ed.), *Accessus ad auctores* (n. 7 above), p. 33; cf. Hexter, *Ovid and Medieval Schooling* (n. 8 above), pp. 46-47.

[96] See Shooner, 'Les *Bursarii Ovidianorum*' (n. 5 above), pp. 408-9 (esp. n. 12), pp. 410-11 (n. 17), 423 (n. 47); cf. Hexter, *Ovid and Medieval Schooling* (n. 8 above), p. 43 (n. 85).

[97] Ed. by Hexter, *Ovid and Medieval Schooling* (n. 8 above), p. 219.

[98] Huygens (ed.), *Accessus ad auctores* (n. 7 above), p. 34.

second book of the *Ars amatoria* rather than the third. Moreover, there is the testimony of an *Ars* translation which we have not as yet mentioned, the work of a certain 'Maistre Elie' who seems to have been a contemporary of the writer responsible for the original *L'Art d'amours*. Elie was interested only in the first two books of Ovid's poem (though he goes no farther than line 336 of Book II).[99] His poem of 1,305 octosyllabic lines adapts and amplifies those parts of the original (while omitting a large number of passages), modernising them considerably with reference to Parisian locations, manners and styles of dress. The third book of the Ars is ignored.

The reasons for this reluctance to engage with Book III can only be guessed at. Bruno Roy makes the eminently plausible suggestion that here were are dealing with 'un phénomène d'ordre sociologique, celui de la répugnance qu'éprouvaient les auteurs didactiques à s'adresser directement aux femmes', which is largely true (with notable exceptions) of the earlier thirteenth century, though by the end of that same century change was well on the way.[100] Roy's statement, however, raises the issue of what exactly a 'didactic' work was in the period under discussion. The poet of the *Ars amatoria* always sat uneasily among 'les auteurs didactiques', and as we have seen this work could easily be adapted to serve the ends of *fine amor*, a tradition wherein direct address to a women or women was utterly commonplace. In this regard one need only think of how Jacques d'Amiens managed to recommend the *Remedia amoris* to a female love-sufferer, albeit with considerable ingenuity. Then again, women were regularly addressed as readers—and sometimes as patrons—of French romances, which often contained highly didactic passages.[101] The *romans antiques* are an obvious case in point (and, incidentally, are highly indebted to the Ovidian tradition of female complaint. But that is another story).[102]

---

[99] *Maître Elies Überarbeitung der ältesten französischen Bearbeitung der Ars amatoria des Ovids*, ed. H. Kühne and E. Stengel, Marburg 1886. Repr. in Finoli (n. 52 above), *Artes amandi*, pp. 1-30.

[100] Introduction to Roy's *L'Art d'amours* edition (n. 12 above), p. 16. For one exception, see the major corpus of English treatises produced for women in the period 1190-1230, in part edited by Bella Millett and Jocelyn Wogan-Browne, *Medieval English Prose for Women*, Oxford, 1990.

[101] On this controversial subject see esp. Roberta L. Krueger, *Women Readers and the Ideology of Gender in Old French Verse Romance*, Cambridge, 1993.

[102] See esp. Barbara Nolan, *Chaucer and the Tradition of the 'Roman Antique'*, Cambridge, 1992.

In general, however, Roy's suggestion that the medieval *ars amandi* tradition had a mainly male audience may be accepted,[103] though it is going too far to say that '*Toute* la littérature des arts d'aimer ... s'adresse aux hommes'.

Another reason for the relative neglect of the third book of the *Ars amatoria* could have been that writers were reluctant to treat of, or unable to use in their own literary works, its blatant sexuality; particularly its unblushing accounts of different types of intercourse, which are far more explicit than anything found in the first two books. The disapproval of the translator responsible for Book III of *L'Art d'amours* becomes evident occasionally. Introducing Ovid's 'lessons' on 'how a woman must perform the labor of Venus' he remarks that 'There are many so clever that no teaching is necessary for them'.[104] A brief review of the sexual practices of experienced women is broken off with the comment, 'There are many other perversions (*faussetez*) which they know better than I'.[105] Ovid's text seems to be confirming some of his worst suspicions about women. He is not above seeing the funny side of the business, however, as when he glosses Ovid's recommendation of alternative sexual positions (the woman on top or the man on top) with a citation of Galatians VI, 2, 'Bear ye one another's burdens, and so you shall fulfil the law of Christ'.[106] But that, of course, is a very donnish, knowing joke. Despite the hope expressed right at the end of his translation, that no one can bear him any ill-will because his work is of benefit to both men and women, it seems aimed at an audience which is largely, though probably not exclusively, male. Which is hardly surprising.

To return to Pierre Col's comparison of Ovid and Jean de Meun: having said that the latter's work is available to women in a way in which the former's was not, Col then changes tack, and argues

---

[103] Just as in the medieval tradition of 'heroic love' the patients were, for the most part, assumed to be male. However, female victims of lovesickness were not unknown, and more attention is paid to them in the later tradition of *Viaticum* commentaries, starting with Peter of Spain. See Wack, *Lovesickness* (n. 36 above), pp. 7, 9, 110-15, 121-25, 174-76; also the cogent comments by Joan Cadden, *Meanings of Sex Difference in the Middle Ages. Medicine, Science, and Culture*, Cambridge, 1993, pp. 138-41. For an elaborately detailed account of a woman who dies of the disease despite the ministrations of many physicians and the correct diagnosis by one of them, see Guillaume de Machaut's *Jugement dou Roy de Navarre*, ll. 1863-2010, ed. R. Burton Palmer, New York and London, 1988, pp. 84-91.

[104] *L'Art d'amours*, ed. Roy (n. 12 above), p. 277; trans. Blonquist, p. 179.

[105] Ibid., p. 277; trans., p. 180.

[106] Ibid., ed. Roy, p. 278; trans., p. 180.

that Ovid was unfairly maligned.[107] Obviously he realises that if this case is made convincingly he will be in a good position to defend the ancient poet's modern counterpart. To this end he accuses the Roman husbands who objected to the *Ars amatoria*, thereby causing Ovid's exile, of being excessively and unreasonably jealous. The national characteristics of the French equip them to take the *Rose* in the spirit in which it was meant, he claims, in contrast with the Romans, who were congenitally disposed to react violently against the *Ars*. Not that the exile of the poet did any lasting damage to the poem's posterity, adds Col, for it endures, will endure, and has endured in all Christendom. Besides, Ovid recanted by writing the *Remedia amoris*. Viewed in the light of these facts, the exiling of Ovid is seen to be unjustifiable by reason, and must have been motivated by enormously cruel jealousy.

What, then, of the argument that Jean drew on works other than the *Ars amatoria*? This made the work even more effective, Col declares, in forewarning the defenders of the lady's castle.[108] The more varied the forms of attack that he describes, the better he teaches them to guard it: and it was for this purpose ('fin') that he wrote the poem. To amplify Col's point through the scholastic critical idiom which he is using, the *finis* of the *Rose* excels that of the *Ars amatoria*. He bolsters his argument by citing the case of a friend who borrowed his copy of the *Rose*: largely due to his reading of the poem, this man managed to disentangle himself from foolish love. The obvious implication is that the *Rose* is a very effective *remedium amoris*. To be more precise, Col is claiming that the poem does something which generations of *accessus* to the *Remedia amoris* had claimed for that book of Ovid's. It would seem, then, that some of the traditional justifications of Ovid's poetry have been appropriated in the defence of the *Rose*.

But Christine de Pizan was not impressed. Pierre Col's claim that Jean de Meun was on the side of the defenders of the castle was, in her view, 'mervilleuse' ('incredible').[109] When Col says that Jean included in his poem the work of many authors other than Ovid, by his own reasoning it is proved that the poet is speaking only to the attackers, just like Ovid, from whom he borrowed. (Here again, it is being assumed that the *Ars* catered exclusively

---

[107] *Le Débat*, ed. Hicks (n. 82 above), p. 105; trans. Baird and Kane, pp. 108-9.
[108] Ibid., pp. 105-6; trans., p. 109.
[109] Letter dated 2 October 1402; Ibid., pp. 137-9; trans., pp. 134-35.

for a male audience.) A proliferation of evil material does not make for a good *fin*. Col has said that the more diverse the methods of attack which are revealed to the guards, the better they are taught the art of defence. This is tantamount to saying that a man who attacks you and tries to kill you is merely showing you how to defend yourself! Thus Christine responded to her opponent's attempt to assign and defend the *utilitas* of Jean de Meun's Ovidian poem.

Here, then, even in this apparently remote province of the Ovidian empire, is further testimony of the longevity and continuous purchase of the critical vocabulary and values which were transmitted in the academic prologues to his poems. Those *accessus* had many adventures. I have been able to discuss only a few of them; a host of others await investigation. It seems obvious, however, that in many of Ovid's medieval travels, the *accessus Ovidiani* went with him, sometimes easing his way but on other occasions making it more difficult, controversial, contested. Ovid's influence on the French art of love is incalculable; the influence of the introductions to his love-poetry is less intimidating to investigate, though the full picture cannot be known until such times as comprehensive editions of the Latin commentaries are with us.

PSEUDOANTIKE LITERATUR ALS PHILOLOGISCHES PROBLEM IN MITTELALTER UND RENAISSANCE

Paul Gerhard Schmidt

Als Paul Lehmann 1927 in den 'Studien der Bibliothek Warburg' seinen Vortrag über *Pseudo-antike Literatur des Mittelalters* veröffentlichte, erschloß er der Forschung ein neues Gebiet und stellte ihr neue Aufgaben. Er machte dabei Werke bekannt, 'deren Verfasser es oft nicht für gut und klug gehalten haben, sich selbst zu nennen und infolgedessen leicht verkannt sind, Werke, die für sich allein genommen zumeist unbedeutend oder mittelmäßig sind und gewöhnlich erst dann an Interesse gewinnen, wenn man ihren Zusammenhang mit der Antike und ihre Wirkungen auf die Umwelt und Nachwelt, auf die sonstige mittellateinische Literatur und besonders auch ihren Einfluß auf die Literatur der modernen Sprachen des Abendlandes abwägt'.[1] Besonders Lehmanns Hinweis auf die zahlreichen Pseudo-Ovidiana des Hoch- und Spätmittelalters, auf die vielen Variationen des *Pyramus und Thisbe*-Stoffes oder auf

---

[1] P. Lehmann, *Pseudo-antike Literatur des Mittelalters*, Studien der Bibliothek Warburg 19, Leipzig-Berlin, 1927 (Rpt. Darmstadt 1964) S. 29. 1983 gab ich eine Überblick über 'Kritische Philologie und pseudoantike Literatur' (in A. Buck und K.Heitmann [Hgg.], *Die Antike-Rezeption in den Wissenschaften während der Renaissance*, Mitteilungen X der Kommission für Humanismusforschung der Deutschen Forschungsgemeinschaft, Weinheim, 1983, S. 117-28). Seitdem sind gewichtige Arbeiten zu Fälschungen erschienen: *Fälschungen im Mittelalter*, Internationaler Kongreß der Monumenta Germaniae Historica, München, 16.-19. September 1986, 6 Bände, Hannover, 1988-1990; K. Arnold, *Johannes Trithemius (1462-1516). Quellen und Forschungen zur Geschichte des Bistums und Hochstifts Würzburg*, 23, Würzburg, 2. Aufl., 1991; Anthony Grafton, *Defenders of the Text. The Traditions of Scholarship in an Age of Science, 1450-1800*, Cambridge, Mass., 1991; ders., *Forgers and Critics. Creativity and Duplicity in Western Scholarship*, Princeton, 1990; J.F. d'Amico, *Theory and Practice in Renaissance Textual Criticism. Beatus Rhenanus between Conjecture and History*, Berkeley-Los Angeles-London, 1988; W. Speyer, *Italienische Humanisten als Kritiker der Echtheit antiker und christlicher Literatur*, Abhandlungen der Geistes- und Sozialwissenschaftlichen Klasse der Akademie der Wissenschaften und der Literatur Mainz, Jahrgang 1993, Nr. 3, Stuttgart, 1993; K. Corino (Hg.), *Gefälscht. Betrug in Politik, Literatur, Wissenschaft, Kunst und Musik*, Nördlingen, 1988 (Hamburg, 1992); H. Ott, 'Die Fälscher hören nimmer auf. Oder: Mundus vult decipi', in W. Schmierer (Hg.), *Aus südwestdeutscher Geschichte. Festschrift für Hans-Martin Maurer*, Stuttgart, 1994, S.764-772.

das angeblich autobiographische Epos *De vetula* ist auf fruchtbaren
Boden gefallen, seine Anregungen sind aufgegriffen und viele ein-
schlägige Texte sind seitdem erstmals oder erneut in kritischer und
verbesserter Form ediert worden; eine zusammenfassende Monographie über Ovids Nachleben im Mittelalter ist jedoch trotz viel-
er Vorarbeiten nach wie vor ein Desiderat.

Es ist nicht meine Absicht, zu jedem einzelnen Pseudepigraphon,
auf das Lehmann aufmerksam machte, den gegenwärtigen Stand
oder die gegenwärtigen Defizite der Forschung anzugeben, so nütz-
lich eine Aktualisierung wäre. Der große Wert seiner Studie liegt
über die konkreten Hinweise hinaus m. E. vor allem darin, daß
seit ihrem Erscheinen die Beschäftigung mit Falsa, mit Pseudepigrapha, mit Spuria, mit Imitationen und Fiktionen keiner Entschul-
digung mehr bedarf. Es wurde ein separater Zweig der Philologie
nicht nur neu etabliert, sondern er wurde grundsätzlich legitimiert.
Gleichzeitig setzte während der zwanziger Jahre in der mediävistischen Forschung ein Mentalitätswechsel ein, der zur Zeit eine
Hochkonjunktur erlebt. Nicht herausragende Originalwerke werden erforscht; das Interesse gilt vielmehr der sekundären, einer
abgeleiteten und vermittelnden Literatur. Es sind die Florilegien,
die seit Berthold Louis Ullman und Anders Gagnér immer stärker Beachtung finden,[2] die Kompilationen, Epitomai, die zahlreichen Variant Versions eines Texts, der neu geformt und adaptiert
wurde für die Bedürfnisse immer neuer und geänderter Schichten
von Lesern.[3] Derartige Bearbeitungen klassischer Texte, auch
Prosaauflösungen von Dichtungen und Versifikationen von Pro-
sawerken gehören in diese Kategorie, haben sich oft als ein-
flußreicher und weiter verbreitet erwiesen als die Originalwerke

---

[2] Ullman hat von 1928-1932 in *Classical Philology* (23-27) Studien zu der Flori-
legienüberlieferung einzelner antiker Autoren publiziert. Gagnér machte 1936 in
seiner in Lund erschienenen Studie auf das *Florilegium Gallicum* aufmerksam. Seine
Studien sind weitergeführt worden von J. Hamacher, *Florilegium Gallicum. Prolegomena und Edition der Exzerpte von Petron bis Cicero, De oratore*, Lateinische Sprache
und Literatur des Mittelalters, 5, Frankfurt, 1975, und R. Burton, *Classical Poets
in the "Florilegium Gallicum"*, Lateinische Sprache und Literatur des Mittelalters,
14, Frankfurt-Bern, 1983; vgl. ferner R.H. Rouse and M.A. Rouse, *Preachers, Florilegia and Sermons: Studies on the Manipulus florum of Thomas of Ireland*, Studies and
Texts 47, Toronto, 1979. Nützliche Literaturhinweise bietet der Artikel 'Florilegien' im *Lexikon des Mittelalters*, IV, München-Zürich, 1987-89, Sp. 566-69.
[3] Aus der mittelalterlichen Literatur wären z. B. die verschiedenen Versionen
von Galfreds von Monmouth *Historia Regum Britanniae* zu nennen. Auch die Enzy-
klopädie des Thomas Cantimpratanus hat nicht in der Originalfassung, sondern
in Redaktionen ihre stärkste Wirksamkeit entfaltet.

selbst. Die Forschung über Nicht-Originale ist in vollem Gang.
Man gelangt immer stärker zu der Einsicht, daß die mittelalterlichen Vorstellungen über einen Autor und sein Werk mehr von
den Falsa als von den authentischen Schriften geprägt sein können. So wird das Hieronymusbild des Spätmittelalters durch drei
Briefe bestimmt, die berühmten Autoren zugewiesen wurden, Eusebius, Augustinus und Cyrillus von Jerusalem. Eusebius handelt in
seinem Brief über die Todesstunde des Heiligen im Kreis seiner
Jünger und erwähnt einige Mirakel des Hieronymus. Der dem
Augustinus zugeschriebene Brief enthält eine Jenseitsvision, der
man entnehmen kann, daß Hieronymus im Himmel den gleichen
Rang besitzt wie Johannes der Täufer und die Propheten. Im drit-
ten Brief, dem des Cyrillus, stehen die schon im Augustinusbrief
kurz erwähnten Miracula Hieronymi im Vordergrund. Auch hier
wird Hieronymus gepriesen, aber zugleich dem Unterhaltungs-
bedürfnis des Lesers Rechnung getragen. Die drei Briefe werden
sehr unterschiedlich datiert;[4] unbestritten ist, daß sie nicht von den
Freunden und Zeitgenossen des heiligen Hieronymus selbst stammen. Soweit ich sehe, gibt es ein breites Spektrum von Datierungs-
vorschlägen, die vom 7. bis zum Ende des 13. Jahrhunderts reichen.
Aus dem 13. Jahrhundert stammen die ältesten Handschriften der
Briefe; bald nach der Mitte des 14. Jahrhunderts setzen die ersten
Übersetzungen in die Volkssprachen ein. Ein Zentrum der Verbrei-
tung war Bologna, wo der Jurist Johannes Andreae den Kult des
Hieronymus förderte. Aus Italien brachte Johann von Neumarkt,
der Kanzler Karls IV., die lateinischen Briefe mit und übertrug
sie ins Deutsche. Übersetzungen ins Niederländische und Nieder-
deutsche folgten. Von der lateinischen Version der Briefe haben
sich annähernd 400 Handschriften erhalten. Texte von derartiger
Wirkungsbreite mögen einen Eindruck von der Omnipräsenz der
Falsa im 14. und 15. Jahrhundert geben. In der Gegenwart werden diese Briefe über St. Hieronymus wohl nur selten gelesen. In
erster Linie interessieren ihre Übersetzungen den Sprachforscher,
der Belege für die sog. Prager Kanzleisprache, für baierische Spe-
zifika oder für Mischdialekte an der Grenze zwischen Nieder-
ländisch und Niederdeutsch sucht. Über den oder die Verfasser
dieser Briefe äußerte man die Vermutung, daß sie in Dominikaner-

---

[4] K. Ruh (Hg.), *Die deutsche Literatur des Mittelalters. Verfasserlexikon*, III, Berlin-
New York 1981, Sp. 1233-38 ('Hieronymus-Briefe'). Migne, *PL* 22, Sp. 239. J.
Klapper (Hg.), *Schriften Johanns von Neumarkt*, Zweiter Teil: *Hieronymus. Die unecht-
en Briefe des Eusebius, Augustin, Cyrill zum Lobe des Heiligen*, Berlin, 1932.

kreisen in Südfrankreich oder Oberitalien zu suchen seien. Ich muß aber gestehen, daß ich in der Literatur bisher keinen Hinweis darauf gefunden habe, wer als erster diese im Spätmittelalter und in der frühen Neuzeit so oft kopierten und gedruckten Briefe als Pseudepigrapha ihren angeblichen Verfassern abgesprochen hat. Migne, der die Briefe abdruckt, weist darauf hin, daß der Praemonstratenser Remy Casimir Oudin (1638-1717) die Briefe dem Papst Formosus aus dem Ende des 9. Jahrhunderts zuschrieb. Daß sie nicht authentisch sind, geht aus dem Umstand hervor, daß Cyrillus vor Hieronymus gestorben ist, also schlecht über den Tod des Hieronymus geschrieben haben kann—es sei denn, er hätte seinen Brief im Jenseits verfaßt und auf die Erde herabgesandt. Damit würde ich das große Gebiet der sogenannten Himmelsbriefe berühren, Briefe, in denen göttliche Befehle, wie das Gebot der Sonntagsheiligung, der Menschheit verkündet wurden. Von derartigen Texten soll hier nicht die Rede sein. Nicht immer ist der Nachweis einer falschen Zuschreibung so leicht zu führen wie in dem vorliegenden Fall, wo der Hinweis auf einen Anachronismus ausreicht, um ohne jeden Zweifel feststellen zu können, daß Cyrillus diesen Brief nicht geschrieben haben kann.

Es wäre sicher auch im 14. Jahrhundert möglich gewesen, anhand chronologischer Argumente ihre Unechtheit zu erweisen; wir müssen aber konstatieren, daß das Corpus dieser drei unzweifelhaft unechten Briefe mit dem Lob des Hieronymus bis in das 17. Jahrhundert hinein intensiv rezipiert wurde. Ich gehe einen Schritt weiter und erinnere daran, daß die Vermischung von echten und unechten Schriften in der patristischen Literatur besonders häufig anzutreffen ist. So gibt es eine immense Zahl an Pseudoaugustiniana, besonders Sermones und Epistolae. Es überrascht daher nicht, daß der Bibliothekar, der kürzlich unbekannte, dem Augustin zugeschriebene Predigten in einer Mainzer Handschrift des 15. Jahrhunderts fand, fast automatisch an Pseudo-Augustin dachte. Erst François Dolbeau gelang der Nachweis, daß es sich wider Erwarten um echte Predigten Augustins handelt. Schließlich hatte, mit Blick auf Hieronymus, schon 1914 Martin Schanz resignierend festgestellt: 'Die Zahl der apokryphen, den Namen des Hieronymus tragenden Schriften erreicht einen Umfang fast wie die echten'.[5]

---

[5] M. Schanz, *Geschichte der römischen Literatur*, IV. Teil, 1. Band. *Handbuch der Altertumswissenschaften*, München, 1914, S. 496. Seit 1989 verfügt dieses Forschungsgebiet über eine Zeitschrift: *Apocrypha. Revue Internationale des Littératures Apocryphes*; vgl. ferner G. Roth, *Sündenspiegel im 15. Jahrhundert. Untersuchungen zum pseudo-augus-*

Unechte Schriften weisen einen Vorteil gegenüber den echten auf: sie bieten das für einen Autor Charakteristische und Typische viel reiner und klarer als der Autor selbst es könnte. So besteht kein Anlaß, an ihrer Echtheit zu zweifeln. Pseudepigrapha—man denke an die apokryphen Evangelien und Apostelgeschichten—sind auch farbiger und unterhaltsamer als die im Kanon des Neuen Testaments akzeptierten vier Evangelien oder die eine Apostelgeschichte. Die biblischen Apokryphen sind im Mittelalter gern und häufig gelesen und literarisch genutzt worden. Man wußte, daß sie nicht als authentisch galten, behalf sich aber—wie Hrotsvit von Gandersheim es tat—mit der Überlegung, daß die in ihnen berichteten Ereignisse zwar nicht wahr seien, aber doch hätten wahr sein können. Mit einer gewissen Übertreibung könnte man sagen, daß man im Mittelalter nicht zwischen echten und unechten Schriften unterschied. Über das unter dem Namen des Boethius kursierende Werk *De disciplina scholarium* sagt seine letzte Herausgeberin: 'Tout le moyen âge, pour lequel la question d'authenticité ne jouait guère de rôle, a accepté, utilisé, commenté le traité comme l'une des oeuvres populaires de Boèce'.[6] Das Falsum wurde nicht als Problem empfunden; man sah bei literarischen Fälschungen keinen Anlaß, sie als unwahr zu eliminieren, sondern spielte eher mit der Möglichkeit, daß ein verdächtiger Text sich als wahr erweisen könnte, nach dem Prinzip 'in dubio pro falso'.

Nachdem jetzt so viele Arbeiten über die Entstehungszeit, die Quellen, die Tendenz und den Erfolg mittelalterlicher Falsa, etwa über Pseudo-Beda *De mundi caelestis terrestrisque constitutione*[7] oder über Pseudo-Aristoteles-Schriften wie das *Secretum secretorum*[8] vorliegen, scheint es notwendig, auch einmal nach dem Ende eines Falsums zu fragen. Wer entlarvte das Werk als unecht, und bedeutete die 'Entlarvung' zugleich das Ende, den Decline eines nicht authentischen Werkes? Die Frage wird selten gestellt und noch seltener beantwortet. Die Herausgeberin von *De disciplina scholarium* gehört

---

tinischen *'Speculum peccatoris'* in deutscher *Überlieferung*, Diss. phil. Bern-Berlin, 1991.

[6] O. Weijers, *Pseudo-Boèce De disciplina scholarium. Édition critique, introduction et notes*, Studien und Texte zur Geistesgeschichte des Mittelalters Band 12. Leiden-Köln, 1976, S. 3

[7] Ch. Burnett, *Pseudo-Bede: De mundi caelestis terrestrisque constitutione. A Treatise on the Universe and the Soul*, Warburg Institute Surveys and Texts 10, London, 1985.

[8] W.F. Ryan and Ch.B. Schmitt, *Pseudo-Aristotle, The Secret of Secrets. Sources and Influences*, Warburg Institute Surveys and Texts 9, London, 1982; Ch.B. Schmitt and D. Knox, *Pseudo-Aristoteles Latinus. A Guide to Latin Works Falsely Attributed to Aristotle before 1500*, Warburg Institute Surveys and Texts 12, London, 1985.

zu den wenigen Philologen, die sich auch für das 'Nachleben' eines Falsums interessieren. Sie nennt einige Humanisten, die mit unterschiedlichen Begründungen Boethius das Werk absprachen: Alexander Hegius nahm am barbarischen Latein Anstoß, am unlateinischen Titel, an der scholastischen Terminologie, an Begriffen wie *natura naturans* und *natura naturata*. Andere Humanisten folgten dieser Argumentation, so Jodocus Badius, Johannes Murmellius und Heinrich Bebel. Jakob Wimpfeling führte zusätzlich das chronologische Argument ein; der echte Boethius könne unmöglich von der Pariser Universität gesprochen haben, die doch erst viele Jahrhunderte nach seinem Tod gegründet worden sei. Man sollte annehmen, daß dieses Argument das Interesse an *De disciplina scholarium* schlagartig beendet habe. Das ist keineswegs der Fall. Der Text wird trotz der Feststellung der Unechtheit weiter in den Schulen gelesen und weiterhin zusammen mit der *Consolatio philosophiae* gedruckt —so von Glareanus noch im Jahre 1564. Es ist als auffällige Tatsache festzuhalten, daß die Philologen des 15. Jahrhunderts, die diese Schrift dem Boethius absprachen, dies mehr nebenbei in einigen Randbemerkungen taten und kein Methodenbewußtsein dabei verrieten. Auch wenn Beatus Rhenanus oder Erasmus von Rotterdam sich kritisch über mittelalterliche Zuschreibungen und Fabeln äußern, geschieht dies in der Regel im Vorübergehen, so als lohne es sich nicht, sich mit einem Werk zu beschäftigen, das nicht antiken Ursprungs ist. Einzig Lorenzo Valla hat mit seiner Studie über die Unechtheit der *Donatio Constantini* eine selbständige Monographie über ein Falsum verfaßt. Zweifel an ihrer Echtheit waren seit dem 12. Jahrhundert zwar schon wiederholt geäußert worden, aber Valla hat eine neue Form der Echtheitskritik zur Norm erhoben, die Stilkritik. Seine Vorgänger, die seit dem 12. Jahrhundert die Echtheit der konstantinischen Schenkung angezweifelt hatten, waren auf philologische Gesichtspunkte nicht eingegangen. Sie standen in der Tradition der Urkundenlehre; die häufig ganz oder teilweise verunechteten Diplomata wurden seit dem 12. Jahrhundert einer Überprüfung unterzogen, die der äußeren Form der Dokumente galt, den Fragen der Besiegelung, der Datierung, der Unterschrift und Titulatur. Mit solchen Argumenten hatte bereits Petrarca einige angeblich von römischen Herrschern stammende Urkunden als Falsa nachgewiesen. Die Geschichtswissenschaft und die Genealogie müssen als Vorläufer der philologischen Echtheitsmethoden angesehen werden. Auf diesem Gebiet werden im Lauf des 15. Jahrhunderts durchgreifende Reformen

durchgeführt, indem man den trojanischen Ursprungssagen zuneh-
mend den Glauben verweigerte. Man wandte sich gegen die Ab-
leitung einzelner Herrscherhäuser von den Trojanern und stellte
dabei fest, daß die Trojaberichte von Dares und Diktys keineswegs
von Zeitgenossen des trojanischen Kriegs stammten, sondern der
Spätantike angehören, daß sie im Mittelalter erweitert und verän-
dert wurden. Auch die Literatur über Karl den Großen wurde in
dieser Zeit von hoch -und spätmittelalterlichen Zutaten befreit, und
man entdeckte Einhard als zuverlässige Quelle wieder.

Als Raphael Rhegius 1491 den Nachweis führte, daß die im Mittelalter und bis zu seiner Zeit unter Ciceros Namen gehende *Rhetorica ad Herennium* kein Werk Ciceros ist, sondern vielleicht von Cor-
nificius stammt, blieb die Diskussion darüber auf den eigentlichen
Anlaß beschränkt. In der Inkunabelzeit war das Interesse viel stärker auf die Entdeckung von Texten und die Emendation von Fehlern
gerichtet als auf die grundsätzlichen Fragen einer Echtheitskritik.
Selbst die spektakulären Fälschungen des Dominikaners Annius von
Viterbo benötigten eine über 100 Jahre andauernde Diskussion,
bis sie endgültig in Scaligers *Thesaurus temporum* von 1606 verwor-
fen wurden.[9] Anthony Grafton hat die einzelnen Phasen dieser Diskussion unter Historikern, Theologen und Philologen aufgezeich-
net. Er hat zu Recht auf den Umstand aufmerksam gemacht, daß
mit Scaliger ein Calvinist gegen einen Dominikanermönch argu-
mentierte. Echtheitsfragen haben im Streit der Konfessionen eine
große Bedeutung gehabt; die Aufmerksamkeit gegenüber Pseudepigrapha und Falsa scheint besonders an neuralgischen Punkten
entwickelt worden zu sein, auf dem Gebiet der Hagiographie und
der Bibelkritik viel stärker als auf dem Feld der klassischen Philologie. Glaubensfragen waren von ungleich größerer Bedeutung als
die abstrakten Regeln einer reinen Philologie. Autoritäten wurden
von den Reformatoren viel stärker in Frage gestellt als von Philologen.

Das Schicksal eines Pseudo-Ovidianums mag das Desinteresse
des Mittelalters an Echtheitsfragen illustrieren. Das im 13. Jahrhundert erstmals aufgetauchte Epos *De vetula*, angeblich im Grab Ovids
gefunden, ist in Sprache und Stil mittelalterlich. Zwar greift es
immer wieder auf Ovids echte Werke zurück, häufiger sogar als

---

[9] M. Wifstrand Schiebe, *Annius von Viterbo und die schwedische Historiographie des
16. und 17. Jahrhunderts*, Acta Societatis Litterarum Humaniorum Regiae Upsalen-
sis 48, Uppsala, 1992; A. Grafton, *Joseph Scaliger. A Study in the History of Classical
Scholarship*. Band 1: *Textual Criticism and Exegesis*, Oxford, 1983.

die letzten Editionen dies nachweisen,[10] aber die Verwandlung des
Liebhabers Ovid in einen abgeklärten Philosophen, der sich nur
noch mit Fragen der Mathematik und Astrologie beschäftigt, paßt
so wenig zur Antike, daß schon Roger Bacon an der Autorschaft
Ovids zweifelte. Petrarca, Pierre d'Ailly und Jean Gerson äußerten
sich ähnlich. Eine große Zahl der Handschriften, die das Werk
überliefern, enthalten Bemerkungen, die erkennen lassen, daß man
seiner Echtheit zweifelte. Der Beliebtheit des Werkes tat das aber
zu keiner Zeit Abbruch. Man las und druckte es bis in das 17.
Jahrhundert. Das Werk bietet nämlich einen Passus, der oft ex-
zerpiert und oft zitiert wurde: Unter Berufung auf einen arabi-
schen Astrologen verkündet Ovid als Prophet, dem Vergil der
vierten Ekloge vergleichbar, daß eine Jungfrau ein Kind gebären
werde. Wer wird einen solchen Text, das Zeugnis eines Heiden
über ein christliches Dogma, als deliramentum unterdrücken wollen,
auch wenn dieser angebliche Ovid wissenschaftliche Texte kennt,
die über 1000 Jahre nach ihm verfaßt wurden? Die Bereitschaft
zum Glauben ist groß. Melchior Goldast von Haiminfeld schrieb
1610: 'Nihil vidi libellis istis de Vetula ineptius, nihil absurdius ...
nihil stolidius'.[11] Man kann dieses Urteil akzeptieren, aber Goldast
muß sich fragen lassen, warum er diesen Text druckte, den er für
so töricht hielt. 1662 wird *De vetula* noch einmal gedruckt als Opus-
culum incerti auctoris, zusammen mit dem *Speculum stultorum* Nigels
von Canterbury. Hier liegt nicht mehr ein Dokument der Fröm-
migkeit vor, sondern es artikuliert sich Interesse an lateinischer Literatur des Mittelalters. Mit der Mitte des 17. Jahrhunderts ist eine
Epochengrenze in der Einstellung zu pseudo-klassischer Literatur
erreicht. Zu diesem Zeitpunkt sind die meisten falschen Zuschreibungen korrigiert—z.B. das Corpus Hermeticum, die *Tabula Cebetis*
und andere Texte. Bentley's *Letters on the Epistles of Phalaris* markieren
nicht den Beginn, sondern den Abschluß einer Konfrontation mit
Falsa. Das Problem wird erst dann theoretisch artikuliert, als die
Bewältigung der praktischen Aufgaben bereits weitgehend abge-
schlossen war. Aber es folgt ein Satyrspiel. Manche der anerkann-

---

[10] P. Klopsch, *Pseudo-Ovidius De vetula. Untersuchungen und Text*, Mittellateinische
Studien und Texte 2, Leiden-Köln, 1967; D.M. Robathan, *The Pseudo-Ovidian De
vetula. Text, Introduction, and Notes*, Amsterdam, 1968; W. Maaz, 'Henricus Boger
(vor 1450-1505)—ein Beitrag zur *Vetula*-Rezeption', in U. Kindermann (Hg.), *Festschrift für Paul Klopsch*, Göppinger Arbeiten zur Germanistik 492, Göppingen, 1988,
S. 345-58.
[11] Zitiert nach Klopsch (wie Anm.10), S. 182f.

te Falsa beweisen eine enorme Lebenskraft, die alle Kritik über-
dauert. So werden einige Texte, deren Unechtheit seit Jahrhun-
derten erwiesen ist, erneut für echt gehalten. Der Briefwechsel zwischen Paulus und Seneca bietet ein Beispiel für die Resistenz und
Vitalität eines Dokuments. Der eher banale Inhalt rechtfertigt keine
lange Diskussion. Dennoch wurde nicht nur 1851 zugunsten der
Echtheit argumentiert, nein erst vor wenigen Jahren fanden die
Briefe einen renommierten Wissenschaftler, der sich in dubio pro
falso aussprach.[12] Offensichtlich kann die Philologie auf Pseudepigrapha und Falsa nicht verzichten.

---

[12] E. Franceschini, 'È veramente apocrifo l'epistolario Seneca—S. Paolo?',
Letterature comparate. Problemi e metodo. Studi in onore di Ettore Paratore, II, Bologna,
1981, S. 827-41. Vgl. dazu B. Bischoff, *Anecdota novissima. Quellen und Untersuchun-*
gen zur lateinischen Philologie des Mittelalters, VII, Stuttgart, 1984, S. 1ff.

BIBLIOGRAPHY OF CLASSICAL SCHOLARSHIP IN THE MIDDLE AGES AND THE EARLY RENAISSANCE (9TH TO 15TH CENTURIES)

KARSTEN FRIIS-JENSEN, BIRGER MUNK OLSEN AND
OLE L. SMITH (†)

This bibliography is an offshoot of the cooperation engendered by the European Science Foundation Network on the 'Classical Tradition in the Middle Ages and the Renaissance'. Its immediate background is the second workshop of the Network, since that workshop, like this bibliography, was centered on classical scholarship in the Middle Ages and the early Renaissance (textual criticism, commentaries and discussions of attribution).

The bibliography constitutes a complement to Pierre Petitmengin and Birger Munk Olsen's *Bibliographie de la réception de la littérature classique du IXe au XVe siècle,* covering the aspects of diffusion, translation and epitomization of classical texts, and published in *The Classical Tradition in the Middle Ages and the Renaissance. Proceedings of the First European Science Foundation Workshop on the Reception of Classical Texts (Florence, Certosa del Galluzzo, 26-27 June 1992).* Spoleto 1995. In general, references to studies on the diffusion of manuscripts are to be found in the Florence volume, whereas those discussing scholarly criticism of and intervention in the state of the text in its various phases are registered in this volume. It has been impossible to achieve complete consistency on this point.

Modern scholars are publishing an increasing number of books and articles on the achievements of their medieval and Renaissance predecessors. These contributions cut across the traditional dividing lines between the disciplines of classical philology, medieval philology and manuscript studies. Even if each field taken separately is well-indexed in bibliographical terms, a comprehensive view of modern literature on medieval and early Renaissance contributions to classical scholarship is nevertheless very difficult to obtain. The present bibliography is meant as the first step towards providing such a view.

For many good reasons completeness has not been aimed at. The diversity of the material just mentioned has imposed its own limits, as have considerations of space. In order to prevent overloading, normally only books and articles that deal entirely or mainly with the themes of the bibliography have been included. A special procedure has been followed in the case of commentaries on Aristotle, so that surveys and repertories have been given first priority.

The nucleus of the material for this bibliography was supplied by Birger Munk Olsen; the other contributors supplemented it with items from their own fields of interest, and assisted in the process of information retrieval and editing.

GENERAL

[1]   BURSIAN, C., *Geschichte der classischen Philologie in Deutschland von den Anfängen bis zur Gegenwart*. Vol. I-II. Munich 1883 (Geschichte der Wissenschaften in Deutschland. Neuere Zeit, 19).
[2]   NOLHAC, Pierre de, *Pétrarque et l'Humanisme*. Nouvelle édition, remaniée et augmentée. Vol. I-II. Paris 1907 (repr. 1965).
[3]   PFEIFFER, Rudolf, *A History of Classical Scholarship from 1300 to 1850*. Oxford 1976.
[4]   REYNOLDS, L.D. & N.G. WILSON, *Scribes & Scholars. A Guide to the Transmission of Greek & Latin Literature*. 3rd edition. Oxford 1991.
[5]   SABBADINI, Remigio, *Le scoperte dei codici latini e greci ne' secoli XIV e XV*. Edizione anastatica con nuove aggiunte e correzioni dell'autore a cura di E. Garin. Florence 1967 (Biblioteca storica del Rinascimento, IV*) [1st ed.: Florence 1905].
[6]   SABBADINI, Remigio, *Le scoperte dei codici latini e greci ne' secoli XIV e XV. Nuove ricerche col riassunto filologico dei due volumi*. Florence 1967 (Biblioteca storica del Rinascimento, IV**) (1st ed.: Florence 1914).
[7]   SANDYS, John Edwin, *A History of Classical Scholarship*. Vol. I-III. Cambridge 1903-1908 (reprint: New York & London 1958).
[8]   WILAMOWITZ-MOELLENDORFF, U. von, *History of Classical Scholarship*. Translated from the German by Alan Harris. Edited with Introduction and Notes by Hugh Lloyd-Jones. London 1982.

TEXTUAL CRITICISM

[9]   BOTFIELD, Beriah, *Prefaces to the First Editions of the Greek and Roman Classics and of the Sacred Scriptures*. London 1861.

[10]   FELD, M.D., *The First Roman Printers and the Idioms of Humanism*, in *Harvard Library Bulletin*, 36 (1988), pp. 7-91.

[11]   GRAFTON, Anthony, *Defenders of the Text: The Tradition of Scholarship in the Age of Science, 1450-1800*. Cambridge (Mass.) 1991.

[12]   KENNEY, E.J., *The Character of Humanist Philology*, in *Classical Influences on European Culture A.D. 500-1500*, ed. by R.R. Bolgar. Cambridge 1971, pp. 119-128.

[13]   PASQUALI, G., *Recentiores, non deteriores. Collazioni umanistiche ed editiones principes*, in his *Storia della tradizione e critica del testo*. 2ª ed. Florence 1962, pp. 41-108.

[14]   PRETE, Sesto, *Observations on the History of Textual Criticism in the Medieval and Renaissance Periods*. Collegeville (Minn.) 1970.

[15]   RIZZO, S., *Gli umanisti, i testi classici e le scritture maiuscole*, in *Atti del convegno internazionale "Il libro e il testo". Urbino, 20-23 settembre 1982*. Urbino 1984, pp. 223-241.

[16]   RUBERTO, L., *Studi sul Poliziano filologo*, in *Rivista di filologia e di istruzione classica*, 12 (1884), pp. 212-260.

Greek

[17]   BOLL, F., *Beiträge zur Überlieferungsgeschichte der griechischen Astrologie und Astronomie*, in *Sitzungsberichte der kgl. Bayerischen Akademie der Wissenschaften. Philosophisch-historische Klasse*, 1899, pp. 77-140.

[18]   BROWNING, R., *"Recentiores non deteriores"*, in *Bulletin of the Institute of Classical Studies*, 7 (1960), pp. 11-21 (= his *Studies on Byzantine History, Literature and Education*. London 1977, no. XII).

[19]   DAIN, A., *La transmission des textes littéraires classiques de Photius à Constantin Porphyrogénète*, in *Dumbarton Oaks Papers*, 8 (1954), pp. 33-47 (= *Griechische Kodikologie und Textüberlieferung*. Darmstadt 1980, pp. 206-224).

[20]   *Graecogermania. Griechischstudien deutscher Humanisten. Die Editionstätigkeit der Griechen in der italienischen Renaissance (1469-1523)*. Weinheim 1989 (Ausstellungskataloge der Herzog August Bibliothek, 59).

[21]   IRIGOIN, J., *Survie et renouveau de la littérature antique à Constantinople (IXe siècle)*, in *Cahiers de civilisation médiévale*, 5 (1962), pp. 287-302 (= *Griechische Kodikologie und Textüberlieferung*. Darmstadt 1980, pp. 173-205).

[22]   IRIGOIN, J., *La tradition manuscrite des tragiques grecs dans l'Italie méridionale au XIIIe et dans les premières années du XIVe siècle*, in *Bisanzio e l'Italia. Raccolta di studi in memoria di Agostino Pertusi*. Milan 1982, pp. 132-143.

[23]   LEMERLE, Paul, *Le premier humanisme byzantin. Notes et remarques sur enseignement et culture à Byzance des origines au Xe siècle*. Paris 1971 (Bibliothèque byzantine. Etudes, 6).

[24]   PONTANI, F.M., *Demetrio Mosco e Alessandro Fortio (rettifiche e postille)*, in *Medioevo e rinascimento veneto con altri studi in onore di Lino Lazzarini*, vol. II. Padua 1979, pp. 39-49.

[25]   SMITH, O.L., *Tricliniana*, in *Classica et Mediaevalia*, 33 (1981-1982), pp. 239-262.

[26]   SMITH, O.L., *Tricliniana II*, in *Classica et Mediaevalia*, 43 (1992), pp. 187-228.

[27]   WILAMOWITZ-MOELLENDORFF, Ulrich von, *Die Textgeschichte der griechischen Lyriker*. Berlin 1900 (*Abhandlungen der königl. Gesellschaft der Wissenschaften zu Göttingen. Phil.-hist. Kl.*, N.F. IV, 3).

[28]   WILAMOWITZ-MOELLENDORFF, Ulrich von, *Die Textgeschichte der griechischen Buko-

liker. Berlin 1906 (Philologische Untersuchungen, 18).

[29]　WILSON, N.G., *Some Remarks on Greek Philology in the Milieu of Aldus Manutius,* in *Dotti bizantini e libri greci nell'Italia del secolo XV. Atti del Convegno internazionale, Trento 22-23 ottobre 1990.* Naples 1992, pp. 29-36.

[30]　WILSON, Nigel G., *Scholars of Byzantium.* London 1983.

[30a]　WILSON, Nigel G., *From Byzantium to Italy. Greek Studies in the Italian Renaissance.* London 1992.

Aeschines

[31]　DILLER, A., *The Manuscript Tradition of Aeschines' Orations,* in *Illinois Classical Studies,* 4 (1979), pp. 34-64.

Aeschylus

[32]　BRYSON, E.A.E., *Contributions to the Study of the Thoman Recension of Aeschylus.* Diss. University of Illinois 1956.

[33]　DAWE, R.D., *The Collation and Investigation of the Manuscripts of Aeschylus.* Cambridge 1964.

[34]　MASSA POSITANO, L., *Osservazioni sull'edizione eschilea di Demetrio Triclinio,* in *Dionisio,* 10 (1947), pp. 247-265.

[35]　SMITH, O.L., *Flogging Dead Horses: The Thoman Recension of Aeschylus,* in *Classica et Mediaevalia,* 37 (1986), pp. 245-254.

[36]　SHOTWELL, M.H., *On the Originality of Demetrius Triclinius in Editing and Commenting on the Byzantine Triad of Aeschylus.* Diss. Brown University, Providence, R.I. 1982 (Cf. Summary in *Dissertation Abstracts* 63, 1983, p. 3587 A).

[37]　TURYN, Alexander, *The Manuscript Tradition of the Tragedies of Aeschylus.* New York 1943 (Polish Institute of Arts and Sciences in America, Series 2) (reprint: Hildesheim 1967).

Anaximenes of Lampsacus

[38]　FUHRMANN, Manfred, *Untersuchungen zur Textgeschichte der pseudo-aristotelischen Alexander-Rhetorik (der* Τέχνη *des Anaximenes von Lampsakos).* Wiesbaden 1965 (Akademie der Wissenschaften und der Literatur [Mainz]. Abhandlungen der Geistes- und Sozialwissenschaftlichen Klasse. Jahrgang 1964. Nr. 7).

Anthologia Graeca

[39]　HUTTON, James, *The Greek Anthology in Italy to the Year 1800.* Ithaca (N.Y.) 1935 (Cornell Studies in English, 23).

[40]　MESCHINI, A., *Il codice Barb. gr. 123 e Giano Làskaris,* in *Rivista di filologia e di istruzione classica,* 103 (1975), pp. 56-70.

[41]　MIONI, E., *L'Antologia greca da Massimo Planude a Marco Musuru,* in *Scritti in onore di Carlo Diano.* Bologna 1975, pp. 267-268.

[42]　MIONI, E., *L'Antologia planudea di Angelo Poliziano,* in *Medioevo e rinascimento veneto, con altri studi in onore di Lino Lazzarini,* vol. I. Padua 1979, pp. 541-555 [Vatican, Vat. gr. 1373].

[43]　SABBADINI, R., *Giovanni Aurispa e l'Antologia palatina,* in *Bollettino di filologia classica,* 35 (1928), pp. 99-100.

[44]　TURYN, A., *Demetrius Triclinius and the Planudean Anthology,* in Λειμὼν προσφορᾶς εἰς τὸν καθηγητὴν Ν. Β. Τωμαδάκην ἐν ᾿Αθήναις 1973, p. 434.

Apollonius Rhodius

[45] FERRI, F., *Basinio e l'Argonautica di Apollonio Rodio*, in *Rendiconti dell'Istituto lombardo di scienze e lettere*, 53 (1920), pp. 147-165.

[16] REGTA, C., *Vegio, Basinio e l'"Argonautica" di Apollonio Rodio*, in *Miscellanea Augusto Campana*, vol. II. Padua 1981, pp. 639-670.

[47] VIAN, F., *La recension 'crétoise' des "Argonautiques" d'Apollonios*, in *Revue d'Histoire des Textes*, 2 (1972), pp. 171-195.

Aratus

[48] MARTIN, J., *Histoire du texte des "Phénomènes" d'Aratos*. Paris 1956 (Études et commentaires, 22).

Aristophanes

[49] BOUDREAUX, P., *Le texte d'Aristophane et ses commentateurs*, publié après la mort de l'auteur par G. Méautis. Paris 1919 (Bibliothèque des Écoles françaises d'Athènes et de Rome, 114).

[50] EBERLINE, Charles N., *Studies in the Manuscript Tradition of the Ranae of Aristophanes*. Meisenheim am Glan 1980 (Beiträge zur klassischen Philologie, 119).

[51] KOSTER, W.J.W., *Autour d'un manuscrit d'Aristophane écrit par Démétrius Triclinius. Études paléographiques et critiques sur les éditions d'Aristophane de l'époque byzantine tardive*. Groningen & Djakarta 1957 (Scripta Academica Groningiana).

[52] KOSTER, W.J.W., *Aristophane dans la tradition byzantine*, in *Revue des études grecques*, 76 (1963), pp. 381-396.

[53] KOSTER, W.J.W., *De priore recensione thomana Aristophanis*, in *Mnemosyne*, ser. IV, 17 (1964), pp. 337-366.

[54] KOSTER, W.J.W., *De duabus recensionibus byzantinis Aristophanis*, in *Serta Turyniana*. Urbana (Ill.) 1974, pp. 311-328.

[55] SMITH, O.L., *On the Problem of a Thoman Recension of Aristophanes*, in *Greek, Roman and Byzantine Studies*, 17 (1976), pp. 75-80.

[56] WILSON, N.G., *The Triclinian Edition of Aristophanes*, in *Classical Quarterly*, 56 (1962), pp. 32-47.

Aristotle

[57] HARLFINGER, D., *Einige Grundzüge der Aristoteles-Überlieferung*, in *Griechische Kodikologie und Textüberlieferung*. Darmstadt 1980, pp. 447-483.

[58] IRIGOIN, J., *La tradition des textes de Platon et d'Aristote de l'Antiquité à la Renaissance*, in *Les humanistes et l'antiquité grecque*. Paris 1991, pp. 175-176.

[59] LOBEL, E., *The Greek Manuscripts of Aristotle's Poetics*. Oxford 1937.

[60] SICHERL, M., *Handschriftliche Vorlagen der Editio princeps des Aristoteles*. Wiesbaden 1976 (Akademie der Wissenschaften und der Literatur in Mainz. Abhandlungen der Geistes- und Sozialwissenschaftlichen Klasse, 1976, 8).

Aristotle (Pseudo)

[61] HARLFINGER, D., *Die Textgeschichte der pseudo-aristotelischen Schrift Περὶ ἀτόμων γραμμῶν. Ein kodikologisch-kulturgeschichtliches Beitrag zur Klärung der Überlieferungsverhältnisse im Corpus Aristotelicum*. Amsterdam 1971.

Athenaeus

[62] IRIGOIN, J., *L'édition princeps d'Athénée et ses sources*, in *Revue des études grecques*, 80 (1967), pp. 418-424.

[63] WILSON, N.G., *Did Arethas read Athenaeus?*, in *Journal of Hellenic Studies*, 82 (1962), pp. 147-148.

Autolycus of Pitane
[64] MOGENET, Joseph, *Autolycus de Pitane. Histoire du texte suivie de l'édition critique des traités de la sphère en mouvement et des levers et couchers*. Leuven 1950 (Université de Louvain. Recueil de travaux d'histoire et de philologie, 3ᵉ sér., fasc. 37).

Callimachus
[64a] HARDER, M.A., *Politian and the Fragments of Callimachus*, in *Res Publica Litterarum*, 12 (1989), pp. 77-84.

Diogenes Laertius
[65] GIGANTE, M., *Francesco Elio Marchese editore della versione ambrosiana di Diogene Laerzio*, in *Quaderni*, 5 (1988), pp. 5-28 [Rome 1472].
[66] SOTTILI, A., *Il Laerzio latino e greco e altri autografi di Ambrogio Traversari*, in *Vestigia. Studi in onore di Giuseppe Billanovich*, vol. II. Rome 1984, pp. 699-745.

Dionysius Periegetes
[67] TSAVARI, Isabelle On., *Histoire du texte de la Description de la terre de Denys le Périégète*. Ioannina 1990 (Πανεπιστήμιο Ιωαννίνων. Επιστημονική επετηρίδα Δωδώνη, παράρτημα, 28).

Euripides
[68] DIGGLE, James, *The Textual Tradition of Euripides*. Oxford 1991.
[69] MASTRONARDE, Donald J. & Jan Maarten BREMER, *The Textual Tradition of Euripides' "Phoenissae"*. Berkeley & Los Angeles 1982 (University of California Publications. Classical Studies, 27).
[70] MATTHIESSEN, K., *Studien zur Textüberlieferung der Hekabe des Euripides*. Heidelberg 1974.
[71] SCHARTAU, B., *Observations on the Activities of the Byzantine Grammarians of the Palaeologian Era. I. Demetrius Triclinius' Early Work on the Euripidean Triad (Gamle Kongelige Samling 3549, 8° and Rylands Hebrew 1689)*, in *Cahiers de l'Institut du moyen âge grec et latin*, 4 (1970), pp. 3-33.
[72] SICHERL, M., *Die Editio Princeps Aldina des Euripides und ihre Vorlagen*, in *Rheinisches Museum*, 118 (1975), pp. 205-225 [Venice 1503].
[73] TUILIER, André, *Recherches critiques sur la tradition du texte d'Euripide*. Paris 1968 (Études et commentaires, 68).
[74] TURYN, Alexander, *The Byzantine Manuscript Tradition of the Tragedies of Euripides*. Urbana (Ill.) 1957 (Illinois Studies in Language and Literature, 43).
[75] ZUNTZ, G., *An Inquiry into the Transmission of the Plays of Euripides*. Cambridge 1965.

Hesiod
[76] WEST, M.L., *The Medieval and Renaissance Manuscripts of Hesiod's Theogony*, in *Classical Quarterly*, N.S. 14 (1964), pp. 165-189.
[77] WEST, M.L., *The Medieval Manuscripts of the Works and the Days*, in *Classical Quarterly*, N.S. 24 (1974), pp. 161-185.

Homer
[78] BROWNING, R., *Homer in Byzantium*, in *Viator*, 6 (1975), pp. 15-33 (= Robert BROWNING, *Studies on Byzantine History, Literature and Education*. London 1977, no. XV).

[79]   DI BENEDETTO, F., *Leonzio, Omero e le "Pandette"*, in *Italia medioevale e umanistica*, 12 (1969), pp. 53-112.

[80]   GRANDOLINI, S., *Sull'edizione moscopulea dell'Iliade*, in *Annali della Facoltà di Lettere e Filosofia. Università di Perugia*, 16-17, 1 (1978-1980), pp. 5-11

[81]   HOWALD, E., *Eustathius und der Venetus A*, in *Rheinisches Museum*, 78 (1929), pp. 171-187.

[82]   PERTUSI, A., *L'Omero inviato al Petrarca da Nicola Sigero, ambasciatore e letterato bizantino*, in *Mélanges Eugène Tisserant*, vol. III. Vatican City 1964, pp. 113-139.

[83]   TOFFANIN, G., *L'Omero del Poliziano*, in *La Rinascita*, 4 (1941), pp. 544-554.

Lucian
[84]   GOLDSCHMIDT, E.P., *The First Edition of Lucian of Samosata*, in *Journal of the Warburg and Courtauld Institutes*, 14 (1951), pp. 7-20 [Florence 1496].

Marcus Aurelius
[85]   SONNY, A., *Zur Überlieferungsgeschichte von M. Aurelius* ΕΙΣ ΕΑΥΤΟΝ, in *Philologus*, 54 (1895), pp. 181-183.

Oppianus
[86]   FAJEN, F., *Überlieferungsgeschichtliche Untersuchungen zu den Halieutika des Oppian*. Meisenheim am Glan 1969 (Beiträge zur klassischen Philologie, 32).

Pausanias
[87]   DILLER, A., *Pausanias in the Middle Ages*, in *Transactions and Proceedings of the American Philological Association*, 87 (1956), pp. 84-97.

[88]   DILLER, A., *The Manuscripts of Pausanias*, in *Transactions and Proceedings of the American Philological Association*, 88 (1957), pp. 169-188.

Pindar
[89]   IRIGOIN, Jean, *Histoire du texte de Pindare*. Paris 1952 (Études et commentaires, 13).

[90]   TESSIER, A., *Demetrio Triclinio revisore della colometria pindarica*, in *Studi italiani di filologia classica*, 5 (1987), pp. 67-76.

[91]   TURYN, A., *De codicibus pindaricis*. Krakow & Warsaw 1932 (Archivum filologiczne Polska Akad. Umiejetnosci, 11).

Plato
[92]   ALLINE, H., *Histoire du texte de Platon*. Paris 1915.

[93]   BIDEZ, J., *Aréthas de Césarée. Éditeur et scholiaste*, in *Byzantion*, 9 (1934), pp. 391-408.

[94]   BOTER, G.J., *The Textual Tradition of Plato's Republic*. Leiden 1988 (Mnemosyne. Supplementum, 107).

[95]   BROCKMANN, Christian, *Die handschriftliche Überlieferung von Platons Symposion*. Wiesbaden 1992 (Serta Graeca. Beiträge zur Erforschung griechischer Texte, 2).

[96]   SICHERL, M., *Platonismus und Textüberlieferung*, in *Griechische Kodikologie und Textüberlieferung*. Darmstadt 1980, pp. 535-576.

Plutarch
[97]   HILLYARD, B., *The Medieval Tradition of Plutarch, "De audiendo"*, in *Revue d'Histoire des Textes*, 7 (1977), pp. 1-56.

[98] IRIGOIN, J., *La formation d'un corpus. Un problème d'histoire des textes dans la tradition des "Vies parallèles" de Plutarque*, in *Revue d'Histoire des Textes*, 12-13 (1982-1983), pp. 1-11.

[99] MANFREDINI, M., *Su alcune aldine di Plutarco*, in *Annali della Scuola Normale Superiore di Pisa*, ser. III^a, 14 (1984), pp. 1-12.

[100] MANFREDINI, M., *Codici plutarchei di umanisti italiani*, in *Annali della Scuola Normale Superiore di Pisa*, ser. III^a, 17 (1987), pp. 1001-1043.

[101] MANFREDINI, M., *Codici plutarchei contenenti 'Vitae' e 'Moralia'*, in *Sulla tradizione manoscritta dei 'Moralia' di Plutarco. Atti del Convegno salernitano del 4-5 dicembre 1986*. Salerno 1987, pp. 103-122 (Università degli studi di Salerno. Quaderni del dipartimento di scienze dell'antichità, 2).

Polyaenus

[102] SCHINDLER, Friedel, *Die Überlieferung der Strategemata des Polyainos*. Vienna 1973 (Sitzungsberichte der Österreichischen Akademie der Wissenschaften. Phil.-hist. Klasse, 284, 1).

Polybius

[103] MOORE, John M., *The Manuscript Tradition of Polybius*. Cambrige 1965.

[104] MOORE, J.M., *Polybiana*, in *Greek, Roman and Byzantine Studies*, 12 (1971), pp. 411-449.

Sophocles

[105] AUBRETON, Robert, *Démétrius Triclinius et les recensions médiévales de Sophocle*. Paris 1949 (Collection d'études anciennes).

[106] DAWE, R.D., *Studies on the Text of Sophocles*, vol. I. Leiden 1973.

[107] DIETZ, Hans Peter, *Thomas Magistros' Recension of the Sophoclean Plays Oedipus Coloneus, Trachiniae, Philoctetes*. Diss. University of Illinois 1965.

[108] HECQUET-DEVIENNE, M., *Lecture nouvelle de l'"Oedipe roi" de Sophocle dans les manuscrits L et A*, in *Revue d'Histoire des Textes*, 24 (1994), pp. 1-59 [Florence, Bibl. Laur., Plut. 37.9; Paris, Bibl. nat., gr. 2712].

[109] KOPFF, E.C., *Thomas Magister and the Text of Sophocles' Antigone*, in *Transactions of the American Philological Association*, 106 (1976), pp. 241-266.

[110] SMITH, O.L., *A Note on the Sophocles Ms "Vat. gr." 1333*, in *Classica et Mediaevalia*, 32 (1971-1980), pp. 35-43.

[111] TURYN, A., *The Sophocles Recension of Manuel Moschopulus*, in *Transactions and Proceedings of the American Philological Asssociation*, 80 (1949), pp. 94-173.

[112] TURYN, A., *Studies in the Manuscript Tradition of the Tragedies of Sophocles*. Urbana (Ill.) 1952 (Illinois Studies in Language and Literature, 36, 1-2) (reprint: Rome 1970).

Strabo

[113] DILLER, Aubrey, *The Textual Tradition of Strabo's Geography. With Appendix: The Manuscripts of Eustathius' Commentary on Dionysius Periegetes*. Amsterdam 1975.

Theocritus

[114] GALLAVOTTI, C., *Edizione teocritea di Moscopulo*, in *Rivista di filologia e di istruzione classica*, 62 (1934), pp. 349-369.

[115] GALLAVOTTI, C., *I codici planudei di Teocrito*, in *Studi italiani di filologia classica*, 11 (1934), pp. 289-313.

[116] GALLAVOTTI, C., *Da Planude e Moscopulo alla prima edizione a stampa di Teocrito*, in *Studi italiani di filologia classica*, 13 (1936), pp. 45-59.

Thucydides

[117] HEMMERDINGER, Bertrand, *Essai sur l'histoire du texte de Thucydide*. Paris 1955 (Collection d'études anciennes).

[118] KLEINLOGEL, Alexander, *Geschichte des Thukydides-Textes im Mittelalter*. Berlin 1965.

[119] KUGÉAS, S., *Zur Geschichte der Münchener Thukydides-Handschrift Augustanus F*, in *Byzantinische Zeitschrift*, (1907), pp. 587-609.

[119a] LUZZATTO, M.-J., *Itinerari di codici antichi: un'edizione di Tucidide tra il II ed il X secolo*, in *Materiali e discussioni per l'analisi dei testi classici*, 30 (1993), pp. 167-203 [Florence, Bibl. Laur., Plut. 69.2].

Xenophon

[120] BANDINI, M., *Osservazioni sulla storia del testo dei Memorabilia di Senofonte in età umanistica*, in *Studi classici e orientali*, 38 (1988), pp. 272-292.

[121] BANDINI, M., *I Memorabilia di Senofonte fra il Bessarione, Isidoro di Kiev e Pier Vettori*, in *Bollettino dei classici*, ser. 3ª, 12 (1991), pp. 83-92.

[122] BANDINI, M., *La costituzione del testo dei "Commentarii Socratici" di Senofonte dal Quattrocento ad oggi*, in *Revue d'Histoire des Textes*, 24 (1994), pp. 61-91.

[123] JACKSON, D.F., *Correction and Contamination in Xenophon's "Hiero"*, in *Studi italiani di filologia classica*, 3ª s., 6 (1988), pp. 68-76.

[124] JACKSON, D.F., *The Mysterious Manuscript A of the "Cynegeticus"*, in *Hermes*, 117 (1989), pp. 157-166 [Vienna, Österreichische Nationalbibl., phil. gr. 37].

[125] PERSSON, Axel W., *Zur Textgeschichte Xenophons*. Lund & Leipzig 1915 (Lunds Universitets Årsskrift, N.F. Afd. 1, Bd. 10, Nr. 2).

[126] SCHMOLL, E., *The Manuscript Tradition of Xenophon's Apologia Socratis*, in *Greek, Roman and Byzantine Studies*, 31 (1990), pp. 313-321.

Latin

[127] BILLANOVICH, Giuseppe, *I primi umanisti e la tradizione dei classici latini*. Freiburg 1953 (Discorsi universitari, n.s. 14).

[128] BILLANOVICH, G., *Il Petrarca e i classici*, in *Studi petrarcheschi*, 7 (1961), pp. 21-33.

[129] BILLANOVICH, G., *Il Petrarca e gli storici latini*, in *Tra latino e volgare. Per Carlo Dionisotti*, vol. I. Padua 1974, pp. 67-145.

[130] BRANCA, V., *Il metodo filologico del Poliziano in un capitolo della "Centuria secunda"*, in *Tra latino e volgare. Per Carlo Dionisotti*, vol. I. Padua 1974, pp. 211-243.

[131] GARIEPY, R.J., *Lupus of Ferrières and the Classics*. Darien (Conn.) 1967.

[132] HERMOLAI BARBARI *Castigationes plinianae et in Pomponium Melam*, edidit Giovanni POZZI. Vol. I-IV. Padua 1973-1979 (Thesaurus mundi).

[133] KENNEY, E.J., *The Classical Text. Aspects of Editing in the Age of the Printed Book*. Berkeley, Los Angeles & London 1974.

[134] MUNK OLSEN, B., *L'édition des textes antiques au moyen âge*, in *The Medieval Text. Editors and Critics. A Symposium*. Odense 1990. pp. 83-100.

[135] PRETE, S., *Plauto, Terenzio e il Petrarca*, in *Studi petrarcheschi*, 5 (1952), pp. 85-94.

[136] SABBADINI, Remigio, *Storia e critica di testi latini*. 2ª ed. Padua 1971 (Medioevo e umanesimo, 11).

[137] *Texts and Transmission. A Survey of the Latin Classics*, edited by L.D. REYNOLDS. Oxford 1983.

Ammianus Marcellinus

[138] CAPPELLETTO, R., *Niccolò Niccoli e il codice di Ammiano Vat. lat. 1873*, in *Bollettino del Comitato per la preparazione dell'edizione nazionale dei classici greci e latini*, 26 (1978), pp. 57-84.

[139] CAPPELLETTO, R., *Marginalia di Poggio in due codici di Ammiano Marcellino (Vat. lat. 1873 e Vat. lat. 2969)*, in *Miscellanea Augusto Campana*, vol. I. Padua, 1981 pp. 189-211.

[140] CAPPELLETTO, Rita, *Recuperi Ammianei da Biondo Flavio*. Rome 1983 (Note e discussioni erudite, 18).

Apicius

[141] MILHAM, M.E., *Toward a Stemma and "fortuna" of Apicius*, in *Italia medioevale e umanistica*, 10 (1967), pp. 259-320.

[142] MILHAM, M.E., *Apicius*, in *Catalogus translationum et commentariorum*, 2 (1971), pp. 324-329.

Ausonius

[143] PRETE, Sesto, *Ricerche sulla storia del testo di Ausonio*. Rome 1960 (Temi e testi, 7).

[144] WEISS, R., *Ausonius in the Fourteenth Century*, in *Classical Influences on European Culture A.D. 500-1500*, ed. by R.R. Bolgar. Cambridge 1971, pp. 67-80.

Caesar

[145] BEESON, C.H., *The Text History of the Corpus Caesarianum*, in *Classical Philology*, 35 (1940), pp. 113-135.

[146] BILLANOVICH, G., *Nella tradizione dei "Commentarii" di Cesare. Roma, Petrarca, i Visconti*, in *Studi petrarcheschi*, n.s. 7 (1990), pp. 262-318.

Catullus

[147] ALBERTINI, A., *Calfurnio Bresciano. La sua edizione di Catullo (1481)*, in *Commentari dell'Ateneo di Brescia per l'anno 1953*, pp. 29-79.

[148] GAISSER, Julia Haig, *Catullus and his Renaissance Readers*. Oxford 1993.

[149] GIL, J., *Crítica textual y humanismo*, in *La crítica textual y los textos clásicos* Murcia 1986 (Universidad de Murcia. Sección de filología clásica. III simposio), pp. 65-85 [Controversy between Marullus and Politianus].

[150] SABBADINI, R., *Se Guarino Veronese abbia fatto una recensione a Catullo*, in *Rivista di filologia e di istruzione classica*, 13 (1884-1885), pp. 266-269.

[151] SABBADINI, R., *Ancora di Catullo e di Guarino Veronese*, in *Rivista di filologia e di istruzione classica*, 14 (1885-1886), pp. 179-181.

Celsus

[152] SABBADINI, R., *Cornelio Celso*, in his *Storia e critica di testi latini*. Padua 1971, pp. 215-237.

Cicero

[153] BARKER-BENFIELD, B.C., *A Ninth-Century Manuscript from Fleury: "Cato de senectute cum Macrobio"*, in *Medieval Learning and Literature. Essays Presented to Richard William Hunt*. Oxford 1976, pp. 145-165 [Vatican, Reg. lat. 1587 + Paris, Bibl. Nat., lat. 16677].

[154]   BEESON, Charles Henry, *Lupus of Ferrières as Scribe and Text Critic. A Study of his Autograph Copy of Cicero's "De oratore" (with a Facsimile of the Manuscript)*. Cambridge (Mass.) 1930 (The Mediaeval Academy of America. Publication No. 4) [London, Brit. Libr., Harley 4927].

[155]   FERA, V., *Un proemio al "De officiis" tra Filelfo e Barzizza*, in *Giornale italiano di filologia*, 35 (1983), pp. 113-131.

[156]   HUNT, T.J., *The Origin of the Deteriores of the "Academicus primus"*, in *Scriptorium*, 27 (1973), pp. 39-42.

[157]   MARCHESI, C., *Un nuovo codice del "De officiis" di Cicerone (cod. di Troyes 552)*, in *Memorie del Reale Istituto lombardo di scienze e lettere. Classe di lettere e scienze morali e storiche*, 22 (1911), pp. 187-212.

[158]   NARDO, D., *Le correzioni nei due codici medicei 49,7 e 49,9 delle "Familiares" di Cicerone*, in *Atti dell'Istituto veneto di scienze, lettere e arti*, 124 (1965-1966), pp. 337-397.

[159]   PECERE, O., *La "subscriptio" di Statilio Massimo e la tradizione delle "Agrarie" di Cicerone*, in *Italia medioevale e umanistica*, 25 (1982), pp. 73-124.

[160]   PELLEGRIN, E. & G. BILLANOVICH, *Un manuscrit de Cicéron annoté de Pétrarque au British Museum*, in *Scriptorium*, 8 (1954), pp. 115-117 [London, Brit. Libr., Harley 4927].

[161]   RAIMONDI, E., *Correzioni medioevali, correzioni umanistiche e correzioni petrarcheschi nella lettera VI del libro XVI delle "Familiares"*, in *Studi petrarcheschi*, 1 (1948), pp. 125-133.

[162]   REEVE, M.D., *Before and After Poggio: Some Manuscripts of Cicero's Speeches*, in *Rivista di filologia e di istruzione classica*, 112 (1984), pp. 266-284.

[163]   REEVE, M.D., *Missing Passages of "Pro Flacco"*, in *Revue d'Histoire des Textes*, 14-15 (1984-1985), pp. 53-57.

[164]   RIZZO, S., *Apparati ciceroniani e congetture del Petrarca*, in *Rivista di filologia e di istruzione classica*, 103 (1975), pp. 5-15.

[165]   RIZZO, Silvia, *La tradizione manoscritta della "Pro Cluentio" di Cicerone*. Genoa 1979 (Pubblicazioni dell'Istituto di filologia classica e medievale dell'Università di Genova, 57).

[166]   SABBADINI, R., *Cicerone*, in his *Storia e critica di testi latini*. Padua 1971, pp. 13-144.

[167]   SCHMIDT, Peter Lebrecht, *Die Überlieferung von Ciceros Schrift "de legibus" in Mittelalter und Renaissance*. Munich 1974 (Studia et testimonia antiqua, 10).

[168]   SCHMIDT, P.L., *Die handschriftliche Überlieferung von De legibus. Resultate und Perspektive*, in *Ciceroniana*, n.s. 1 (1973), pp. 83-89.

[169]   SCHMIDT, P.L., *Il Gudiano lat. 2 nella trasmissione dei testi ciceroniani*, in *Italia medioevale e umanistica*, 28 (1985), pp. 48-56.

[170]   THURN, H., *M.p.th. f. 185 der Universitätsbibliothek Würzburg, ein unbearbeiteter karolingischer Textzeuge von Ciceros De inventione*, in *Würzburger Jahrbücher für Altertumswissenschaft*, N.F. 3 (1977), pp. 227-230.

Cicero (Pseudo)

[171]   SPALLONE, M., *La trasmissione della "Rhetorica ad Herennium" nell'Italia meridionale tra XI e XII secolo*, in *Bollettino dei classici*, ser. IIIª, 1 (1980), pp. 158-190.

Claudian

[172]   HALL, J.B., *Prolegomena to Claudian*. London 1986 (Institute of Classical Studies. Bulletin Supplement, 45).

Columella
[173] HEDBERG, S., *Contamination and Interpolation. A Study of the 15th Century Columella Manuscripts.* Uppsala 1968.
[174] PRETE, S., *Il codice di Columella di Stefano Guarnieri: studio critico.* Fano 1974 (Fonti e studi, 2) [Florence, 1452].

Curtius
[175] SMITS, E.R., *A Medieval Supplement to the Beginning of Curtius Rufus's Historia Alexandri. An Edition with Introduction,* in *Viator,* 18 (1987), pp. 89-124.

Dictys Cretensis
[176] FRANCESCHINI, E., *Intorno alla tradizione manoscritta di Ditti Cretese,* in *Atti del Reale istituto Veneto di scienze, lettere ed arti.* Anno accademico 1937-1938, vol. 97 (II), pp. 141-178 (= his *Scritti di filologia latina medievale,* vol. I. Padua 1976, pp. 166-204) [Milan, Bibl. Ambr., C 72 inf.].
[177] MALTESE, E.V., *Il diario della guerra di Troia (Ditti Cretese) tra Ciriaco d'Ancona e Giorgio Gemisto Pletone,* in *Res Publica Litterarum,* 10 (1987), pp. 209-214.

Donat
[178] HOLTZ, Louis, *Donat et la tradition de l'enseignement grammatical. Etude sur l'"Ars Donati" et sa diffusion (IVᵉ-IXᵉ siècle) et édition critique.* Paris 1981 (Documents, études et répertoires publiés par l'Institut de Recherche et d'Histoire des Textes).

Florus
[179] HAVAS, L., *Textgeschichte des Florus von der Antike bis zu frühen Neuzeit,* in *Athenaeum,* 80 (1992), pp. 433-469.

Gellius
[180] BARON, H., *Aulus Gellius in the Renaissance and a Manuscript from the School of Guarino,* in *Studies in Philology,* 48 (1951), pp. 107-125.
[181] LIEFTIENCK, G.I., *Le manuscrit d'Aulu-Gelle à Leeuwarden, exécuté à Fulda en 836,* in *Bullettino dell'"Archivio paleografico italiano",* n.s. 1 (1955), pp. 11-17 [Leeuwarden, Prov. Bibl., B.A. Fr. 55].
[182] MARE, A.C. de la, P.K. MARSHALL & R.H. ROUSE, *Pietro da Montagna and the Text of Aulus Gellius in Paris, B.N. lat. 13038,* in *Scriptorium,* 30 (1976), pp. 219-225.
[183] MEAGHER, L., *The Gellius Manuscript of Lupus of Ferrières.* Chicago 1936 [Vatican, Reg. lat. 597].

Historia Augusta
[184] BALLOU, S.H., *The Manuscript Tradition of the Historia Augusta.* Leipzig & Berlin 1914.
[185] BANTI, L., *Annotatori del manoscritto Vaticano Palatino latino 899 della "Historia Augusta",* in *Studi in onore di Ugo Enrico Paoli.* Florence 1956, pp. 59-70.
[185a] CALLU, J.-P., *L'"Histoire Auguste" de Pétrarque,* in *Bonner Historia Augusta Colloqium 1984/1985.* Bonn 1987, pp. 81-115.
[186] CALLU, J.-P. & O. DESBORDES, *Le 'Quattrocento' de l'Histoire Auguste,* in *Revue d'Histoire des Textes,* 19 (1989), pp. 253-275.
[187] HOHL, E., *Petrarca und der Palatinus 899 der Historia Augusta,* in *Hermes,* 51 (1916), pp. 154-159.

Horace

[188]   CAMPAUX, A., *De la critique du texte d'Horace avant Peerlkamp du 1er au XVIIIe siècle*, in *Annales de l'Est*, 4 (1880), pp. 189-204.

[189]   ROSTAGNO, E., *L'Orazio Laurenziano già di Francesco Petrarca*. Rome 1933 [Florence, Bibl. Laur., Plut. 34.1].

Livy

[190]   BILLANOVICH, G., *Petrarch and the Textual Tradition of Livy*, in *Journal of the Warburg and Courtauld Institutes*, 14 (1951), pp. 137-208.

[191]   BILLANOVICH, G., *Dal Livio di Raterio (Laur. 63, 19) al Livio del Petrarca (B.M., Harl. 2493)*, in *Italia medioevale e umanistica*, 2 (1959), pp. 103-178.

[192]   BILLANOVICH, G., *Per la fortuna di Tito Livio nel Rinascimento italiano: Un altro Livio corretto dal Valla (Valenza, Biblioteca della Cattedrale, 173)*, in *Italia medioevale e umanistica*, 1 (1958), pp. 265-275.

[193]   BILLANOVICH, G., *Da Dante a Petrarca: il Virgilio Ambrosiano e l'Orazio Morgan*, in *Accademia Nazionale dei Lincei. Adunanze Straordinarie per il conferimento dei Premi della Fondazione Antonio Feltrinelli*, I, 3 (1966), pp. 61-67.

[194]   BILLANOVICH, Giuseppe, *La tradizione del testo di Livio e le origini dell'umanesimo*. Vol. I, 1 and II. Padua 1981-1983 (Studi sul Petrarca, 9 & 11).

[195]   BILLANOVICH, G., *Il Livio di Pomposa e i primi umanisti padovani*, in *Bibliofilia*, 85 (1983), pp. 125-148.

[196]   BILLANOVICH, G., *Il testo di Livio. Da Roma a Padova, a Avignone, a Oxford*, in *Italia medioevale e umanistica*, 32 (1989), pp. 53-100.

[197]   BILLANOVICH, G. & M. FERRARIS, *Per la fortuna di Tito Livio nel Rinascimento italiano: le "Emendationes in T. Livium" del Valla e il Codex Regius di Livio*, in *Italia medioevale e umanistica*, 1 (1958), pp. 245-264.

[197a] BORGHI, A., *Il codice Valenciano della terza Deca di Tito Livio e la sua tradizione*, in *Rendiconti dell'Istituto lombardo di scienze e lettere. Classe di lettere e scienze morali e storiche*, 108 (1974), pp. 803-818.

[198]   DOREY, T.A., *Livy XXI-XXV. Petrarch and the Codices Deteriores*, in *Euphrosyne*, 3 (1969), pp. 59-72.

[199]   REEVE, M.D., *The Third Decade of Livy in Italy: The Family of the Puteaneus*, in *Rivista di filologia e di istruzione classica*, 115 (1987), pp. 129-164.

[200]   REEVE, M.D., *The Third Decade of Livy in Italy: The Spirensian Tradition*, in *Rivista di filologia e di istruzione classica*, 115 (1987), pp. 405-440.

[201]   REGOLIOSI, M., *Lorenzo Valla, Antonio Panormita, Giacomo Curlo e le emendazioni a Livio*, in *Italia medioevale e umanistica*, 24 (1981), pp. 287-316.

[202]   REGOLIOSI, M., *Le congetture a Livio del Valla: Metodo e problemi*, in *Lorenzo Valla e l'umanesimo italiano. Atti del Convegno internazionale di studi umanistici (Parma, 18-19 ottobre 1984)*. Padua 1986, pp. 51-71.

[203]   SABBADINI, R., *Le "Periochae Livianae" del Petrarca possedute dai Barzizza*, in *F. Petrarca e la Lombardia*. Milan 1904, pp. 195-201 [Naples, Bibl. Naz., IV C 32].

[204]   SHIPLEY, F.W., *Certain Sources of Corruption in Latin MSS: A Study Based upon Two MSS of Livy: Cod. Putaneus (Fifth Century), and its Copy: Codex Reginensis 762 (Ninth Century)*, in *American Journal of Archaeology*, 2nd Ser., 7 (1903), pp. 1-25, 157-197, 405-428.

[205]   VALENTINI, R., *Il Codex Regius di T. Livio*, in *Studi italiani di filologia classica*, 14 (1906), pp. 206-238.

[206]   VALENTINI, R., *Le "Emendationes in T. Livium"*, in *Studi italiani di filologia classica*, 15 (1907), pp. 262-302.

[207]   WALTERS, W.C.F., *On Some Symbols of Omission in Livian MSS*, in *Classical Review*, 17 (1903), pp. 161-162.

[208] WALTERS, W.C.F., *"Codex Agenensis" (Brit. Mus. Harl. 2493) and Laurentius Valla*, in *Classical Quarterly*, 11 (1917), pp. 154-158.

Lucan

[209] GOTOFF, Harold C., *The Transmission of Lucan in the Ninth Century*. Cambridge (Mass.) 1971 (Loeb Classical Monographs).

Lucretius

[210] PELLEGRIN, É., *Le "Codex Pomponii Romani" de Lucrèce*, in *Latomus*, 7 (1948), pp. 77-82.

[211] REEVE, M.D., *The Italian Tradition of Lucretius*, in *Italia medioevale e umanistica*, 23 (1980), pp. 27-48.

Macrobius

[212] LA PENNA, A., *Studi sulla tradizione dei "Saturnalia" di Macrobio*, in *Annali della Scuola Normale Superiore di Pisa*, ser. IIª, 22 (1953), pp. 225-252.

Martial

[213] CARRATELLO, U., *L'editio princeps di Valerio Marziale e l'incunabolo ferrarese di Leida*, in *Giornale italiano di filologia*, n.s. 4, = 25 (1973), pp. 295-299 [Ferrara 1471].

[214] CARRATELLO, U., *L'"Epigrammaton liber" di Marziale nella tradizione tardomedievale e umanistica*, in *Giornale italiano di filologia*, n.s. 5, = 26 (1974), pp. 1-17.

[215] DELLA CORTE, F., *Nicolò Perotti e gli epigrammi di Marziale*, in *Res Publica Litterarum*, 9 (1986), pp. 97-107.

[215a] HAUSMANN, F.-R., *Martial in Italien*, in *Studi medievali*, ser. III, 17 (1976), pp. 173-218.

Mela (Pomponius)

[216] MILHAM, M.E., *The Renaissance Tradition of Pomponius Mela*, in *Conventus Neo-Latini Amstelodamensis*. Munich 1979, pp. 786-793.

[217] PARRONI, P., *Il contributo dei codici umanistici al testo di Pomponio Mela*, in *Rivista di filologia e di istruzione classica*, 107 (1979), pp. 157-179.

Nepos

[218] MARSHALL, Peter K., *The Manuscript Tradition of Cornelius Nepos*. London 1977 (University of London. Institute of Classical Studies. Bulletin Supplement, 37).

Nonius Marcellus

[219] GATTI, P., *Interpolazioni umanistiche in un codice di Nonio Marcello (Vat. lat. 1554)*, in *Studi Noniani*, 6 (1980), pp. 103-115.

Ovid

[220] LUCK, Georg, *Untersuchungen zur Textgeschichte Ovids*. Heidelberg 1969 (Bibliothek der klassischen Altertumswissenschaften, N.F., 2. Reihe, 29).

[221] MOSS, Ann, *Ovid in Renaissance France, A Survey of the Latin Editions of Ovid and Commentaries Printed in France before 1600*. London 1982 (Warburg Institute Surveys, 8).

[222] PEETERS, F., *Les "Fastes" d'Ovide. Histoire du texte*. Brussels 1939 [Brussels, Bibl. royale, 5369-5373].

[223] QUESTA, C., *I "Tristia" in un nuovo codice dell'XI-XII secolo*, in *Atti del Convegno internazionale ovidiano. Sulmona, maggio 1958*, vol. I. Rome 1959, pp. 81-91 [Vatican, Ott. lat. 1469].

[224]   QUESTA, C., *Ovidio nell'Ottoboniano lat. 1469*, in *Scriptorium*, 13 (1959), pp. 217-232.
[225]   STEINER, G., *Source-Editions of Ovid's "Metamorphoses", 1471-1500*, in *Transactions and Proceedings of the American Philological Association*, 82 (1951), pp. 219-231.

Persius
[226]   CLAUSEN, W., *Codex Vat. Reginensis 1560 of Persius*, in *Transactions and Proceedings of the American Philological Asssociation*, 80 (1949), pp. 238-244.
[227]   KUBITSCHEK, W., *Die Persiushandschrift der Peterskirche in Rom*, in *Wiener Studien*, 8 (1886), pp. 125-130 [Vatican, Arch. S. Pietro H. 36].
[228]   OWEN, S.G., *On the Montpellier Manuscripts of Persius and Juvenal*, in *Classical Review*, 19 (1905), pp. 218-223 [Montpellier, Fac. de Médecine, 125 & 212].

Phaedrus
[229]   BOLDRINI, Sandro, *Fedro e Perrotti. Ricerche sulla storia della traditione*. Urbino 1988.
[230]   BOLDRINI, Sandro, *Note sulla tradizione manoscritta di Fedro (i tre codici di età carolingia)*. Rome 1990 (Suppl. n. 9 al "Bollettino dei classici").

Plautus
[231]   CAPPELLETTO, R., *Congetture di Niccolò Niccoli al testo delle "dodici commedie" di Plauto*, in *Rivista di filologia e di istruzione classica*, 105 (1977), pp. 43-56.
[232]   LINDSAY, W.M., *The Palatine Text of Plautus*. Oxford 1896.
[233]   LINDSAY, W.M., *The Mss. of the First Eight Plays of Plautus*, in *Classical Review*, 10 (1896), pp. 319-321.
[234]   PRETE, S., *Gli studi del Poliziano su un codice delle Commedie di Terenzio*, in *Civiltà dell'Umanesimo. Atti del VI, VII, VIII convegno internazionale del Centro di studi umanistici*. Florence 1972, pp. 307-312 [Vatican, Vat. lat. 3226].
[235]   QUESTA, C., *Plauto diviso in atti prima di G.B. Pio (Codd. Vatt. latt. 3304 e 2711)*, in *Rivista di cultura classica e medievale*, 4 (1962), pp. 209-230.
[236]   QUESTA, Cesare, *Per la storia del testo di Plauto nell'Umanesimo. I. La "recensio" di Poggio Bracciolini*. Rome 1968 (Quaderni Athena, 6).
[237]   QUESTA, C., *Il testo dello "Pseudolus" nei codici C D (Plauto dagli 'scriptoria' medievali a Poggio)*, in *Miscellanea Augusto Campana*, vol. II. Padua 1981, pp. 611-638 [Heidelberg, Universitätsbibl., Pal. lat. 1613 & Vatican, Vat. lat. 3870].
[238]   QUESTA, Cesare, *Parerga plautina. Struttura e tradizione manoscritta delle Commedie*. Urbino 1985 (Pubblicazioni dell'Università di Urbino. Scienze umane. Serie di linguistica letteratura arte, 5).
[239]   SABBADINI, R., *Plauto*, in his *Storia e critica di testi latini*. Padua 1971, pp. 241-259.
[240]   TONTINI, A., *Note sulla presentazione del testo di Plauto nella famiglia palatina: le maiuscole interne del codice Pal. lat. 1615*, in *Studi Urbinati* B 3, 61 (1988), pp. 229-296.

Pliny (the Elder)
[241]   DESANGES, J., *Le manuscrit (Ch) et la classe des "recentiores" perturbés de l'"Histoire naturelle" de Pline l'Ancien*, in *Latomus*, 25 (1966), pp. 508-525.
[242]   MARUCCHI, A., *Note sul manoscritto (Vat. lat. 5991) di cui si è servito Giovanni Andrea Bussi per l'edizione di Plinio del 1470*, in *Bulletin d'information de l'Institut de Recherche et d'Histoire des Textes*, 15 (1967-1968), pp. 175-182.

[243]   MEYVAERT, P., *The Duke Pliny*, in *Library Notes*, 42 (1971), pp. 23-34.

[244]   PUGLIESE CARRATELLI, G., *Due epistole di Giovanni Brancati su la "Naturalis historia" di Plinio e la versione di Cristoforo Landino*, in *Atti della Accademia Pontaniana*, n.s. 3 (1949-1950), pp. 179-192.

[245]   SABBADINI, R., *Edizioni quattrocentistiche della Storia naturale di Plinio*, in *Studi italiani di filologia classica*, 8 (1900), pp. 439-445.

Pliny (the Younger)

[246]   SABBADINI, R., *Plinio*, in his *Storia e critica di testi latini*. Padua 1971, pp. 263-279.

[247]   STOUT, S.E., *Scribe and Critic at Work in Pliny's Letters*. Bloomington (Ind.) 1954 (Indiana University Publications, Humanities Series, No. 30).

Priscian

[248]   DE NONNO, M., *Contributo alla tradizione di Prisciano in area beneventano-cassinese: il Vallicell. C 9*, in *Revue d'Histoire des Textes*, 9 (1979), pp. 123-139.

[249]   MAZZINI, G., *Il codice Vaticano latino 3313 della grammatica di Prisciano*, in *Archivum latinitatis medii aevi*, 1 (1924), pp. 213-222.

Propertius

[250]   BUTRICA, James L., *The Manuscript Tradition of Propertius*. Toronto 1984 (Phoenix. Supplementary volume, 17).

[251]   COPPINI, D., *Filologi del Quattrocento al lavoro su due passi di Properzio*, in *Rinascimento*, 2ᵃ ser.,16 (1976), pp. 219-229.

[252]   JAMES, M.R., *The "Codex Neapolitanus" of Propertius*, in *Classical Review*, 17 (1903), pp. 462-463 [Wolfenbüttel, Herzog August Bibl., 224 Gud. lat.].

[253]   ULLMAN, B.L., *The Manuscripts of Propertius*, in *Classical Philology*, 6 (1911), pp. 282-301.

Quintilian

[254]   CECCHETTI, D., *La "traditio" quintilianea nel Quattrocento francese. Gli umanisti francesi precedettero quelli italiani nella riscoperta della "Institutio oratorio" integra?* in *L'arte dell'interpretare. Studi critici offerti a Giovanni Getto*. Cuneo 1984, pp. 145-165.

[255]   COUSIN, Jean, *Recheches sur Quintilien. Manuscrits et éditions*. Paris 1975.

[256]   SABBADINI, R., *Quintiliano*, in his *Storia e critica di testi latini*. Padua 1971, pp. 283-302.

[257]   WINTERBOTTOM, M., *Fifteenth-century Manuscripts of Quintilian*, in *Classical Quarterly*, 17 (1967), pp. 356-367.

Sallust

[258]   MAURENBRECHER, B., *Sallustiana I. Die Überlieferung der Jugurthalücke*. Halle a. S. 1903 (Festschrift der 47. Versammlung deutscher Philologen und Schulmänner in Halle a. S. zum Willkommen zugeeignet).

[259]   REYNOLDS, L.D., *The Lacuna in Sallust's "Jugurtha"*, in *Revue d'Histoire des Textes*, 14-15 (1984-1985), pp. 59-69.

[260]   SCHLEE, Friedrich, *Zwei Berliner Sallusthandschriften*. Sorau 1899 [Berlin, Deutsche Staatsbibl., Phill. 1901 & 1902].

[261]   ULLMAN, B.L., *The Dedication Copy of Pomponius Letus's Edition of Sallust and the "Vita" of Sallust*, in his *Studies in the Italian Renaissance*. Rome 1955, pp. 365-372 [Vatican, Ott. lat. 2989].

Seneca

[262] EDEN, P.T., *The Manuscript Tradition of Seneca's "Apocolocyntosis"*, in *Classical Quarterly*, 73, = N.S. 29 (1979), pp. 149-161.

[263] MAZZOLI, G., *Ricerche sulla tradizione medievale del "De beneficiis" e del "De clementia" di Seneca. I. "Nachleben" fino al sec. XII: Ugo di Flavigny.—II. Il posto del ms. Monac. 2544*, in *Bollettino del Comitato per la preparazione dell'edizione nazionale dei classici greci e latini*, n.s. 26 (1978), pp. 85-109.

[264] MAZZOLI, G., *Ricerche sulla tradizione medievale del "De beneficiis" e del "De clementia". III. Storia della tradizione manoscritta*, in *Bollettino dei classici*, ser. 3ª, 3 (1982), pp. 165-223.

[265] MCGREGOR, A.P., *The Manuscript Tradition of Seneca's Tragedies, "ante renatas in Italia litteras"*, in *Transactions and Proceedings of the American Philological Association*, 102 (1971), pp. 327-356.

[266] REYNOLDS, L.D., *The Medieval Tradition of Seneca's "Letters"*. Oxford 1965.

[267] REYNOLDS, L.D., *The Medieval Tradition of Seneca's "Dialogues"*, in *Classical Quarterly*, N.S. 18 (1968), pp. 355-372.

[268] ROUSE, R.H., *The A Text of Seneca's Tragedies in the Thirteenth Century*, in *Revue d'histoire des textes*, 1 (1971), pp. 93-121.

[269] SABBADINI, R., *Il testo interpolato del "Ludus" di Seneca*, in *Rivista di filologia e di istruzione classica*, 47 (1919), pp. 338-345.

[270] SCHMIDT, P.L., *Rezeption und Überlieferung der Tragödien Senecas bis zum Ausgang des Mittelalters*, in *Der Einfluss Senecas auf das europäische Drama*. Darmstadt 1978, pp. 12-73.

[271] VILLA, C., *La tradizione delle "Ad Lucilium" e la cultura di Brescia dall'età carolingia ad Albertano*, in *Italia medioevale e umanistica*, 12 (1969), pp. 9-51.

Silius Italicus

[272] HEITLAND, W.E., *The "Great Lacuna" in the Eighth Book of Silius Italicus*, in *The Journal of Philology*, 24 (1896), pp. 188-211.

Solinus

[273] BELL, H.I., *A Solinus Manuscript from the Library of Coluccio Salutati*, in *Speculum*, 4 (1929), pp. 451-461 [London, Brit. Libr., Egerton 818].

[274] CHATELAIN, É., *Un manuscrit de Solin révélé par les notes tironiennes*, in *Revue de philologie*, n.s. 26 (1902), pp. 38-43 [Leiden, Bibl. der Rijksuniv., Voss. lat. Q. 87].

Statius

[275] CESARINI MARTINELLI, L., *Le "Selve" di Stazio nella critica testuale del Poliziano*, in *Studi italiani di filologia classica*, n.s. 47 (1975), pp. 130-174.

[275a] REEVE, M.D., *Statius' "Silvae" in the Fifteenth Century*, in *Classical Quarterly*, 27 (1977), pp. 202-225.

Suetonius

[276] BILLANOVICH, G., *Uno Svetonio della biblioteca del Petrarca (Berlinese lat. fol. 337)*, in *Studi petrarcheschi*, 6 (1954), pp. 23-33.

[277] BILLANOVICH, G., *Nella biblioteca del Petrarca. II. Un altro Svetonio del Petrarca (Oxford, Exeter College, 186)*, in *Italia medioevale e umanistica*, 3 (1960), pp. 28-58.

[278] CESARINI MARTINELLI, L., *Il Poliziano e Svetonio. Osservazioni su un recente contributo alla filologia umanistica*, in *Rinascimento*, 2ª ser., 16 (1976), pp. 111-131.

[279] FERA, V., *Polemiche filologiche intorno allo Svetonio di Beroaldo*, in *The Uses of Greek and Latin. Historical Essays*, ed. by A.C. Dionisotti, A. Grafton & J. Kraye. London 1988 (Warburg Institute Surveys and Texts, 16), pp. 71-87.

[280] GARDENAL, Gianna, *Il Poliziano e Svetonio. Contributo alla storia della filologia uma-

nistica. Florence 1975 (Università di Padova. Pubblicazioni della facoltà di lettere e filosofia, 53).

[280a] VENIER, M., *Giovanni Battista Egnazio editore. I. Il "De vita Caesarum" di Svetonio*, in *Res Publica Litterarum*, 16 (1993), pp. 175-183.

Tacitus

[281] SABBADINI, R., *Tacito*, in his *Storia e critica di testi latini*. Padua 1971, pp. 185-211.

[282] ULERY, R.W., *The Text of Tacitus in 15th-Century Italy and the Guarnieri Brothers*, in *Res Publica litterarum*, 12 (1989), pp. 237-250 [Stefano & Francesco Guarnieri].

Terentius

[283] CERETTI, L., *Critica testuale a Terenzio in una lettera del Faerno a Paolo Manuzio*, in *Aevum*, 28 (1954), pp. 522-551.

[284] CESARINI MARTINELLI, L., *Uno sconosciuto incunabolo di Terenzio postillato dal Poliziano*, in *Rinascimento*, 2ª ser., 24 (1984), pp. 239-246 [Florence, Bibl. Naz. Centrale, B.R. 97; a. 1475].

[285] GEPPERT, G., *Zur Geschichte der terentianischen Texteskritik*, in *Neue Jahrbücher für Philologie und Pädagogik*, 18 (1852), pp. 28-87.

[286] GRANT, John N., *Studies in the Textual Tradition of Terence*. Toronto 1986 (Phoenix. Supplementary volume, 20).

[287] RIBUOLI, Riccardo, *La collazione polizianea del codice Bembino di Terenzio con le postille inedite del Poliziano e note su Pietro Bembo*. Rome 1981 (Note e discussioni erudite, 17).

[288] SABBADINI, R., *La "Philologia" del Petrarca e Terenzio*, in *Bollettino di filologia classica*, 22 (1915), pp. 53-55.

[289] VILLA, Claudia, *La "Lectura Terentii"*. Volume primo. *Da Ildemaro a Francesco Petrarca*. Padua 1984 (Studi sul Petrarca, 17).

[290] VILLA, C., *Petrarca e Terenzio*, in *Studi petrarcheschi*, n.s. 6 (1989), pp. 1-22.

Valerius Flaccus

[291] CAMBIER, G., *L'"édition princeps" des "Argonautiques" de Valerius Flaccus, Bologne 1474*, in *Revue belge de philologie et d'histoire*, 42 (1964), p. 1419.

[292] CAMBIER, G., *Attribution du manuscrit de Florence, Laur. 39.38 à Niccolò Niccoli*, in *Scriptorium*, 19 (1965), pp. 236-243.

[293] EHLERS, W. Wolfgang, *Untersuchungen zur handschriftlichen Überlieferung der Argonautica des C. Valerius Flaccus*. Munich 1970 (Zetemata, 52).

[294] FERA, V., *Il primo "testo critico" di Valerio Flacco*, in *Giornale italiano di filologia*, n.s. 10, = 31 (1979), pp. 230-254 [Bartolomeo Fonzio, s. XV].

[295] LABARDI, L., *Congetture del Niccoli e tradizione estranea all'archetipo sui margini del Laurenziano 39, 18 di Valerio Flacco*, in *Italia medioevale e umanistica*, 26 (1983), pp. 189-214.

[296] SCHMIDT, P.L., *Polizian und der italienische Archetyp der Valerius-Flaccus-Überlieferung*, in *Italia medioevale e umanistica*, 19 (1976), pp. 241-256.

Valerius Maximus

[297] SCHNETZ, Joseph, *Ein Kritiker des Valerius Maximus im 9. Jahrhundert*. Neuburg a. D. 1901 [Lupus Ferrariensis; Berne, Burgerbibl., 366].

Varro

[298] FERRERO, L., *Un codice torinese e l'edizione principe del "De lingua latina" di*

Varrone, in *Atti della Accademia delle scienze di Torino. Classe di scienze morali, storiche e filologiche*, 84 (1949-1950), pp. 130-160.

Virgil

[299] AUSTIN, R.G., *Ille ego qui quondam...*, in *Classical Quarterly*, N.S. 18, = 62 (1968), pp. 107-115.

[300] BILLANOVICH, G., *Il Virgilio del Petrarca. Da Avignone a Milano*, in *Studi Petrarcheschi*, n.s. 2 (1985), pp. 15-52 [Milan, Bibl. Ambros., S.P. 10/27].

[301] ESPOSITO, E., *Edizioni*, in *Enciclopedia Virgiliana*, vol. II. Rome 1985, pp. 169-174.

[302] DELISLE, L., *Virgile copié au Xe siècle par le moine Rahingus*, in *Mélanges d'archéologie et d'histoire*, 6 (1886), pp. 239-250 [Vatican, Vat. lat. 1570].

[303] KALLENDORF, C., *Cristoforo Landino's "Aeneid" and the Humanist Critical Tradition*, in *Renaissance Quarterly*, 36 (1983), pp. 519-546.

[304] RATTI, A., *Ancora del celebre cod. ms. delle opere di Virgilio già di Francesco Petrarca ed ora della Biblioteca Ambrosiana*, in *Francesco Petrarca e la Lombardia*. Milan 1904, pp. 219-242.

[305] SABBADINI, R., *Dal "Virgilius Petrarcae" dell'Ambriosiana*, in *Giornale storico della letteratura italiana*, 45 (1905), pp. 169-175 [Milan, Bibl. Ambros., S.P. 10/27].

[306] SABBADINI, R., *Pomponio Leto e il codice Mediceo di Virgilio*, in *Rivista di filologia e di istruzione classica*, 48 (1920), pp. 212-213.

[307] SABBADINI, R., *Del Virgilio Ambrosiano di Francesco Petrarca*, in *Historia*, 5 (1931), pp. 416-420 [Milan, Bibl. Ambros., S.P. 10/27].

Virgil (Pseudo)

[308] COURTNEY, E., *The Textual Transmission of the Appendix Vergiliana*, in *Institute of Classical Studies. Bulletin*, 15 (1968), pp. 133-141.

[309] LORD, M.L., *Boccaccio's "Virgiliana" in the "Miscellanea Latina"*, in *Italia medioevale e umanistica*, 34 (1991), pp. 127-198 [Florence, Bibl. Laur., Plut. 31.31].

[310] REEVE, M.D., *The Textual Tradition of the "Appendix Virgiliana"*, in *Maia*, n.s. 28 (1976), pp. 233-254.

Vitruvius

[311] CIAPPONI, L.A., *Il "De architectura" di Vitruvio nel primo umanesimo (dal ms. Bodl. Auct. F.5.7)*, in *Italia medioevale e umanistica*, 3 (1960), pp. 59-99.

[312] JUREN, V., *Politien et Vitruve (Note sur le ms. 7382 de la Bibliothèque nationale)*, in *Rinascimento*, n.s. 18 (1978), pp. 285-292.

[313] PELLATI, F., *Giovanni Sulpicio da Veroli, primo editore di Vitruvio*, in *Atti del II Congresso nazionale di studi romani*, vol. III. Rome 1931, pp. 382-386.

COMMENTARIES

Greek

[314] HOPFNER, Th., *Thomas Magister, Demetrius Triclinius, Manuel Moschopoulos. Eine Studie über ihren Sprachgebrauch in den Scholien zu Aischylos, Sophokles, Euripides, Aristophanes, Hesiod, Pindar und Theokrit*, in *Sitzungsberichte der Kaiserlichen Akademie der Wissenschaften zu Wien*, 172, 3 (1913).

[315] WILSON, N.G., *A Chapter in the History of Scholia*, in *Classical Quarterly*, 17 (1967), pp. 244-256.

Aelianus
[316] MARCHESELLI, L.L., *Note schedografiche inedite del Marc. gr. Z 487=883*, in *Rivista di studi bizantini e neoellenici*, 8-9 (1971-1972), pp. 241-260.

Aeschines
[317] *Scholia in Aeschinem*, ed. Mervin R. DILTS. Leipzig 1992 (Bibl. Teubn.).

Aeschylus
[318] ALLEGRINI, S., *Gli scolii thomani alla triade bizantina nel Perusinus gr. 571*, in *Giornale italiano di filologia*, n.s. 8 (1977), pp. 34-39.
[319] ALLEGRINI, S., *Note di Giovanni Tzetzes ad Eschilo*, in *Annali della facoltà di lettere e filosofia dell'Università di Perugia*, 9 (1971-1972), pp. 221-233.
[320] BÜHLER, W., *Kleine Korrekturen zu den byzantinischen Scholien zu Aesch. Septem*, in *Quaderni dell'Istituto di filologia greca*, 2 (1967), p. 107.
[321] DEMETRII TRICLINII *in Aeschyli Persas Scholia*, iterum edidit Lydia MASSA POSITANO. Naples 1963.
[322] HERINGTON, C.J., *The Older Scholia on the Prometheus Bound*. Leiden 1972.
[323] JEFFREYS, M. J. & O. L. SMITH, *Political Verse for Queen Atossa*, in *Classica et Mediaevalia*, 42 (1991), pp. 301-304.
[324] JORSAL, F., *Vaticanus graecus 2222 and its Relation to Laur. 32, 9*, in *Classica et Mediaevalia*, 31 (1970), pp. 339-388.
[325] MASSA POSITANO, L., *Frustula I. Gli scolii ai Persiani nel Cod. Vindobonense 334*, in *Giornale italiano di filologia*, 5 (1952), pp. 198-202.
[326] ROMAGNOLI, E., *Il contenuto degli scolî laurenziani di Eschilo*, in *Atti del R. Istituto veneto di scienze, lettere ed arti*, 75 (1915-1916), pp. 849-893.
[327] *Scholia graeca in Aeschylum quae extant omnia. Pars I. Scholia in Agamemnonem Choephoros Eumenides Supplices continens*, edidit Ole L. SMITH. Leipzig 1976; *Pars II, fasc. II. Scholia in septem adversus Thebas continens*, edidit Ole L. SMITH. Leipzig 1982 (Bibliotheca Teubneriana).
[328] *Scholia in Aeschyli Septem adversus Thebas*, ed. Gaspar MOROCHO GAYO. León 1989.
[329] SEALEY, R., *A Note on the Metrical Scholia to the Agamememnon*, in *Classical Quarterly*, N.S. 5 (1955), pp. 119-122.
[330] SEELMANN, G., *De propagatione scholiorum Aeschyleorum*. Halle 1875 (Diss.).
[331] SMITH, O.L., *Notes and Observations on some Manuscripts of the Scholia on Aescylus*, in *Classica et Mediaevalia*, 31 (1970), pp. 14-48.
[332] SMITH, O.L., *The Commentary in the Manuscript "P" of Aeschylus*, in *Classica et Mediaevalia*, 32 (1970-1980), pp. 11-34 [Paris, Bibl. nat., gr. 2787].
[333] SMITH, O.L., *A New Source for Triclinius's Commentary on Aeschylus, Prometheus Vinctus*, in *Rheinisches Museum*, 117 (1974), pp. 176-180.
[334] SMITH, Ole L., *Studies in the Scholia on Aeschylus 1: The Recensions of Demetrius Triclinius*. Leiden 1975 (Mnemosyme. Supplementum, 33).
[335] SMITH, O.L., *The Scholia on the Eumenides in the Early Triclinian Recension of Aeschylus*, in *Philologus*, 123 (1979), pp. 328-336.
[336] SMITH, O.L., *The A Commentary on Aeschylus. Author and Date*, in *Greek, Roman and Byzantine Studies*, 21 (1980), pp. 395-399.
[337] SMITH, O.L., *Classification of MSS of the Scholia on Aeschylus*, in *Illinois Classical Studies*, 6 (1981), pp. 44-55.
[338] SMITH, O.L., *The So-Called "sch. rec." in the Editions of the Scholia on Aeschylus*, in *Philologus*, 126 (1982), pp. 138-140.
[339] SMYTH, H.W., *The Commentary on Aeschylus' Prometheus in the Codex Neapolitanus*, in *Harvard Studies in Classical Philology*, 32 (1921), pp. 1-98 [Demetrius Triclinius; Naples, Bibl. Naz., II F 31].

[340] WILAMOWITZ-MOELLENDORFF, U. von, *Die Überlieferung der Aischylosscholien*, in *Hermes*, 25 (1890), pp. 161-170.

[341] ZABROWSKI, C.J., *The Commentary in the Manuscript Ne of Aeschylus*, in *Classica et Mediaevalia*, 34 (1983), pp. 269-272 [Vatican, Vat. gr. 58].

[342] ZABROWSKI, C.J., *A Note on the Interlinear Glosses in the Aeschylean Codex Marc. Gr. 468 (nunc 653) (V)*, in *American Journal of Philology*, 108 (1987), pp. 528-531.

[343] ZABROWSKI, C.J., *The Annotation "sch. rec." in Dindorf's and Wecklein's Editions of the Medicean Scholia on Aeschylus' "Persae"*, in *Classica et Mediaevalia*, 38 (1987), pp. 287-303.

[344] ZABROWSKI, Charles J., *The Scholia and Glosses on Aeschylus's Persae in the Codex Parisinus Gr. 2884 (Q)*: Summary in *American Philological Association. Abstracts*, 1989, p. 175.

Anthologia Graeca

[345] CALDERINI, A., *Alcuni testi per lo studio degli scolî greci dell'Antologia planudea*, in *Classici e neolatini*, 8 (1912), pp. 261-271.

[346] CALDERINI, A., *Scoli greci all'Antologia Planudea*. Milan 1912 (Memorie del R. Istituto Lombardo. Classe di lettere, 22, 8).

[347] CASSIO, A.C., *Le note del Poliziano all'"Antologia greca"*, in *Italia medioevale e umanistica*, 16 (1973), pp. 272-290.

[348] LUPPINO, A., *Scholia graeca inedita in Anthologiae epigrammata selecta*, in *Atti della Accademia Pontaniana*, n.s. 9 (1959-1960), pp. 25-62.

[349] TURYN, A., *Demetrius Triclinius and the Planudean Anthology*, in Ἐπετηρὶς Ἑταιρείας Βυζαντινῶν Σπουδῶν, 39-40 (1972-1973), pp. 409-411.

Apollonius Rhodius

[350] WENDEL, Carl, *Die Überlieferung der Scholien zu Apollonios von Rhodos*. Berlin 1932 (Abhandlungen der Gesellschaft der Wissenschaften zu Göttingen. Phil.-hist. Kl., 3. F., Nr. 1).

Aratus

[351] *Scholia in Aratum vetera*, edidit Jean MARTIN. Stuttgart 1974 [Triclinius' notes].

Aristides

[352] LENZ, F., *Untersuchungen zu den Aristeidesscholien*. Berlin 1934 (Problemata, 8).

Aristophanes

[353] HOLWERDA, D., *De Tzetza in Eustathii reprehensiones incurrenti*, in *Mnemosyne*, ser. IV, 13 (1960), pp. 323-326.

[354] HOLZINGER, K., *Kritische Bemerkungen zu den spätbyzantinischen Aristophanesscholien*, in *Charisteria Alois Rzach zum achtzigsten Geburtstag dargebracht*. Reichenberg 1930, pp. 58-85.

[355] HOLZINGER, K., *Vorstudien zur Beurteilung der Erklärertätigkeit des Demetrios Triklinios zu den Komödien des Aristophanes*. Munich 1939 (Sitzungsberichte der Bayerischen Akademie der Wissenschaften, Phil.-hist. Klasse, 217, 4).

[356] HUNGER, H., *Zur Interpretation polemischer Stellen im Aristophanes-Kommentar des Johannes Tzetzes*, in ΚΩΜΩΙΔΟΤΡΑΓΗΜΑΤΑ. *Studia Aristophanea viri Aristophanei W.J.W. Koster in honorem*. Amsterdam 1967, pp. 59-64.

[357] JORSAL, F., M. KIIL JØRGENSEN & O.L. SMITH, *A Byzantine Metrical Commentary on Aristophanes' "Frogs"*, in *Classica et Mediaevalia*, 31 (1970), pp. 324-338.

[358] KEANEY, J.J., *Notes on Moschopoulos and Aristophanes-Scholia*, in *Mnemosyne*, ser. IV, 25 (1972), pp. 123-128.

[359]   KEIL, H., *Ioannis Tzetzae scholiorum in Aristophanem prolegomena*, in *Rheinisches Museum*, 6 (1848), pp. 108-134, 243-257.

[360]   KOSTER, W.J.W., *Quaestiones criticae ad scholia Aristophanea pertinentes*, in *Mnemosyne*, n.s. 60 (1933), pp. 113-134.

[361]   KOSTER, W.J.W. & D. HOLWERDA, *De Eustathio, Tzetza, Moschopulo, Planude Aristophanis commentatoribus*, in *Mnemosyne*, s. IV, 7 (1954), pp. 136-156; 8 (1955), pp. 196-206.

[362]   *Scholia graeca in Aristophanem*, edidit Fr. DÜBNER. Paris 1842.

[363]   *Scholia in Aristophanem. Pars I. Prolegomena de comoedia. Scholia in Acharnenses, Equites, Nubes.* Fasc. I A continens *Prolegomena de comoedia*, edidit W.J.W. KOSTER. Groningen 1975.—Fasc. I B continens *Scholia in Aristophanis Acharnenses*, edidit Nigel G. WILSON. Groningen 1975.—Fasc. II continens *Scholia vetera in Aristophanis Equites*, edidit D. MERVYN JONES, et *Scholia Tricliniana in Aristophanis Equites*, edidit Nigel G. WILSON. Groningen & Amsterdam 1969.—Fasc. III 1 continens *Scholia vetera in Nubes*, edidit D. HOLWERDA, cum duabus appendicibus, quas subministravit W.J.W. KOSTER. Groningen 1977.—Fasc. III 2 continens *Scholia recentiora in Nubes*, edidit W.J.W. KOSTER. Groningen 1974.

[364]   *Scholia in Aristophanem. Pars II. Scholia in Vespas; Pacem; Aves et Lysistratam.* Fasc. I continens *Scholia vetera et recentiora in Aristophanis Vespas*, edidit W.J.W. KOSTER. Groningen 1978.—Fasc. II continens *Scholia vetera et recentiora in Aristophanis Pacem*, edidit D. HOLWERDA. Groningen 1982.—Fasc. III continens *Scholia vetera et recentiora in Aristophanis Aves*, edidit D. HOLWERDA. Groningen 1991.

[365]   *Scholia in Aristophanem. Pars IV. JO. TZETZAE Commentarii in Aristophanem.* Fasc. I continens *Prolegomena et commentarium in Plutum*, quem edidit Lydia MASSA POSITANO. Groningen & Amsterdam 1960.—Fasc. II continens *Commentarium in Nubes*, quem edidit D. HOLWERDA. Groningen & Amsterdam 1960.—Fasc. III continens *Commentarium in Ranas et in Aves, Argumentum Equitum*, quae edidit W.J.W. KOSTER. Groningen & Amsterdam 1962 (Scripta Academica Groningana).

[366]   *Scholia in Aristophanis Plutum et Nubes vetera, Thomae Magistri, Demetrii Triclinii nec non anonyma recentiora partim inedita*, edidit, varias lectiones adiecit, commentariis instruxit W.J.W. KOSTER. Leiden 1927.

[367]   WHITE, J.W., *The Scholia on the Aves of Aristophanes, with an Introduction on the Origin, Development, Transmission and Extant Sources of the Old Commentary of his Comedies.* Boston & London 1914.

[368]   ZACHER, K., *Die Handschriften und Classen der Aristophanesscholien*, in *Jahrbücher für classische Philologie*, Supplementsband 16. Leipzig 1888, pp. 501-746.

[369]   ZURETTI, C.O., *Scolii al Pluto ed alle Rane d'Aristofane dal codice Veneto 472 e dal codice Cremonese 12229, L, 6, 28.* Torino 1890.

Aristotle

[370]   ARGYROPOULOS, Roxane D. & Iannis CARAS, *Inventaire des manuscrits grecs d'Aristote et de ses commentateurs. Contribution à l'histoire du texte d'Aristote. Supplément.* Paris 1980 (Centre de recherches néohelléniques, 23).

[371]   BIANCHI, L., *Un commento 'umanistico' ad Aristotele. L'"Expositio super libros Ethicorum" di Donato Acciaiuoli*, in *Rinascimento*, 2ª ser., 30 (1990), pp. 29-55.

[372]   CACOUROS, M., *Recherches sur le commentaire inédit de Théodore Prodrome au second livre des "Analytiques postérieurs" d'Aristote*, in *Atti della Accademia Pontaniana*, n.s. 38 (1990), pp. 313-338.

[373]   CACOUROS, M., *Un commentaire byzantin inédit au deuxième livre des "Seconds analytiques" attribuable à Jean Chortasménos*, in *Revue d'histoire des textes*, 24 (1994), pp. 149-198.

[374]   DE RIJK, Lambertus Maria & Olga WEIJERS, *Repertorium commentariorum medii aevi in Aristotelem latinorum quae in bibliothecis publicis neerlandicis asservantur.* Amsterdam

1981 (Koninklijke Nederlandse Akademie van Wetenschappen. Afdeling Let-
terkunde. Verhandelingen, N.R. 109).

[374a] EBBESEN, S., *Medieval Glosses and Commentaries on Aristotelian Logical Texts of the
Twelfth and Thirteenth Centuries*, in *Glosses and Commentaries on Aristotelian Logical
Texts. The Syriac, Arabic and Medieval Latin Traditions*, ed. by Charles Burnett. Lon-
don 1993 (Warburg Institute. Surveys and Texts, 23), pp. 129-177.

[375] FLÜELER, C., *Mittelalterliche Kommentare zur "Politik" des Aristoteles und zur Pseudo-
Aristotelischen "Oekonomik"*, in *Bulletin de philosophie médiévale*, 29 (1987), pp. 193-
229.

[376] HARLFINGER, D. & J. WIESNER, *Die griechischen Handschriften des Aristoteles und seiner Kommentatoren*, in *Scriptorium*, 18 (1964), pp. 238-257.

[377] KOROLEC, Georgius B., *Repertorium commentariorum medii aevi in Aristotelem latinorum quae in Bibliotheca olim Universitatis Pragensis nunc Státní knihovna CSR vocata asservantur*. Wroclaw 1977.

[378] KRISTELLER, P.O., *Un codice padovano di Aristotele postillato da Francesco ed Ermolao
Barbaro: il manoscritto Plimpton 17 della Columbia University Library*, in his *Studies in
Renaissance Thought and Letters*. Rome 1956, pp. 337-353.

[379] LOHR, C.H., *Medieval Latin Aristotle Commentaries. Authors: A-F*, in *Traditio*, 24
(1967), pp. 313-413.

[380] LOHR, C.H., *Medieval Latin Aristotle Commentaries. Authors: G-J*, in *Traditio*, 25
(1968), pp. 149-245.

[381] LOHR, C.H., *Medieval Latin Aristotle Commentaries. Authors: Johannes de Kanthi-Myn-
godus*, in *Traditio*, 27 (1971), pp. 251-351.

[382] LOHR, C.H., *Medieval Latin Aristotle Commentaries. Authors: Narcissus-Wilgelmus*, in
Traditio, 28 (1972), pp. 281-396.

[383] LOHR, C.H., *Medieval Latin Aristotle Commentaries. Authors: Robertus-Wilgelmus*, in
Traditio, 29 (1973), pp. 93-197.

[384] LOHR, C.H., *Medieval Latin Commentaries on Aristotle in Manuscripts in Libraries out-
side of Italy (according to Kristeller, Iter italicum III)*, in *Freiburger Zeitschrift für Philosophie und Theologie*, 34 (1987), p. 531-542.

[385] LOHR, C.H., *Latin Aristotle Commentaries. II. Renaissance Authors*. Florence 1988
(Unione Accademica Nazionale. Corpus Philosophorum Medii Aevi. Subsidia,
6).

[386] LOHR, Charles H., *Commentateurs d'Aristote au Moyen-Age latin. Bibliographie de la
littérature secondaire récente*. Fribourg & Paris 1988 (Vestigia, 2).

[387] MARENBON, J., *Medieval Latin Glosses and Commentaries on Aristotelian Logical Texts,
Before c. 1150 AD*, in *Glosses and Commentaries on Aristotelian Logical Texts. The Sy-
riac, Arabic and Medieval Latin Traditions*, ed. by Charles Burnett. London 1993
(Warburg Institute. Surveys and Texts, 23), pp. 77-127.

[388] MARKOWSKI, Miecislaus, *Repertorium commentariorum medii aevi in Aristotelem latinorum quae in bibliothecis Wiennae asservantur*. Wroclaw 1985.

[389] MARKOWSKI, Miecislaus, *Repertorium commentariorum medii aevi in Aristotelem latinorum quae in Bibliotheca Amploniana Erffordiae asservantur*. Wroclaw 1987 (Polska
Akademia Nauk. Instytut Filozofii i Socjologii).

[389a] MARKOWSKI, Miecislaus & Sophia WLODEK, *Repertorium commentariorum medii aevi
in Aristotelem latinorum quae in Bibliotheca Iagellonica Cracoviae asservantur*. Krakow
1974.

[390] MERCATI, G., *Fra i commentatori greci di Aristotele*, in *Mélanges de l'École française de
Rome*, 1915, pp. 191-219 [Vatican, Vat. gr. 290; 13th c.].

[391] OLIVIERI, L., *Intorno ai "Problemata" di Aristotele: le glosse del codice Antoniano XVII
370 (ff. 1r-2v) e il commento di Pietro d'Abano*, in *Italia medioevale e umanistica*, 28
(1985), pp. 221-275.

[392] PATTIN, Adriaan, *Repertorium commentariorum medii aevi in Aristotelem latinorum quae*

in bibliothecis belgicis asservantur. Leuven & Leiden 1978 (Ancient and Medieval Philosophy. De Wulf-Mansion Centre, Ser. 1, 1).

[393] POLIZIANO, Angelo, *Lamia. Praelectio in Priora Aristotelis Analytica. Critical Edition, Introduction and Commentary* by A. WESSELING. Leiden 1986 (Studies in Medieval and Renaissance Thought) [a. 1492].

[394] RIZZO, S., *Una prolusione del Poliziano e i commentatori greci di Aristotele,* in *Studi in onore di Anthos Ardizzoni,* vol. II. Rome 1978, pp. 759-768.

[395] SENKO, Wladyslaw, *Repertorium commentariorum medii aevi in Aristotelem latinorum quae in bibliothecis publicis Parisiis asservantur (Bibliothèque Nationale, Arsenal, Mazarine, Sorbonne, Ste Geneviève),* vol. I-II. Warsaw 1982 (Textus et studia, 5).

[396] SLOMSZYNSKA, A., *Repertorium commentariorum in Aristotelis «Economica» latinorum quae in bibliothecis europaeis asservantur,* in *Mediaevalia Philosophica Polonorum,* 28 (1987), pp. 167-200.

[397] VENNEBUSCH, Joachim, *Ein anonymer Aristoteleskommentar des XIII. Jahrhunderts. Questiones in tres libros de Anima (Admont, Stiftsbibliothek, cod. lat. 367). Textedition und philosophisch-historische Einleitung.* Paderborn 1963.

[398] WARTELLE, A., *Inventaire des manuscrits grecs d'Aristote et de ses commentateurs. Contribution à l'histoire du texte d'Aristote.* Paris 1963 (Études anciennes).

[399] ZAMPONI, Stefano, *Commenti ad Aristotele nella Biblioteca Fortegueriana di Pistoia,* in *Atti e memorie dell'Accademia toscana di scienze e lettere La Colombaria,* 42, = n.s. 28 (1977), pp. 77-108.

[400] ZAMPONI, Stefano, *Commenti ad Aristotele nell'Archivio capitolare di Pistoia,* in *Atti e memorie dell'Accademia toscana di scienze e lettere La Colombaria,* 43, = n.s. 29 (1978), pp. 1-93.

[401] ZIMMERMANN, A. (ed.), *Verzeichnis ungedruckter Kommentare zur Metaphysik und Physik des Aristoteles aus der Zeit von etwa 1250-1350,* vol. I. Leiden 1971 (Studien und Texte zur Geistesgeschichte des Mittelalters, 9).

Aristotle (Pseudo)

[402] GOLDBRUNNER, H., *Leonardo Brunis Kommentar zu seiner Übersetzung der pseudo-aristotelischen Ökonomik: ein humanistischer Kommentar,* in *Der Kommentar in der Renaissance,* hrsg. v. August Buck & Otto Herding. Boppard 1975 (Kommission für Humanismusforschung. Mitteilung 1), pp. 99-118.

Demosthenes

[403] TEODORO METOCHITES, *Saggio critico su Demostene e Aristide,* a cura di Marcello GIGANTE. Milan 1969 (Testi e documenti per lo studio dell'antichità, 27).

Dio Chrysostomus

[404] SONNY, Adolfus, *Ad Dionem Chrysostomum analecta.* Kiev 1897.

Dionysius Periegetes

[405] DILLER, Aubrey, *The Textual Tradition of Strabo's Geography. With Appendix: The Manuscripts of Eustathius' Commentary on Dionysius Periegetes.* Amsterdam 1975.

[406] DIONYSIUS PERIEGETES *graece et latine cum vetustis commentariis et interpretationibus ex recensione et cum annotatione Godofredi* BERNHARDY. Pars prior. Leipzig 1828, pp. 64-316 (Eusthatii Epistola & Commentarii).

Diophantus
[407] DIOPHANTI ALEXANDRINI *Opera omnia cum graecis commentariis*, ed. et latine interpretatus est Paulus TANNERY, vol. II. Leipzig 1895 (Bibl. Teubn.).

Epictetus
[408] *Epicteti dissertationes ab Arriano digestae*, ad fidem codicis Bodleiani recensuit Henricus SCHENKL. *Accedunt fragmenta, enchiridion ex recensione Schweighaeseri, gnomologiorum epicteteorum reliquiae*. Editio minor. Leipzig 1898 (Bibliotheca Teubneriana).

Euclid
[409] HEIBERG, J.L., *Om Scholierne til Euklids Elementer*. Copenhagen 1888 (Det Kgl. Danske Videnskabernes Selskabs Skrifter, 6. Række. Historisk og philosophisk Afdeling, II, 3).

Euripides
[410] SCHARTAU, Bjarne, *Observations II. The Impact of Thomas Magistros' Introductory Matter to the Euripidean Triad*. Odense 1973.
[411] SCHARTAU, B., *Observations on the Commentary on Euripides' "Phoenissae" in the MSS Parma 154 and Modena, α.U.9.22*, in *Illinois Classical Studies*, 6 (1981), pp. 221-241.
[412] *Scholia graeca in Euripidis tragoedias*, ex codicibus aucta et emendata edidit Gulielmus DINDORFIUS. Vol. I-IV. Oxford 1863 [Included are also scholia by Moschopoulos, Planudes, Thomas Magister and Triclinius].
[413] *Scholia metrica anonyma in Euripidis Hecubam, Orestem, Phoenissas*, edited with Prolegomena, Critical Apparatus, Appendix and Index by Ole L. SMITH. Copenhagen 1977.
[414] WAGENVOORT, H., *Demetrii Triclinii scholia metrica e codice angelico aucta et emendata*, in *Mnemosyne*, n.s. 41 (1913), pp. 313-332 [Rome, Bibl. Angelica, gr. 14].

Hesiod
[415] CALDERONE, S., *L'Exegesis ad "Opera et Dies" di Tzetzes e il Codex Messianius*, in *Giornale italiano di filologia*, 1 (1948), pp. 363-371.
[416] COLONNA, A., *I "Prolegomeni" ad Esiodo e la "Vita esiodea" di Giovanni Tzetze*, in *Bollettino per la preparazione dell'Edizione nazionale dei classici greci e latini*, 2 (1953), pp. 27-39.
[417] DAHLÉN, Carl, *Zu Johannes Tzetzes' Exegesis der hesiodeischen Erga*. Uppsala 1933 (Diss.).
[418] DERENZINI, G., *Demetrio Triclinio e il codice Marciano greco 464*, in *Scrittura e Civiltà*, 3 (1979), pp. 222-241.
[419] LJUNGVIK, H., *Kritische und exegetische Bemerkungen zu einigen Stellen der Erga-Exegesis des Johannes Tzetzes*, in *Byzantinische Zeitschrift*, 34 (1934), pp. 262-271.
[420] MANUELIS MOSCHOPOLI *Commentarium in Hesiodi Opera et dies*, ed. Simonetta GRANDOLINI. Rome, 1991 (Biblioteca del Giornale italiano di filologia, 8).
[421] PERTUSI, A., *La tradizione manoscritta degli scolii alle "Opere e giorni" e le note inedite attribuite a Massimo Planude*, in *Studi bizantini e neoellenici*, 7 (1953), pp. 177-182.

[422]   PERTUSI, A., *Scholia vetera in Hesiodi Opera et dies*. Milan 1955 (Pubblicazioni dell'Università Cattolica del Sacro Cuore, n.s. 53).

[423]   SCHULTZ, Hermann, *Die handschriftliche Überlieferung der Hesiod-Scholien*. Berlin 1910 (Abhandlungen der königlichen Gesellschaft der Wissenschaften zu Göttingen. Phil.-hist. Kl., N.F. 12, 4).

Homer

[424]   BAAR, Johannes, *Index zu den Ilias-Scholien. Die wichtigeren Ausdrücke der grammatischen, rhetorischen und ästhetischen Textkritik*. Baden-Baden 1961 (Deutsche Beiträge zur Altertumswissenschaft, 15).

[425]   BACHMANN, Ludovicus, *Scholia in Homeri Iliadem quae in codice Bibl. Publ. Acad. Lips. leguntur*. 1835, pp. 689-845.

[426]   BOISSONNADE, J.F., *Tzetzae Allegoriae Iliadis. Accedunt Pselli Allegoriae quarum una inedita*. Paris 1851.

[427]   ERBSE, H., *Die Genfer Iliasscholien*, in *Rheinisches Museum*, 95 (1952), pp. 171-191 [Genoa, Bibl. et univ., gr. 44].

[428]   ERBSE, H., *Zur handschriftlichen Überlieferung der Iliasscholien*, in *Mnemosyne*, 4ª ser., 6 (1953), pp. 1-38.

[429]   ERBSE, Hartmut, *Beiträge zur Übelieferung der Iliasscholien*. Munich 1960 (Zetemata, 24).

[430]   EVSTATHIVS THESSALONICENSIS, *Commentarii ad Homeri Iliadem pertinentes ad fidem codicis Laurentiani editi*, curavit Marchinus VAN DER VALK. Vol. I-IV. Leiden 1971-1987.

[431]   EVSTATHIVS archiepiscopus THESSALONICENSIS, *Commentarii ad Homeri Odysseam*, ad fidem exempli Romani editi [G. STALLBAUM]. Vol. I-II. Leipzig 1825-1826 (Reprint: Hildesheim 1960).

[431a] EVSTATHII archiepiscopi THESSALONICENSIS, *Commentarii ad Homeri Iliadem*, ad fidem exempli Romani editi. Vol. I-IV. Leipzig 1827-1830 (Reprint: Hildesheim 1960).

[432]   FELBER, Hans, *Quellen der Ilias-Exegesis des Joannes Tzetzes*. Zürich 1925 (Diss.).

[433]   GRANDOLINI, S., *La parafrasi al primo libro dell'Iliade di Manuel Moschopulos*, in *Studi in onore di Aristide Colonna*. Perugia 1982, pp. 131-149.

[434]   GRANDOLINI, S., *La parafrasi del secondo libro dell'Iliade di Manuel Moschopulos*, in *Annali della Facoltà di lettere e filosofia. Università di Perugia*, 18, 1 (1980-1981), pp. 7-22.

[435]   HEDBERG, T., *Eustathios als Attizist*. Uppsala 1935 (Diss.).

[436]   HEDBERG, T., *Das Interesse des Eustathius für die Verhältnisse und die Sprache seiner eigenen Zeit*, in *Eranos*, 44 (1946), pp. 208-218.

[437]   ISAAC PORPHYROGENITUS, *Praefatio in Homerum*, ed. with Introduction and Notes by Jan Fredrik KINDSTRAND. Uppsala 1979 (Acta Universitatis Upsaliensis. Studia graeca Upsaliensia, 14).

[438]   JOHANNES TZETZES, *Allegorien zur Odysse, I-XII*. Kommentierte Textausgabe von H. HUNGER, in *Byzantinische Zeitschrift*, 49 (1956), pp. 249-310.

[439]   JOHANNES TZETZES, *Allegoriae in Odysseae libros XIII-XVIII*, ed. F. FINOCCHIARO, in *Bollettino per la preparazione dell'edizione nazionale dei classici greci e latini*, n.s. 5 (1957), pp. 45-61.

[440]   LINDBERG, G., *Eustathius on Homer. Some of his Approaches to the Text, Exemplified from his Comments on the First Book of the Iliad*, in *Eranos*, 83 (1985), pp. 125-140.

[441]   MAÏER, I., *Une page inédite de Politien: la note du Vat. lat. 3617 sur Démétrius Triclinius commentateur d'Homère*, in *Bibliothèque d'Humanisme et Renaissance*, 16 (1954), pp. 7-17.

[442]   MAN. MOSCOPULI *byzantini scholia ad Homeri Iliados librum I & II adhuc inedita*, cum notis et animadversionibus Joannis SCHEERPEZEELII. Utrecht 1719.

[443]   MAVROUDIS, E. D., *Commentaires sur certains passages de caractère médical de l''Εξήγησις τῆς 'Ιλιάδος de Jean Tzetzes*, in *Hellenica*, 40 (1989), pp. 387-402.

[444]   MELANDRI, E., *La parafrasi di M. Moschopulo ad Hom. A-B493 e la tradizione esegetica e lessicografica dell'Iliade*, in *Prometheus*, 9 (1983), pp. 177-192.

[445]   MELANDRI, E., *Rapporti fra scolii e parafrasi nel commentario di M. Moscopulo*, in *Studi in onore di Adelmo Barigazzi*, vol. II, = *Sileno*, 11 (1985), pp. 41-60.

[446]   MELANDRI, E., *Per un'edizione della "Technologia" di M. Moschopoulo ad Hom. A-B 493*, in *Prometheus*, 7 (1981), pp. 215-224.

[447]   PAPATHOMOPOULOS, M., *Pour une nouvelle édition de l'Exégèse à l'Iliade de Jean Tzetzès*, in *Dodone*, 16 (1987), pp. 193-204.

[448]   RUBINSTEIN, A.L., *The Notes to Poliziano's "Iliad"*, in *Italia medioevale e umanistica*, 25 (1982), pp. 205-239.

[448a] *Scholia in Homeri Odysseae A 1-309 auctiora et emendatiora*, edidit A. Ludwich. Königsberg 1888-1890 (Reprint: Hildesheim 1966).

[448b] *Les scolies genevoises de l'Iliade*, publiées avec une étude historique, descriptive et critique sur le Genevensis 44 ou Codex ignotus d'Henri Estienne et une collation complète de ce manuscrit par Jules NICOLE. Vol. I-II. Geneva & Basle 1891 (Reprint: Hildesheim 1966).

[449]   *Der unbekannte Teil der Ilias-Exegesis des Iohannes Tzetzes (A 97-609)*, hrsg. von A. LOLOS. Königstein 1981 (Beiträge zur klassischen Philologie, 130).

[450]   VAN DER VALK, M., *Zum Odysseekommentar des Eustathius*, in *Mnemosyne*, 24 (1981), pp. 385-388.

Lucian

[451]   RABE, H., *Die Überlieferung der Lukianscholien*, in *Nachrichten von der königl. Gesellschaft der Wissenschaften zu Göttingen. Phil.-hist. Kl.*, 1901 (1902).

[452]   RABE, H., *Die Lukianstudien des Arethas*, in *Nachrichten der königl. Gesellschaft der Wissenschaften zu Göttingen. Phil.-hist. Kl.*, 1903 (1904).

[453]   *Scholia in Lucianum*, edidit Hugo RABE. Leipzig 1906 (Bibliotheca Teubneriana).

Lycophron

[453a] GUALANDRI, Isabel, *Index nominum propriorum quae in scholiis Tzetzianis ad Lycophronem laudantur*. Milan 1962 (Testi e documenti per lo studio dell'antichità, 6).

[453b] GUALANDRI, Isabel, *Index glossarum quae in scholiis Tzetzianis ad Lycophronem laudantur*. Milan 1965 (Testi e documenti per lo studio dell'antichità, 12).

[454]   LYCOPHRONIS *Alexandra*, rec. E. SCHEER, vol. II *Scholia continens*. Berlin 1908.

[455]   LEONE, P., *Excerpta Vaticana ex Ioannis Tzetzae commentario in Lycophronem et Historiis*, in *Atti dell'Accademia delle scienze di Torino. Classe di scienze morali, storiche e filologiche*, 99 (1964-1965), pp. 381-488.

Oppian

[456]   COLONNA, A., *Il commento di Giovanni Tzetzes agli "Halieutica" di Oppiano*, in *Lanx satura N. Terzaghi oblata*. Genoa 1963, pp. 101-104.

[457]   LEVERENZ, Lynn M., *The Scholia on Oppian's Halieutica from the Z Family of Manuscripts*. Diss. University of Iowa, Iowa City 1991 [Summary in *Dissertation Abstracts* 52, 1991-1992, 4312 A].

[458] NAPOLITANO, F., *Esegesi bizantina degli "Halieutica" di Oppiano*, in *Rendiconti dell'Accademia di archeologia, lettere e belle arti di Napoli,* 48 (1973), pp. 237-254.

Pausanias
[459] SPIRO, F., *Pausanias-Scholien,* in *Hermes,* 29 (1894), pp. 143-149.

Philostratus
[460] LINDSTAM, S., *Die Philostratoskommentare und die Moschopoulos-Sylloga,* in *Göteborg Högskolas Årsskrift,* 31 (1925), pp. 173-184.

Pindar
[461] ABEL, Eugenius, *Scholia in Pindari Epinicia.* Pars III. *Scholia recentia.* Vol. I. *Scholia in Olympia et Pythia.* Budapest & Berlin 1891.
[462] EUSTATHIOS VON THESSALONIKE, *Prooimion zum Pindarkommentar. Einleitung, kritischer Text, Indices,* besorgt von Athanasios KAMBYLIS. Göttingen, 1991 (Veröffentlichungen der Joachim-Jungius-Gesellschaft, 65).
[463] IRIGOIN, J., *Les scholies métriques de Pindare.* Paris 1958 (Bibliothèque de l'École des hautes études. Sciences historiques et philologiques, 310).
[464] ISAAC TZETZAE *De metris pindaricis commentarius,* edidit A.B. DRACHMANN. Copenhagen 1925 (Det Kgl. Danske Videnskabernes Selskab. Historisk-filologiske Meddelelser, IX, 3).
[465] KAMBYLIS, Athanasios, *Eustathios über Pindars Epinikiendichtung: ein Kapitel der klassischen Philologie in Byzanz.* Göttingen, 1991 (Berichte aus den Sitzungen der Joachim-Jungius-Gesellschaft der Wissenschaften, 9).
[466] LEHRS, K., *Die Pindarscholien. Eine kritische Untersuchung zur philologischen Quellenkunde. Nebst einem Anhange über den falschen Hesychius Milesius und den falschen Philemon.* Leipzig 1874.
[467] MOMMSEN, Th., *Scholia recentiora Thomano-Tricliniana in Pindari Nemea et Isthmia,* e codicibus antiquis hoc libello primum eduntur. Frankfurt am Main 1865 (Progr.)
[468] SCHMIDT, M., *Zu den Scholien des Pindaros,* in *Philologus,* 17 (1861), pp. 360-361.
[469] SCHNEIDER, C.E.C., *Apparatus Pindarici supplementum ex codicibus Vratislaviensibus. I. Thomae Magistri et Demetrii Triclinii scholia in Pythia quattuor prima ex codice Vratisl. E. II. Varia Olymp. scriptura ex codicibus Vratisl. A et B. III. Vita Pindari et vetera in Ol. I et II scholia ex codice Vratisl. A.* Wroclaw 1844.
[470] *Scholia Germani in Pindari Olympia e codice Cesareo Vindobonensi* edidit, aliorum scholiorum specimina adjecit, epistolarum criticarum triadem praemisit Theodor MOMMSEN. Kiel 1861.
[470a] *Scholia metrica vetera in Pindari carmina,* edidit Andrea TESSIER. Leipzig 1989 (Bibl. Teubn.).
[471] *Scholia Thomano-Tricliniana in Pindari Pythia V-XII ex codice florentino* edidit Th. MOMMSEN. Frankfurt am Main 1867 (Progr.).
[472] *Scholia vetera in Pindari carmina,* edidit A.B. DRACHMANN, vol. III. Leipzig 1927, pp. 285-306 [Eustathius's introduction to Pindar].

Plato
[473] ALLEN, M.J.B., *The Platonism of Marsilio Ficino. A Study of his Phaedrus Commentary, its Sources, and Genesis.* Berkeley & Los Angeles 1984 (UCLA Center for Medieval & Renaissance Studies, 21).
[474] COULTER, J., *Literary Criticism in the Platonic Scholia,* in *Florilegium Columbianum. Essays in Honor of Paul Oskar Kristeller.* New York 1987, pp. 63-72.
[475] GREENE, Guilielmus Chase, *Scholia Platonica.* Haverford (Penn.) 1938 (Philolo-

gical Monographs Published by the American Philological Association, 8) (Reprint: Chico, CA 1981).

[476]   HANKINS, James, *Plato in the Italian Renaissance*. Vol. I-II. Leiden 1990 (Columbia Studies in the Classical Tradition, 17).

[477]   *Icastes. Marsilio Ficino's Interpretation of Plato's Sophist: Five Studies and a Critical Edition with Translation*, by Michael J. B. ALLEN. Berkeley 1989.

[478]   LENZ, Fr., *Der Vaticanus Gr. 1, eine Handschrift des Arethas*, in *Nachrichten von der Gesellschaft der Wissenschaften zu Göttingen. Philol.-hist. Klasse*, 1933, pp. 193-218.

[479]   LENZ, F., *Bemerkungen zu den Platonscholien*, in *Philologische Wochenschrift*, 53 (1933), pp. 128-134.

[480]   MENCHELLI, M., *Un codice viennese tra i manoscritti platonici del Ficino*, in *Studi classici e orientali*, 39 (1989), pp. 355-358 [Vienna, Österreichische Nationalbibl., phil. gr. 109].

[481]   MINIO PALUELLO, L., *Il "Fedone" latino con note autografe del Petrarca*, in *Rendiconti dell'Accademia nazionale dei Lincei. Classe di scienze morali, storiche e filologiche*, ser. VIII, 4 (1949), pp. 107-113.

[481a] PERCIVAL, W.K., *Ficino's "Cratylus" Commentary: A Transcription and Edition*, in *Res Publica Litterarum*, 14 (1991), pp. 185-196.

Plutarch

[482]   MANFREDINI, M., *Gli scoli alle Vite di Plutarco*, in *Jahrbuch der Österreichischen Byzantinistik*, 28 (1979), pp. 83-119.

[483]   MANFREDINI, M., *Gli scolî alle Vite di Plutarco e i lessici bizantini coevi*, in *Studi bizantini e neogreci. Atti del IV congresso nazionale di studi bizantini, Lecce, 21-23 aprile 1980—Calimera, 24 aprile 1980*. Galatina 1983, pp. 445-455.

[484]   TARTAGLIA, L., *Il saggio su Plutarco di Teodoro Metochita*, in ΤΑΛΑΡΙΣΚΟΣ. *Studia graeca Antonio Garzya sexagenario a discipulis oblata*. Naples 1987, pp. 339-362.

Sophocles

[485]   BEVILACQUA, F., *Il commento di Giovanni Tzetzes a Sofocle*, in *Annali della Facoltà di lettere e filosofia dell'Università di Perugia*, 11 (1973-1974), pp. 559-570.

[486]   CHRISTODOLOU, G.A., Τὰ ἀρχαῖα σχόλια εἰς Αἴαντα τοῦ Σοφοκλέους. Athens 1977.

[487]   COLONNA, A., *La recensione moscopulea della "Vita Sophoclis"*, in *Koinonia*, 12 (1988), pp. 169-180.

[488]   HOPFNER, Th., *Die thomano-triklinischen Scholien zu Sophocles Elektra*. Prague 1913 (Jahresbericht des K.-K. Staats-Gymnasiums mit deutscher Unterrichtssprache in Prag-Neustadt).

[489]   LONGO, Oddone, *Scholia byzantina in Sophoclis Oedipum Tyrannum*. Padua 1971 (Proagones, 2) [*Scholia Moschopuli—Planudea—Thomae—Triclinii*].

[490]   *Scholia in Sophoclis tragoedias septem*, e codice ms. laurentiano descripsit Petrus ELMSLEY. Oxford 1825 [Florence, Bibl. Laurenziana, Plut. 32.9].

[491]   TURYN, A., *On the Sophoclean Scholia in the Manuscript Paris 2712*, in *Harvard Studies in Classical Philology*, 63 (1958), pp. 161-170.

Strabo

[492]   DILLER, A., *The Scholia of Strabo*, in *Traditio*, 10 (1954), pp. 29-50.

Theocritus

[493]   GARIN, E., *La "Expositio Theocriti" di A. Poliziano nello Studio fiorentino*, in *Rivista di filologia classica*, 42 (1914), pp. 272-282.

[494]   WENDEL, Carl, *Überlieferung und Entstehung der Theokrit-Scholien*. Berlin 1920 (Ab-

handlungen der Königlichen Gesellschaft der Wissenschaften zu Göttingen. Phil.-hist. Kl., N.F., Bd. XVII, 2).

Thucydides
[495] DOVER, K.J., *The Patmos Scholia and the Text of Thucydides*, in *Classical Review*, N.S. 5 (1955), pp. 134-137.
[496] LUSCHNAT, O., *Die Thukydidesscholien. Zu ihrer handschriftlichen Grundlage, Herkunft und Geschichte*, in *Philologus*, 98 (1954), pp. 14-58.
[497] POWELL, J.E., *The Bâle and Leiden Scholia to Thucydides*, in *Classical Quarterly*, 30 (1936), pp. 80-93 [Basle, Universitätsbibl., E III 4, & Leiden, Bibl. der Rijksuniv., Periz. 40 4°].
[498] POWELL, J.E., *The Aldine Scholia to Thucydides*, in *Classical Quarterly*, 30) (1936), pp. 146-150 [Paris, Bibl. Nat., Suppl. gr. 256].
[499] POWELL, J.E., *A Byzantine Critic*, in *Classical Review*, 52 (1938), pp. 2-4 [Heidelberg, Universitätsbibl., Pal. gr. 252].

Latin

[500] *Accessus ad auctores—Bernard d'Utrecht—Conrad d'Hirsau, Dialogus super auctores.* Édition critique entièrement revue et augmentée par R.B.C. HUYGENS. Leiden 1970.
[501] ALLEN, Judson Boyce, *The Friar as Critic. Literary Attitudes in the Later Middle Ages.* Nashville (Tenn.) 1971.
[502] BIANCHI, R., *Note di Francesco Filelfo al "De natura deorum", al "De oratore" e all'"Eneide" negli appunti di un notaio senese*, in *Francesco Filelfo nel quinto centenario della morte. Atti del XVII convegno di studi maceratesi (Tolentino, 27-30 settembre 1981).* Padua 1986, pp. 325-368 [Vatican, Chig. H.IV.99].
[503] BISCHOFF, B., *Living with the Satirists*, in *Classical Influences on European Culture A.D. 500-1500*, ed. by R.R. Bolgar. Cambridge 1971, pp. 83-94.
[504] CASELLA, M.T., *Il metodo dei commentatori umanistici esemplato sul Beroaldo*, in *Studi medievali*, 3ª ser., 16 (1975), pp. 627-701.
[505] *Catalogus Translationum et Commentariorum: Medieval and Renaissance Latin Translations and Commentaries. Annotated Lists and Guides.* Editor in chief: Paul Oskar KRISTELLER (F. Edward CRANZ; Virginia BROWN). Vol. I-VII. Washington (D.C.) 1960-1992.
[506] FÖRSTER, M. & A.S. NAPIER, *Englische Cato- und Ilias-Glossen des 12. Jahrhunderts*, in *Archiv für das Studium der neueren Sprachen und Literaturen*, 117 (1906), pp. 17-28.
[507] GARZYA, A., *Sobre los comentarios de autores antiguos hechos por Poliziano*, in *Vichiana*, 3ª ser., 2 (1991), pp. 217-230.
[508] HAURÉAU, B., *Additions et corrections*, in *Histoire littéraire de la France*, vol. 29. Paris 1885, pp. 568-583.
[509] HUNT, J., *Three New Incunables with Marginalia by Politian*, in *Rinascimento*, ser. IIª, 24 (1986), pp. 251-259 [Munich, Bayerische Staatsbibl., 2° Inc. c.a. 467: Cicero & Sallust].
[510] HUNT, R.W., *The Introduction to the "Artes" in the Twelfth Century*, in *Studia mediaevalia in honorem admodum reverendi patris Raymundi Josephi Martin.* Bruges 1948, pp. 85-111 (= his *The History of Grammar in the Middle Ages. Collected Papers.* Amsterdam 1980, pp. 117-144, cf. M.T. Gibson & S.P. Hall in *The Bodleian Library Record*, 11 (1982), pp. 14-17).
[511] JEAUNEAU, É., *L'usage de la notion d'"integumentum" à travers les gloses de Guillaume de Conches*, in *Archives d'histoire doctrinale et littéraire du moyen âge*, 24 (1957), pp. 35-

100 (= Édouard JEAUNEAU, *"Lectio philosophorum"*. *Recherches sur l'école de Chartres*. Amsterdam 1973, pp. 127-192).

[512] LANDINO, Cristoforo, *Scritti critici e teorici*. Edizione, introduzione e commento a cura di Roberto CARDINI. Vol. I-II. Rome 1974 (I critici italiani, 1-2) [Vol. I, pp. 1-15: *Praefatio in Tusculanis;* pp. 17-28: *Praefatio in Virgilio;* pp. 193-202: *Proemio al commento oraziano;* pp. 203-223: *Proemio al commento virgiliano e Introduzione all'Eneide*].

[513] LAPIDGE, M., *The Study of Latin Texts in Late Anglo-Saxon England. The Evidence of Latin Glosses*, in *Latin and the Vernacular Languages in Early Medieval Britain*. Leicester 1982, pp. 99-140.

[514] LEONARDI, Cl., *I commenti altomedievali ai classici medievali: da Severino Boezio a Remigio d'Auxerre*, in *La cultura antica nell'Occidente latino dal VII all'XI secolo*. Spoleto 1975 (Settimane di studi del Centro italiano di studi sull'alto medioevo, 22), pp. 459-504.

[515] LO MONACO, F., *Alcune osservazioni sul commento umanistico ai classici nel secondo Quattrocento*, in *Il commento ai testi. Atti del seminario di Ascona, 2-9 ottobre 1989*. Basle 1992, pp. 103-154.

[516] MERCATI, G., *Tre dettati universitari dell'umanista Martino Filetico sopra Persio, Giovenale ed Orazio*, in *Classical and Mediaeval Studies in Honor of Edward Kennard Rand*. New York 1938, pp. 221-230 (= his *Opere minori*, vol. VI. Vatican City 1984, pp. 13-24).

[517] MINNIS, Alistair J., *Medieval Theory of Authorship. Scholastic Literary Attitudes in the Later Middle Ages*. London 1984.

[518] MINNIS, A.J. & A.B. SCOTT, *Medieval Literary Theory and Criticism c. 1100-c. 1375. The Commentary Tradition*. Oxford 1987.

[519] MUNK OLSEN, Birger, *L'étude des auteurs classiques latins aux XIᵉ et XIIᵉ siècle*, vol. I. *Catalogue des manuscrits classiques latins copiés du IXᵉ au XIIᵉ siècle: Apicius—Juvénal;* vol. II. *Catalogue des manuscrits classiques latins copiés du IXᵉ au XIIᵉ siècle: Livius—Vitruvius. Florilèges—Essais de plume*. Paris 1982-1985 (Documents, études et répertoires publiés par l'Institut de Recherche et d'Histoire des Textes); cf. t. III, 2. *Addenda et corrigenda—Tables*. Paris 1989, pp. 3-157, 190-192.

[520] QUAIN, E.A., *The Medieval Accessus ad Auctores*, in *Traditio*, 3 (1945), pp. 215-264.

[521] SABBADINI, R., *Guarino Veronese e gli archetipi di Celso e Plauto con un'appendice sull'Aurispa*. Livorno 1886.

[522] SMALLEY, Beryl, *English Friars and Antiquity in the Early Fourteenth Century*. Oxford 1960.

[523] SPALLONE, M., *I percorsi medievali del testo: "accessus", commentari, florilegi*, in *Lo spazio letterario di Roma antica*. Vol. III. *La ricezione del testo*, Rome 1990, pp. 387-471.

[524] TRISTANO, C., *Le postille del Petrarca nel Vaticano lat. 2193 (Apuleio, Frontino, Vegezio, Palladio)*, in *Italia medioevale e umanistica*, 17 (1974), pp. 365-468.

[525] WESSNER, P., *Bericht über die Erscheinungen auf dem Gebiete der lateinischen Grammatiker mit Einschluss der Scholienliteratur und Glossographie für 1908-1920*, in *Jahresbericht über die Fortschritte der klassischen Altertumswissenschaft*. Jahrgang 47, Bd. 188 (1921), pp. 34-254.

[526] WHITBREAD, L.G., *Conrad of Hirsau as Literary Critic*, in *Speculum*, 47 (1972), pp. 234-245.

[527] WIELAND, G., *The Glossed Manuscript: Classbook or Library Book*, in *Anglo-Saxon England*, 14 (1986), pp. 153-173.

[528] ZETZEL, J.E., *On the History of Latin Scholia*, in *Harvard Studies in Classical Philology*, 79 (1975), pp. 335-354.

Ammianus Marcellinus

[529] CAPPELLETTO, R., *Niccolò Niccoli e il codice di Ammiano Vat. lat. 1873*, in *Bollettino*

del comitato per la preparazione dell'edizione nazionale dei classici, 26 (1978), pp. 57-84.

Apuleius
[530] KRAUTTER, K., *Philologische Methode und humanistiche Existenz, Filippo Beroaldo und sein Kommentar zum Goldenen Esel des Apuleius.* Munich 1971 (Humanistiche Bibliothek, Reihe I: Abhandlungen, Bd. 9).

Apuleius (Pseudo)
[531] LUCENTINI, P., *Il commento all'"Asclepius" del Vaticano Ottoboniano lat. 811*, in *Filosofia e cultura. Per Eugenio Garin*, vol. I. Rome 1991, pp. 39-59.

Ausonius
[532] FELBER, H.L. & S. PRETE, *Decimus Magnus Ausonius*, in *Catalogus Translationum et Commentariorum*, 4 (1980), pp. 193-222.

Boethius
[533] BRIGHT, J.W., *Anglo-Saxon Glosses to Boethius*, in *American Journal of Philology*, 5 (1884), pp. 488-492.
[534] BROWN, V., *Lupus of Ferrières on the Metres of Boethius*, in *Festschrift Ludwig Bieler. Latin Script and Letters A.D. 400-900.* Leiden 1976, pp. 63-79.
[535] COURCELLE, P., *Étude critique sur les commentaires de la Consolation de Boèce (IXe-XVe siècles)*, in *Archives d'histoire doctrinale et littéraire du moyen âge*, 14 (1939), pp. 5-140.
[536] CRESPO, R., *Il prologo alla traduzione della "Consolatio Philosophiae" di Jean de Meun e il commento di Guglielmo d'Aragona*, in *Romanitas et Christianitas. Studia I.H. Waszink oblata.* Amsterdam & London 1983, pp. 55-70.
[537] DEAN, R.J., *The Dedication of Nicholas Trevet's Commentary on Boethius*, in *Studies in Philology*, 63 (1966), pp. 593-603.
[538] FORTIN, John R., *Clarembald of Arras as a Boethian Commentator.* Diss. University of Notre Dame South Bend, Ind. 1991 [Summary in *Dissertation Abstracts 52*, 1991-1992, 3624 A].
[539] FRATI, L., *Pietro da Moglio e il suo commento a Boezio*, in *Studi e memorie per la storia dell'Università di Bologna*, 5 (1920), pp. 237-276.
[540] HUYGENS, R.B.C., *Mittelalterliche Kommentare zum "O qui perpetua..."*, in *Sacris erudiri*, 6 (1954), pp. 373-427.
[541] JEAUNEAU, É., *Un commentaire inédit sur le chant "O qui perpetua" de Boèce*, in *Rivista critica di storia della filosofia*, 14 (1959), pp. 60-80 (= Édouard JEAUNEAU, *"Lectio philosophorum". Recherches sur l'école de Chartres.* Amsterdam 1973, pp. 310-331).
[542] JOURDAIN, C., *Des commentaires inédits de Guillaume de Conches et de Nicolas Triveth sur la Consolation de la philosophie de Boèce*, in *Notices et extraits de la Bibliothèque impériale*, 20, 2 (1862), pp. 40-82.
[543] OLMEDILLA HERRERO, Carmen, *Comentarios a la Consolatio Philosophiae de Boecio: Guillermo de Aragón y la versión castellana anónima del comentario de Nicolás de Trevet*, in *Cuadernos de filología clásica (L)*, 2 (1992), pp. 277-288.
[543a] PIZZANI, U., *I metri di Boezio nell'interpretazione di N. Perotti*, in *Res Publica Litterarum*, 8 (1985), pp. 245-254.
[544] *Saeculi noni auctoris in Boetii consolationem philosophiae commentarius*, edidit Edmund T. SILK. Rome 1935 (Papers and Monographs of the American Academy in Rome, 9).
[545] SILK, E.T., *Pseudo-Johannes Scottus, Adalbold of Utrecht, and the Early Commentaries on Boethius*, in *Mediaeval and Renaissance Sudies*, 3 (1954), pp. 1-40.
[546] SILVESTRE, H., *Le commentaire inédit de Jean Scot Erigène au mètre IX du livre III du*

"De consolatione Philosophiae" de Boèce, in Revue d'histoire ecclésiastique, 47 (1952), pp. 44-122.

[546a] STEWART, H.F., A Commentary by Remigius Autissiodoriensis on the De consolatione philosophiae of Boethius, in Journal of Theological Studies, 17 (1916), pp. 22-42.

[547] THOMAS, A., Notice sur le manuscrit latin 4788 du Vatican contenant une traduction française avec commentaire par Maître Pierre de Paris de la "Consolatio philosophiae" de Boèce, in Notices et extraits des manuscrits de la Bbliohèque nationale, 41 (1923), pp. 29-90.

[548] TRONCARELLI, F., Per una ricerca sui commenti altomedievali al "De consolatione" di Boezio, in Miscellanea in memoria di Giorgio Cencetti. Turin 1973, pp. 363-380.

Caesar

[549] BROWN, V., Caesar, Gaius Julius, in Catalogus Translationum et Commentariorum, 3 (1976), pp. 87-139 [Aulus Janus Parrhasius].

[550] HEDICKE, E., Scholia in Caesarem et Sallustium. Quedlinburg 1879 [Paris, Bibl. Nat., 6256].

[551] MCGRATH, G.K., An Unknown Fourteenth-Century Commentary on Suetonius and Caesar, in Classical Philology, 65 (1970), pp. 182-185 [Vatican, Barb. lat., 148].

Calcidius

[552] DUTTON, P.E., The Uncovering of the Glosae super Platonem of Bernard of Chartres, in Mediaeval Studies, 46 (1984), pp. 192-221.

[553] The "Glosae super Platonem" of Bernard of Chartres. Edited with an Introduction by Paul Edward DUTTON. Toronto 1991 (Pontifical Institute of Mediaeval Studies. Studies and Texts, 107).

[554] GUILLAUME DE CONCHES, Glosae super Platonem. Texte critique avec introduction, notes et tables par Édouard JEAUNEAU. Paris 1965 (Textes philosophiques du Moyen Age, 13).

[555] JEAUNEAU, É., Gloses sur le "Timée" et commentaire du "Timée" dans deux manuscrits du Vatican, in Revue des études augustiniennes, 8 (1962), pp. 365-373 (= Édouard JEAUNEAU, "Lectio philosophorum". Recherches sur l'école de Chartres. Amsterdam 1973, pp. 195-203) [Vatican, Arch. S. Pietro H. 51 & Chig. E.V. 152].

[556] JEAUNEAU, É., Gloses marginales sur le "Timée" de Platon du manuscrit 226 de la Bibliothèque municipale d'Avranches, in Sacris erudiri, 17 (1966), pp. 71-89 (= Édouard JEAUNEAU, "Lectio philosophorum". Recherches sur l'école de Chartres. Amsterdam 1973, pp. 209-227).

[557] JEAUNEAU, É., Gloses sur le "Timée" du manuscrit Digby 217 de la Bodléienne à Oxford, in Sacris erudiri, 17 (1966), pp. 365-400 (= Édouard JEAUNEAU, "Lectio philosophorum". Recherches sur l'école de Chartres. Amsterdam 1973, pp. 229-264).

[558] LÖFSTEDT, B., Zu den Glosae super Platonem des Wilhelm von Conches, in Arctos, 20 (1986), pp. 93-99.

Carmina Priapea

[559] HAUSMANN, F.-R., Carmina Priapea, in Catalogus Translationum et Commentariorum, 4 (1980), pp. 423-450 [Bernardinus Cyllenius, Nicolaus Fabritius Sacca, Hieronymus Avantius, Ludovicus Pretinus]

Cato (Pseudo)

[560] DE MARCO, M., Una nuova redazione del commento di Remigio d'Auxerre ai "Disticha Catonis", in Aevum, 26 (1952), p. 466-467 [Vatican, Reg. lat., 1560].

[561] HAZELTON, R., The Christianization of "Cato". The "Disticha Catonis" in the Light of Late Mediaeval Commentaries, in Mediaeval Studies, 19 (1957), pp. 157-173.

[562] HUYGENS, R.B.C., *Remigiana*, in *Aevum*, 28 (1954), p. 330-344.
[563] MANCINI, A., *Un commento ignoto di Remy d'Auxerre ai "Disticha Catonis"*, in *Rendiconti della Reale Accademia dei Lincei*, Ser. Vᵃ, 11 (1902), p. 175-198, 369-382 [Lucca, Bibl. Statale, 1433].
[564] MANITIUS, M., *Remigiusscholien*, in *Münchener Museum für Philologie*, 2 (1913), p. 79-113 [Rouen, Bibl. mun., O. 32 (1470)].
[565] ORTOLEVA, V., *Gli scholia alla traduzione planudea dei Disticha Catonis*, in *Siculorum Gymnasium*, 44 (1991), pp. 275-280.
[566] ORTOLEVA, V., *Glosse in καθαρεύουσα alla traduzione planudea dei Disticha Catonis*, in *Eikasmos*, 3 (1992), pp. 265-276.

Catullus

[567] GAISSER, J.H., *Catullus and his First Interpreters: Antonius Parthenius and Angelo Poliziano*, in *Transactions of the American Philological Association*, 112 (1982), pp. 83-106.
[568] GAISSER, J.H., *Catullus, Gaius Valerius*, in *Catalogus Translationum et Commentariorum*, 7 (1992), pp. 197-292 [Antonius Parthenius Lacisius, Angelus Polizianus, Marcus Antonius Coccius (Sabellicus), Hieronymus Avantius, Palladius Fuscus, Franciscus Puccius].
[569] JOCELYN, D., *On Some Unneccessarily Indecent Interpretations of Catullus 2 and 3*, in *American Journal of Philology*, 101 (1980), pp. 420-441 [Angelus Politianus].
[570] RESTANI, M., *Le Commentationes in Catullum di Antonio Partenio Veronese*, in *Giornale italiano di filologia*, 42 (1990), pp. 275-294 [Brescia, 1486].
[571] RICHARDSON, B., *Pucci, Parrasio and Catullus*, in *Italia medioevale e umanistica*, 19 (1976), pp. 277-289.

Cicero

[572] BILLANOVICH, G., *Il Cicerone di Rolando da Piazzola*, in *Italia medioevale e umanistica*, 28 (1985), pp. 37-47 [Wolfenbüttel, Herzog August Bibl., 2 Gud. lat.].
[573] BLANC, P., *Pétrarque lecteur de Cicéron: les scolies pétrarquiennes du "De oratore" et de l'"Orator"*, in *Studi petrarcheschi*, 9 (1978), pp. 109-166 [Troyes, Bibl. mun., 552].
[574] DICKEY, M., *Some Commentaries on the "De inventione" and "Ad Herennium" of the Eleventh and Early Twelfth Centuries*, in *Mediaeval and Renaissance Studies*, 6 (1968), pp. 1-41.
[575] FREDBORG, K.M., *Petrus Helias on Rhetoric*, in *Cahiers de l'Institut du Moyen Age grec et latin*, 13 (1974), pp. 31-41.
[576] FREDBORG, K.M., *The Commentaries on Cicero's De inventione and Rhetorica ad Herennium by William of Champeaux*, in *Cahiers de l'Institut du Moyen Age grec et latin*, 17 (1976), pp. 1-39.
[577] JUREN, V., *Les notes de Politien sur les Lettres de Cicéron à Brutus, Quintus et Atticus*, in *Rinascimento*, 2ᵃ ser., 28 (1988), pp. 235-256 [Paris, Bibl. Nat., Rés. Z. 121; a. 1470].
[578] *The Latin Rhetorical Commentaries by Thierry of Chartres*, ed. by K.M. FREDBORG. Toronto 1988 (Pontifical Institute of Mediaeval Studies. Studies and Texts, 84).
[579] MILLER, I.E., *The Commentary on Cicero's Paradoxa Stoicorum in Codex Reginensis Latinus 1624*. Diss. St. Louis University. St. Louis (Missouri) 1985 [Summary in *Dissertation Abstracts* 46, 1986, p. 3713 A].
[580] MURPHY, J.J., *Cicero's Rhetoric in the Middle Ages*, in *The Quarterly Journal of Speech*, 53 (1967), pp. 334-341.
[581] PELLEGRIN, E., *Quelques "accessus" au "De amicitia" de Cicéron*, in *Hommages à André Boutemy*. Brussels 1976, p. 274-298.
[582] PIGMAN, G.W., *Barzizza's Studies of Cicero*, in *Rinascimento*, 21 (1981), pp. 123-163.

[583] ROMMICK, M.V., *Manuscripts and Commentaries of the Paradoxa Stoicorum*, in *Rivista di cultura classica e medioevale*, 32 (1990), pp. 119-137.

[584] WARD, J.O., *From Antiquity to the Renaissance: Glosses and Commentaries on Cicero's Rhetorica*, in *Medieval Eloquence. Studies in the Theory and Practice of Medieval Rhetoric*, ed. by J.J. Murphy. Berkeley, Los Angeles & London 1978, pp. 25-67.

[585] WARD, J.O., *Renaissance Commentators on Ciceronian Rhetoric*, in *Renaissance Eloquence. Studies in the Theory and Practice of Renaissance Rhetoric*, ed. by J.J. Murphy. Berkeley, Los Angeles & London 1983, pp. 126-173.

Cicero (Pseudo)

[586] CAPLAN, H., *A Mediaeval Commentary on the "Rhetorica ad Herennium"*, in *Of Eloquence. Studies in Ancient and Mediaeval Rhetoric*. Ithaca & London 1970, pp. 247-270.

[587] FILELFO, Francesco, *In rhethoricam ad Herennium commentarii*, in *Francesco Filelfo educatore e il "Codice Sforza" della Biblioteca Reale di Torino*, a cura di L. FIRPO. Turin 1967, pp. 38-52 [Turin, Bibl. Reale, Varia 75].

[588] WERTIS, S.K., *The Commentary of Bartolinus de Benincasa de Canulo on the "Rhetorica ad Herennium"*, in *Viator*, 10 (1979), pp. 283-310.

[589] WISÉN, Magne, *De Scholiis Rhetoricis ad Herennium codice Holmiensi traditis*. Stockholm 1905.

Claudian

[590] CHATELAIN, E., *Fragments de scholies sur Claudien*, in *Revue de philologie*, 8 (1884), pp. 81-91.

[591] CLARKE, A.K. & H.L. LEVY, *Claudius Claudianus*, in *Catalogus Translationum et Commentariorum*, 3 (1976), pp. 141-171.

[592] *The Commentary of Geoffrey of Vitry on Claudian "De raptu Proserpinae"*. Transcribed by A.K. CLARKE and P.M. GILES, with an Introduction and Notes by A.K. CLARKE. Leiden 1973 (Mittellateinische Studien und Texte, 7).

[593] HAVERFIELD, *Scholia on Claudian*, in *Journal of Philology*, 17 (1888), pp. 271-273.

Columella

[594] BROWN, V., *Columella, Lucius Junius Moderatus*, in *Catalogus Translationum et Commentariorum*, 3 (1976), pp. 173-193 [Julius Pomponius Laetus, Curius Lancilottus Pasius, Philippus Beroaldus].

Donatus

[594a] *Ars Laureshamensis. Expositio in Donatum maiorem*, edidit Bengt LÖFSTEDT. Turnhout 1977 (Corpus Christianorum. Continuatio Mediaeualis, 40A).

[595] *Commentum Sedulii Scotti in maiorem Donatum*, ed. by Denis BREARLY. Toronto 1975 (Pontifical Institute of Mediaeval Studies. Studies and Texts, 27).

[596] HOLTZ, L., *Sur trois commentaires irlandais de l'Art majeur de Donat au IXe siècle*, in *Revue d'Histoire des Textes*, 2 (1972), pp. 45-72.

[597] JEUDY, C., *Israël le grammairien et la tradition manuscrite du commentaire de Rémi d'Auxerre à l'"Ars minor" de Donat*, in *Studi medievali*, 18 (1977), pp. 185-248.

[598] JEUDY, C., *Donat et commentateurs de Donat à l'abbaye de Ripoll au Xe siècle (ms. Barcelone, Archivo de la Corona de Aragón, Ripoll 46)*, in *Lettres latines du moyen âge et de la Renaissance*, recueil édité par G. Cambier, C. Deroux, J. Préaux. Brussels 1978 (Collection Latomus, 158), pp. 56-75.

[598a] MVRETHACH (MVRIDAC) *In Donati artem maiorem*, edidit Louis HOLTZ. Turnhout 1977 (Corpus Christianorum. Continuatio Mediaeualis, 40).

[598b] PAVLVS DIACONVS, *Expositio artis Donati seu Incipit ars Donati quam Paulus Diaconus*

exposuit, a cura di M.F. BUFFA GIOLITO. Genoa 1990 (Collana di grammatici latini).

[598c] ROBERTVS KILWARDBY, O.P., *In Donati artem maiorem III*, edidit Laurentius SCHMUECKER. Brixen 1984.

[598d] SEDVLIVS SCOTTVS, *In Donati artem maiorem*, edidit Bengt LÖFSTEDT. Turnhout 1977 (Corpus Christianorum. Continuatio Mediaeualis, 40B).

[598e] SMARAGDVS, *Liber in partibus Donati*, cura et studio B. LÖFSTEDT, L. HOLTZ, A. KIBRE. Turnhout 1986 (Corpus Christianorum. Continuatio Mediaeualis, 68).

Germanicus

[599]   DELL'ERA, A., *Una miscellanea astronomica medievale. Gli "Scholia Strozziana" a Germanico*, in *Atti della Accademia nazionale dei Lincei. Classe di scienze morali storiche e filologiche. Memorie*, ser. VIIIª, 23.2 (1979), pp. 145-268.

[600]   DELL'ERA, A., *Un "codex descriptus" di Germanico con gli "Scholia Basilensia"*, in *Letterature comparate. Problemi e metodi. Studi in onore di Ettore Paratore*, vol. II. Bologna 1981, pp. 581-583.

[601]   GERMANICI CAESARIS *Aratea cum scholiis*, edidit Alfredus BREYSIG. Berlin 1867 (reprint: Hildesheim 1967).

[602]   MAAS, E., *Commentariorum in Aratum reliquiae*. Berlin 1898 (reprint: Berlin 1958).

Horace

[603]   BORZSÁK, I., *Die Scholien des Horatius Bodmerianus (P). Zur Überlieferungsgeschichte des Horaztextes*, in *Acta Antiqua Academiae Scientiarum Hungaricae*, 25 (1977), pp. 417-437.

[604]   BOTSCHUYVER, H.J., *Scholia in Horatium*. Vol. I, III & IV. Amsterdam 1935, 1939, 1942.

[605]   BOTSCHUYVER, H.J., *Quelques remarques sur les scholies parisiennes* λ φ ψ *d'Horace*, in *Latomus*, 3 (1939), pp. 25-51.

[606]   BOTSCHUYVER, H.J., *Les scholies du Suevovaticanus (= R)*, in *Latomus*, 5 (1946), pp. 229-231 [Vatican, Reg. lat. 1703].

[607]   BÜHLER, W., *Die Pariser Horazscholien, eine neue Quelle der Mythographi Vaticani 1 und 2*, in *Philologus*, 105 (1961), pp. 123-135.

[608]   CURCIO, G., *Commenti medioevali ad Orazio*, in *Rivista di filologia e di istruzione classica*, 35 (1907), pp. 43-64.

[609]   CURCIO, G., *Un manoscritto vaticano di scoli pseudo-acroniani*, in *Rivista di filologia e di istruzione classica*, 35 (1907), pp. 65-68.

[610]   CURCIO, Gaetano, *Q. Orazio Flacco, studiato in Italia dal secolo XIII al XVIII*. Catania 1913 (Biblioteca di filologia classica, 7).

[610a] DI BENEDETTO, F., *Fonzio e Landino su Orazio*, in *Tradizione classica e letteratura umanistica. Per Alessandro Perosa*. Rome 1985, pp. 437-453.

[611]   ENDT, Johann, *Die Glossen des Vaticanus Latinus 3257, besonders mit Rücksicht auf die Ausgabe der Pseudoacronischen Scholien von O. Keller*. Smichow 1904-1905 (Sonderdruck aus dem 31. Jahresbericht des kk. deutschen Staatsgymnasiums in Smichow).

[612]   ENDT, Johann, *Studien zum Commentator Cruquianus*. Leipzig & Berlin, 1906.

[613]   FRASSO, G., *Erudizione classica e letterature romanze in terra trevigiana. L'Orazio Ambrosiano Q. 75 sup.*, in *Italia medioevale e umanistica*, 27 (1984), pp. 30-55.

[614]   FREDBORG, K.M., *Difficile est proprie communia dicere (Horats, A. P. 128). Horatsfortolkningens bidrag til middelalderens poetik*, in *Museum Tusculanum*, 40-43 (1980), pp. 583-597.

[615]   FRIIS-JENSEN, K., *Horatius liricus et ethicus. Two Twelfth-Century School Texts on Horace's Poems*, in *Cahiers de l'Institut du Moyen Age grec et latin*, 57 (1988), pp. 81-147.

[616] FRIIS-JENSEN, K., *The "Ars Poetica" in Twelfth-Century France. The Horace of Matthew of Vendôme, Geoffrey of Vinsauf and John of Garland*, in *Cahiers de l'Institut du Moyen Age grec et latin*, 60 (1990), pp. 319-388.

[017] FRIIS-JENSEN, K., *Addenda et Corrigenda to CIMAGL 60 1990 319-88*, in *Cahiers de l'Institut du Moyen Age grec et latin* 61 (1991), p. 184.

[618] FRIIS-JENSEN, K., *The Medieval Horace and his Lyrics*, in *Horace. L'Oeuvre et les imitations. Un siècle d'interprétation*. Genève 1993 (Entretiens sur l'Antiquité classique, 39), pp. 257-303.

[619] FRIIS-JENSEN, K., *Horace and the Early Writers of Arts of Poetry*, in *Sprachtheorien in Spätantike und Mittelalter*. Tübingen 1995 (Geschichte der Sprachtheorie, 3), pp. 360-401.

[620] HAJDÚ, I., *Ein Zürcher Kommentar aus dem 12. Jahrhundert zur Ars poetica des Horaz*, in *Cahiers de l'Institut du Moyen Age grec et latin*, 63 (1993), pp. 231-293 [Zürich, Zentralbibl., Rheinau 76].

[621] KURSCHAT, A., *Unedierte Horazscholien des Cod. Paris. lat. 7975, etc.* Tilsit 1884.

[622] MANCINI, A., *Sul commento oraziano del codice della Biblioteca pubblica di Lucca n. 1433 (Trattato di origine alcuiniana)*, in *Atti del Congresso internazionale di scienze storiche (Roma, 1-9 aprile 1903)*, vol. II. Rome 1905, pp. 243-248.

[623] MASSARO, M., *Un commento medievale inedito ad Orazio*, in *Atene e Roma*, 23 (1978), pp. 190-193 [Vatican, Vat. lat. 3866].

[624] NOLTE, A., *Scholia marginalia e cod. Franequerano Horatii ad Oden II libri Epodon*, in *Philologus*, 8 (1853), pp. 566-570 [Leeuwarden, Prov. Bibl., B.A. Fr. 45].

[625] NOSKE, Gottfried, *Quaestiones pseudacroneae*. Munich 1969.

[626] PETSCHENIG, M., *Zu den Scholiasten des Horaz*. Graz 1873.

[627] PIRRONE, N., *Thomae Schifaldi commentaria atque Persii et Horatii vitae ex eis sublatae*, in *Atti dell'Accademia Properziana di Assisi*, 2 (1905), p. 12.

[628] *Pseudoacronis scholia in Horatium vetustiora*, recensuit Otto KELLER, vol. I-II. Leipzig 1902-1904 (Bibliotheca Teubneriana).

[629] PYRITZ, H., *Althochdeutsche Horaz-Glossen*, in *Zeitschrift für deutsches Altertum und deutsche Literatur*, 68 (1931), pp. 215-216.

[630] SCHWEIKERT, E., *Zur Überlieferung der Horaz-Scholien*. Paderborn 1915 (Studien zur Geschichte und Kultur des Altertums, VIII, 1) (reprint: New York & London 1967).

[631] SIEWERT, Klaus, *Die althochdeutsche Horazglossierung*. Göttingen 1986 (Studien zum Althochdeutschen, 8).

[632] TSENG, Marie Shively, *Paolo da Perugia and his Influence on the Beginning of Italian Humanism as Seen through his Commentary on Horace's "Ars poetica"* Diss. University of Southern California 1984 [Summary in *Dissertation Abstracts* 45, section A, p. 2516].

[633] VILLA, C., *Per una tipologia del commento mediolatino: l'"Ars poetica" di Orazio*, in *Il commento ai testi. Atti del seminario di Ascona 2-9 ottobre 1989*. Basle 1992, pp. 19-46.

[634] VILLA, C., *I manoscritti di Orazio. III*, in *Aevum*, 68 (1994), pp. 117-146 [pp. 127-146: *I manoscritti di commenti oraziani*].

[635] WEGSTEIN, W., *Horaz für Anfänger? Über die volkssprachliche Glossierung lateinischer Liebeslyrik*, in *Liebe in der deutschen Literatur des Mittelalters. St-Andrews-Colloquium 1985*. Tübingen 1987 (Publications of the Institute of Germanic Studies. University of London, 40), pp. 27-35.

[636] ZECHMEISTER, Josephus, *Scholia Vindobonensia ad Horatii artem poeticam*. Vienna 1877 [Vienna, Österreichische Nationalbibl., 223].

Justinus
[637]   PELLEGRIN, E., *Un manuscrit de Justin annoté par Landolfo Colonna (Leyde, Voss. lat. Q. 101)*, in *Italia medioevale e umanistica*, 3 (1960), pp. 241-249.

Juvenal
[638]   BARNETT, Robert John, *An Anonymous Medieval Commentary on Juvenal*. Diss. Univ. of Chapel Hill 1964 [Summary in *Dissertation Abstracts* 26/3, 1965, p. 1638].
[639]   BEER, R., *De nova scholiorum in Iuuenalem recensione instituenda*, in *Wiener Studien*, 6 (1884), pp. 297-314; 7 (1885), pp. 311-324.
[640]   BELDAME, C., *Scolies inédites de Juvénal*, in *Revue de philologie*, n.s. 6 (1882), pp. 76-103.
[641]   BOYER, B.B., *Traces of Insular Tradition in the Ancient Scholia of Juvenal*, in *Classical Philology*, 29 (1934), pp. 240-250.
[642]   CRANZ, F.E. & P.O. KRISTELLER, *Juvenalis. Addenda et Corrigenda*, in *Catalogus Translationum et Commentariorum*, 3 (1976), pp. 432-445.
[643]   DÜRR, J., *Das Leben Iuvenalis*. Ulm 1883 (Wisenschaftliche Beilage zum Programm des kgl. Gymnasiums in Ulm).
[644]   GNILKA, Chr., *"Scholiastenweisheit" und moderne Exegese Zu Juv. sat. 6, 231 ff und 247 ff*, in *Wiener Studien*, 81, = N.F. 2 (1968), pp. 193-205.
[645]   GUILLAUME DE CONCHES, *Glosae in Iuuenalem*. Edited with an Introduction and Notes by Bradford WILSON. Paris 1980 (Textes philosophiques du Moyen Age, 18).
[646]   GUSTARELLI, A., *Un commento umanistico inedito alle Satire di Giovenale*, in *Reale Accademia Peloritana. Rendiconti*, 1907, pp. 14-21 [Florence, Bibl. Laur., Ashb. 263; c. 1470/80].
[647]   HIGHET, G., *The Life of Juvenal*, in *Transactions and Proceedings of the American Philological Association*, 68 (1937), pp. 480-506.
[648]   HÖHLER, W., *Die Cornutus-Scholien zum ersten Buche der Satiren des Juvenals*, in *Jahrbücher für classische Philologie*, Supplementsband 23 (1867), pp. 379-442.
[649]   *In D. Iunii Iuvenalis satiras commentarii vetusti*, post P. Pithoei curas auxit virorum doctorum suisque notis instruxit A.G. CRAMER. Hamburg 1823.
[650]   MANITIUS, M., *Lesarten und Scholien zu Juvenal aus dem Dresdensis Dc 153*, in *Rheinisches Museum für Philologie*, N.F. 66 (1905), pp. 202-228.
[651]   PROCACCI, G., *Scolii a Giovenale di Battista Guarini in un codice ferrarese*, in *Studi italiani di filologia classica*, 20 (1913), pp. 425-437 [Ferrara, Bibl. Civica, II 103; s. XV].
[652]   RÖNSCH, H., *Lexicalisches aus Leidener lateinischen Juvenal-Scholien der Karolingerzeit*, in *Romanische Forschungen*, 2 (1886), pp. 302-313.
[653]   SABBADINI, R., *Uno scoliasta di Giovenale: Giovanni Tortelli*, in *Rivista Etnea di lettere, arti e scienze*, 1 (1893), pp. 97-99.
[654]   SANFORD, E.M., *Tortelli's Commentary on Juvenal*, in *Transactions and Proceedings of the American Philological Association*, 82 (1951), pp. 207-218.
[655]   SANFORD, E.M., *Juvenalis, Decimus Junius*, in *Catalogus Translationum et Commentariorum*, 1 (1960), pp. 175-238 [Guilelmus de Conchis, Gaspar Veronensis, Guarinus Veronensis, Omnibonus Leonicenus, Christophorus Landinus, Peregrinus Allius, Martinus Phileticus, Baptista Guarinus, Franciscus Philelphus, Petrus Philippus Pandolphinus, Angelus Cneus Sabinus, Domitius Calderinus, Georgius Merula, Georgius Valla, Angelus Politianus, Johannes Baptista Cantalycius, Bartholomaeus Fontius, Antonius Mancinellus, Jodocus Badius Ascensius, Johannes Britannicus]
[656]   *Scholia in Iuvenalem vetustiora*, collegit, recensuit, illustravit Paulus WESSNER. Leipzig 1931 (Bibliotheca Teubneriana).
[657]   *Scholiasta Iuuenalis e codice Sangallensi*, cura I.C. ORELLII. Suppletus et emendatus.

Zürich 1833 (Index lectionum in Academia Turicensi 1833-1834) [St. Gall, Stiftsbibl., 870]

[658]   STEPHAN, Chr., *De Pithoeanis in Iuuenalem scholis*. Bonn 1882 [Montpellier, Faculté de Médecine, 125 & St. Gall, Stiftsbibl., 870].

[659]   VITELLI, C., *De codice Roncioniano scholiorum in Iuuenalem*, in *Studi italiani di filologia classica*, 10 (1902), pp. 29-39 [Pisa, Bibl. Universitaria, 690; a. 1452].

Livy

[660]   DEAN, R.J., *The Earliest Known Medieval Commentary on Livy is by Nicholas Trevet*, in *Medievalia et Humanistica*, 3 (1945), pp. 86-98; 4 (1946), p. 110.

[661]   MCDONALD, A.H., *Livius, Titus*, in *Catalogus Translationum et Commentariorum*, 2 (1971), pp. 331-348 [Nicolaus Trevet].

[662]   TITUS LIVIUS, *Ab urbe condita I.1-9. Ein mittellateinischer Kommentar mit sechs romanischen Übersetzungen und Kürzungen aus dem Mittelalter*. Aus den Handschriften hrsg. v. Curt J. WITTLIN. Tübingen 1970 (Romanische Paralleltexte, 2).

[663]   VAN ACKER, L., *Nicolas Trevet et son interprétation de quelques passages de Tite-Live*, in *L'Antiquité classique*, 31 (1962), pp. 252-257.

[664]   VOIT, L., *Marginalnoten zur 1. Dekade des Livius*, in *Philologus*, 91, = N.F. 45 (1936), pp. 308-322 [Florence, Bibl. Laur., Plut. 63.19].

Lucan

[665]   BADALÌ, R., *Sulle glosse del Vat. lat. 3284*, in *Letterature comparate. Problemi e metodo. Studi in onore di Ettore Paratore*, vol. II. Rome 1981, pp. 609-618.

[666]   BIANCHI, R., *Il commento a Lucano e il "Natalis" di Paolo Marsi*, in *Miscellanea Augusto Campana*, vol. I. Padua, 1981, pp. 71-100.

[667]   BRAIDOTTI, Cecilia, *Le vite antiche di M. Anneo Lucano. Introduzione e testo critico*. Bologna 1972.

[668]   BRAIDOTTI, C., *La "Vita" svetoniana di Lucano nel Reginensis lat. 1634*, in *Letterature comparate. Problemi e metodo. Studi in onore di Ettore Paratore*, vol. II. Rome 1981, pp. 713-718.

[669]   CAVAJONI, G.A., *La tradizione degli scholia vetera a Lucano nelle Glosule super Lucanum di Arnolfo di Orléans*, in *Rendiconti dell'Istituto lombardo. Classe di lettere, scienze morali e storiche*, 101 (1967), pp. 184-194.

[670]   CAVAJONI, G.A., *Scholia inediti a Lucano nel Codice Bernensis litt. 45 saec. X*, in *ACME*, 28 (1975), pp. 79-114.

[671]   CAVAJONI, G.A., *Glosse antico alto tedesche in Lucano (dai codici Monacensis 14505 e Berolinensis fol. 35)*, in *Scripta filologica*, 1 (1977), pp. 105-116.

[672]   CAVAJONI, G.A., *Supplementum adnotationum super Lucanum. I (libri I-V)*. Milan 1979 (Testi e documenti per lo studio dell'antichità, 63).

[673]   CAVAJONI, G.A., *Supplementum adnotationum super Lucanum. II (libri VI-VII)*. Milan 1984 (Testi e documenti per lo studio dell'antichità, 63, 2).

[674]   CRESCINI, V., *Di un codice ignoto contenente il commento di Benvenuto da Imola su la "Pharsalia" di Lucano*, in *Studi editi dall'Università di Padova a commemorare l'VIII centenario dello Studio Bolognese*, vol. III. Padua 1888, pp. 1 sqq.

[675]   ENDT, J., *Zur Überlieferung der Adnotationes super Lucanum*. Smichow 1906 (Zweiunddreissigster Jahresbericht des k.k. deutschen Staatsgymnasiums in Smichow, veröffentlicht am Schlusse des Schuljahres 1905-1906).

[676]   ENDT, J., *Der Parisinus latinus 10403 und die Adnotationes super Lucanum*, in *Wiener Studien*, 31 (1909), pp. 177-179.

[677]   ENDT, J., *Adnotationes super Lucanum*. Leipzig 1909 (Bibliotheca Teubneriana) (reprint: Stuttgart 1969).

[678]   ENDT, J., *Ein Kommentar zu Lucan aus dem Mittelalter*, in *Wiener Studien*, 32 (1910), pp. 123-155. 272-295.

[679] ENDT, J., *Aus dem Sangallensis 864*, in *Wiener Studien*, 32 (1910), pp. 324-325.

[680] GENTHE, H., *Scholia vetera in Lucanum e codice Montepessulano*. Berlin 1868 [Montpellier, Faculté de Médecine, 113].

[681] KALINKA, E., *Analecta latina. II. Adnotationes super Lucanum*, in *Wiener Studien*, 16 (1894), pp. 85-93 [Paris, Bibl. Nat., lat. 10403].

[682] KNEEPKENS, C.H., *Ralph of Beauvais, Liber Tytan*. Nijmegen 1991 (Artistarium, 8).

[683] MARTI, B.M., *Literary Criticism in the Medieval Commentaries on Lucan*, in *Transactions and Proceedings of the American Philological Association*, 72 (1941), pp. 245-254.

[684] MARTI, B.M., *Arnulfi Aurelianensis Glosule super Lucanum*. Rome 1958 (Papers and Monographs of the American Academy in Rome, 18).

[685] QUADLBAUER, F., *Lukan im Schema des ordo naturalis / artificialis. Ein Beitrag zur Geschichte der Lukanwertung im lateinischen Mittelalter*, in *Grazer Beiträge*, 6 (1977), pp. 67-105.

[686] RAMMINGER, J., *Quellen und Genese der Scholien und Glossen zu Lukan, "Pharsalia", 2,335-371*, in *Hermes*, 114 (1986), pp. 479-490.

[687] ROSSI, L.C., *Benvenuto da Imola lettore di Lucano*, in *Il commento ai testi. Atti del seminario di Ascona, 2-9 ottobre 1989*. Basle 1992, pp. 47-102; in *Benvenuto da Imola, lettore degli antichi e dei moderni. Atti del Convegno internazionale, Imola, 26 e 27 maggio 1989*. Ravenna 1991, pp. 165-203.

[688] SANFORD, E.M., *The Manuscripts of Lucan. Accessus and Marginalia*, in *Speculum*, 9 (1934), pp. 278-295.

[689] SZELEST, H., *Die nach-augusteischen Autoren in den Adnotationes super Lucanum*, in *Eos*, 78 (1990), pp. 187-194.

[690] USENER, Hermann, *M. Annaei Lucani commenta Bernensia*. Leipzig 1869 (reprint: Hildesheim 1967) [Berne, Burgerbibl., 370]

[691] USSANI, V., *Il testo di Lucano e gli scolii Bernesi*, in *Studi italiani di filologia classica*, 11 (1903), pp. 29-83 [Berne, Burgerbibl., 370].

[692] USSANI, V., *Le annotazioni di Pomponio Leto a Lucano*, in *Rendiconti della Reale Accademia dei Lincei. Classe di scienze morali*, ser. Vª, 13 (1904), pp. 366-385.

[693] WEBER, Car. Fried., *Vitae M. Annaei Lucani collectae*. Part. I-III. Marburg 1856, 1857 & 1858 (Indices lectionum... Academiae Marburgensis).

[694] WERNER, S., *The Scholia to Lucan in Beinecke MS 673*, in *Traditio*, 45 (1989-1990), pp. 347-364 [New Haven, Yale Univ., Beinecke Libr. 673].

[695] WERNER, Shirley J., *The Transmission and Scholia to Lucan's Bellum civile*. Diss. Yale Univ., New Haven, Conn. 1992 [Summary in *Dissertation Abstracts* 53, 1992-1993, 3892 A].

Macrobius

[696] JEAUNEAU, É., *Gloses de Guillaume de Conches sur Macrobe. Note sur les manuscrits*, in *Archives d'histoire doctrinale et littéraire du moyen âge*, 27 (1960), pp. 17-28 (= Édouard JEAUNEAU, *"Lectio philosophorum". Recherches sur l'école de Chartres*. Amsterdam 1973, pp. 267-278).

[697] JEAUNEAU, É., *La lecture des auteurs classiques à l'école de Chartres durant la première moitié du XIIᵉ siècle. Un témoignage privilégié: les "Glosae super Macrobium" de Guillaume de Conches*, in *Classical Influences on European Culture A.D. 500-1500*, ed. by R.R. Bolgar. Cambridge 1971, pp. 95-102.

Martial

[698] HAUSMANN, F.-R., *Martialis, Marcus Valerius*, in *Catalogus Translationum et Commentariorum*, 4 (1980), pp. 249-296 [Domitius Calderinus, Georgius Merula, Nicolaus Perottus, Angelus Politianus].

[699] MONROE SIMMONS, J., *Martial in the Renaissance: Three "Lost" Commentaries Found*,

in *Acta Conventus Neo-latini Torontonensis*. Binghamton (N.Y.) 1991, pp. 689-696.

Martianus Capella

[700] *The Berlin Commentary on Martianus Capella's "De Nuptiis Philologiae et Mercurii", Book I*, edited by Haijo Jan WESTRA. Leiden 1994 (Mittellateinische Studien und Texte, 20).

[701] *The Commentary on Martianus Capella's "De nuptiis Philologiae et Mercurii" Attributed to Bernardus Silvestris*, ed. by Haijo Jan WESTRA. Toronto 1986 (Pontifical Institute of Mediaeval Studies. Studies and Texts, 80).

[702] DRONKE, P., *William of Conches's Commentary on Martianus Capella*, in *Études de civilisation médiévale (IXᵉ-XIIᵉ siècle). Mélanges offerts à Edmond-René Labande*. Poitiers 1974, pp. 223-235.

[703] HAURÉAU, B., *Commentaire de Jean Scot Érigène sur Martianus Capella. Manuscrit de Saint-Germain-des-Prés, N° 1110*, in *Notices et extraits des manuscrits de la Bibliothèque impériale*, 20, 2 (1862), pp. 1-39.

[704] HERREN, M., *The Commentary on Martianus Attributed to John Scottus: its Hiberno-Latin Background*, in *Jean Scot écrivain. Actes du IVᵉ Colloque international. Montréal, 28 août—2 septembre 1983*. Montreal & Paris 1986, pp. 265-286.

[705] LABOWSKI, L., *A New Version of Scotus Eriugena's Commentary on Martianus Capella*, in *Mediaeval and Renaissance Studies*, 1 (1941-1943), pp. 187-193.

[706] LEONARDI, Cl., *Glosse eriugeniane a Marziano Capella in un codice leidense*, in *Jean Scot Erigène et l'histoire de la philosophie. Laon, 7-12 juillet 1975*. Paris 1977, pp. 171-182 [Leiden, Bibl. der Rijksuniv., B.P.L. 88].

[707] LIEBESCHÜTZ, H., *Zur Geschichte der Erklärung des Martianus Capella bei Eriugena*, in *Philologus*, 104 (1960), pp. 127-137.

[708] LIEBESCHÜTZ, H., *The Place of the Martianus "Glossae" in the Development of Eriugena's Thought*, in *The Mind of Eriugena. Papers of a Colloquium, Dublin, 14-18 July 1970*. Dublin 1973, pp. 49-58.

[709] LUTZ, Cora E., *Iohannis Scotti Annotationes in Marcianum*. Cambridge (Mass.) 1939.

[710] LUTZ, Cora E,, *Dunchad Glossae in Martianum*. Lancaster (Pa.) 1944 (American Philological Asociation. Monographs, 12).

[711] LUTZ, C., *The Commentary of Remigius of Auxerre on Martianus Capella*, in *Mediaeval Studies*, 19 (1957), pp. 137-156.

[712] LUTZ, Cora E., *Remigii Autissiodorensis Commentum in Martianum Capellam*. Vol. I-II. Leiden 1962-1965.

[713] LUTZ, C., *Martianus Capella*, in *Catalogus Translationum et Commentariorum*, 2 (1971), pp. 367-381 [Martinus Laudensis, Johannes Scotus Eriugena, Remigius Autissiodorensis, Bernardus Silvester, Alexander Neckam].

[714] NARDUCCI, E., *Intorno ad un commento inedito di Remigio d'Auxerre al "Satyricon" di Marziano Capella*, in *Bullettino di bibliografia e di storia delle scienze matematiche e fisiche*, 15 (1882), pp. 505-580.

[715] PRÉAUX, J.G., *Le commentaire de Martin de Laon sur l'oeuvre de Martianus Capella*, in *Latomus*, 12 (1953), pp. 437-459.

[716] PRÉAUX, J., *Jean Scot et Martin de Laon en face du "De nuptiis" de Martianus Capella*, in *Jean Scot Erigène et l'histoire de la philosophie. Laon, 7-12 juillet 1975*. Paris 1977, pp. 161-170.

[717] RAND, E.K., *How Much of the "Annotationes in Marcianum" is the Work of John the Scot?*, in *Transactions and Proceedings of the American Philological Association*, 71 (1940), pp. 507-508.

[718] SCHRIMPF, G., *Zur Frage der Authentizität unserer Texte von Johannes Scottus' "Annotationes in Martianum"*, in *The Mind of Eriugena. Papers of a Colloquium, Dublin, 14-18 July 1970*. Dublin 1973, pp. 125-139.

[719] STOKES, W., *The Old Welsh Glosses on Martianus Capella*, in *Archaeologia Cambrensis*, IVth Ser., 4 (1873), pp. 1-20.

Mela (Pomponius)
[720] MILHAM, M.E., *Mela, Pomponius*, in *Catalogus Translationum et Commentariorum*, 5 (1984), pp. 257-285 [Anonymus Remensis (Guillermus Philastrius?)].

Ovid
[721] *Acessus ovidiani*, prolegomenis epilegomenis instruxit Gustavus PRZYCHOCKI, in *Rozprawy Akademii umiejetnosci. Wydzial filologiczny*. Serya III. Tom. 4. Krakow 1911, pp. 65-126.

[722] ALTON, E.H., *The Mediaeval Commentators of Ovid's Fasti*, in *Hermathena*, 20, n. 44 (1926), pp. 119-151.

[723] COULSON, F.T., *Manuscripts of the 'Vulgate' Commentary on Ovid's Metamorphoses. A Checklist*, in *Scriptorium*, 39 (1985), pp. 118-129.

[724] COULSON, F.T., *MSS of the 'Vulgate' Commentary on Ovid's Metamorphoses. Addendum*, in *Scriptorium*, 41 (1987), pp. 263-264.

[725] COULSON, F.T., *Hitherto Unedited Medieval and Renaissance Lives of Ovid (I)*, in *Mediaeval Studies*, 49 (1987), pp. 152-207.

[726] COULSON, F.T., *New Manuscript Evidence for Sources of the "Accessus" of Arnoul d'Orléans to the "Metamorphoses" of Ovid*, in *Manuscripta*, 30 (1986), pp. 103-107.

[727] COULSON, F.T., *New Manuscripts of the Medieval Interpretations of Ovid's Metamorphoses*, in *Scriptorium*, 44 (1990), pp. 272-275.

[728] COULSON, Frank T., *The "Vulgate" Commentary on Ovid's "Metamorphoses". The Creation Myth and the Story of Orpheus. Ed. from Sélestat, Bibliothèque humaniste, MS. 92*. Toronto 1991 (Toronto Medieval Latin Texts, 20).

[729] COULSON, F.T. & U. MOLYVIATI-TOPTSIS, *Vaticanus Latinus 2877: A Hitherto Unedited Allegorization of Ovid's "Metamorphoses"*, in *The Journal of Medieval Latin*, 2 (1992), pp. 134-202 [s. XIV m.].

[730] DEMATS, Paule, *Fabula. Trois études de mythographie antique et médiévale*. Geneva 1973 (Publications romanes et françaises, 122).

[731] DONNINI, M., *L'accessus Ovidii epistularum del cod. Asis. Bibl. Civ. 302*, in *Giornale italiano di filologia*, 31 (1979), pp. 121-129.

[732] ELLIOTT, A.G., *Accessus ad auctores: Twelft-Century Introductions to Ovid*, in *Allegorica*, 5 (1980), pp. 12-17 [Mostly translations of `accessus` into English].

[733] ENGELBRECHT, W., *"Bursarii Ovidianorum"—ein Ovid-Kommentar des Wilhelm von Orléans (um 1200)*, in *Mittellateinisches Jahrbuch*, 26 (1991), pp. 357-358.

[734] GANZ, P.F., *"Archani celestis non ignorans". Ein unbekannter Ovid-Kommentar*, in *Verbum et signum. Beiträge zur mediävistischen Bedeutungsforschung. Friedrich Ohly zum 60. Geburtstag überreicht*, vol. I. Munich 1975, pp. 195-208 [Oxford, Bodl. Libr., Bodl. 807].

[735] GHISALBERTI, F., *Arnolfo d'Orléans, un cultore di Ovidio nel sec. XII*, in *Memorie del R. Istituto Lombardo di scienze e lettere*, 24 (1932), pp. 157-234.

[736] GHISALBERTI, F., *Giovanni del Virgilio, espositore delle "Metamorfosi"*, in *Giornale dantesco*, 34 (1933), pp. 1-110.

[737] GHISALBERTI, F., *Mediaeval Biographies of Ovid*, in *Journal of the Warburg and Courtauld Institutes*, 9 (1946), pp. 10-59.

[738] GHISALBERTI, F., *Il commentario medioevale all'"Ovidius maior" consultato da Dante*, in *Rendiconti dell'Istituto lombardo. Classe di Lettere, scienze morali e storiche*, 100 (1966), pp. 267-275.

[739] GIOVANNI DI GARLANDIA, *Integumenta Ovidii, poemetto inedito del secolo XIII*, a cura di Fausto GHISALBERTI. Messina & Milan 1933 (Testi e documenti inediti o rari, 2).

[740] GUTHMÜLLER, B., *Lateinische und volkssprachliche Kommentare zu Ovids "Metamorphosen"*, in *Der Kommentar in der Renaissance*, hrsg. v. August Buck & Otto Herding. Boppard 1975 (Kommission für Humanismusforschung. Mitteilung 1), pp. 119-140.

[741] HAURÉAU, B., *Mémoire sur un commentaire des Métamorphoses d'Ovide*, in *Mémoires de l'Institut national de France. Académie des inscriptions et belles-lettres*, 30 (1881), pp. 45-55.

[742] HEXTER, R.J., *Ovid and Medieval Schooling. Studies in Medieval School Commentaries on Ovid's "Ars amatoria", "Epistulae ex Ponto" and "Epistulae Heroidum"*. Munich 1986 (Münchener Beiträge zur Mediävistik und Renaissance-Forschung, 38).

[743] JAHNKE, R., *Eine neue Ovid-Vita*, in *Rheinisches Museum*, 47 (1892), pp. 460-462.

[744] LEOTTA, R., *Un accessus ovidiano*, in *Giornale italiano di filologia*, 33 (1981), pp. 141-144 [Vatican, Vat. lat. 11597].

[745] LO MONACO, F., *Dal commento medievale al commento umanistico: il caso dei "Fasti" di Ovidio*, in *Studi italiani di filologia classica*. 85, = 3ª s., 10 (1992), pp. 848-860 (= *Giornate pisane. Atti del IX congresso della F.I.E.C., 24-30 agosto 1989*, vol. II).

[746] MEISER, C., *Über einen Commentar zu den Metamorphosen des Ovid*, in *Sitzungsberichte der Königl. Bayerischen Akademie der Wissenschaften. Philosophisch-philologische und historische Classe*, 1885, pp. 47-89 [Munich, Bayerische Staatsbibl., Clm 4610].

[747] MEYER, R.T., *Coll. Cambridge, MS No. 280 of the "Fasti" of Ovid*, in *Linguistic and Literary Studies in Honor of Helmut H. Hatzfeld*. Washington (D.C.) 1964, pp. 255-262 [Cambridge, Pembroke Coll., 280].

[748] MUNARI, Franco, *Il codice Hamilton 471 di Ovidio (Ars amatoria—Remedia amoris—Amores)*, in appendice *Pontano's Marginalia in Berlin, Hamilton 471*, by B.L. ULLMAN. Rome 1965 (Note e discussioni erudite, 9) [Berlin, Deutsche Staatsbibl., Hamilton 471].

[749] NOGARA, B., *Di alcune vite e commenti medioevali di Ovidio*, in *Miscellanea Ceriani*. Milan 1910, pp. 415-431.

[750] POLIZIANO, Angelo, *Commento inedito all'Epistola ovidiana di Saffo a Faone*, a cura di Elisabetta LAZZERI. Florence 1971 (Istituto Nazionale di studi sul Rinascimento. Studi e testi, 2).

[751] POLIZIANO, Angelo, *Commento inedito ai Fasti di Ovidio*, a cura di Francesco LO MONACO. Florence 1991 (Istituto nazionale di studi sul Rinascimento. Studi e testi, 23).

[752] PRETE, S., *Osservazioni sul commento ai Fasti di Ovidio dell'umanista Antonio Costanzi*, in *Cultura, poesia, ideologia nell'opera di Ovidio*, a cura di I. Gallo & L. Nicastri. Naples 1991 (Pubbl. dell'Univ. degli studi di Salerno. Sez. Atti, convegni, miscellanee, 33), pp. 213-220 [Rome, 1489].

[753] ROSA, L., *Su alcuni commenti inediti alle opere di Ovidio*, in *Annali della Facoltà di lettere e filosofia della Università di Napoli*, 5 (1955), pp. 191-231.

[754] ROSA, L., *Due biografie medievali di Ovidio*, in *La parola del passato*, 13 (1958), pp. 168-172.

[755] ROY, Bruno, *L'art d'amours. Traduction et commentaire de l'"Ars amatoria" d'Ovide. Edition critique*. Leiden 1974.

[756] *Scholia in P. Ovidii Nasonis Ibin*, a cura di A. LA PENNA. Florence 1959 (Biblioteca di studi superiori. Filologia latina, 35).

[757]   SEDLMAYER, H.S., *Beiträge zur Geschichte der Ovidstudien im Mittelalter*, in *Wiener Studien*, 6 (1884), pp. 142-158.

[758]   SENIS, G., *Le "Narrationes ovidianae" e il cod. Neap. IV F 3*, in *Maia*, 42 (1990), pp. 167-178.

[759]   SHOONER, H.-V., *Les Bursarii Ovidianorum de Guillaume d'Orléans*, in *Mediaeval Studies*, 43 (1981), pp. 405-424.

[760]   YOUNG, K., *Chaucer's Appeal to the Platonic Deity*, in *Speculum*, 19 (1944), pp. 1-13.

Palladius

[761]   RODGERS, R.H., *Palladius Rutilius Taurus Aemilianus*, in *Catalogus Translationum et Commentariorum*, 3 (1976), pp. 195-199 [Antonius Urceus 'Codrus', Philippus Beroaldus].

Persius

[762]   *AULI PERSII FLACCI satirarum liber, cum scholiis antiquis*, edidit Otto JAHN. Leipzig 1843 (reprint: Hildesheim 1967).

[763]   BERGER, A., *Zum sogenannten Cornuti Commentum*, in *Wiener Studien*, 32 (1911), pp. 157-158.

[764]   BISCHOFF, B., *Anonymus Leodiensis (c. 1077-80)*, in *Catalogus Translationum et Commentariorum*, vol. III (1976), pp. 239-243 [St. Gall, Stiftsbibl., 868].

[765]   ELDER, J.P., *A Mediaeval Cornutus on Persius*, in *Speculum*, 22 (1947), pp. 240-248.

[766]   GHISALBERTI, F., *Paolo da Perugia, commentatore di Persio*, in *Rendiconti del Reale Istituto Lombardo di scienze e lettere*, ser. IIª, 62 (1929), pp. 535-598 [Cremona, Bibl. Gov., 109, s. XV in].

[767]   HÖHLER, W., *Die Cornutus-Scholien*, in *Jahrbücher für classische Philologie*, 23 (1897), pp. 379-442.

[768]   IANNACCONE, S., *Rapporti di codici nella tradizione degli scolii a Persio*, in *Giornale italiano di filologia*, 12 (1959), pp. 198-213.

[769]   IANNACCONE, S., *Il codice inedito "Londinensis British Museum Additional 15601" (sec. X-XI in.) e la scoliografia alle Satire di Persio*, in *Quaderni dell'Istituto di lingua e letteratura latina (Università degli studi di Roma "La Sapienza". Facoltà di magistero)*, 4 (1982), pp. 29-40.

[770]   IANNACCONE, S., *Glosse e scolii inediti alle Satire di Persio nel codice "Oxoniensis Bibl. Bodleianae Auct. F 1, 15"*, in *Giornale italiano di filologia*, 36, = n.s. 15 (1985), pp. 105-119.

[771]   KURZ, E., *Die Persius-Scholien nach Berner Handschriften (mit den Scholien zum Prolog und zur ersten Satira und der Vita Persii)*. Burgdorf 1875 (Beilage zum Jahresbericht des Burgdorfer Gymnasiums für 1875).

[772]   KURZ, E., *A. Über den Octavius des Minucius Felix. B. Die Persius-Scholien nach den Berner Handschriften. II. Die Scholien zu Sat. II und III, nebst dem Text von Sat. II und III, nach Cod. Bern. 257*. Burgdorf 1888 (Beilage zum Jahresbericht über das Gymnasium in Burgdorf am Schlusse des Schuljahres 1887/88).

[773]   KURZ, E., *Die Persius-Scholien nach den Berner Handschriften III. Die Scholien zu Sat. IV-VI*. Burgdorf 1889 (Beilage zum Jahresbericht über das Gymnasium in Burgdorf am Schlusse des Schuljahres 1889).

[774]   LANGBROEK, E., *Die althochdeutschen Glossen des Codex Adv. Ms. 18.5.10 der National Library of Scotland Edinburg (2)*, in *Amsterdamer Beiträge zur älteren Germanistik*, 19 (1983), pp. 79-104.

[775]   LIEBL, Hans, *Beiträge zu den Persius-Scholien*. Straubing 1883 (Programm

der k. b. Studien-Anstalt Straubing für das Studienjahr 1882-1883).

[776]   MANITIUS, M., *Zur lateinischen Scholienliteratur. I. Zur Vita und den Scholien des Persius*, in *Philologus*, 64 (1905), pp. 567-569 [Munich, Bayerische Staatsbibl., Clm 14490].

[777]   MARCHESI, Concetto, *Gli scoliasti di Persio*, in his *Scritti minori di filologia e di letteratura*, vol. II. Florence 1978, pp. 907-983.

[778]   MARIANI, F., *Persio nella scuola di Auxerre e l'"Adnotatio secundum Remigium"*, in *Giornale italiano di filologia*, 18 (1965), pp.145-161.

[779]   PIRRONE, N., *Thomae Schiphaldi commentaria atque Persii et Horatii vitae ex eis sublatae*, in *Atti dell'Accademia Properziana di Assisi*, 2 (1905) [a. 1461].

[780]   POLIZIANO, Angelo, *Commento inedito alle Satire di Persio*, a cura di Lucia CESARINI MARTINELLI & Roberto RICCIARDI. Florence 1985 (Istituto nazionale di studi sul Rinascimento. Studi e testi, 11).

[781]   PRÉAUX, J., *Propositions sur l'histoire des textes des "Satires" de Perse et du "Commentum Cornuti"*, in *Hommages à André Boutemy*. Brussels 1976, pp. 299-314.

[782]   RAMORINO, F., *De duobus Persii codicibus qui inter ceteros Laurentianae Bibliothecae servantur*, in *Studi italiani di filologia classica*, 12 (1904), pp. 229-260 [Florence, Bibl. Laur., Plut. 37.19 & 33.31].

[783]   ROBATHAN, D.M. & F.E. CRANZ, *A. Persius Flaccus*, in *Catalogus Translationum et Commentariorum*, 3 (1976), pp. 201-339 [Remigius Autissiodorensis, Ventura de Foro de Longulo, Johannes de Levedale, Magister Salibene, Paulus Perusinus, Franciscus de Butis, Sozomenus Pistoriensis, Guarinus Veronensis, Omnibonus Leonicenus, Thomas Schifaldus, Martinus Phileticus, Christophorus Landinus, Philippinus Italus, Johannes Lachus, Bartholomaeus Fontius, Johannes Britannicus, Raphael Regius, Johannes Baptista Cantalicius, Johannes Taberius, Antonius Volscus Pipernas, Jodocus Badius Ascensius].

[784]   SCARCIA PIACENTINI, Paola, *Saggio di un censimento dei manoscritti contenenti il testo di Persio e gli scoli e i commenti al testo*. Rome 1973 (Istituto di lingua e letteratura latina. Facoltà di lingue e letterature straniere. Università di Pisa. Studi su Persio e la scolastica persiana, Ser. 2).

[785]   SCARCIA PIACENTINI, Paola, *Corrigenda e addenda al censimento dei manoscritti, note bibliografiche, indici, concordantiae siglorum*. Rome 1975 (Studi su Persio e la scolastica persiana, 3, 2).

[786]   SCHOLZ, U.W., *Zur Persius-Kommentierung um 1500. Scholia und Kommentare*, in *Wissensorganisierende & wissensvermittelnde Literatur im Mittelalter*. Wiesbaden 1987, pp. 143-156.

[787]   SIEWERT, K., *Die althochdeutsche Persiusglossierung im Lichte neuer Quellen*, in *Althochdeutsch*, hrsg. v. R. Bergmann, H. Tiefenbach & L. Voetz, vol. I. Heidelberg 1987, pp. 608-624.

[788]   STAMPACCHIA, G., *Gli scoli a Persio*, in *Studi sulla tradizione di Persio e la scolastica persiana*, 2 (Rome 1972), pp. 61-89.

[789]   THOMAS, *Miscellen aus Handschriften der Münchener Staatsbibliothek. 1. Zu Persius*, in *Sitzungsberichte der königl. Bayerischen Akademie der Wissenschaften. Philosophisch-philologische und historische Klasse*, 1863 (II), pp. 254-260 [Munich, Bayerische Staatsbibl., Clm 19477].

[790]   UCCELLI, P.A., *Un foglio di Persio con commenti del XIII secolo*, in *Archivio storico italiano*, 22 (1875), pp. 138-156.

[791]   WESSNER, P., *Zu den Persius-Scholien*, in *Wochenschrift für klassische Philologie*, 34 (1917), pp. 473-480, 496-502.

[792]   ZETZEL, J.E.G., *On the History of Latin Scholia II. The "Commentum Cornuti" in the Ninth Century*, in *Mediaevalia et Humanistica* 10 (1981), pp. 19-31.

[793]   ZINGERLE, A., *Zu den Persius-Scholien*, in *Sitzungsberichte der k. Academie der Wissenschaften Wien. Philos.-hist. Classe*, 97 (1881), pp. 731 ss.

Petronius
[794]   SOCHATOFF, F., *Petronius Arbiter*, in *Catalogus Translationum et Commentario-rum*, 3 (1976), pp. 313-339.

Plautus
[795]   CAPPELLETTO, Rita, *La 'Lectura Plauti' del Pontano con edizione delle postille del cod. Vindob. lat. 3168 e osservazioni sull'"Itala recensio"*. Urbino 1988.

Pliny (the Elder)
[796]   NAUERT, C.G., *Caius Plinius Secundus*, in *Catalogus Translationum et Com-mentariorum*, 4 (1980), pp. 297-422 [Ludovicus de Guastis, Nicolaus Pe-rottus, Cornelius Vitellius, Philippus Beroaldus the Elder, Bartholomaeus Platina, Raphael Regius, Hermolaus Barbarus, Marcus Antonius Coc-cius, called Sabellicus, Robertus de Valle, Georgius Valla, Marinus Beci-chemus].

Priscian
[797]   DE MARCO, M., *Un nuovo codice del Commentum di Remigio d'Auxerre alle "Par-titiones duodecim versuum Aeneidos principalium" di Prisciano*, in *Aevum*, 26 (1952), pp. 465-466.
[798]   FREDBORG, K.M., *The Dependence of Petrus Helias "Summa super Priscianum" on William of Conches "Glose super Priscianum"*, in *Cahiers de l'Institut du Moyen Age grec et latin*, 27 (1960), pp. 212-247.
[799]   GIBSON, M., *The Early Scholastic "Glosule" to Priscian, "Institutiones Gram-maticae": the Text and its Influence*, in *Studi medievali*, 20 (1979), pp. 235-254.
[799a] GIBSON, M., *Milestones in the Study of Priscian, circa 800—circa 1200*, in *Via-tor*, 23 (1992), pp. 17-33.
[800]   GLÜCK, Manfred, *Priscians Partitiones und ihre Stellung in der spätantike Schule. Mit einer Beilage: Commentarii in Prisciani Partitiones medio aevo compositi*. Hildesheim 1967 (Spudasmata, 12) [Remigius Autissiodorensis].
[801]   HUNT, R.W., *Studies on Priscian in the Eleventh and Twelfth Centuries, I*, in *Mediaeval and Renaissance Studies*, 1 (1941-1943), pp. 194-231; *Studies on Priscian in the Twelfth Century. II*, in *Mediaeval and Renaissance Studies*, 2 (1950), pp. 1-56 (= his *The History of Grammar in the Middle Ages*. Amsterdam 1980, pp. 1-94).
[802]   JEAUNEAU, É., *Deux rédactions des gloses de Guillaume de Conches sur Priscien*, in *Recherches de théologie ancienne et médiévale*, 27 (1960), pp. 212-247 (= Édouard JEAUNEAU, *"Lectio philosophorum". Recherches sur l'école de Chartres*. Amsterdam 1973, pp. 335-370).
[803]   JEUDY, C., *La tradition manuscrite des "Partitiones" de Priscien et la version longue du commentaire de Rémi d'Auxerre*, in *Revue d'histoire des textes*, 1 (1971), pp. 123-143.
[804]   JEUDY, C., *L'"Institutio de nomine, praenomine et verbo" de Priscien: manuscrits et commentaires médiévaux*, in *Revue d'histoire des textes*, 2 (1972), pp. 73-144.
[805]   JEUDY, C., *A Glossed Manuscript of Priscian's "Institutio"*, Vatican, MS Reg. Lat. 1578, in *Intellectual Life in the Middle Ages. Essays Presented to Margaret Gibson*. London & Rio Grande 1992, pp. 61-70.
[806]   PETRUS HELIAS, *(ca. 1100-1166?) Summa super Priscianum*, edited by Leo REILLY. Vol. I-II. Toronto 1993 (Pontifical Institute of Mediaeval Stu-dies. Studies and Texts, 113).
[806a] SEDVLIVS SCOTTVS, *In Donati artem minorem, In Priscianum, In Eutychem*, edidit Bengt LÖFSTEDT. Turnhout 1977 (Corpus Christianorum. Con-tinuatio Mediaeualis, 40C).

Properzio
[806b] COPPINI, D., *Il commento a Properzio di D. Calderini*, in *Annali della Scuola Normale Superiore di Pisa*, ser. III, 9 (1979), pp. 1119-1173.

Quintilian
[807] ACCAME LANZILLOTTA, Maria, *Le postille del Petrarca a Quintiliano (Cod. Parigino lat. 7720)*. Florence 1989 (Quaderni petrarcheschi, 5).
[808] CESARINI MARTINELLI, L., *Le postille di Lorenzo Valla all'"Institutio oratoria" di Quintiliano*, in *Lorenzo Valla e l'umanesimo italiano. Atti del Convegno internazionale di studi umanistici (Parma, 18-19 ottobre 1984)*. Padua 1986, pp. 21-50.
[809] PEROSA, A., *L'edizione veneta di Quintiliano coi commenti del Valla, di Pomponio Leto e di Sulpizio da Veroli*, in *Miscellanea Augusto Campana*, vol. II. Padua 1981, pp. 575-610 [Venice 1493 & 1494].

Sallust
[809a] CORTESI, M., *Per il commento a Sallustio di Lorenzo Valla*, in *Res Publica Litterarum*, 14 (1991), pp. 49-59,
[810] HEDICKE, E., *Scholia in Caesarem et Sallustium*. Quedlinburg 1879 (Progr. Gymn. Quedlinburg) [Paris, Bibl. Nat., lat. 6253].
[811] MOLLWEIDE, Richard, *Über die Glossen zu Sallust*. Strasbourg 1888 (Lyceum zu Strassburg in Elsass. Beilage zum Programm für das Schuljahr 1887-1888) [Munich, Bayerische Staatsbibl., Clm 14515].

Seneca
[812] BILLANOVICH, G., *Abozzi e postille del Mussato nel Vaticano lat. 1769*, in *Italia medioevale e umanistica*, 28 (1985), pp. 7-35.
[813] CLAIRMONT, R., *A Commentary on Seneca's Apocolocyntosis Divi Claudii*. Chicago 1980.
[814] CLAIRMONT, R. E., *Glose in librum de ludo Claudii Annei Senece*, in *Rivista di cultura classica e medioevale*, 16 (1974), pp. 235-266.
[815] CODOÑER, C., *Un nuevo manuscrito del comentario de G. Barzizza a las Epístolas de Séneca*, in *Emerita*, 55 (1987), pp. 265-271 [Salamanca, Bibl. Univ., 12]
[816] DE MARCO, M., *Sulla fortuna di un commento alle tragedie di Seneca*, in *Aevum*, 30 (1956), pp. 363-368.
[817] DUERING, T., *Zur Überlieferung von Seneka's Tragödien. II. Der Kommentar des N. Treveth (um 1315) und sein Verhältnis zu C.*, Lingen 1913 (Beilage zum Programm des königlichen Gymnasium Georgianum zu Lingen. Ostern 1913).
[818] FABRIS, V., *Il commento di Nicola Trevet all'"Hercules furens" di Seneca*, in *Aevum*, 27 (1953), pp. 498-509.
[819] FRANCESCHINI, E., *Il commento di Nicola Trevet al Tieste di Seneca. Testo critico*. Milan 1938 (Orbis romanus, 11).
[820] FRANCESCHINI, E., *Glosse e commenti medievali a Seneca tragico*, in his *Studi e note di filologia latina medievale*. Milan 1938 (Pubblicazioni dell'Università Cattolica del Sacro Cuore, ser. IVª, Scienze filologiche, 30), pp. 1-105.
[820a] GIANNOZZO MANETTI, *Vita Socratis et Senecae*. Introduzione, testo e apparati a cura di Alfonso de PETRIS. Florence 1979.
[821] HIJMANS, B.L., *Two Seneca Manuscripts and a Commentary*, in *Mnemosyne*, 21 (1968), pp. 240-253 [Copenhagen, Det kgl. Bibliotek, Ny kgl. S. 57 b 2°; Vatican, Pal. lat. 1541].
[822] KAEPPELI, Th., *Luca Mannelli († 1362) e la sua Tabulatio et expositio Senecae*,

in *Archivum Fratrum Praedicatorum*, 18 (1948), pp. 249-250.

[823] McGregor, A., *Mussato's Commentary on Seneca's Tragedies. New Fragments*, in *Illinois Classical Studies*, 5 (1980), pp. 149-162.

[824] Megas, Anastasios X., *Albertini Mussati, Argumenta tragoediarum Senecae. Commentarii in L.A. Senecae tragoedias fragmenta nuper reperta*. Saloniki 1969.

[825] Nicola Trevet, *Commento alle "Troades" di Seneca*, a cura di Marco Palma. Rome 1977 (Temi e testi, 22).

[826] Nicolai Treveti *Expositio Herculis Furentis*, ed. Vincentius Ussani, vol. II. Rome 1959 (Biblioteca degli scrittori greci e latini).

[827] Nicolai Treveti *Expositio L. Annaei Senecae Agamemnonis*, ed. Petrus Meloni. Palermo 1961 (Università di Cagliari. Facoltà di lettere e di magistero, 3).

[828] Nicolai Treveti *Expositio L. Annaei Senecae Herculis Oetaei*, ed. Petrus Meloni. Palermo 1962 (Università di Cagliari. Facoltà di lettere e di magistero, 7).

[829] Palma, M., *Note sulla storia di un codice di Seneca tragico col commento di Nicola Trevet (Vat. lat. 1650)*, in *Italia medioevale e umanistica*, 16 (1973), pp. 317-322.

[830] Panizza, L.A., *Gasparino Barzizza's Commentaries on Seneca's Letters*, in *Traditio*, 33 (1977), pp.. 297-358,

[831] Panizza, L.A., *Textual Interpretation in Italy, 1350-1450: Seneca's Letter I to Lucilius*, in *Journal of the Warburg and Courtauld Institutes*, 46 (1983), pp. 40-62.

[832] Pascal, C., *Glosse giuridiche ai Dialoghi di Seneca*, in *Bolletino di filologia classica*, 13 (1906), pp. 13-16 [Milano, Bibl. Ambros., C 90 inf.].

[833] Russo, C.F., *Glose in librum De ludo Claudii Annei Senecae*, in *La parola del passato*, 7 (1952), pp. 48-65 [Oxford, Bodl. Libr., Bodl. 192].

[834] Questa, C., *"Accessus" medioevali al "De moribus" dello Pseudo-Seneca*, in *Rivista di cultura classica e medioevale*, 2 (1960), pp. 183-190.

[835] Villa, C., *La tradizione dell'Ad Lucilium' e la cultura di Brescia dall'età carolingia ad Albertano*, in *Italia medioevale e umanistica*, 12 (1969), pp. 9-51.

Serenus Sammonicus (Quintus)

[836] Reuss, F.A., *Lectionum Samonicearum particula I*. Würtzburg 1836 (Lectiones de scientiarum naturalium historia per semestre hyemale MDCCCXXXVI-XXXVII habendas...) [Zürich, Zentralbibl., C. 78].

Silius Italicus

[837] Bassett, E.L., J. Delz & A.J. Dunston, *Silius Italicus, Tiberius Catius Asconius*, in *Catalogus Translationum et commentariorum*, 3 (1976), pp. 341-398 [Sicco Polentonus, Marcellus Virgilius Adrianus, Petrus Odus Montopolitanus, Iulius Pomponius Laetus, Domitius Calderinus, Petrus Marsus].

[838] Dunston, A.J., *Studies in Domizio Calderini*, in *Italia medioevale e umanistica*, 11 (1968), pp. 71-150 [pp. 86-106: *Calderini and the "Punica" of Silius Italicus*].

Statius

[839] Brugnoli, G., *Due note dantesche*, in *Rivista di cultura classica e medioevale*, 7 (1965), pp. 246-251.

[840] Cesarini Martinelli, L., *In margine al commento di Angelo Poliziano alle "Selve" di Stazio*, in *Interpres*, 1 (1978), pp. 96-145.

[841] Cesarini Martinelli, L., *Un ritrovamento polizianesco: il fascicolo perduto del commento alle Selve di Stazio*, in *Rinascimento*, ser. II^a, 22 (1982), pp. 183-212 [Florence, Bibl. Naz., II.I.99].

[842] Clogan, P.M., *A Preliminary List of Anonymous Glosses on Statius' Achilleid*, in *Manuscripta*, 9 (1965), pp. 104-109.

[843] Clogan, P.M., *Medieval Glossed Mss of the Thebaid*, in *Manuscripta*, 11 (1967), pp. 102-112.

[844]   CLOGAN, P.M., *The Mss of Lactantius Placidus' Commentary on the Thebaid*, in *Scriptorium*, 22 (1968), pp. 87-91.
[845]   CLOGAN, P.M., *The Latin Commentaries to Statius. A Bibliographical Project*, in *Acta Conventus Neo Latini Lovaniensis*. Munich & Leuven 1973, pp. 149-157.
[846]   CLOGAN, P.M., *Lactantius Placidus' Commentary on the "Thebaid"*, in *Acta Conventus Neo-Latini Guelpherbytani*. Binghamton (N.Y.) 1988, pp. 25-32.
[847]   CLOGAN, P.M., *The Renaissance Commentators on Statius*, in *Acta Conventus Neo-Latini Torontonensis*. Binghamton (N.Y.) 1991, pp. 689-696.
[848]   DE ANGELIS, V., *Petrarca, Stazio, Liegi*, in *Studi petrarcheschi*, n.s. 2 (1985), pp. 53-84.
[849]   DE ANGELIS, V., *Un apografo del Virgilio ambrosiano*, in *Studi petrarcheschi*, n.s. 3 (1986), pp. 203-233 [Vatican, Reg. lat. 1828].
[850]   FUNAIOLI, C., *Da un codice di Valenciennes*, in *Studi italiani di filologia classica*, 21 (1915), pp. 1-73.
[851]   JAKOBI, R., *Versprengungen in den Statius-Scholien*, in *Hermes*, 120 (1992), pp. 364-374.
[852]   KLOTZ, A., *Die Statiusscholien*, in *Philologus*, 33 (1874), pp. 485-525.
[853]   KOHLMANN, P., *Neue Scholien zur Thebais des Statius aus einer Pariser Handschrift*. Posen 1873 (Programm des kgl. Friedrich-Wilhelms-Gymnasium zu Posen für das Schuljahr 1872/73) [Paris, Bibl. Nat., lat. 10317].
[854]   KOHLMANN, P., *Beiträge zur Kritik der Statius-Scholiasten*, in *Philologus*, 33 (1874), pp. 128-138.
[855]   LANDI, C., *Di un commento medievale inedito della "Tebaide" di Stazio*, in *Atti e memorie dell'Accademia di scienze e lettere di Padova*, 30 (1914), pp. 315-344 [Padua, Seminario, 41]
[856]   *The Mediaeval Achilleid of Statius*, ed. with Introduction, Variant Readings, and Glosses by Paul M. CLOGAN. Leiden 1968.
[857]   POLIZIANO, Angelo, *Commento inedito alle "Selve" di Stazio*, a cura di L. CESARINI MARTINELLI. Florence 1978 (Istituto Nazionale di Studi sul Rinascimento. Studi e testi, 5).
[858]   STOCK, B., *A Note on Thebaid Commentaries. Paris, B.N. lat. 3012*, in *Traditio*, 27 (1971), pp. 468-471.
[859]   SWEENEY, R.D., *Prolegomena to an Edition of the Scholia to Statius*. Leiden 1969 (Mnemosyne. Supplementum, 8)
[860]   VAN DE WOESTIJNE, P., *Les scolies à la Thébaïde de Stace. Remarques et suggestions*, in *Antiquité classique*, 19 (1950), pp. 149-163.
[861]   WASSERSTEIN, A., *Politian's Commentary on the Silvae of Statius*, in *Scriptorium*, 10 (1956), pp. 83-89.

Suetonius
[862]   FERA, V., *Una ignota "Expositio Suetoni" del Poliziano*. Messina 1983.
[863]   FERA, V., *Tra Poliziano e Beroaldo: l'ultimo scritto filologico di Giorgio Merula*, in *Studi umanistici*, 2 (1991), pp. 7-88.
[864]   IHM, M., *Beiträge zur Textgeschichte des Sueton. 2. Glossen in Suetonhandschriften*, in *Hermes*, 36 (1901), pp. 356-363.
[865]   McGRATH, G.K., *An Unknown Fourteenth-Century Commentary on Suetonius and Caesar*, in *Classical Philology*, 65 (1970), pp. 182-185 [Vatican, Barb. lat., 148].

Terentius
[866]   ÁBEL, J., *Az ó-és középkori Terentiusbiographiák*, in *Értekezések à nyelv-és széptudományok köréből*, 14 (1887), pp. 36-62.
[867]   BALLAIRA, G., *Praefatio "Monacensis" ad Terentium quae integra in Cod. Vat. lat. 11455*

asservatur, in *Bollettino del Comitato per la preparazione dell'edizione nazionale dei classici greci e latini*, n.s. 16 (1968), pp. 13-24.

[868] BILLANOVICH, G., *I commenti a Terenzio di Giacomino Robazzi e di Pietro da Moglio*, in *Italia medioevale e umanistica*, 17 (1974), pp. 15-42.

[869] BOZZOLO, C., *Laurent de Premierfait et Térence*, in *Vestigia. Studi in onore di Giuseppe Billanovich*, vol. I. Rome 1984, pp. 93-129.

[870] DZIATZKO, K., *Zu Terentius im Mittelalter*, in *Neue Jahrbücher für Philologie und Paedagogik*, 149 (1894), pp. 465-477 [Munich, Bayerische Staatsbibl., Clm 14420].

[871] GRAFTON, A., *Pietro Bembo and the "Scholia Bembina"*, in *Italia medioevale e umanistica*, 24 (1981), pp. 405-408.

[872] GRANT, J.N., *The "Commentum Monacense" and the MS Tradition of Terence*, in *Manuscripta*, 22 (1978), pp. 83-90.

[872a] IACOBI CURULI *Epitoma Donati in Terentium*. Edizione critica a cura di Giuseppe GERMANO. Naples 1987

[873] KALINKA, E., *Analecta latina I. Scholia ad Terentium*, in *Wiener Studien*, 16 (1894), pp. 78-85 [Paris, Bibl. Nat., lat. 12322 + 12244].

[874] LAMMERT, F., *Zu den Terentiusscholien*, in *Jahresbericht über die Fortschritte der klassischen Altertumswissenschaft*, 231 (1931), pp. 82-85.

[875] POLIZIANO, Angelo, *La commedia antica e l'Andria di Terenzio*. Appunti inediti a cura di R. LATTANZI ROSELLI. Florence 1973 (Istituto nazionale di studi sul Rinascimento. Studi e testi, 3).

[876] RAND, E.K., *Early Medieval Commentaries on Terence*, in *Classical Philology*, 4 (1909), pp. 359-389.

[877] RIOU, Y.-F., *Essai sur la tradition manuscrite du "Commentum Brunsianum" des Comédies de Térence*, in *Revue d'histoire des textes*, 3 (1973), pp. 79-113.

[878] RIOU, Y.-F., *Le "Commentum Brunsianum" des Comédies de Térence et les gloses des manuscrits "Vaticanus" (3868) et "Basilicanus" (H 19)*, in Y.-F. RIOU & C. JEUDY, *Tradition textuelle et commentaire des auteurs classiques latins conservés dans les manuscrits de la Bibliothèque Vaticane*, in *Settimane di studio del Centro di studi sull'alto medioevo*, 22 (1975), pp. 183-189.

[879] RIOU, Y.-F., *Le "Commentum Brunsianum" des Comédies de Térence dans le Clm 29004 c*, in *Mélanges André Boutemy*. Brussels 1976, pp. 325-323 [Munich, Bayerische Staatsbibl., Clm 29214/3].

[880] RIOU, Y.-F., *Gloses et commentaires des Comédies de Térence dans les manuscrits de la bibliothèque du monastère San Lorenzo el Real de l'Escorial*, in *Lettres latines du moyen âge et de la Renaissance*, recueil édité par G. Cambier, C. Deroux, J. Préaux. Brussels, 1978 (Collection Latomus, 158), pp. 5-55.

[881] SABBADINI, R., *Biografi e commentatori di Terenzio (Un nuovo codice del commento di Donato a Terenzio; Emendamenti agli scolii terenziani di Donato; Una biografia di Terenzio e un trattato sulla commedia; Altre biografie di Terenzio; Commenti medievali a Terenzio)*, in *Studi italiani di filologia classica*, 5 (1897), pp. 289-327.

[882] SABBADINI, R., *Giacomino da Mantova commentatore di Terenzio*, in *Atti e memorie della Accademia virgiliana di Mantova*, n.s. 8 (1915), pp. 3-19.

[883] SCHLEE, F., *Scholia Terentiana*. Leipzig 1893.

[884] STUDEMUND, W., *Über die Editio Princeps der Terenz-Scholien des Codex Bembinus*, in *Neue Jahrbücher für Philologie und Paedagogik*, 97 (1868), pp. 546-571.

[885] VILLA, C., *Petrarca e Terenzio*, in *Studi petrarcheschi*, n.s. 6 (1989), pp. 1-22.

[886] WARREN, M., *Unpublished Scholia from the Vaticanus (C) of Terence*, in *Harvard Studies in Classical Philology*, 12 (1901), pp. 125-136 [Vatican, Vat. lat. 3868].

[887] WESSNER, P., *Die Donatscholien des Codex Parisinus 7899 (P) des Terenz*, in *Philologische Wochenschrift*, 41 (1921), col. 428-432, 449-455.
[888] WESSNER, P., *Zu den Donatauszügen in Codex Victorinus (D) des Terenz*, in *Philologische Wochenschrift*, 47 (1927), col. 443-448.

Valerius Flaccus
[889] SABBADINI, R., *Del commento di Pomponio Leto a Valerio Flacco*, in *Bollettino di filologia classica*, 2 (1895-1896), pp. 165-166.

Valerius Maximus
[890] BERLINCOURT, A., *The Relationship of Some Fourteenth Century Commentaries on Valerius Maximus*, in *Mediaeval Studies*, 34 (1972), pp. 362-387.
[891] DE MARCO, M., *Un nuovo codice del commento di Frater Petrus a Valerio Massimo*, in *Aevum*, 30 (1956), pp. 554-558.
[892] DI STEFANO, G., *Per la fortuna di Valerio Massimo nel Trecento: le glosse di Pietro da Monteforte ed il commento di Dionigi di Borgo S. Sepolcro*, in *Atti della Accademia delle scienze di Torino*, 96 (1961-1962), pp. 272-314.
[893] DI STEFANO, G., *Tradizione esegetica e traduzioni di Valerio Massimo nel primo umanesimo francese*, in *Studi francesi*, 21 (1963), pp. 401-417 [Pierre Hérard de Reims].
[894] DI STEFANO, G., *La diffusion de Valère-Maxime au XIVe siècle: le commentaire attribué à Frater Lucas*, in *Acta conventus Neo-Latini Lovaniensis*. Munich & Leuven 1973, pp. 219-227.
[895] FOHLEN, J., *Les deux accessus de l'"Epitome" de Iulius Paris*, in *Revue d'histoire des textes*, 1 (1971), pp. 211-213.
[896] KOHL, B.G., *Valerius Maximus in the Fourteenth Century: The Commentary of Giovanni Conversini da Ravenna*, in *Acta Conventus Neo-latini Hafniensis. Proceedings of the Eighth International Congress of Neo-Latin Studies. Copenhagen 12 August to 17 August 1991*. Binghamton (N.Y.) 1994, pp. 537-546.
[897] LARKIN, John William, *A Critical Edition of the First Book of the Commentary of Dionigi da Borgo San Sepolcro on the "Facta and Dicta Memorabilia urbis Romae" of Valerius Maximus*. New York 1967 (Diss. Fordham University).
[898] SCHULLIAN, D.M., *Valerius Maximus*, in *Catalogus Translationum et Commentariorum*, 5 (1984), pp. 287-403 [Dionysius de Burgo Sancti Sepulchri, Milanus de Spoleto, Frater Lucas, Johannes Caballinus de Cerronibus, Conradus Waldhauser, Petrus de Muglio, Johannes de Ravenna, Lucas de Penna, Marzagaia, Benvenutus de Imola, Frater Petrus, Petrus Herardi, Johannes de Floremontis, Guarinus Veronensis, Pallacinus (Omnibonus Leonicenus?), Oliverius Arzignanensis].

Varro
[899] ACCAME LANZILLOTTA, M., *Il commento varroniano di Pomponio Leto*, in *Miscellanea greca e romana*, 15 (1990), pp. 309-345.
[900] BROWN, V., *Varro, Marcus Terentius*, in *Catalogus Translationum et Commentariorum*, 4 (1980), pp. 451-500.

Virgil
[901] ALESSIO, G.C., *Glossografia altomedievale alle Georgiche*, in *L'ambiente vegetale nell'alto medioevo*, vol. I. Spoleto 1990 (Settimane di studi del Centro italiano di studi sull'alto medioevo, 37, I), pp. 55-102.
[902] BARABINO, G., *Gli scholia del Virgilio di Tours [Bern, 165] e l'esegesi virgiliana di Nonio*, in *Studi Noniani*, 9 (Genoa 1984), pp. 9-34.
[903] BASWELL, Chr., *The Medieval Allegorization of the "Aeneid". Ms. Cambridge, Peterhouse 158*, in *Traditio*, 41 (1985), pp. 181-237.

[904]   BEESON, C.H., *Insular Symptoms in the Commentaries of Virgil*, in *Studi medievali*, n.s. 5 (1932), pp. 81-100.

[905]   BERSCHIN, W., *Glossierte Virgil-Handschriften dreier "Aetates virgilianae"*, in *The Role of the Book in Medieval Culture*, vol. II. Turnhout 1986, pp. 115-127.

[906]   BERTINI, F., *Interpreti medievali di Virgilio. Fulgenzio e Bernardo Silvestri*, in *Sandalion*, 6-7 (1983-1984), pp. 151-164.

[907]   BILLANOVICH, G., *L'Orazio Morgan e gli studi del giovane Petrarca*, in *Tradizione classica e letteratura umanistica. Per Alessandro Perosa*, vol. I. Rome 1985, pp. 121-138 [New York, Pierpont Morgan Library, M. 404].

[908]   BOUCHERIE, A., *Fragment d'un commentaire sur Virgile*. Montpellier 1875, pp. 7-25 [Montpellier, Faculté de Médecine, 358].

[909]   BROWN, V., *A Twelfth Century Virgilian Miscellany-Commentary of German Origin (Vatican Ms. Pal. lat. 1965)*, in *Scire litteras. Forschungen zum mittelalterlichen Geistesleben*. Munich 1988, pp. 73-86.

[910]   BROWN, V. & C. KALLENDORFF, *Two Humanist Annotators of Virgil: Coluccio Salutati and Giovanni Tortelli*, in *Supplementum Festivum. Studies in Honor of Paul Oskar Kristeller*. Binghamton (N.Y.) 1987, pp. 65-148 [Basle, Universitätsbibl., F II 23 & Oxford, Bodl. Libr., Auct. F.2.6].

[911]   CASTANO MUSICÒ, L., *Il commento di Angelo Poliziano alle Georgiche di Virgilio*, in *Materiali e discussioni per l'analisi dei testi classici*, 24 (1990), pp. 181-190 [Paris, Bibl. nat., Rés. g. Yc. 236].

[912]   CONTRENI, John J., *Codex Laudunensis 468. A Ninth Century Guide to Virgil, Sedulius and the Liberal Arts*. Turnhout 1984 (Armarium codicum insignium, 3).

[913]   CORMIER, R., *Early Medieval Glossed "Aeneid" Manuscripts*, in *Studi medievali*, 32 (1991), pp. 971-979.

[914]   DAINTREE, D., *Glosse irlandesi*, in *Enciclopedia Virgiliana*, vol. II. Rome 1985, pp. 774-776.

[915]   DE MARCO, M., *Un nuovo codice del commento di Bernardo Silvestris all'Eneide*, in *Aevum*, 28 (1954), pp. 178-183 [Paris, Bibl. Nat., lat. 3804 A].

[916]   DESMOND, M., *Bernard Silvestris and the "Corpus" of the "Aeneid"*, in *The Classics in the Middle Ages. Papers of the Twentieth Annual Conference of the Center for Medieval and Early Renaissance Studies*. Binghamton (N.Y.) 1990, pp. 129-139.

[917]   DIONIOSOTTI, C., *"Lavinia venit litora". Polemica virgiliana di M. Filetico*, in *Italia medioevale e umanistica*, 1 (1958), pp. 283-315.

[918]   DYCKMANS, M., *La "Vita Pomponiana" de Virgile*, in *Humanistica Lovaniensia*, 36 (1987), pp. 85-111.

[919]   DRONKE, P., *"Integumenta Virgilii"*, in *Lectures médiévales de Virgile. Actes du Colloque organisé par l'Ecole française de Rome (Rome, 25-28 octobre 1982)*. Rome 1985, pp. 313-329.

[920]   FASBENDER, J., *Die Schlettstädter Vergilglossen und ihre Verwandten*. Strasbourg 1907 (Diss.).

[921]   FIELD, A., *A Manuscript of Cristoforo Landino's First Lectures on Virgil, 1462-1463 (Codex 1368, Biblioteca Casanatense, Rome)*, in *Renaissance Quarterly*, 31 (1978), pp. 17-20.

[922]   FINCH, C.F., *Fragment of a New Vita Vergiliana in Codex Reg. lat. 1669*, in *American Journal of Philology*, 95 (1974), pp. 56-61.

[923]   FUNAIOLI, G., *Chiose e leggende virgiliane del medio evo*, in *Studi medievali*, n.s. 5 (1932), pp. 154-163 [Wolfenbüttel, Herzog August Bibl., 70 Gud. lat.].

[924]   GERSH, S., *(Pseudo-?) Bernard Silvestris and the Revival of Neoplatonic Virgilian Exegesis*, in ΣΟΦΙΗΣ ΜΑΙΗΤΟΡΕΣ. *"Chercheurs de sagesse". Hommages à Jean Pépin*. Paris 1992, pp. 573-593.

[925]   GEYMONAT, M., *Glosse*, in *Enciclopedia Virgiliana*, vol. II. Rome 1985, pp. 771-773.

[926]   GHISALBERTI, F., *Le chiose virgiliane di Benvenuto da Imola*, in *Studi virgiliani pubbli-cati in occasione delle celebrazioni bimillenarie (1930) dalla Reale Accademia virgiliana*. Mantua 1930, pp. 69-77.

[927]   CIOFFETTI, Massimo, *Studi sul commento a Virgilio dello Pseudo-Probo*. Florence 1991 (Pubbl. della Fac. di lettere e filosofia del'Univ. di Milano, 143; Sez. a cura dell'Ist. di filologia classica, 3).

[928]   GIUSTINIANI, V.R., *Il Filelfo, l'interpretazione allegorica di Virgilio e la tripartizione pla-tonica dell'anima*, in *Umanesimo e rinascimento. Studi offerti a Paul Oskar Kristeller*. Florence 1980, pp. 33-44.

[929]   HAGEN, H., *Scholia Bernensia ad Vergilii Bucolica atque Georgica*, in *Jahrbücher für clas-sische Philologie. Supplementband* 4 (1867), pp. 673-1014 (reprint: Hildesheim 1967).

[930]   HOFFMAN, R., *Some New Facts Concerning the Knowledge of Vergil in Early Medieval Ireland*, in *Études celtiques*, 25 (1988), pp. 189-212 [St. Gall, Stiftsbibl., 904].

[931]   JONES, Julian Ward & Elizabeth Frances JONES, *The Commentary of the First Six Books on the "Aeneid" of Vergil Commonly Attributed to Bernardus Silvestris. A New Cri-tical Edition*. Lincoln & London 1977.

[932]   JONES, J.W., *A Twelfth-century Interpretation of Vergil*, in *Vergilius*, 28 (1982), pp. 51-57 [Bernardus Silvestris].

[933]   JONES, J.W., *The So-Called Silvestris Commentary of the Aeneid and the Two Other Inter-pretations*, in *Speculum*, 64 (1989), pp. 835-848.

[934]   KALLENDORF, C., *Cristoforo Landino's Aeneid and the Humanist Critical Tradition*, in *Renaissance Quarterly*, 36 (1983), pp. 519-546.

[935]   KLUGE, F., *Zu den Oxforder Vergilglossen Auct. F. 1, 16*, in *Zeitschrift für deutsches Altertum und deutsche Literatur*, 26, = N.F. 16 (1884), p. 260.

[936]   LAMBERT, P.-Y., *Les gloses celtiques aux commentaires de Virgile*, in *Études celtiques*, 23 (1986), pp. 81-128.

[937]   LAMBERT, P.-Y., *Gloses celtiques aux commentaires de Virgile. Addendum*, in *Études cel-tiques*, 24 (1987), pp. 327-328.

[938]   LEGENDRE, Paul, *Études tironiennes. Commentaire sur la VIᵉ églogue de Virgile tiré d'un manuscrit de Chartres avec divers appendices et un fac-similé*. Paris 1907 (Bibliothèque de l'École des hautes études, 165) [Chartres, Bibl. mun., 13].

[939]   LOBRICHON, G., *Saint Virgile Auxerrois et les avatars de la IVᵉ eclogue*, in *Lectures médié-vales de Virgile. Actes du Colloque organisé par l'École française de Rome (Rome, 25-28 octobre 1982)*. Rome 1985, pp. 375-393.

[940]   LORD, M.L., *Petrarch and Vergil's First Eclogue. The Codex Ambrosianus*, in *Harvard Studies in Philology*, 86 (1982), pp. 253-276.

[941]   LORD, M.L., *A Commentary on Aeneid 6: Ciones de Magnali, not Nicholas Trivet*, in *Medievalia et Humanistica*, 15 (1987), pp. 147-160.

[942]   LORD, M.L., *Virgil's "Eclogues", Nicholas Trevet, and the Harmony of the Spheres*, in *Mediaeval Studies*, 54 (1992), pp. 186-273.

[943]   LUNELLI, A., *Il commento virgiliano di Pomponio Leto*, in *Atti del Convegno virgiliano di Brindisi nel bimillenario della morte (Brindisi 15-18 ottobre 1981)*. Perugia 1983, pp. 309-322.

[944]   LUUKKAINEN, Matti, *Untersuchungen zur morphematischen Transferenz im Frühdeutschen dargestellt an den Tegernseer Vergilglossen. Ein Beitrag zur Transferenzlexikologie*. Helsin-ki 1982 (Annales Academiae Scientiarum Fennicae. Diss. Hum. Litt., 32).

[945]   MOMMSEN, Th., *Aus und über Leydener und Münchener Handschriften. 3. Virgilische Scholien*, in *Rheinisches Museum*, N.F. 16 (1861), pp. 137-140.

[946]   MOMMSEN, Th., *Zu den Scholien der virgilischen "Georgica"*, in *Rheinisches Museum*, N.F. 16 (1861), pp. 442-453 [Berne, Burgerbibl., 165].

[947]   NASCIMENTO, A.A., *Um comentador medieval das Bucólicas de Virgílio, Nicolau Trivet*, in *Euphrosyne*, 11 (1981-1982), pp. 180-186 [Evora, Bibl. publ., Inc. 307-12, & Florence, Bibl. Laur., Plut. 77.3].

[948]   NASCIMENTO, A.A., *Os auctores no commentário de Nicolau Trivet às Bucólicas de Virgilio. Aspectos formais de uso e sua significação*, in *Euphrosyne*, 12 (1983-1984), pp. 209-221.

[949]   NICOLAS TRIVET ANGLICO, *Comentario a las Bucólicas de Virgilio. Estudio y edición crítica*, por A.A. NASCIMENTO & J.-M. DÍAZ DE BUSTAMANTE. Santiago de Compostela 1984 (Monografias de la Universidad de Santiago de Compostela, 97).

[950]   O'DONNELL, J.R., *The Sources and Meaning of Bernard Silvester's Commentary on the Aeneid*, in *Mediaeval Studies*, 24 (1962), pp. 233-249.

[951]   PADOAN, G., *Tradizione e fortuna del commento all'"Eneide" di Bernardo Silvestre*, in *Italia medioevale e umanistica*, 3 (1960), pp. 227-240.

[952]   PETSCHENIG, M., *Eine uita Uergilii*, in *Wiener Studien*, 4 (1882), pp. 168-169 [Sankt Paul im Lavanttal, Stiftsbibl., 86 b/1].

[953]   POLIZIANO, Angelo, *Commento inedito alle Georgiche di Virgilio*, a cura di Livia CASTANO MUSICÒ. Florence 1990 (Istituto nazionale di studi sul Rinascimento. Studi e testi, 18).

[954]   PRZYCHOCKI, G., *De vitis vel accessibus Vergilianis*, in *Eos*, 80 (1927), pp. 27-37.

[955]   ROCCARO, C., *Glossari medievali*, in *Enciclopedia Virgiliana*, vol. II. Rome 1985, pp. 773-774.

[956]   SABBADINI, R., *Una biografia medievale di Virgilio*, in *Studi italiani di filologia classica*, 7 (1899), pp. 37-43.

[957]   SABBADINI, R., *Quali biografie fossero note al Petrarca*, in *Rendiconti dell'Istituto Lombardo di scienze e lettere*, 39 (1906), pp. 193-198.

[958]   SABBADINI, R., *Le biografie di Virgilio antiche, medievali e umanistiche*, in *Studi italiani di filologia classica*, 15 (1907), pp. 197-261.

[959]   SAVAGE, J.J., *De scholiis in Turonensi Vergilii codice scriptis*, in *Harvard Studies in Classical Philology*, 35 (1924), p. 173 [Berne, Burgerbibl., 165].

[960]   SAVAGE, J.J., *The Scholia in the Virgil of Tours, Bernensis 165*, in *Harvard Studies in Classical Philology*, 36 (1925), pp. 91-164.

[961]   SAVAGE, J.J., *Notes on some Unpublished Scholia in a Paris Manuscript of Virgil*, in *Transactions and Proceedings of the American Philological Association*, 56 (1925), pp. 229-241 [Paris, Bibl. Nat., lat. 7930].

[962]   SAVAGE, J.J., *The Scholia on Virgil's "Eclogues" in Harleian 2782*, in *Classical Philology*, 24 (1929), pp. 274-278.

[963]   SAVAGE, J.J., *Mediaeval Notes on the Sixth Aeneid in Parisinus 7930*, in *Speculum*, 9 (1934), pp. 204-212.

[964]   SKIMIA, S., *De Bernardo Silvestri Vergilii interprete*. Krakow 1930.

[965]   SMITS, E.R., *New Evidence for the Authorship of the Commentary on the First Six Books of Virgil's "Eneid" Commonly Attributed to Bernardus Silvestris?*, in *Non nova, sed nove. Mélanges de civilisation médiévale dédiés à Willem Noomen*. Groningen 1984, pp. 239-246.

[965a]   STOK, F., *Il rinascimento della biografia virgiliana*, in *Res Publica Litterarum*, 14 (1991), pp. 229-240.

[965b]   STOK, F., *La "Vita di Virgilio" di Zono de' Magnalis*, in *Rivista di cultura classica e medioevale*, 33 (1991), pp. 145-181.

[965c]   STOK, F., *Il Virgilio di Domenico di Bandino*, in *Giornale italiano di filologia*, 44 (1992), pp. 3-28.

[966]   STOKES, H., *Hibernica—The Glosses on the Bucolics*, in *Zeitschrift für vergleichende Sprachforschung*, 33 (1894), pp. 62-80, 313-315.

[967]   SUERBAUM, W., *Von der "Vita Vergiliana" über die "Accessus Vergiliani" zum Zauberer Vergil*, in *Aufstieg und Niedergang der römischen Welt*, II.31.2 (1981), pp. 1156-1262.

[968]   THILO, C., *Beiträge zur Kritik der Scholiasten des Vergilius*, in *Rheinisches Museum*, 15 (1860), pp. 119-152.

[969]   THOMPSON, H.J., *A New Supplement to the Berne Scholia on Virgil*, in *Journal of Philology*, 35 (1920), pp. 357-386.
[970]   UPSON, H.R., *Medieval Lives of Virgil*, in *Classical Philology*, 38 (1943), pp. 103-111.
[971]   VELTHUIS, H.J., *De Tegernseër Glossen op Vergilius*. Groningen 1892.
[972]   VIANELLO, R., *Appunti sul commento alle "Bucoliche" virgiliane nel codice 1084 della Biblioteca universitaria di Padova*, in *Atti e memorie dell'Accademia patavina di scienze, lettere e arti. Classe di scienze morali, lettere e arti*, 99 (1986-1987), pp. 51-86.
[973]   VIARRE, S., *L'interprétation de l'Énéide, à propos d'un commentaire du XIIe siècle*, in *Présence de Virgile. Actes du Colloque des 9, 11 et 12 décembre 1976 (Paris, É.N.S., Tours)*. Paris 1976, pp. 223-232 [Bernardus Silvestris].
[974]   WIESER, K., *Der Zusammenhang der Vergilviten*. Erlangen 1926 (Diss.).
[975]   WOLF, E., *Die allegorische Vergilerklärung des Cristoforo Landino*, in *Neue Jahrbücher für das klassische Altertum*, 1 (1919), pp. 453-480.
[976]   ZABUGHIN, V., *Scholiastarum Vergilianorum reliquiae in Pomponii Laeti codicibus servatae*. Grottaferrata 1911.
[977]   ZABUGHIN, V., *L'umanesimo nella storia della scienza. Il commento vergiliano di Zono de' Magnalis. Noterelle di Benvenuto de Imola. Commento di Giovanni di Virgilio alle "Metamorfosi" d'Ovidio*, in *L'Arcadia*, 1 (1917), pp. 1-18, 2 (1917), pp. 87-110.
[978]   ZABUGHIN, V., *L'umanesimo nella storia della scienza. III. L'autografo delle chiose Vergiliane di Pomponio Leto*, in *L'Arcadia*, 3 (1918), pp. 135-151.
[979]   ZINTZEN, C., *Zur Aeneis-Interpretation [1472/1480] des Cristoforo Landino*, in *Mittellateinisches Jahrbuch*, 20 (1985), pp. 193-215.

Virgil (Pseudo)
[980]   PASTORE STOCCHI, M., *Il commento del Poliziano al "De rosis"*, in *Umanesimo e Rinascimento a Firenze e Venezia. Miscellanea di studi in onore di V. Branca*, vol. III, part 1. Florence 1983, pp. 397-422.

Vitruvius
[981]   JUREN, V., *Politien et Vitruve (Note sur le ms. lat. 7382 de la Bibliothèque nationale)*, in *Rinascimento*, 2ª ser. 18 (1978), pp. 285-292.

DISCUSSIONS OF ATTRIBUTION

[982]   SPEYER, Wolfgang, *Italienische Humanisten als Kritiker der Echtheit antiker und christlicher Literatur*. Stuttgart 1993 (Abhandlungen der Geistes- und Sozialwissenschaftlichen Klasse der Akademie der Wissenschaften und der Literatur Mainz. Jahrgang 1993, Nr. 3).

Cato (Pseudo)
[983]   NAVONE, P., *Catones perplurimi*, in *Sandalion*, 5 (1982), pp. 311-327.

Homerus Latinus
[984]   SCAFFAI, M., *Pindarus seu Homerus: un'ipotesi sul titolo dell'Ilias Latina*, in *Latomus*, 38 (1979), pp. 932-939 [Oxford, Bodl. Libr., Rawl. G. 57].

Seneca
[985]   MARTELLOTTI, G., *La questione dei due Seneca da Petrarca a Benvenuto*, in *Italia medioevale e umanistica*, 15 (1972), pp. 149-169.
[986]   RONCALI, R., *L'anonima 'Apoteosi del Divo Claudio'*, in *Belfagor*, 29 (1974), pp. 571-573.

INDEX TO THE BIBLIOGRAPHY
The references are to the numbered items in the bibliography

GENERAL INDEX

For the Bibliography, see the separate index on pp. 249-59

MITTELLATEINISCHE STUDIEN UND TEXTE